JOHN KEATS

Complete Poems

JOHN KEATS

Complete Poems

edited by

Jack Stillinger

*The Belknap Press of
Harvard University Press
Cambridge, Massachusetts
and London, England*

Copyright © 1978, 1982 by the President and Fellows of Harvard College
All rights reserved
Printed in the United States of America

Ninth printing, 2003

Library of Congress Cataloging in Publication Data

Keats, John, 1795-1821.
 Complete poems.

 Reading ed. based on: The poems of John Keats /
edited by Jack Stillinger. 1978.
 Bibliography: p.
 Includes index.
 I. Stillinger, Jack. II. Title.
PR4831.S75   1982   821'.7   82-6091
ISBN 0-674-15431-2 (pbk.)   AACR2

Preface

THIS IS INTENDED to be an all-purpose reading edition of Keats's complete poetical works arranged in chronological order according to the dates of composition or (for works written over a long period) substantial completion. The texts here have been produced from the same tapes used in the parent edition, *The Poems of John Keats*, published by the Belknap Press of Harvard University Press in 1978, and should be identical with the 1978 texts in every respect save page division and pagination. For information concerning strictly textual matters—specification of the individual copy-texts (with reasons for the choice in each case), details of the emendation of substantives and accidentals, and a full record of variants in authoritative MS and printed versions—the reader should consult the introduction, footnotes, and textual notes to that edition.

The Commentary at the back of this book gives the date of composition (as well as the place when Keats was away from home) and details of first publication for each poem, identifies quotations and allusions that Keats expected the reader to recognize, and glosses names and words that are not included in the ordinary college or desk dictionary. For practical reasons, but even more so as a matter of editorial principle, the notes generally do not identify or suggest sources; a full account of recognizable "echoes and borrowings" would require several hundred additional pages, and to very little purpose (see the Commentary for *La Belle Dame sans Merci*, where, as a special illustration, sources are enumerated at some length). Similarly, historical and philological explanations have in most instances been reduced to a bare minimum. Some of the space that might have been given to interpretation of difficult passages has instead been used for reference to the best recent scholarship and criticism (the Selected Bibliography lists the standard book-length studies, while the Commentary concentrates more on specialized treatments of the separate works).

I continue to be under obligation to the individuals and institutions who helped me in my original editing, and on this occasion am further indebted to the scholars and critics—more than 140, all told—who figure in the Selected Bibliography and Commentary. Some of them, I hope, will approve of a presentation in which Keats is allowed largely to speak for himself.

J.S.

Contents

Introduction

THE MOST IMPORTANT details of Keats's outward life are given in the Chronology following this introduction. The Contents lists his poems in the approximate order in which he wrote them, and the Commentary provides information about the circumstances of composition and publication. An appendix at the end describes the arrangement of poems in his first and third volumes. The Selected Bibliography and the Commentary cite a great deal of recent Keats scholarship, including some excellent biographies and the essential editions of Keats's letters and related papers. Here I wish simply to introduce a few central facts about Keats's life and career, then describe the predominant subject matter and themes of his best work, and finally speculate briefly on the causes of his greatness as a poet.

THE FIRST and most obvious fact about Keats is how young he was. Born in London on 31 October 1795, dead in Rome at the age of twenty-five on 23 February 1821, he was a young man all his adult life. Of the half-dozen other most highly regarded English poets, only Spenser, who died in his later forties, did not live at least twice as long as Keats. Chaucer and Shakespeare were alive in their fifties; Milton reached the age of sixty-five; Yeats and Wordsworth, dying at seventy-three and eighty, lived three times as long. These poets would be virtually unknown today had they stopped writing as early as Keats did (their most enduring works, collectively, would be *The Book of the Duchess, On the Morning of Christ's Nativity, An Evening Walk,* and *Descriptive Sketches*), and the same is true of our major writers in fiction and other forms. By contrast, between the ages of twenty-one and twenty-four Keats published three volumes of poetry—*Poems* (1817), *Endymion* (1818), and *Lamia, Isabella, The Eve of St. Agnes, and Other Poems* (1820). The last of these, containing among the "other poems" the five great odes and *Hyperion,* is universally regarded as one of the landmark volumes of English literature.

Paradoxically, for all this youthful productivity Keats actually made a late start as a poet and then progressed relatively slowly. The second fact for consideration here is what might be called the shape of his poetic career, in which the most prominent feature is the striking suddenness of his development to maturity. He wrote his first poem at the age of eighteen and produced another twenty or so occasional pieces during the next two years, while finishing an apprenticeship to an apothecary-surgeon at Edmonton and taking a year's course in medicine at Guy's Hospital in London. But he did not seriously embark on a career as poet until after he passed the apothecaries' examination toward the end of July 1816, three months before he turned twenty-one. His terminal illness (tuberculosis, which had killed his mother and his brother Tom) lasted more than a year, and he wrote no work of any consequence later than the final months of 1819. Thus, if we set aside the juvenile effusions, his entire writing career amounts to little more than three and a half years.

Within that span, Keats's major achievement comes only at the very end. There are 150 titles in this complete edition. If we number the items consecutively, the long "poetic romance" *Endymion,* which critics usually class among the youthful preliminary works and which Keats himself (in the printed preface to the poem) characterized as the product of "great inexperience, immaturity, and every error denoting a feverish attempt," is actually sixty-third in the chronological array. The serious shorter poems of the winter of 1817–18 are approximately in the middle of the list (*Welcome joy, and welcome sorrow* is seventy-fifth of the 150). *Isabella,* another poem that seems stylistically more like an earlier than a later work, is eighty-eighth. The fifteen poems written during the walking tour of the summer of 1818 (*Give me your patience* through *On Some Skulls in Beauley Abbey*) are numbers 91–105—and at this point, more than two thirds through the list, Keats is still tuning up, still making his preparations to win immortal fame. *The Eve of St. Agnes,* which is the first of what we call the poems of Keats's maturity, is number 117. The works of 1819—the final thirty-four items minus *In after time a sage,* which is assignable to 1820—constitute an astonishing outpouring that includes some of the most famous poems in the language. And they are products of just the last few months of Keats's poetic life. The ripening between the "early" three fourths (or even four fifths) of the career and the mature remainder is a phenomenon unparalleled in literary history.

A third central fact has to do with an important aspect of Keats's character—a commonsense practicality that helped make him extraordinarily levelheaded, perceptive, and wise. This is difficult to convey in a single word, but all those who study Keats recognize its presence and significance; it is a quality that pervades the incidents of his daily life and the pages of his letters, and obviously was a substantial element in the attraction that his wide circle of loyal friends felt toward him. Douglas

Bush admirably depicts the quality in his introduction to Keats's *Selected Poems and Letters* (1959), commenting on a now outdated view of the poet as extravagant sensualist:

> though Keats's name is identified with sensuous richness, he was never the aesthete or voluptuary of sensation that, to the later nineteenth century, he often seemed to be. For one thing, he was—except in genius—too normal and sensible: if we can imagine ourselves contemporaries, and in urgent need of wise advice, we would never think of consulting Shelley or Byron or Blake or Coleridge or even Wordsworth, but we would turn with confidence to Keats, the youngest of the lot. It is part of his fundamental wisdom that he was never carried away by ideological mirages or into misjudgments of other people or himself; along with a manly self-respect and high ambition, he had a healthy and humble capacity for self-criticism, an incapacity for self-deception.

Keats also had a hearty sense of humor, and he was never the least bit stuffy. But the terms "normal," "sensible," "fundamental wisdom" do approach the essence of the kind of person he was.

The fourth central fact that I would set down here (though its "factuality" resides primarily in the poems rather than in the poet's life) is Keats's prolonged concern, from almost the beginning of his career to the very end, with dreams, visions, and the kind of imagination that he took them to represent. Forms of "dream" as noun and verb (plus adjectives and adverbs like "dreamy" and "dreamingly") occur about 125 times in the poems, and "vision" and "visionary" another forty times. Dreaming plays a part in all the narrative poems except *Hyperion;* it is fundamental to the plots of *Endymion, The Eve of St. Agnes, Lamia,* and *The Fall of Hyperion* and also figures significantly in *Isabella* and *La Belle Dame sans Merci.* In addition, we have the dreamlike or visionary situations of Bertha in *The Eve of St. Mark* and of the speakers in *Ode to Psyche, Ode to a Nightingale,* and *Ode on a Grecian Urn* (in some places the dreamlike character of the situation is just hinted at, while in others it is made more explicit with questions like "Surely I dreamt to-day, or did I see . . . with awaken'd eyes?" "Was it a vision, or a waking dream?"); and there are numerous passages about dreaming in the lesser poems —for example, the "barren dream" of romance in *On Sitting Down to Read "King Lear" Once Again,* the descriptions of dreams and the theorizing about them in *Dear Reynolds, as last night I lay in bed,* the dreamlike unreality of the setting in *On Visiting the Tomb of Burns,* and the dream that Keats experienced after reading Dante as recreated in *As Hermes once took to his feathers light.* Keats also describes dreams in his correspondence with friends, and in the best known of the early letters, to Benjamin Bailey, 22 November 1817 (see the Commentary note to *Endymion* I.777–781), he likens the imagination to Adam's dream in *Paradise Lost:* Adam, he says, "awoke and found it truth."

The earliest manifestation of dreaming in Keats's poems (apart from offhand references to "fair dreams" before the "mind's eye" in *To Hope* and swans "dream[ing] so sweetly" in *Calidore*) takes the form of an interest in poetic trances and visionary flights—the result, apparently, of accepting seriously and literally a couple of the oldest motifs in literary tradition. We see this prominently in poems of the closing months of 1816, most notably the epistle *To My Brother George, Sleep and Poetry,* and *I stood tip-toe upon a little hill.* In these poems, thus early, Keats has already arrived at a basic metaphor: poetic flight to another, higher realm. With *Endymion,* the principal work of the following year, 1817, the extraworldly excursion becomes a main element of narrative plot, while dreaming becomes a major symbol (for visionary imagination) and the "authenticity" or truth of dreams is a major thematic interest. From this point on, characters in the poems (and sometimes Keats outside the poems, as in the letter to Bailey) puzzle over the reality of their dream experiences, become engrossed in other worlds that they have reached or created by means of their imagination, and sometimes go too far and cannot return to the real world from which they took flight. It is a most interesting paradox in literary history that Keats the man of commonsense practicality, the one whom above all others we would seek out for wise advice, also appears to be the Romantic poet most concerned with dreams and visionary excursions into the unreal. It may well be that this paradox is itself a chief component of the rich complexity of Keats's best poetry: the visionary and down-to-earth tendencies frequently exist simultaneously, in an ongoing tug-of-war.

THERE IS a basic Keatsian structure—a literally spatial conception of two realms in opposition and a mythlike set of actions involving characters shuttling back and forth between them—that appears in a great many of the poems and can usefully serve as a device for relating poems, passages, and situations one to another in a view of what Keats's work as a whole is preponderantly "about." This structure can be illustrated by means of a simplified cosmography of the poems. Here is a diagram I have used many times in the classroom (and published in a 1968 essay on the odes that is reprinted in *The Hoodwinking of Madeline*) to represent the typical lyric poem of Keats's time as a literal or metaphorical excursion and return:

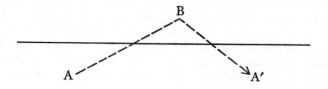

The horizontal line stands for a boundary separating the actual world (below) and the ideal (above). The two realms have many familiar labels —for example, earth and heaven, mortality and immortality, time and eternity, materiality and spirituality, the known and the unknown, the finite and the infinite, realism and romance, the natural and the supernatural. The ideal is represented above the line because it is, so to speak, a higher reality. Characteristically, the speaker in a Romantic lyric begins in the real world (A), takes off in mental flight to visit the ideal (B), and then—for a variety of reasons, but most often because he finds something wanting in the imagined ideal or because, being a native of the real world, he discovers that he does not or cannot belong permanently in the ideal—returns home to the real (A'). But he has not simply arrived back where he began (hence A' rather than A at the descent). He has acquired something—a new understanding of a situation, a change in attitude toward it—from the experience of the flight, and for better or worse he is never the same afterward.

Now if we emphasize that the actual world is the realm of mortals and is associated with mutability, natural process, and death, while the ideal world is the realm of gods and fairies and is associated most significantly with permanence—the absence of all that mutability, process, and death imply—then the diagram becomes a type of map on which we can locate the characters and actions not only of Keats's lyrics but of the major narrative poems as well.

Thematically, the most serious problem that Keats's characters face is, at the outset, the painful half of the pleasure-pain complexity of mortal life. The characters—Endymion, Madeline in *The Eve of St. Agnes,* the knight at arms in *La Belle Dame,* the speakers in *Nightingale* and *Grecian Urn,* Lycius in *Lamia,* to list the most obvious examples—want to "unperplex bliss from its neighbour pain" (*Lamia* I.192), to separate the two so as to be able to get rid of the pain entirely and enjoy pure bliss. This is something that mortals, because of their mortal nature, cannot succeed in doing, as almost all the characters in the course of their experiences and meditations come to learn. Typically the attempt to solve the problem takes the form of a mortal-nonmortal pairing—Endymion with the moon goddess, the knight at arms with the fairy Belle Dame, the ode speakers with the ode objects ("immortal Bird," the "eternity" of ancient Greece), Lycius with the serpent-woman Lamia—a pairing that promises bliss but turns out to be an ideal impossible of permanent realization. The action of a poem, whether narrative or lyric, involves first some kind of union between a mortal and the nonmortal ideal by means of a dream (or a visionary entrancement that is like a dream), and then a gradual or sudden end to the union, as the dreamer awakens to reality. The conclusions of the poems are frequently ambiguous—they end in questions, doubtful circumstances, "wonderment"—but a new and more positive view of the pleasure-pain complexity is sometimes inferable: where there is no death there is no life; the complexity is better than no life at all.

Endymion is Keats's earliest and most literal embodiment of these thematic and narrative materials. Having become enamored of an unknown goddess who visits him in a dream, Endymion renounces the real world and sets forth to wander through caverns, under the ocean, and through the air (all realms that are out of the real world, therefore figuratively above the line in the diagram) seeking reunion with his dream goddess. After numerous adventures (and numerous long speeches) he returns to the real world, meets and falls in love with an Indian maiden, and vows to abandon his search for the goddess. On several occasions while he is out of the world he laments his situation as a solitary, an alien, an "exil'd mortal" suffering "homeward fever," as in the speech at II.302–332, ending, "let me see my native bowers! / Deliver me from this rapacious deep!" Much of Books I and IV focus on the question of the reality of the dream he is pursuing, and his renunciation toward the end of his wanderings has an impressive fervency:

> I have clung
> To nothing, lov'd a nothing, nothing seen
> Or felt but a great dream! O I have been
> Presumptuous against love, against the sky,
> Against all elements, against the tie
> Of mortals each to each. . . .
>
> . . . so my story
> Will I to children utter, and repent.
> There never liv'd a mortal man, who bent
> His appetite beyond his natural sphere,
> But starv'd and died. . . .
>
> . . . gone and past
> Are cloudy phantasms. Caverns lone, farewel!
> And air of visions, and the monstrous swell
> Of visionary seas! No, never more
> Shall airy voices cheat me. . . .   (IV.636–654)

The action of the poem accords with the structure outlined above until the very end, when, in the final thirty lines, the Indian maiden reveals to Endymion that she is his dream goddess in disguise, and the two are blissfully and permanently united, vanishing "far away." This of course represents a last-minute reversion to the realm of the ideal, but the conclusion was inherent in the legend that Keats was retelling; the emphasis in his elaboration, since so many lines are given to it, would seem to fall on the necessity of Endymion's coming to terms with the real world and human existence.

Almost all of the subsequent major poems have at least partial elements of this basic structure. In *The Eve of St. Agnes,* the hostile castle, Porphyro, physical love, and the icy storm are various aspects of the reality below the line; Madeline's ritual and dream state, as unnatural as a rose that can "shut, and be a bud again," are the realm of the ideal, and the consequences of her attempt to attain this ideal are, in some interpretations of the poem, first isolation, then deception by "stratagem," and finally possibly even death. There is a similarly isolated character in *The Eve of St. Mark,* which, although it is only a fragment, presents a clear contrast between the everyday reality of the town (and the church and churchgoers) and the separation from this reality represented by Bertha's indoor confinement and her "captive" absorption in the "curious volume" containing the life of St. Mark. The mortal knight at arms in *La Belle Dame* is still another instance of dreamer separated from reality; his enthrallment to a beautiful fairy lady who sings, feeds him, and takes him to her "elfin grot" (again figuratively above the line) results in a nightmare "horrid warning" by "pale kings, and princes . . . Pale warriors, death pale," and he awakens in a barren landscape, seemingly paralyzed by the outcome of his excursion into the ideal.

The odes have a place in this scheme as well. Psyche's "fane / In some untrodden region" of the speaker's mind is an ideal realm somewhere above the line; and so are the supernature of the nightingale's forest, the art world of the Grecian urn's piper, lovers, trees, and sacrificial procession, and (though they are referred to only in a single line) the "songs of spring" in *To Autumn,* while the mortal speaker in each case makes an imaginative excursion and return. (*Ode on Melancholy,* the shortest of the odes, advises against the excursion, tells what to do instead, and explains why.) Lamia's palace is still another ideal realm, and the mortal Lycius lingers there contentedly until "a thrill / Of trumpets" reminds him of the claims of "the noisy world almost forsworn," whereupon he holds a wedding feast at which the piercing eye of his old tutor exposes his beloved Lamia as a serpent and causes her to vanish; Lycius falls dead, too engrossed in his dream to survive such a precipitous return to reality.

Many lesser poems embody elements of the basic structure. I have already mentioned the trances and visionary flights to a higher realm in the long poems of Keats's first volume, the epistle *To My Brother George, Sleep and Poetry,* and *I stood tip-toe,* each of which prefigures significant actions in *Endymion,* which in turn prefigures much of the rest. The structure of excursion and return shows up in a variety of types of poem, some less serious than others—for example, *Lines on the Mermaid Tavern* and *Robin Hood* (in both of which the speaker makes brief contact with an ideal realm of the past, fully aware at the same time that the poets are "dead and gone," the days "gone away"), *God of the meridian* ("worldly fear . . . when the soul is fled / Too high"), *Dear Reynolds* (on the dangers of seeing both "beyond our bourn" and "Too far into the sea"), *There was a naughty boy* (a whimsical excursion "to the north" to find out that Scotland is after all much the same as England), *There is a joy in footing slow* (sober depiction of "the gentle anchor" of mortality bringing man back to "the sweet and bitter world"), and the *Bright star* sonnet (imaginative flight to a situation of "lone splendor . . . aloft," followed by descent to "earth's human shores" and "my fair love's ripening breast").

Although this scheme identifies a basic structure in Keats's poems, it must be modified to accommodate some special difficulties. There are two complications in particular that cannot be ignored. One of them has to do with Keats's intermittent interest in the dividing line or space *between* the two realms. There are a great many images of midwayness in the poems—bourns, brinks, bars, edges, and boundaries. In *I stood tip-toe* 185–192 "the invisible world," an "unearthly" region that is beyond "our mortal bars," is equated with "the *middle* air," which may or may not be the same as the "middle air" in which Endymion is said to be lost when he comes to a dispirited halt early in his travels outside the world (II.653, 656). Endymion's life in the mortal world is described as a journey "through this middle earth" (I.723). The epistle *Dear Reynolds* speculates on a halfway situation in which the imagination is "brought / Beyond its proper bound, yet still confined,— / Lost in a sort of purgatory blind," so that it "Cannot refer to any standard law / Of either earth or heaven." Madeline appears to enter some sort of state between worlds when she falls asleep and is "Blissfully haven'd both from joy and pain . . . Blinded alike from sunshine and from rain." The knight at arms may be similarly immobilized between realms; having awakened from his dream in La Belle Dame's "grot," he still seems unable to rejoin the real world (the richness suggested by the squirrel's full granary and the completed harvest, in contrast to the knight's bleak surroundings "On the cold hill's side"). In *Ode on a Grecian Urn* the sacrificial procession is stopped forever midway between source and destination. The "space of life between" (Keats's phrase in the preface to *Endymion*) sometimes constitutes a third realm that a two-realm scheme does not sufficiently recognize.

The other complication is more strictly a matter of ideas than of imagery or structure. In the oppositions between reality and the hypothetical ideal, the values attributed to the ideal—most often the permanence that, if only it were possible, would exempt mortals from time, change, and mortality—are clear enough. But the values attached to the contrasting realm of reality are not always so readily graspable; this is the source of some serious problems of interpretation. One likes to think of Keats as a poet who ultimately affirmed reality and disapproved of fanciful and impossible attempts to escape. Yet in many of the poems there seems to be something wrong with the reality. Consider just three instances. In *The Eve of St. Agnes* the sought-after perfection lies in the ritual that Madeline practices and the dream that it produces; unlike Madeline (until too late), we are allowed to see some faults of the alternative to reality—the ritual is an old wives' tale, Madeline is said to be "hoodwink'd," Porphyro displays some of the characteristics of peeping Tom and cowardly seducer, and he and Madeline are last seen fleeing "into the storm." But where, exactly, is a clearly contrasting reality? The chapel in the opening stanzas is freezing cold and full of associations with death, and the Beadsman is an old man who has renounced life and is about to die; the revelers, Madeline's kinsmen and the warrior-guests, are "barbarian hordes," "bloated wassaillers," who are later punished with nightmares of witch, demon, and coffin worm; Porphyro not only is the worker of a "stratagem" but is (in the imagery of speeches and description) associated with fairy lore, witchcraft, and sorcery; Angela is morally as well as physically decrepit (she too dies before the night is over); Madeline's room is a scene of deception and, when she awakens, dismay; the nature outside the castle is ominously dark, icy, and gusting. It may be that there is no genuinely attractive reality anywhere in the poem.

Then we have the curious circumstance that in *Ode to a Nightingale* the real world that the speaker wishes to escape in stanza 3—the world of weariness, fever, fret, and so on—has an entirely different set of references from the real world that, after he imaginatively succeeds in escaping, he longs to return to in stanza 5. In stanza 3 the transient reality is depicted exclusively in human terms (old men, youth, Beauty, Love); in stanza 5 it is conveyed in images of nature (flowers, trees, the season, grass, summer flies). If the two are combined in a concept that rejects weariness, fever, and fret while retaining the flowers and flies, it may be that the "reality" of the poem is just as unreal, and just as impossible of attainment, as the timeless perfection represented by the "immortal Bird." And where, to turn briefly to the third example of complication, is the reality in *Lamia?* It is clear that Lamia's palace and its furnishings are (in the words of the quotation from Burton printed at the end of the poem) "no substance but mere illusions." But the "world almost forsworn" is clamorous, Lycius' prideful nature in Part II is singularly unattractive, the Corinthians at the wedding feast are a "gossip rout" and a "herd," and the exposer of the illusion, Apollonius, is not admired by anybody in the poem, including the narrator. There are other notable instances of the problem, as in the "heart high-sorrowful and cloy'd . . . burning forehead . . . parching tongue" of human passion in *Ode on a Grecian Urn* and the final situation ("among her cloudy trophies," an image of defeat) of the burster of Joy's grape in *Ode on Melancholy.* Possibly Keats was of a divided mind about reality in these poems. When his images and attitudes are translated into ideas, the results are sometimes puzzling in their inconsistency.

KEATS IS NOT, however, primarily a poet of ideas. His letters, reflecting not only the happenings of his outward life but some of the most important events of his day-to-day mental life, do teem with ideas about life and poetry. He writes to Benjamin Bailey, 22 November 1817, about sensation, thought, and "the authenticity of the Imagination"; to his brothers, late December 1817, about "Negative Capability" in philosophy and literature; to John Hamilton Reynolds, 3 February 1818, about egotism in modern poetry; to John Taylor, 27 February 1818, about his "Axioms" in poetry; to Reynolds again, 3 May 1818, about Wordsworth and Milton, "axioms in philosophy," and human life as a "Mansion of Many Apartments"; to Richard Woodhouse, 27 October 1818, about the "poetical Character"; to George and Georgiana Keats, 14 February–3 May 1819, about life as "a continual allegory," the ideal of disinterestedness, and the world as a "vale of Soul-making." These letters (and many more by Keats) are among the most readable and most admired in English literature; the ideas in them have pervaded our intellectual culture, and they surface everywhere—in theology and philosophy, literary criticism, novels, plays, detective fiction, even crossword puzzles. But the ideas are not central in his best poems. They form a background to the poetry, a context in which the poems were written, but are not themselves the explicit or implicit content of the poetry.

The content of Keats's best poems, if reduced to their themes, would be, just as with the best work of Shakespeare and Dickens, quite banal ("life is very difficult," "the imagination is not to be relied on," "everybody has to die," "nature consoles"). But Keats's concerns with dreaming, illusion, problems of time and mortality, and the pleasure-pain complexity of life should not be translated in this way; they give a pleasurable and requisite seriousness of content to the poems, but they cannot be taken as the equivalent of the poems. The same may be said of the most characteristic tensions in the poems—the conflicting claims of human and immortal realms of existence, the opposition of attitudes toward the actual and the ideal. These provide structure and dramatic conflict, but they are not the equivalent of poems either. And the ideas and tensions cannot be invoked to account for Keats's sudden rise to greatness in the poems of the last nine months of his career, because they are in his work all along, from late 1816 to the end. Something else is needed to explain the excellence of his mature poetry.

That "something else," I suggest, is Keats's style. This is a topic that was comprehensively considered in the 1940s (by W. J. Bate and R. H. Fogle in particular) but has been relatively slighted in more recent decades, possibly because critics have become increasingly aware of the methodological difficulties seemingly inherent in stylistic analysis of a literary text. Nowadays there is a great deal of argument about what "style" is and where it resides, if at all, in literary works. But it is still practically useful, while the debate goes on, to retain a concept of style in the old-fashioned sense of "mode of expression," referring to such things as choice of words and images, sentence structure, rhythms and sound patterns, figures of speech. These fundamentals are, or used to be, taught in a freshman Introduction to Poetry, with a textbook like James R. Kreuzer's *Elements of Poetry* or Laurence Perrine's *Sound and Sense*. It would be a mistake, even if we cannot precisely describe or account for their effects, to underestimate the importance of these elements in literary art. All works have subject matter, themes, structures, incidents, ideas, and feelings; it is ultimately the language in which these are contained and transmitted that makes some works more pleasing and more moving than others.

Below are three passages of description that are characteristic of Keats's writing at its best. I propose that these passages are self-evidently excellent as poetry and that their excellence lies not in their content (interesting as that may be—our first view of the deposed monarch Saturn, the atmosphere both outside and inside Madeline's castle, and the sights and sounds of autumn) but in various components of their style: the sounds of the words, the rhythmical variations played upon the basic iambic pattern, the concreteness and textural density of the words and images, and some special qualities deriving from the character of the speaker or narrator (or, to be more accurate, Keats himself speaking through these). The first passage was written sometime toward the end of 1818; the second and third belong to January and September 1819.

(1)   Deep in the shady sadness of a vale
        Far sunken from the healthy breath of morn,
        Far from the fiery noon, and eve's one star,
        Sat gray-hair'd Saturn, quiet as a stone,
        Still as the silence round about his lair;
        Forest on forest hung above his head
        Like cloud on cloud. No stir of air was there,
        Not so much life as on a summer's day
        Robs not one light seed from the feather'd grass,
        But where the dead leaf fell, there did it rest.

A stream went voiceless by, still deadened more
By reason of his fallen divinity
Spreading a shade: the Naiad 'mid her reeds
Press'd her cold finger closer to her lips.

   Along the margin-sand large foot-marks went,
No further than to where his feet had stray'd,
And slept there since. Upon the sodden ground
His old right hand lay nerveless, listless, dead,
Unsceptred; and his realmless eyes were closed;
While his bow'd head seem'd list'ning to the Earth,
His ancient mother, for some comfort yet.

(Hyperion I.1–21)

(2)   St. Agnes' Eve—Ah, bitter chill it was!
The owl, for all his feathers, was a-cold;
The hare limp'd trembling through the frozen grass,
And silent was the flock in woolly fold:
Numb were the Beadsman's fingers, while he told
His rosary, and while his frosted breath,
Like pious incense from a censer old,
Seem'd taking flight for heaven, without a death,
Past the sweet Virgin's picture, while his prayer he saith.

(The Eve of St. Agnes 1–9)

(3)   Where are the songs of spring? Ay, where are they?
   Think not of them, thou hast thy music too,—
While barred clouds bloom the soft-dying day,
   And touch the stubble-plains with rosy hue;
Then in a wailful choir the small gnats mourn
   Among the river sallows, borne aloft
      Or sinking as the light wind lives or dies;
And full-grown lambs loud bleat from hilly bourn;
   Hedge-crickets sing; and now with treble soft
   The red-breast whistles from a garden-croft;
      And gathering swallows twitter in the skies.

(To Autumn 23–33)

    Though his friend Woodhouse once commented on how badly he read his own poetry aloud, Keats obviously heard well enough when he was composing. The lines in these passages abound in both repetition and variation of vowel sounds and consonants; we can say, without specifying why, that they are pleasing to listen to, even when one pays no attention to the meanings of the words (they would be musically pleasing to auditors who knew no English). Keats is reported to have had a theory about "melody in Verse . . . particularly in the management of open & close vowels" (see the Commentary note to *Hyperion* I.1–7), but of course the contrasts and interchanges originated spontaneously, according to ear rather than principle. The same is true of the rhythmical qualities of the lines. Departures from the metrical norm occur almost everywhere (there are only two or three regular iambic pentameter lines in the opening paragraph of *Hyperion,* and very few in the other passages); caesuras and enjambments—the rhetorical pauses within lines and the run-on continuations of sense from one line to the next—are similarly varied. One can count up and tabulate these things (the percentage of caesuras occurring after the fourth syllable in the line, the percentage after the fifth, and so on), but the results never explain, except in the bare fact of its existence, how or why such variation creates pleasure. There is, however, no denying the pleasure.

Two of the chief qualities of the diction and imagery in these passages are particularity and concreteness. On a rough scale that runs from the abstractness of Shelley's "loftiest star . . . Pinnacled dim in the intense inane" (where there is no pinnacle in sight, and "star" and "dim" are only very faint visual images, which is just what Shelley intended) to the specificity of Shakespeare's "enginer / Hoist with his own petar" (a clear picture, with sound effects, of an artilleryman being blown up by his own bomb), Keats is definitely "with Shakespeare." This is not to say that his lines contain no abstractions. The first line of *Hyperion* refers to a vale's "sadness" and the second to the vale's distance from "the healthy breath of morn"; but even here the words "Deep," "shady," and "Far sunken" give a topographical spatiality and particularity to the abstractions that create a picture even while the primary emphasis is on tone. Consider the progression from concreteness to abstraction and back to concreteness in the fourth and fifth lines of the second paragraph of the same work: "nerveless" and "listless" are both physical description (terms, say, in a medical report at Guy's Hospital); "dead" is partly physical (motionless) and partly abstract (referring to the state of being dead); "Unsceptred" is both literal (the hand has no sceptre) and abstract (Saturn is no longer king); "realmless" is almost fully abstract, but then "eyes were closed" returns to purely physical description. In these two lines, which may serve to epitomize the large results of Keats's strong lines generally, we get extremely sharp pictorial effects, political implications, and a moral tone all at once. The physical quality in these opening paragraphs of *Hyperion* is sometimes called "sculpturesque," referring to the three-dimensional solidity of "Forest on forest," the dead leaf falling and then not moving, the Naiad pressing her finger to her lips, the large footprints ending at Saturn's feet, the implied massiveness of his bowed head. But there is almost as much physicality in the images of cold and silence in the second of the passages above, and in the many sounds, shapes, and motions of the third.

The textural density of the imagery in these passages is again Shake-

spearean (and not Shelleyan). There is a striking quantity of things in
the lines, things that can be visualized or that stimulate the auditory and
other senses. The last five lines of the opening stanza of *The Eve of St.
Agnes*, for example, contain seven distinct visual images (the Beadsman's
fingers, his rosary, the action of fingering the beads, the vapor of exhaled breath, the vapor of burning incense, the censer, and the Virgin's
picture), some tactile images (the numbness of the fingers, the sensation
of fingers in contact with the beads), and a nonvisual notion of wafting
upward in the words "Seem'd taking flight for heaven." The fourth line
from the end of *To Autumn* begins with the shortest possible compassing
of a sheep's lifespan ("full-grown lambs"), creates a picture of sheep and
the sound of their bleating, and then, with a cameralike zoom, distances
them on hilly ground. It is surely this kind of textural density that Keats
had in mind when he advised Shelley, in a letter of 16 August 1820, to
"be more of an artist, and 'load every rift' of your subject with ore."
Keats's own lines at their best show a remarkable concentration in this
way.

Obviously Keats had an exceptionally keen sensitivity to the minute
particulars of objects, sounds (as well as various shades of silence), and
motions in the world around him. He was also the least egotistical of all
the Romantic poets, both in his life and in his poetry (even in the odes
and other lyrics having a first-person speaker throughout), and on the
basis of this personal trait he developed a now famous theory about the
"poetical Character," which, as he wrote about it to Woodhouse in a
letter of 27 October 1818, "has no self—it is every thing and nothing—
It has no character—it enjoys light and shade; it lives in gusto, be it foul
or fair, high or low, rich or poor, mean or elevated—It has as much delight in conceiving an Iago as an Imogen. What shocks the virtuous phi-
losop[h]er, delights the camelion Poet. . . . A Poet is the most unpoeti-
cal of any thing in existence; because he has no Identity—he is
continually . . . filling some other Body." Woodhouse, telling Keats's
publisher Taylor about this letter, comments, "The highest order of Poet
will . . . be able to throw his own soul into any object he sees or imag-
ines, so as to see feel be sensible of, & express, all that the object itself wo^d
see feel be sensible of or express—& he will speak out of that object—so
that his own self will . . . be 'annihilated'"—and he adds that Keats
said he could conceive of a billiard ball's "sense of delight from its own
roundness, smoothness volubility. & the rapidity of its motion."

The sympathetic imaginative activity that these quotations describe is
responsible for the most peculiarly Keatsian characteristic of all, the ability to identify with an object perceived and convey to the reader—certainly to the reader who reads the poems imaginatively—what it feels
like to *be* that object. The tenth line of *Hyperion* pictures a dead leaf at

rest and simultaneously somehow, perhaps more than anything else by the sounds and rhythm of the line, gives a sense of the experience of falling, coming to a stop, and feeling contact with the ground (the final word "rest" has a dead-leaf crispness about it). The second and third lines of *The Eve of St. Agnes,* with clear visual images of the owl and the hare, carry a sense of what it is like to be cold inside a coat of feathers and to be limping and to put tender feet down, one at a time, on frozen grass; and there may be a further sensation of how frozen grass itself feels when it is walked upon. The density in these passages is the product of several different kinds of sensation coming simultaneously, and the reader makes very intimate contact with the objects depicted.

These are some of the most prominent qualities of Keats's mature poetic style, but pointing them out is not the same as explaining how Keats arrived at them or succeeded in bringing them all together in the final months of his career. One contributing factor, obviously, is that by the beginning of 1819 he had served a relatively long apprenticeship to poetry, had done his journeywork, so to speak, and had put his juvenilia and "transitional" works behind him. Another clear cause is his steady absorption of the works of the greatest writers who preceded him. When he first began writing seriously, his principal models included the eighteenth-century Spenserians and contemporaries and near-contemporaries like James Beattie, Mary Tighe, Tom Moore, G. F. Mathew, and Leigh Hunt. But he matured as a reader as well as a writer; the better influences of Shakespeare, Milton, Wordsworth, and Dante certainly had their effect.

There is a third cause, however, largely independent of these, in Keats's intellectual and emotional experiences of the twelve-month period preceding his major achievement. The year 1818, which began with a somewhat reluctant rewriting and copying out of *Endymion* and what Keats characterized as "a little change . . . in my intellect lately" (see the Commentary on the *King Lear* sonnet), was a year of accelerated growing-up. His shorter poems become more serious, more cognizant of the hardships of human life; and the narrative *Isabella,* along with flowery and sentimental stanzas describing adolescent love, attempts realistic psychological portrayal that in places is quite moving. The walking tour through the Lake District and Scotland gave Keats firsthand acquaintance with mountains, lakes, and other beauties of nature but also with the realities of rural poverty. He became ill with a sore throat and had to break off his travels to return home, where he took several weeks to recover. He nursed his brother Tom in a lengthy illness that ended in death on December 1st of this year, and as an added complication he met and fell in love with Fanny Brawne.

More than anything else, I think, it is this combined experience of suffering, death, and love all at once, against a background of serious conversation, reading, and thinking, that accounts for Keats's sudden rise to excellence in his poetry. He approaches 1819 with what Wordsworth called "an eye / That hath kept watch o'er man's mortality"; he has arrived at a more sober view of the subjects and themes he was writing about. Now images of death pervade his descriptions ("dead leaf," "stream . . . still deadened more," "listless, dead," "soft-dying day," "light wind lives or dies" in the first and third of the passages quoted above—and the opening stanza of *The Eve of St. Agnes* leads into an account of the "sculptur'd dead" in the chapel and mention of the Beadsman's "deathbell"); there are many indications of sadness and discomfort ("shady sadness," "Far sunken," "fallen," "sodden," "bitter chill," "trembling," "wailful . . . the small gnats mourn," "lambs . . . bleat"). At the same time there are countering consolations: Saturn may be comforted yet; the owl and the hare will survive the night, and the Beadsman's prayer may get to heaven; the crickets, robin, and swallows are still singing away. The mature Keats confronts the human predicaments implied in these passages—change, old age, death, for none of which is there any practical solution—and by the stylistic expression of a complexity of attitudes and feelings, and with a steadfast honesty concerning the good and the less good aspects of reality, seems to make these human predicaments bearable and even ennobling.

Keats at one time quietly predicted that he would, after his death, be "among the English Poets." This edition, as a complete poetical works in chronological order, allows the reader to follow his poem-by-poem progress toward that end. Some of the pieces are today regarded as among the very best achievements in literary art in any language; many others are much less successful and have to be considered of interest mainly because they are the work of the same poet who wrote the major narratives and the great odes. All told, there are nearly fifteen thousand lines of verse here. That is an impressive quantity for so short a career.

Chronology

1795   John Keats is born in London on 31 October, the eldest son of Thomas Keats, manager of a livery stable, and Frances Keats, née Jennings. Subsequent children are George (1797–1841), Thomas (1799–1818), Edward (1801–1802), and Frances Mary, called Fanny (1803–1889).

1803–   With George and, later, Tom, attends John Clarke's school at Enfield,
1811   a dozen miles north of London.

1804   His father dies in a riding accident in April. His mother remarries in June, and the children go to live with their maternal grandparents, John and Alice Jennings, at Ponders End, Enfield.

1805   John Jennings dies in March. Alice Jennings and the Keats children move to Edmonton.

1810   His mother dies of tuberculosis in March.

1811–   Apprenticeship to Thomas Hammond, an apothecary-surgeon at Ed-
1815   monton.

1814   Writes first poems (beginning with *Imitation of Spenser*). His grandmother Alice Jennings dies in December.

1815   Enters Guy's Hospital, London, in October to begin further medical training. Takes lodgings in St. Thomas's Street, near Guy's.

1816   His first published poem (the sonnet *O Solitude*) appears in the *Examiner* in May. Passes apothecaries' examination in July. Visits Margate with Tom Keats in August. Accelerated poetic activity from August to the end of the year. Becomes acquainted with Joseph Severn, Leigh Hunt, Benjamin Robert Haydon, John Hamilton Reynolds. At the end of the year is living with his brothers at 76 Cheapside, London.

1817   His first volume, *Poems,* published by C. and J. Ollier at the beginning of March. With his brothers, moves to 1 Well Walk, Hampstead, in March. Spends much of the rest of the year writing *Endymion* (April–November). Visits the Isle of Wight and Margate in April, Canterbury and

Hastings in May, Oxford in September. Becomes acquainted with Benjamin Bailey, Charles Wentworth Dilke, Charles Brown, and, at the end of the year, Wordsworth.

1818   Writes *Isabella* (February–April). Joins Tom Keats at Teignmouth in March–April. *Endymion* published by Taylor and Hessey toward the end of April. George Keats and his bride emigrate to America in June. Walking tour with Charles Brown through northern England and Scotland in late June–early August. Meets and falls in love with Fanny Brawne sometime in the fall. Begins *Hyperion* perhaps in October. Tom Keats dies of tuberculosis in December. Moves in with Brown at Wentworth Place (now the Keats House), Hampstead.

1819   Visits Chichester and Bedhampton with Brown in January, Shanklin on the Isle of Wight in July–August, and Winchester in August–October. Fanny Brawne and her family move into the other half of Wentworth Place in April. In a nine-month span, writes the poems that put him "among the English Poets": *The Eve of St. Agnes* (January–February), *La Belle Dame sans Merci* (April), the odes *Psyche, Nightingale, Grecian Urn,* and *Melancholy* (some of them assignable to April–May), *Lamia* and *The Fall of Hyperion* (July–September), *To Autumn* (September).

1820   Severe hemorrhage in the lungs in February (the final illness by now well established). Moves to 2 Wesleyan Place, Kentish Town, in May, to Leigh Hunt's house nearby in June, and then back to Wentworth Place in August. His third volume, *Lamia, Isabella, The Eve of St. Agnes, and Other Poems,* published by Taylor and Hessey at the end of June. Sails for Italy with Joseph Severn in September; arrives at Rome and takes lodgings at 26 Piazza di Spagna in November.

1821   Dies on 23 February and is buried three days later in the Protestant Cemetery at Rome.

The Poems

Imitation of Spenser

* * * * * *

Now Morning from her orient chamber came,
And her first footsteps touch'd a verdant hill;
Crowning its lawny crest with amber flame,
Silv'ring the untainted gushes of its rill;
5   Which, pure from mossy beds, did down distill,
And after parting beds of simple flowers,
By many streams a little lake did fill,
Which round its marge reflected woven bowers,
And, in its middle space, a sky that never lowers.

10   There the king-fisher saw his plumage bright
Vieing with fish of brilliant dye below;
Whose silken fins and golden scalès light
Cast upward, through the waves, a ruby glow:
There saw the swan his neck of arched snow,
15   And oar'd himself along with majesty;
Sparkled his jetty eyes; his feet did show
Beneath the waves like Afric's ebony,
And on his back a fay reclined voluptuously.

Ah! could I tell the wonders of an isle
20   That in that fairest lake had placed been,
I could e'en Dido of her grief beguile;
Or rob from aged Lear his bitter teen:
For sure so fair a place was never seen,
Of all that ever charm'd romantic eye:
25   It seem'd an emerald in the silver sheen
Of the bright waters; or as when on high,
Through clouds of fleecy white, laughs the cœrulean sky.

And all around it dipp'd luxuriously
    Slopings of verdure through the glassy tide,
30   Which, as it were in gentle amity,
    Rippled delighted up the flowery side;
    As if to glean the ruddy tears, it tried,
    Which fell profusely from the rose-tree stem!
    Haply it was the workings of its pride,
35   In strife to throw upon the shore a gem
Outvieing all the buds in Flora's diadem.

* * * * * * *

On Peace

Oh Peace! and dost thou with thy presence bless
    The dwellings of this war-surrounded isle;
Soothing with placid brow our late distress,
    Making the triple kingdom brightly smile?
5   Joyful I hail thy presence; and I hail
    The sweet companions that await on thee;
Complete my joy—let not my first wish fail,
    Let the sweet mountain nymph thy favorite be,
With England's happiness proclaim Europa's liberty.
10   Oh Europe, let not sceptred tyrants see
    That thou must shelter in thy former state;
Keep thy chains burst, and boldly say thou art free;
    Give thy kings law—leave not uncurbed the great;
    So with the horrors past thou'lt win thy happier fate.

Lines Written on 29 May,
the Anniversary of Charles's Restoration,
on Hearing the Bells Ringing

Infatuate Britons, will you still proclaim
His memory, your direst, foulest shame?
    Nor patriots revere?
Ah! when I hear each traitorous lying bell,
5   'Tis gallant Sydney's, Russell's, Vane's sad knell,
    That pains my wounded ear.

Stay, ruby breasted warbler, stay

TUNE—"Julia to the Wood Robin"

1

Stay, ruby breasted warbler, stay,
    And let me see thy sparkling eye;
Oh brush not yet the pearl strung spray,
    Nor bow thy pretty head to fly.

2

5 Stay while I tell thee, fluttering thing,
    That thou of love an emblem art;
Yes! patient plume thy little wing,
    Whilst I my thoughts to thee impart.

3

When summer nights the dews bestow,
10   And summer suns enrich the day,
Thy notes the blossoms charm to blow,
    Each opes delighted at thy lay.

4

So when in youth the eye's dark glance
    Speaks pleasure from its circle bright,
15 The tones of love our joys enhance,
    And make superiour each delight.

5

And when bleak storms resistless rove,
    And ev'ry rural bliss destroy,
Nought comforts then the leafless grove
20   But thy soft note—its only joy.

6

E'en so the words of love beguile,
    When pleasure's tree no longer bears,
And draw a soft endearing smile,
    Amid the gloom of grief and tears.

Fill for me a brimming bowl

"What wondrous beauty! From this moment I efface from my mind all women." Terence's *Eunuch*. Act 2. Sc. 4

Fill for me a brimming bowl,
And let me in it drown my soul:
But put therein some drug design'd
To banish Woman from my mind.
5   For I want not the stream inspiring,
That heats the sense with lewd desiring;
But I want as deep a draught
As e'er from Lethe's waves was quaft,
From my despairing breast to charm
10   The image of the fairest form
That e'er my rev'ling eyes beheld,
That e'er my wand'ring fancy spell'd!

'Tis vain—away I cannot chace
The melting softness of that face—
15   The beaminess of those bright eyes—
That breast, earth's only paradise!

My sight will never more be blest,
For all I see has lost its zest;
Nor with delight can I explore
20   The classic page—the muse's lore.

Had she but known how beat my heart
And with one smile reliev'd its smart,
I should have felt a sweet relief,
I should have felt "the joy of grief"!
25   Yet as a Tuscan 'mid the snow
Of Lapland thinks on sweet Arno;
So for ever shall she be
The halo of my memory.

As from the darkening gloom a silver dove

As from the darkening gloom a silver dove
     Upsoars, and darts into the eastern light,
     On pinions that nought moves but pure delight;

So fled thy soul into the realms above,
5   Regions of peace and everlasting love;
      Where happy spirits, crowned with circlets bright
      Of starry beam, and gloriously bedight,
Taste the high joy none but the bless'd can prove.
There thou or joinest the immortal quire
10   In melodies that even heaven fair
Fill with superior bliss, or, at desire
      Of the omnipotent Father, cleavest the air,
On holy message sent.—What pleasures higher?
      Wherefore does any grief our joy impair?

To Lord Byron

Byron, how sweetly sad thy melody,
    Attuning still the soul to tenderness,
    As if soft Pity with unusual stress
Had touch'd her plaintive lute; and thou, being by,
5   Hadst caught the tones, nor suffered them to die.
      O'ershading sorrow doth not make thee less
      Delightful: thou thy griefs dost dress
With a bright halo, shining beamily;
As when a cloud a golden moon doth veil,
10   Its sides are tinged with a resplendent glow,
Through the dark robe oft amber rays prevail,
      And like fair veins in sable marble flow.
Still warble, dying swan,—still tell the tale,
      The enchanting tale—the tale of pleasing woe.

Oh Chatterton! how very sad thy fate

Oh Chatterton! how very sad thy fate!
    Dear child of sorrow! son of misery!
    How soon the film of death obscur'd that eye,
Whence genius wildly flash'd, and high debate!
5   How soon that voice, majestic and elate,
      Melted in dying murmurs! O how nigh
      Was night to thy fair morning! Thou didst die
A half-blown flower, which cold blasts amate.*

* Affright—Spenser.

But this is past. Thou art among the stars
10   Of highest heaven; to the rolling spheres
Thou sweetly singest—nought thy hymning mars
    Above the ingrate world and human fears.
On earth the good man base detraction bars
    From thy fair name, and waters it with tears!

Written on the Day That Mr. Leigh Hunt Left Prison

What though, for showing truth to flatter'd state,
    Kind Hunt was shut in prison, yet has he,
    In his immortal spirit, been as free
As the sky-searching lark, and as elate.
5   Minion of grandeur! think you he did wait?
    Think you he nought but prison walls did see,
    Till, so unwilling, thou unturn'dst the key?
Ah, no! far happier, nobler was his fate!
In Spenser's halls he strayed, and bowers fair,
10   Culling enchanted flowers; and he flew
With daring Milton through the fields of air:
    To regions of his own his genius true
Took happy flights. Who shall his fame impair
    When thou art dead, and all thy wretched crew?

To Hope

When by my solitary hearth I sit,
    And hateful thoughts enwrap my soul in gloom;
When no fair dreams before my "mind's eye" flit,
    And the bare heath of life presents no bloom;
5   Sweet Hope, ethereal balm upon me shed,
        And wave thy silver pinions o'er my head.

Whene'er I wander, at the fall of night,
    Where woven boughs shut out the moon's bright ray,
Should sad Despondency my musings fright,
10   And frown, to drive fair Cheerfulness away,
        Peep with the moon-beams through the leafy roof,
        And keep that fiend Despondence far aloof.

Should Disappointment, parent of Despair,
   Strive for her son to seize my careless heart;
15 When, like a cloud, he sits upon the air,
    Preparing on his spell-bound prey to dart:
      Chace him away, sweet Hope, with visage bright,
      And fright him as the morning frightens night!

Whene'er the fate of those I hold most dear
20   Tells to my fearful breast a tale of sorrow,
  O bright-eyed Hope, my morbid fancy cheer;
    Let me awhile thy sweetest comforts borrow:
      Thy heaven-born radiance around me shed,
      And wave thy silver pinions o'er my head!

25 Should e'er unhappy love my bosom pain,
    From cruel parents, or relentless fair;
  O let me think it is not quite in vain
    To sigh out sonnets to the midnight air!
      Sweet Hope, ethereal balm upon me shed,
30   And wave thy silver pinions o'er my head!

In the long vista of the years to roll,
   Let me not see our country's honour fade:
  O let me see our land retain her soul,
    Her pride, her freedom; and not freedom's shade.
35   From thy bright eyes unusual brightness shed—
      Beneath thy pinions canopy my head!

Let me not see the patriot's high bequest,
   Great Liberty! how great in plain attire!
  With the base purple of a court oppress'd,
40   Bowing her head, and ready to expire:
      But let me see thee stoop from heaven on wings
      That fill the skies with silver glitterings!

And as, in sparkling majesty, a star
   Gilds the bright summit of some gloomy cloud;
45 Brightening the half veil'd face of heaven afar:
    So, when dark thoughts my boding spirit shroud,
      Sweet Hope, celestial influence round me shed,
      Waving thy silver pinions o'er my head.

February, 1815

Ode to Apollo

1

In thy western halls of gold
    When thou sittest in thy state,
Bards, that erst sublimely told
    Heroic deeds, and sung of fate,
    With fervour seize their adamantine lyres,
Whose cords are solid rays, and twinkle radiant fires.

2

There Homer with his nervous arms
    Strikes the twanging harp of war,
And even the western splendour warms
    While the trumpets sound afar;
But, what creates the most intense surprize,
His soul looks out through renovated eyes.

3

Then, through thy temple wide, melodious swells
    The sweet majestic tone of Maro's lyre;
    The soul delighted on each accent dwells,—
    Enraptured dwells,—not daring to respire,
The while he tells of grief, around a funeral pyre.

4

'Tis awful silence then again:
    Expectant stand the spheres;
    Breathless the laurel'd peers;
Nor move, till ends the lofty strain,
Nor move till Milton's tuneful thunders cease,
And leave once more the ravish'd heavens in peace.

5

Thou biddest Shakspeare wave his hand,
    And quickly forward spring
The Passions—a terrific band—
    And each vibrates the string
That with its tyrant temper best accords,
While from their master's lips pour forth the inspiring words.

5

10

15

20

25

6

30   A silver trumpet Spenser blows,
      And as its martial notes to silence flee,
    From a virgin chorus flows
      A hymn in praise of spotless chastity.
    'Tis still!—Wild warblings from the Æolian lyre
35 Enchantment softly breathe, and tremblingly expire.

7

    Next, thy Tasso's ardent numbers
      Float along the pleased air,
    Calling youth from idle slumbers,
      Rousing them from pleasure's lair:—
40   Then o'er the strings his fingers gently move,
And melt the soul to pity and to love.

8

    But when *Thou* joinest with the Nine,
    And all the powers of song combine,
      We listen here on earth:
45   The dying tones that fill the air,
    And charm the ear of evening fair,
From thee, great God of Bards, receive their heavenly birth.

To Some Ladies

What though while the wonders of nature exploring,
    I cannot your light, mazy footsteps attend;
Nor listen to accents that, almost adoring,
    Bless Cynthia's face, the enthusiast's friend:

5 Yet over the steep, whence the mountain stream rushes,
    With you, kindest friends, in idea I muse;
Mark the clear tumbling crystal, its passionate gushes,
    Its spray that the wild flower kindly bedews.

Why linger you so, the wild labyrinth strolling?
10   Why breathless, unable your bliss to declare?
Ah! you list to the nightingale's tender condoling,
    Responsive to sylphs, in the moon beamy air.

'Tis morn, and the flowers with dew are yet drooping,
   I see you are treading the verge of the sea:
15   And now! ah, I see it—you just now are stooping
   To pick up the keep-sake intended for me.

If a cherub, on pinions of silver descending,
   Had brought me a gem from the fret-work of heaven;
And, smiles with his star-cheering voice sweetly blending,
20   The blessings of Tighe had melodiously given;

It had not created a warmer emotion
   Than the present, fair nymphs, I was blest with from you,
Than the shell, from the bright golden sands of the ocean
   Which the emerald waves at your feet gladly threw.

25   For, indeed, 'tis a sweet and peculiar pleasure,
   (And blissful is he who such happiness finds,)
To possess but a span of the hour of leisure,
   In elegant, pure, and aerial minds.

On Receiving a Curious Shell,
and a Copy of Verses, from the Same Ladies

Hast thou from the caves of Golconda, a gem
   Pure as the ice-drop that froze on the mountain?
Bright as the humming-bird's green diadem,
   When it flutters in sun-beams that shine through a fountain?

5   Hast thou a goblet for dark sparkling wine?
   That goblet right heavy, and massy, and gold?
And splendidly mark'd with the story divine
   Of Armida the fair, and Rinaldo the bold?

Hast thou a steed with a mane richly flowing?
10   Hast thou a sword that thine enemy's smart is?
Hast thou a trumpet rich melodies blowing?
   And wear'st thou the shield of the fam'd Britomartis?

What is it that hangs from thy shoulder, so brave,
   Embroidered with many a spring peering flower?
15   Is it a scarf that thy fair lady gave?
   And hastest thou now to that fair lady's bower?

Ah! courteous Sir Knight, with large joy thou art crown'd;
   Full many the glories that brighten thy youth!
I will tell thee my blisses, which richly abound
20   In magical powers to bless, and to sooth.

On this scroll thou seest written in characters fair
   A sun-beamy tale of a wreath, and a chain;
And, warrior, it nurtures the property rare
   Of charming my mind from the trammels of pain.

25 This canopy mark: 'tis the work of a fay;
   Beneath its rich shade did King Oberon languish,
When lovely Titania was far, far away,
   And cruelly left him to sorrow, and anguish.

There, oft would he bring from his soft sighing lute
30   Wild strains to which, spell-bound, the nightingales listened;
The wondering spirits of heaven were mute,
   And tears 'mong the dewdrops of morning oft glistened.

In this little dome, all those melodies strange,
   Soft, plaintive, and melting, for ever will sigh;
35 Nor e'er will the notes from their tenderness change;
   Nor e'er will the music of Oberon die.

So, when I am in a voluptuous vein,
   I pillow my head on the sweets of the rose,
And list to the tale of the wreath, and the chain,
40   Till its echoes depart; then I sink to repose.

Adieu, valiant Eric! with joy thou art crown'd;
   Full many the glories that brighten thy youth;
I too have my blisses, which richly abound
   In magical powers, to bless and to sooth.

O come, dearest Emma! the rose is full blown

1

O come, dearest Emma! the rose is full blown,
And the riches of Flora are lavishly strown;
The air is all softness, and chrystal the streams,
And the west is resplendently cloathed in beams.

2

5   We will hasten, my fair, to the opening glades,
     The quaintly carv'd seats, and the freshening shades;
     Where the fairies are chaunting their evening hymns,
     And in the last sun-beam the sylph lightly swims.

3

     And when thou art weary, I'll find thee a bed,
10   Of mosses, and flowers, to pillow thy head;
     There, beauteous Emma, I'll sit at thy feet,
     While my story of love I enraptur'd repeat.

4

     So fondly I'll breathe, and so softly I'll sigh,
     Thou wilt think that some amorous zephyr is nigh;
15   Ah! no—as I breathe it, I press thy fair knee,
     And then, thou wilt know that the sigh comes from me.

5

     Then why, lovely girl, should we lose all these blisses?
     That mortal's a fool who such happiness misses;
     So smile acquiescence, and give me thy hand,
20   With love-looking eyes, and with voice sweetly bland.

Woman! when I behold thee flippant, vain

     Woman! when I behold thee flippant, vain,
         Inconstant, childish, proud, and full of fancies;
         Without that modest softening that enhances
     The downcast eye, repentant of the pain
5   That its mild light creates to heal again:
         E'en then, elate, my spirit leaps, and prances,
         E'en then my soul with exultation dances
     For that to love, so long, I've dormant lain:
     But when I see thee meek, and kind, and tender,
10   Heavens! how desperately do I adore
     Thy winning graces;—to be thy defender
         I hotly burn—to be a Calidore—
     A very Red Cross Knight—a stout Leander—
         Might I be loved by thee like these of yore.

15   Light feet, dark violet eyes, and parted hair;
      Soft dimpled hands, white neck, and creamy breast,
      Are things on which the dazzled senses rest
    Till the fond, fixed eyes forget they stare.
    From such fine pictures, heavens! I cannot dare
20   To turn my admiration, though unpossess'd
      They be of what is worthy,—though not drest
    In lovely modesty, and virtues rare.
    Yet these I leave as thoughtless as a lark;
      These lures I straight forget,—e'en ere I dine,
25   Or thrice my palate moisten: but when I mark
      Such charms with mild intelligences shine,
    My ear is open like a greedy shark,
      To catch the tunings of a voice divine.

    Ah! who can e'er forget so fair a being?
30   Who can forget her half retiring sweets?
      God! she is like a milk-white lamb that bleats
    For man's protection. Surely the All-seeing,
    Who joys to see us with his gifts agreeing,
      Will never give him pinions, who intreats
35   Such innocence to ruin,—who vilely cheats
    A dove-like bosom. In truth there is no freeing
    One's thoughts from such a beauty; when I hear
      A lay that once I saw her hand awake,
    Her form seems floating palpable, and near;
40   Had I e'er seen her from an arbour take
    A dewy flower, oft would that hand appear,
      And o'er my eyes the trembling moisture shake.

O Solitude! if I must with thee dwell

    O Solitude! if I must with thee dwell,
      Let it not be among the jumbled heap
      Of murky buildings; climb with me the steep,—
    Nature's observatory—whence the dell,
5   Its flowery slopes, its river's crystal swell,
      May seem a span; let me thy vigils keep
      'Mongst boughs pavillion'd, where the deer's swift leap
    Startles the wild bee from the fox-glove bell.
    But though I'll gladly trace these scenes with thee,

10   Yet the sweet converse of an innocent mind,
        Whose words are images of thoughts refin'd,
      Is my soul's pleasure; and it sure must be
        Almost the highest bliss of human-kind,
      When to thy haunts two kindred spirits flee.

To George Felton Mathew

      Sweet are the pleasures that to verse belong,
      And doubly sweet a brotherhood in song;
      Nor can remembrance, Mathew! bring to view
      A fate more pleasing, a delight more true
5   Than that in which the brother Poets joy'd,
      Who with combined powers, their wit employ'd
      To raise a trophy to the drama's muses.
      The thought of this great partnership diffuses
      Over the genius loving heart, a feeling
10   Of all that's high, and great, and good, and healing.

        Too partial friend! fain would I follow thee
      Past each horizon of fine poesy;
      Fain would I echo back each pleasant note
      As o'er Sicilian seas, clear anthems float
15   'Mong the light skimming gondolas far parted,
      Just when the sun his farewell beam has darted:
      But 'tis impossible; far different cares
      Beckon me sternly from soft "Lydian airs,"
      And hold my faculties so long in thrall,
20   That I am oft in doubt whether at all
      I shall again see Phœbus in the morning:
      Or flush'd Aurora in the roseate dawning!
      Or a white Naiad in a rippling stream;
      Or a rapt seraph in a moonlight beam;
25   Or again witness what with thee I've seen,
      The dew by fairy feet swept from the green,
      After a night of some quaint jubilee
      Which every elf and fay had come to see:
      When bright processions took their airy march
30   Beneath the curved moon's triumphal arch.

        But might I now each passing moment give
      To the coy muse, with me she would not live

In this dark city, nor would condescend
'Mid contradictions her delights to lend.
35   Should e'er the fine-eyed maid to me be kind,
Ah! surely it must be whene'er I find
Some flowery spot, sequester'd, wild, romantic,
That often must have seen a poet frantic;
Where oaks, that erst the Druid knew, are growing,
40   And flowers, the glory of one day, are blowing;
Where the dark-leav'd laburnum's drooping clusters
Reflect athwart the stream their yellow lustres,
And intertwined the cassia's arms unite,
With its own drooping buds, but very white;
45   Where on one side are covert branches hung,
'Mong which the nightingales have always sung
In leafy quiet: where to pry, aloof,
Atween the pillars of the sylvan roof,
Would be to find where violet beds were nestling,
50   And where the bee with cowslip bells was wrestling.
There must be too a ruin dark, and gloomy,
To say "joy not too much in all that's bloomy."

Yet this is vain—O Mathew, lend thy aid
To find a place where I may greet the maid—
55   Where we may soft humanity put on,
And sit, and rhyme and think on Chatterton;
And that warm-hearted Shakspeare sent to meet him
Four laurell'd spirits, heaven-ward to intreat him.
With reverence would we speak of all the sages
60   Who have left streaks of light athwart their ages:
And thou shouldst moralize on Milton's blindness,
And mourn the fearful dearth of human kindness
To those who strove with the bright golden wing
Of genius, to flap away each sting
65   Thrown by the pitiless world. We next could tell
Of those who in the cause of freedom fell;
Of our own Alfred, of Helvetian Tell;
Of him whose name to ev'ry heart's a solace,
High-minded and unbending William Wallace.
70   While to the rugged north our musing turns
We well might drop a tear for him, and Burns.

Felton! without incitements such as these,
How vain for me the niggard muse to tease:

For thee, she will thy every dwelling grace,
75   And make "a sun-shine in a shady place":
For thou wast once a flowret blooming wild,
Close to the source, bright, pure, and undefil'd,
Whence gush the streams of song: in happy hour
Came chaste Diana from her shady bower,
80   Just as the sun was from the east uprising;
And, as for him some gift she was devising,
Beheld thee, pluck'd thee, cast thee in the stream
To meet her glorious brother's greeting beam.
I marvel much that thou hast never told
85   How, from a flower, into a fish of gold
Apollo chang'd thee; how thou next didst seem
A black-eyed swan upon the widening stream;
And when thou first didst in that mirror trace
The placid features of a human face:
90   That thou hast never told thy travels strange,
And all the wonders of the mazy range
O'er pebbly crystal, and o'er golden sands;
Kissing thy daily food from Naiad's pearly hands.

November, 1815

Had I a man's fair form, then might my sighs

Had I a man's fair form, then might my sighs
   Be echoed swiftly through that ivory shell
   Thine ear, and find thy gentle heart; so well
Would passion arm me for the enterprize:
5   But ah! I am no knight whose foeman dies;
   No cuirass glistens on my bosom's swell;
   I am no happy shepherd of the dell
Whose lips have trembled with a maiden's eyes.
Yet must I dote upon thee,—call thee sweet,
10   Sweeter by far than Hybla's honied roses
    When steep'd in dew rich to intoxication.
Ah! I will taste that dew, for me 'tis meet,
   And when the moon her pallid face discloses,
    I'll gather some by spells, and incantation.

Hadst thou liv'd in days of old

Hadst thou liv'd in days of old,
O what wonders had been told
Of thy lively countenance,
And thy humid eyes that dance
In the midst of their own brightness;
In the very fane of lightness.
Over which thine eyebrows, leaning,
Picture out each lovely meaning:
In a dainty bend they lie,
Like to streaks across the sky,
Or the feathers from a crow,
Fallen on a bed of snow.
Of thy dark hair that extends
Into many graceful bends:
As the leaves of hellebore
Turn to whence they sprung before.
And behind each ample curl
Peeps the richness of a pearl.
Downward too flows many a tress
With a glossy waviness;
Full, and round like globes that rise
From the censer to the skies
Through sunny air. Add too, the sweetness
Of thy honied voice; the neatness
Of thine ankle lightly turn'd:
With those beauties, scarce discern'd,
Kept with such sweet privacy,
That they seldom meet the eye
Of the little loves that fly
Round about with eager pry.
Saving when, with freshening lave,
Thou dipp'st them in the taintless wave;
Like twin water lillies, born
In the coolness of the morn.
O, if thou hadst breathed then,
Now the Muses had been ten.
Couldst thou wish for lineage higher
Than twin sister of Thalia?
At least for ever, evermore,
Will I call the Graces four.

Hadst thou liv'd when chivalry
Lifted up her lance on high,
Tell me what thou wouldst have been?
Ah! I see the silver sheen
45   Of thy broidered, floating vest
Cov'ring half thine ivory breast;
Which, O heavens! I should see,
But that cruel destiny
Has placed a golden cuirass there;
50   Keeping secret what is fair.
Like sunbeams in a cloudlet nested
Thy locks in knightly casque are rested:
O'er which bend four milky plumes
Like the gentle lilly's blooms
55   Springing from a costly vase.
See with what a stately pace
Comes thine alabaster steed;
Servant of heroic deed!
O'er his loins, his trappings glow
60   Like the northern lights on snow.
Mount his back! thy sword unsheath!
Sign of the enchanter's death;
Bane of every wicked spell;
Silencer of dragon's yell.
65   Alas! thou this wilt never do:
Thou art an enchantress too,
And wilt surely never spill
Blood of those whose eyes can kill.

I am as brisk

I am as brisk
As a bottle of whisk-
Ey and as nimble
As a milliner's thimble.

Give me women, wine, and snuff

Give me women, wine, and snuff
Untill I cry out "hold, enough!"

You may do so sans objection
Till the day of resurrection;
5   For, bless my beard, they aye shall be
My beloved Trinity.

Specimen of an Induction to a Poem

Lo! I must tell a tale of chivalry;
For large white plumes are dancing in mine eye.
Not like the formal crest of latter days:
But bending in a thousand graceful ways;
5   So graceful, that it seems no mortal hand,
Or e'en the touch of Archimago's wand,
Could charm them into such an attitude.
We must think rather, that in playful mood,
Some mountain breeze had turned its chief delight,
10   To show this wonder of its gentle might.
Lo! I must tell a tale of chivalry;
For while I muse, the lance points slantingly
Athwart the morning air: some lady sweet,
Who cannot feel for cold her tender feet,
15   From the worn top of some old battlement
Hails it with tears, her stout defender sent:
And from her own pure self no joy dissembling,
Wraps round her ample robe with happy trembling.
Sometimes, when the good knight his rest would take,
20   It is reflected, clearly, in a lake,
With the young ashen boughs, 'gainst which it rests,
And th' half seen mossiness of linnets' nests.
Ah! shall I ever tell its cruelty,
When the fire flashes from a warrior's eye,
25   And his tremendous hand is grasping it,
And his dark brow for very wrath is knit?
Or when his spirit, with more calm intent,
Leaps to the honors of a tournament,
And makes the gazers round about the ring
30   Stare at the grandeur of the ballancing?
No, no! this is far off:—then how shall I
Revive the dying tones of minstrelsy,
Which linger yet about lone gothic arches,
In dark green ivy, and among wild larches?
35   How sing the splendour of the revelries,

When butts of wine are drunk off to the lees?
And that bright lance, against the fretted wall,
Beneath the shade of stately banneral,
Is slung with shining cuirass, sword, and shield,
40   Where ye may see a spur in bloody field?
Light-footed damsels move with gentle paces
Round the wide hall, and show their happy faces;
Or stand in courtly talk by fives and sevens:
Like those fair stars that twinkle in the heavens.
45   Yet must I tell a tale of chivalry:
Or wherefore comes that steed so proudly by?
Wherefore more proudly does the gentle knight
Rein in the swelling of his ample might?

Spenser! thy brows are arched, open, kind,
50   And come like a clear sun-rise to my mind;
And always does my heart with pleasure dance,
When I think on thy noble countenance:
Where never yet was ought more earthly seen
Than the pure freshness of thy laurels green.
55   Therefore, great bard, I not so fearfully
Call on thy gentle spirit to hover nigh
My daring steps: or if thy tender care,
Thus startled unaware,
Be jealous that the foot of other wight
60   Should madly follow that bright path of light
Trac'd by thy lov'd Libertas; he will speak,
And tell thee that my prayer is very meek;
That I will follow with due reverence,
And start with awe at mine own strange pretence.
65   Him thou wilt hear; so I will rest in hope
To see wide plains, fair trees and lawny slope:
The morn, the eve, the light, the shade, the flowers;
Clear streams, smooth lakes, and overlooking towers.

Calidore:
A Fragment

Young Calidore is paddling o'er the lake;
His healthful spirit eager and awake
To feel the beauty of a silent eve,

Which seem'd full loath this happy world to leave;
5   The light dwelt o'er the scene so lingeringly.
He bares his forehead to the cool blue sky,
And smiles at the far clearness all around,
Until his heart is well nigh over wound,
And turns for calmness to the pleasant green
10 Of easy slopes, and shadowy trees that lean
So elegantly o'er the waters' brim
And show their blossoms trim.
Scarce can his clear and nimble eye-sight follow
The freaks, and dartings of the black-wing'd swallow,
15 Delighting much, to see it half at rest,
Dip so refreshingly its wings, and breast
'Gainst the smooth surface, and to mark anon,
The widening circles into nothing gone.

And now the sharp keel of his little boat
20 Comes up with ripple, and with easy float,
And glides into a bed of water lillies:
Broad leav'd are they and their white canopies
Are upward turn'd to catch the heavens' dew.
Near to a little island's point they grew;
25 Whence Calidore might have the goodliest view
Of this sweet spot of earth. The bowery shore
Went off in gentle windings to the hoar
And light blue mountains: but no breathing man
With a warm heart, and eye prepared to scan
30 Nature's clear beauty, could pass lightly by
Objects that look'd out so invitingly
On either side. These, gentle Calidore
Greeted, as he had known them long before.

The sidelong view of swelling leafiness,
35 Which the glad setting sun in gold doth dress;
Whence ever and anon the jay outsprings,
And scales upon the beauty of its wings.

The lonely turret, shatter'd, and outworn,
Stands venerably proud; too proud to mourn
40 Its long lost grandeur: fir trees grow around,
Aye dropping their hard fruit upon the ground.

The little chapel with the cross above

Upholding wreaths of ivy; the white dove,
That on the window spreads its feathers light,
45   And seems from purple clouds to wing its flight.

Green tufted islands casting their soft shades
Across the lake; sequester'd leafy glades,
That through the dimness of their twilight show
Large dock leaves, spiral foxgloves, or the glow
50   Of the wild cat's eyes, or the silvery stems
Of delicate birch trees, or long grass which hems
A little brook. The youth had long been viewing
These pleasant things, and heaven was bedewing
The mountain flowers, when his glad senses caught
55   A trumpet's silver voice. Ah! it was fraught
With many joys for him: the warder's ken
Had found white coursers prancing in the glen:
Friends very dear to him he soon will see;
So pushes off his boat most eagerly,
60   And soon upon the lake he skims along,
Deaf to the nightingale's first under-song;
Nor minds he the white swans that dream so sweetly:
His spirit flies before him so completely.

And now he turns a jutting point of land,
65   Whence may be seen the castle gloomy, and grand:
Nor will a bee buzz round two swelling peaches,
Before the point of his light shallop reaches
Those marble steps that through the water dip:
Now over them he goes with hasty trip,
70   And scarcely stays to ope the folding doors:
Anon he leaps along the oaken floors
Of halls and corridors.

Delicious sounds! those little bright-eyed things
That float about the air on azure wings,
75   Had been less heartfelt by him than the clang
Of clattering hoofs; into the court he sprang,
Just as two noble steeds, and palfreys twain,
Were slanting out their necks with loosened rein;
While from beneath the threat'ning portcullis
80   They brought their happy burthens. What a kiss,
What gentle squeeze he gave each lady's hand!
How tremblingly their delicate ancles spann'd!
Into how sweet a trance his soul was gone,

While whisperings of affection
85 Made him delay to let their tender feet
Come to the earth; with an incline so sweet
From their low palfreys o'er his neck they bent:
And whether there were tears of languishment,
Or that the evening dew had pearl'd their tresses,
90 He feels a moisture on his cheek, and blesses
With lips that tremble, and with glistening eye,
All the soft luxury
That nestled in his arms. A dimpled hand,
Fair as some wonder out of fairy land,
95 Hung from his shoulder like the drooping flowers
Of whitest cassia, fresh from summer showers:
And this he fondled with his happy cheek
As if for joy he would no further seek;
When the kind voice of good Sir Clerimond
100 Came to his ear, like something from beyond
His present being: so he gently drew
His warm arms, thrilling now with pulses new,
From their sweet thrall, and forward gently bending,
Thank'd heaven that his joy was never ending;
105 While 'gainst his forehead he devoutly press'd
A hand heaven made to succour the distress'd;
A hand that from the world's bleak promontory
Had lifted Calidore for deeds of glory.

Amid the pages, and the torches' glare,
110 There stood a knight, patting the flowing hair
Of his proud horse's mane: he was withal
A man of elegance, and stature tall:
So that the waving of his plumes would be
High as the berries of a wild ash tree,
115 Or as the winged cap of Mercury.
His armour was so dexterously wrought
In shape, that sure no living man had thought
It hard, and heavy steel: but that indeed
It was some glorious form, some splendid weed,
120 In which a spirit new come from the skies
Might live, and show itself to human eyes.
'Tis the far-fam'd, the brave Sir Gondibert,
Said the good man to Calidore alert;
While the young warrior with a step of grace
125 Came up,—a courtly smile upon his face,
And mailed hand held out, ready to greet

The large-eyed wonder, and ambitious heat
Of the aspiring boy; who as he led
Those smiling ladies, often turned his head
130 To admire the visor arched so gracefully
Over a knightly brow; while they went by
The lamps that from the high-roof'd hall were pendent,
And gave the steel a shining quite transcendent.

Soon in a pleasant chamber they are seated;
135 The sweet-lipp'd ladies have already greeted
All the green leaves that round the window clamber,
To show their purple stars, and bells of amber.
Sir Gondibert has doff'd his shining steel,
Gladdening in the free, and airy feel
140 Of a light mantle; and while Clerimond
Is looking round about him with a fond,
And placid eye, young Calidore is burning
To hear of knightly deeds, and gallant spurning
Of all unworthiness; and how the strong of arm
145 Kept off dismay, and terror, and alarm
From lovely woman: while brimful of this,
He gave each damsel's hand so warm a kiss,
And had such manly ardour in his eye,
That each at other look'd half staringly;
150 And then their features started into smiles
Sweet as blue heavens o'er enchanted isles.

Softly the breezes from the forest came,
Softly they blew aside the taper's flame;
Clear was the song from Philomel's far bower;
155 Grateful the incense from the lime-tree flower;
Mysterious, wild, the far heard trumpet's tone;
Lovely the moon in ether, all alone:
Sweet too the converse of these happy mortals,
As that of busy spirits when the portals
160 Are closing in the west; or that soft humming
We hear around when Hesperus is coming.
Sweet be their sleep. * * * * * * * * *

To one who has been long in city pent

To one who has been long in city pent,
    'Tis very sweet to look into the fair

And open face of heaven,—to breathe a prayer
Full in the smile of the blue firmament.
5   Who is more happy, when, with heart's content,
    Fatigued he sinks into some pleasant lair
    Of wavy grass, and reads a debonair
And gentle tale of love and languishment?
Returning home at evening, with an ear
10   Catching the notes of Philomel,—an eye
Watching the sailing cloudlet's bright career,
    He mourns that day so soon has glided by:
E'en like the passage of an angel's tear
    That falls through the clear ether silently.

Oh! how I love, on a fair summer's eve

Oh! how I love, on a fair summer's eve,
    When streams of light pour down the golden west,
    And on the balmy zephyrs tranquil rest
The silver clouds, far—far away to leave
5   All meaner thoughts, and take a sweet reprieve
    From little cares:—to find, with easy quest,
    A fragrant wild, with Nature's beauty drest,
And there into delight my soul deceive.
There warm my breast with patriotic lore,
10   Musing on Milton's fate—on Sydney's bier—
    Till their stern forms before my mind arise:
Perhaps on the wing of poesy upsoar,—
    Full often dropping a delicious tear,
    When some melodious sorrow spells mine eyes.

To a Friend Who Sent Me Some Roses

As late I rambled in the happy fields,
    What time the sky-lark shakes the tremulous dew
    From his lush clover covert;—when anew
Adventurous knights take up their dinted shields:
5   I saw the sweetest flower wild nature yields,
    A fresh-blown musk-rose; 'twas the first that threw
    Its sweets upon the summer: graceful it grew
As is the wand that queen Titania wields.
And, as I feasted on its fragrancy,
10   I thought the garden-rose it far excell'd:

But when, O Wells! thy roses came to me
  My sense with their deliciousness was spell'd:
Soft voices had they, that with tender plea
  Whisper'd of peace, and truth, and friendliness unquell'd.

Happy is England! I could be content

Happy is England! I could be content
  To see no other verdure than its own;
  To feel no other breezes than are blown
Through its tall woods with high romances blent:
5   Yet do I sometimes feel a languishment
  For skies Italian, and an inward groan
  To sit upon an Alp as on a throne,
And half forget what world or worldling meant.
Happy is England, sweet her artless daughters;
10   Enough their simple loveliness for me,
    Enough their whitest arms in silence clinging:
Yet do I often warmly burn to see
    Beauties of deeper glance, and hear their singing,
And float with them about the summer waters.

To My Brother George

Many the wonders I this day have seen:
  The sun, when first he kist away the tears
  That fill'd the eyes of morn;—the laurel'd peers
Who from the feathery gold of evening lean;—
5   The ocean with its vastness, its blue green,
  Its ships, its rocks, its caves, its hopes, its fears,—
  Its voice mysterious, which whoso hears
Must think on what will be, and what has been.
E'en now, dear George, while this for you I write,
10   Cynthia is from her silken curtains peeping
So scantly, that it seems her bridal night,
    And she her half-discover'd revels keeping.
But what, without the social thought of thee,
Would be the wonders of the sky and sea?

To My Brother George

Full many a dreary hour have I past,
My brain bewilder'd, and my mind o'ercast
With heaviness; in seasons when I've thought
No spherey strains by me could e'er be caught
5   From the blue dome, though I to dimness gaze
On the far depth where sheeted lightning plays;
Or, on the wavy grass outstretch'd supinely,
Pry 'mong the stars, to strive to think divinely:
That I should never hear Apollo's song,
10 Though feathery clouds were floating all along
The purple west, and, two bright streaks between,
The golden lyre itself were dimly seen:
That the still murmur of the honey bee
Would never teach a rural song to me:
15 That the bright glance from beauty's eyelids slanting
Would never make a lay of mine enchanting,
Or warm my breast with ardour to unfold
Some tale of love and arms in time of old.

But there are times, when those that love the bay,
20 Fly from all sorrowing far, far away;
A sudden glow comes on them, nought they see
In water, earth, or air, but poesy.
It has been said, dear George, and true I hold it,
(For knightly Spenser to Libertas told it,)
25 That when a Poet is in such a trance,
In air he sees white coursers paw, and prance,
Bestridden of gay knights, in gay apparel,
Who at each other tilt in playful quarrel,
And what we, ignorantly, sheet-lightning call,
30 Is the swift opening of their wide portal,
When the bright warder blows his trumpet clear,
Whose tones reach nought on earth but Poet's ear.
When these enchanted portals open wide,
And through the light the horsemen swiftly glide,
35 The Poet's eye can reach those golden halls,
And view the glory of their festivals:
Their ladies fair, that in the distance seem
Fit for the silv'ring of a seraph's dream;
Their rich brimm'd goblets, that incessant run
40 Like the bright spots that move about the sun;

And, when upheld, the wine from each bright jar
Pours with the lustre of a falling star.
Yet further off, are dimly seen their bowers,
Of which no mortal eye can reach the flowers;
45   And 'tis right just, for well Apollo knows
'Twould make the Poet quarrel with the rose.
All that's reveal'd from that far seat of blisses,
Is, the clear fountains' interchanging kisses,
As gracefully descending, light and thin,
50   Like silver streaks across a dolphin's fin,
When he upswimmeth from the coral caves,
And sports with half his tail above the waves.

These wonders strange he sees, and many more,
Whose head is pregnant with poetic lore.
55   Should he upon an evening ramble fare
With forehead to the soothing breezes bare,
Would he naught see but the dark, silent blue
With all its diamonds trembling through and through?
Or the coy moon, when in the waviness
60   Of whitest clouds she does her beauty dress,
And staidly paces higher up, and higher,
Like a sweet nun in holy-day attire?
Ah, yes! much more would start into his sight—
The revelries, and mysteries of night:
65   And should I ever see them, I will tell you
Such tales as needs must with amazement spell you.

These are the living pleasures of the bard:
But richer far posterity's award.
What does he murmur with his latest breath,
70   While his proud eye looks through the film of death?
"What though I leave this dull, and earthly mould,
Yet shall my spirit lofty converse hold
With after times.—The patriot shall feel
My stern alarum, and unsheath his steel;
75   Or, in the senate thunder out my numbers
To startle princes from their easy slumbers.
The sage will mingle with each moral theme
My happy thoughts sententious; he will teem
With lofty periods when my verses fire him,
80   And then I'll stoop from heaven to inspire him.
Lays have I left of such a dear delight

That maids will sing them on their bridal night.
Gay villagers, upon a morn of May,
When they have tired their gentle limbs with play,
85   And form'd a snowy circle on the grass,
And plac'd in midst of all that lovely lass
Who chosen is their queen,—with her fine head
Crowned with flowers purple, white, and red:
For there the lily, and the musk-rose, sighing,
90   Are emblems true of hapless lovers dying:
Between her breasts, that never yet felt trouble,
A bunch of violets full blown, and double,
Serenely sleep:—she from a casket takes
A little book,—and then a joy awakes
95   About each youthful heart,—with stifled cries,
And rubbing of white hands, and sparkling eyes:
For she's to read a tale of hopes, and fears;
One that I foster'd in my youthful years:
The pearls, that on each glist'ning circlet sleep,
100 Gush ever and anon with silent creep,
Lured by the innocent dimples. To sweet rest
Shall the dear babe, upon its mother's breast,
Be lull'd with songs of mine. Fair world, adieu!
Thy dales, and hills, are fading from my view:
105 Swiftly I mount, upon wide spreading pinions,
Far from the narrow bounds of thy dominions.
Full joy I feel, while thus I cleave the air,
That my soft verse will charm thy daughters fair,
And warm thy sons!" Ah, my dear friend and brother,
110 Could I, at once, my mad ambition smother,
For tasting joys like these, sure I should be
Happier, and dearer to society.
At times, 'tis true, I've felt relief from pain
When some bright thought has darted through my brain:
115 Through all that day I've felt a greater pleasure
Than if I'd brought to light a hidden treasure.
As to my sonnets, though none else should heed them,
I feel delighted, still, that you should read them.
Of late, too, I have had much calm enjoyment,
120 Stretch'd on the grass at my best lov'd employment
Of scribbling lines for you. These things I thought
While, in my face, the freshest breeze I caught.
E'en now I'm pillow'd on a bed of flowers
That crowns a lofty clift, which proudly towers

125 Above the ocean-waves. The stalks, and blades,
    Chequer my tablet with their quivering shades.
    On one side is a field of drooping oats,
    Through which the poppies show their scarlet coats;
    So pert and useless, that they bring to mind
130 The scarlet coats that pester human-kind.
    And on the other side, outspread, is seen
    Ocean's blue mantle streak'd with purple, and green.
    Now 'tis I see a canvass'd ship, and now
    Mark the bright silver curling round her prow.
135 I see the lark down-dropping to his nest,
    And the broad winged sea-gull never at rest;
    For when no more he spreads his feathers free,
    His breast is dancing on the restless sea.
    Now I direct my eyes into the west,
140 Which at this moment is in sunbeams drest:
    Why westward turn? 'Twas but to say adieu!
    'Twas but to kiss my hand, dear George, to you!

    August, 1816

To Charles Cowden Clarke

    Oft have you seen a swan superbly frowning,
    And with proud breast his own white shadow crowning;
    He slants his neck beneath the waters bright
    So silently, it seems a beam of light
5   Come from the Galaxy: anon he sports,—
    With outspread wings the Naiad Zephyr courts,
    Or ruffles all the surface of the lake
    In striving from its crystal face to take
    Some diamond water drops, and them to treasure
10 In milky nest, and sip them off at leisure.
    But not a moment can he there insure them,
    Nor to such downy rest can he allure them;
    For down they rush as though they would be free,
    And drop like hours into eternity.
15 Just like that bird am I in loss of time,
    Whene'er I venture on the stream of rhyme;
    With shatter'd boat, oar snapt, and canvass rent,
    I slowly sail, scarce knowing my intent;

Still scooping up the water with my fingers,
20   In which a trembling diamond never lingers.

    By this, friend Charles, you may full plainly see
Why I have never penn'd a line to thee:
Because my thoughts were never free, and clear,
And little fit to please a classic ear;
25   Because my wine was of too poor a savour
For one whose palate gladdens in the flavour
Of sparkling Helicon:—small good it were
To take him to a desert rude, and bare,
Who had on Baiæ's shore reclin'd at ease,
30   While Tasso's page was floating in a breeze
That gave soft music from Armida's bowers,
Mingled with fragrance from her rarest flowers:
Small good to one who had by Mulla's stream
Fondled the maidens with the breasts of cream;
35   Who had beheld Belphœbe in a brook,
And lovely Una in a leafy nook,
And Archimago leaning o'er his book:
Who had of all that's sweet tasted, and seen,
From silv'ry ripple, up to beauty's queen;
40   From the sequester'd haunts of gay Titania,
To the blue dwelling of divine Urania:
One who, of late, had ta'en sweet forest walks
With him who elegantly chats, and talks—
The wrong'd Libertas,—who has told you stories
45   Of laurel chaplets, and Apollo's glories;
Of troops chivalrous prancing through a city,
And tearful ladies made for love, and pity:
With many else which I have never known.
Thus have I thought; and days on days have flown
50   Slowly, or rapidly—unwilling still
For you to try my dull, unlearned quill.
Nor should I now, but that I've known you long;
That you first taught me all the sweets of song:
The grand, the sweet, the terse, the free, the fine;
55   What swell'd with pathos, and what right divine:
Spenserian vowels that elope with ease,
And float along like birds o'er summer seas;
Miltonian storms, and more, Miltonian tenderness;
Michael in arms, and more, meek Eve's fair slenderness.
60   Who read for me the sonnet swelling loudly

Up to its climax and then dying proudly?
Who found for me the grandeur of the ode,
Growing, like Atlas, stronger from its load?
Who let me taste that more than cordial dram,
65   The sharp, the rapier-pointed epigram?
Shew'd me that epic was of all the king,
Round, vast, and spanning all like Saturn's ring?
You too upheld the veil from Clio's beauty,
And pointed out the patriot's stern duty;
70   The might of Alfred, and the shaft of Tell;
The hand of Brutus, that so grandly fell
Upon a tyrant's head. Ah! had I never seen,
Or known your kindness, what might I have been?
What my enjoyments in my youthful years,
75   Bereft of all that now my life endears?
And can I e'er these benefits forget?
And can I e'er repay the friendly debt?
No, doubly no;—yet should these rhymings please,
I shall roll on the grass with two-fold ease:
80   For I have long time been my fancy feeding
With hopes that you would one day think the reading
Of my rough verses not an hour misspent;
Should it e'er be so, what a rich content!
Some weeks have pass'd since last I saw the spires
85   In lucent Thames reflected:—warm desires
To see the sun o'er peep the eastern dimness,
And morning shadows streaking into slimness
Across the lawny fields, and pebbly water;
To mark the time as they grow broad, and shorter;
90   To feel the air that plays about the hills,
And sips its freshness from the little rills;
To see high, golden corn wave in the light
When Cynthia smiles upon a summer's night,
And peers among the cloudlet's jet and white,
95   As though she were reclining in a bed
Of bean blossoms, in heaven freshly shed.
No sooner had I stepp'd into these pleasures
Than I began to think of rhymes and measures:
The air that floated by me seem'd to say
100   "Write! thou wilt never have a better day."
And so I did. When many lines I'd written,
Though with their grace I was not oversmitten,
Yet, as my hand was warm, I thought I'd better

Trust to my feelings, and write you a letter.
105   Such an attempt required an inspiration
Of a peculiar sort,—a consummation;—
Which, had I felt, these scribblings might have been
Verses from which the soul would never wean:
But many days have past since last my heart
110   Was warm'd luxuriously by divine Mozart;
By Arne delighted, or by Handel madden'd;
Or by the song of Erin pierc'd and sadden'd:
What time you were before the music sitting,
And the rich notes to each sensation fitting;
115   Since I have walk'd with you through shady lanes
That freshly terminate in open plains,
And revel'd in a chat that ceased not
When at night-fall among your books we got:
No, nor when supper came, nor after that,—
120   Nor when reluctantly I took my hat;
No, nor till cordially you shook my hand
Mid-way between our homes:—your accents bland
Still sounded in my ears, when I no more
Could hear your footsteps touch the grav'ly floor.
125   Sometimes I lost them, and then found again;
You chang'd the footpath for the grassy plain.
In those still moments I have wish'd you joys
That well you know to honour:—"Life's very toys
With him," said I, "will take a pleasant charm;
130   It cannot be that ought will work him harm."
These thoughts now come o'er me with all their might:—
Again I shake your hand,—friend Charles, good night.

September, 1816

How many bards gild the lapses of time

How many bards gild the lapses of time!
    A few of them have ever been the food
    Of my delighted fancy,—I could brood
Over their beauties, earthly, or sublime:
5   And often, when I sit me down to rhyme,
    These will in throngs before my mind intrude:
    But no confusion, no disturbance rude
Do they occasion; 'tis a pleasing chime.

So the unnumber'd sounds that evening store;
10   The songs of birds—the whisp'ring of the leaves—
The voice of waters—the great bell that heaves
With solemn sound,—and thousand others more,
That distance of recognizance bereaves,
Make pleasing music, and not wild uproar.

On First Looking into Chapman's Homer

Much have I travell'd in the realms of gold,
And many goodly states and kingdoms seen;
Round many western islands have I been
Which bards in fealty to Apollo hold.
5   Oft of one wide expanse had I been told
That deep-brow'd Homer ruled as his demesne;
Yet did I never breathe its pure serene
Till I heard Chapman speak out loud and bold:
Then felt I like some watcher of the skies
10   When a new planet swims into his ken;
Or like stout Cortez when with eagle eyes
He star'd at the Pacific—and all his men
Look'd at each other with a wild surmise—
Silent, upon a peak in Darien.

Keen, fitful gusts are whisp'ring here and there

Keen, fitful gusts are whisp'ring here and there
Among the bushes half leafless, and dry;
The stars look very cold about the sky,
And I have many miles on foot to fare.
5   Yet feel I little of the cool bleak air,
Or of the dead leaves rustling drearily,
Or of those silver lamps that burn on high,
Or of the distance from home's pleasant lair:
For I am brimfull of the friendliness
10   That in a little cottage I have found;
Of fair-hair'd Milton's eloquent distress,
And all his love for gentle Lycid drown'd;
Of lovely Laura in her light green dress,
And faithful Petrarch gloriously crown'd.

On Leaving Some Friends at an Early Hour

Give me a golden pen, and let me lean
   On heap'd up flowers, in regions clear, and far;
   Bring me a tablet whiter than a star,
Or hand of hymning angel, when 'tis seen
5   The silver strings of heavenly harp atween:
   And let there glide by many a pearly car,
   Pink robes, and wavy hair, and diamond jar,
And half discovered wings, and glances keen.
The while let music wander round my ears,
10   And as it reaches each delicious ending,
    Let me write down a line of glorious tone,
And full of many wonders of the spheres:
   For what a height my spirit is contending!
   'Tis not content so soon to be alone.

To My Brothers

Small, busy flames play through the fresh laid coals,
   And their faint cracklings o'er our silence creep
   Like whispers of the household gods that keep
A gentle empire o'er fraternal souls.
5   And while, for rhymes, I search around the poles,
   Your eyes are fix'd, as in poetic sleep,
   Upon the lore so voluble and deep,
That aye at fall of night our care condoles.
This is your birth-day, Tom, and I rejoice
10   That thus it passes smoothly, quietly.
Many such eves of gently whisp'ring noise
   May we together pass, and calmly try
What are this world's true joys,—ere the great voice,
   From its fair face, shall bid our spirits fly.

November 18, 1816

Addressed to Haydon

Highmindedness, a jealousy for good,
   A loving-kindness for the great man's fame,
   Dwells here and there with people of no name,

In noisome alley, and in pathless wood:
5   And where we think the truth least understood,
    Oft may be found a "singleness of aim,"
    That ought to frighten into hooded shame
A money mong'ring, pitiable brood.
How glorious this affection for the cause
10   Of stedfast genius, toiling gallantly!
What when a stout unbending champion awes
    Envy, and Malice to their native sty?
Unnumber'd souls breathe out a still applause,
    Proud to behold him in his country's eye.

Addressed to the Same

Great spirits now on earth are sojourning;
    He of the cloud, the cataract, the lake,
    Who on Helvellyn's summit, wide awake,
Catches his freshness from archangel's wing:
5   He of the rose, the violet, the spring,
    The social smile, the chain for freedom's sake:
    And lo!—whose stedfastness would never take
A meaner sound than Raphael's whispering.
And other spirits there are standing apart
10   Upon the forehead of the age to come;
These, these will give the world another heart,
    And other pulses. Hear ye not the hum
Of mighty workings?——
    Listen awhile ye nations, and be dumb.

To G. A. W.

Nymph of the downward smile, and sidelong glance,
    In what diviner moments of the day
    Art thou most lovely? When gone far astray
Into the labyrinths of sweet utterance?
5   Or when serenely wand'ring in a trance
    Of sober thought? Or when starting away,
    With careless robe, to meet the morning ray,
Thou spar'st the flowers in thy mazy dance?
Haply 'tis when thy ruby lips part sweetly,

10 And so remain, because thou listenest:
But thou to please wert nurtured so completely
   That I can never tell what mood is best.
I shall as soon pronounce which Grace more neatly
   Trips it before Apollo than the rest.

To Kosciusko

Good Kosciusko, thy great name alone
   Is a full harvest whence to reap high feeling;
   It comes upon us like the glorious pealing
Of the wide spheres—an everlasting tone.
5 And now it tells me, that in worlds unknown,
   The names of heroes, burst from clouds concealing,
   Are changed to harmonies, for ever stealing
Through cloudless blue, and round each silver throne.
It tells me too, that on a happy day,
10   When some good spirit walks upon the earth,
     Thy name with Alfred's and the great of yore
   Gently commingling, gives tremendous birth
To a loud hymn, that sounds far, far away
     To where the great God lives for evermore.

Sleep and Poetry

"As I lay in my bed slepe full unmete
Was unto me, but why that I ne might
Rest I ne wist, for there n'as erthly wight
[As I suppose] had more of hertis ese
Than I, for I n'ad sicknesse nor disese."
          Chaucer

What is more gentle than a wind in summer?
What is more soothing than the pretty hummer
That stays one moment in an open flower,
And buzzes cheerily from bower to bower?
5 What is more tranquil than a musk-rose blowing
In a green island, far from all men's knowing?
More healthful than the leafiness of dales?
More secret than a nest of nightingales?

More serene than Cordelia's countenance?
10   More full of visions than a high romance?
What, but thee, Sleep? Soft closer of our eyes!
Low murmurer of tender lullabies!
Light hoverer around our happy pillows!
Wreather of poppy buds, and weeping willows!
15   Silent entangler of a beauty's tresses!
Most happy listener! when the morning blesses
Thee for enlivening all the cheerful eyes
That glance so brightly at the new sun-rise.

But what is higher beyond thought than thee?
20   Fresher than berries of a mountain tree?
More strange, more beautiful, more smooth, more regal,
Than wings of swans, than doves, than dim-seen eagle?
What is it? And to what shall I compare it?
It has a glory, and nought else can share it:
25   The thought thereof is awful, sweet, and holy,
Chacing away all worldliness and folly;
Coming sometimes like fearful claps of thunder,
Or the low rumblings earth's regions under;
And sometimes like a gentle whispering
30   Of all the secrets of some wond'rous thing
That breathes about us in the vacant air;
So that we look around with prying stare,
Perhaps to see shapes of light, aerial lymning,
And catch soft floatings from a faint-heard hymning;
35   To see the laurel wreath, on high suspended,
That is to crown our name when life is ended.
Sometimes it gives a glory to the voice,
And from the heart up-springs, rejoice! rejoice!
Sounds which will reach the Framer of all things,
40   And die away in ardent mutterings.

No one who once the glorious sun has seen,
And all the clouds, and felt his bosom clean
For his great Maker's presence, but must know
What 'tis I mean, and feel his being glow:
45   Therefore no insult will I give his spirit,
By telling what he sees from native merit.

O Poesy! for thee I hold my pen
That am not yet a glorious denizen

Of thy wide heaven—Should I rather kneel
50   Upon some mountain-top until I feel
A glowing splendour round about me hung,
And echo back the voice of thine own tongue?
O Poesy! for thee I grasp my pen
That am not yet a glorious denizen
55   Of thy wide heaven; yet, to my ardent prayer,
Yield from thy sanctuary some clear air,
Smoothed for intoxication by the breath
Of flowering bays, that I may die a death
Of luxury, and my young spirit follow
60   The morning sun-beams to the great Apollo
Like a fresh sacrifice; or, if I can bear
The o'erwhelming sweets, 'twill bring to me the fair
Visions of all places: a bowery nook
Will be elysium—an eternal book
65   Whence I may copy many a lovely saying
About the leaves, and flowers—about the playing
Of nymphs in woods, and fountains; and the shade
Keeping a silence round a sleeping maid;
And many a verse from so strange influence
70   That we must ever wonder how, and whence
It came. Also imaginings will hover
Round my fire-side, and haply there discover
Vistas of solemn beauty, where I'd wander
In happy silence, like the clear Meander
75   Through its lone vales; and where I found a spot
Of awfuller shade, or an enchanted grot,
Or a green hill o'erspread with chequered dress
Of flowers, and fearful from its loveliness,
Write on my tablets all that was permitted,
80   All that was for our human senses fitted.
Then the events of this wide world I'd seize
Like a strong giant, and my spirit teaze
Till at its shoulders it should proudly see
Wings to find out an immortality.

85   Stop and consider! life is but a day;
A fragile dew-drop on its perilous way
From a tree's summit; a poor Indian's sleep
While his boat hastens to the monstrous steep
Of Montmorenci. Why so sad a moan?
90   Life is the rose's hope while yet unblown;

The reading of an ever-changing tale;
The light uplifting of a maiden's veil;
A pigeon tumbling in clear summer air;
A laughing school-boy, without grief or care,
95   Riding the springy branches of an elm.

O for ten years, that I may overwhelm
Myself in poesy; so I may do the deed
That my own soul has to itself decreed.
Then will I pass the countries that I see
100   In long perspective, and continually
Taste their pure fountains. First the realm I'll pass
Of Flora, and old Pan: sleep in the grass,
Feed upon apples red, and strawberries,
And choose each pleasure that my fancy sees;
105   Catch the white-handed nymphs in shady places,
To woo sweet kisses from averted faces,—
Play with their fingers, touch their shoulders white
Into a pretty shrinking with a bite
As hard as lips can make it: till agreed,
110   A lovely tale of human life we'll read.
And one will teach a tame dove how it best
May fan the cool air gently o'er my rest;
Another, bending o'er her nimble tread,
Will set a green robe floating round her head,
115   And still will dance with ever varied ease,
Smiling upon the flowers and the trees:
Another will entice me on, and on
Through almond blossoms and rich cinnamon;
Till in the bosom of a leafy world
120   We rest in silence, like two gems upcurl'd
In the recesses of a pearly shell.

And can I ever bid these joys farewell?
Yes, I must pass them for a nobler life,
Where I may find the agonies, the strife
125   Of human hearts: for lo! I see afar,
O'er sailing the blue cragginess, a car
And steeds with streamy manes—the charioteer
Looks out upon the winds with glorious fear:
And now the numerous tramplings quiver lightly
130   Along a huge cloud's ridge; and now with sprightly

Wheel downward come they into fresher skies,
Tipt round with silver from the sun's bright eyes.
Still downward with capacious whirl they glide;
And now I see them on a green-hill's side
135 In breezy rest among the nodding stalks.
The charioteer with wond'rous gesture talks
To the trees and mountains; and there soon appear
Shapes of delight, of mystery, and fear,
Passing along before a dusky space
140 Made by some mighty oaks: as they would chase
Some ever-fleeting music on they sweep.
Lo! how they murmur, laugh, and smile, and weep:
Some with upholden hand and mouth severe;
Some with their faces muffled to the ear
145 Between their arms; some, clear in youthful bloom,
Go glad and smilingly athwart the gloom;
Some looking back, and some with upward gaze;
Yes, thousands in a thousand different ways
Flit onward—now a lovely wreath of girls
150 Dancing their sleek hair into tangled curls;
And now broad wings. Most awfully intent,
The driver of those steeds is forward bent,
And seems to listen: O that I might know
All that he writes with such a hurrying glow.

155   The visions all are fled—the car is fled
Into the light of heaven, and in their stead
A sense of real things comes doubly strong,
And, like a muddy stream, would bear along
My soul to nothingness: but I will strive
160 Against all doubtings, and will keep alive
The thought of that same chariot, and the strange
Journey it went.

                    Is there so small a range
In the present strength of manhood, that the high
Imagination cannot freely fly
165 As she was wont of old? prepare her steeds,
Paw up against the light, and do strange deeds
Upon the clouds? Has she not shewn us all?
From the clear space of ether, to the small
Breath of new buds unfolding? From the meaning
170 Of Jove's large eye-brow, to the tender greening

Of April meadows? Here her altar shone,
E'en in this isle; and who could paragon
The fervid choir that lifted up a noise
Of harmony, to where it aye will poise
175   Its mighty self of convoluting sound,
Huge as a planet, and like that roll round,
Eternally around a dizzy void?
Ay, in those days the Muses were nigh cloy'd
With honors; nor had any other care
180   Than to sing out and sooth their wavy hair.

    Could all this be forgotten? Yes, a schism
Nurtured by foppery and barbarism,
Made great Apollo blush for this his land.
Men were thought wise who could not understand
185   His glories: with a puling infant's force
They sway'd about upon a rocking horse,
And thought it Pegasus. Ah dismal soul'd!
The winds of heaven blew, the ocean roll'd
Its gathering waves—ye felt it not. The blue
190   Bared its eternal bosom, and the dew
Of summer nights collected still to make
The morning precious: beauty was awake!
Why were ye not awake? But ye were dead
To things ye knew not of,—were closely wed
195   To musty laws lined out with wretched rule
And compass vile: so that ye taught a school
Of dolts to smooth, inlay, and clip, and fit,
Till, like the certain wands of Jacob's wit,
Their verses tallied. Easy was the task:
200   A thousand handicraftsmen wore the mask
Of Poesy. Ill-fated, impious race!
That blasphemed the bright Lyrist to his face,
And did not know it,—no, they went about,
Holding a poor, decrepid standard out
205   Mark'd with most flimsy mottos, and in large
The name of one Boileau!

                    O ye whose charge
It is to hover round our pleasant hills!
Whose congregated majesty so fills
My boundly reverence, that I cannot trace
210   Your hallowed names, in this unholy place,

So near those common folk; did not their shames
Affright you? Did our old lamenting Thames
Delight you? Did ye never cluster round
Delicious Avon, with a mournful sound,
215 And weep? Or did ye wholly bid adieu
To regions where no more the laurel grew?
Or did ye stay to give a welcoming
To some lone spirits who could proudly sing
Their youth away, and die? 'Twas even so:
220 But let me think away those times of woe:
Now 'tis a fairer season; ye have breathed
Rich benedictions o'er us; ye have wreathed
Fresh garlands: for sweet music has been heard
In many places;—some has been upstirr'd
225 From out its crystal dwelling in a lake,
By a swan's ebon bill; from a thick brake,
Nested and quiet in a valley mild,
Bubbles a pipe; fine sounds are floating wild
About the earth: happy are ye and glad.

230   These things are doubtless: yet in truth we've had
Strange thunders from the potency of song;
Mingled indeed with what is sweet and strong,
From majesty: but in clear truth the themes
Are ugly clubs, the poets Polyphemes
235 Disturbing the grand sea. A drainless shower
Of light is poesy; 'tis the supreme of power;
'Tis might half slumb'ring on its own right arm.
The very archings of her eye-lids charm
A thousand willing agents to obey,
240 And still she governs with the mildest sway:
But strength alone though of the Muses born
Is like a fallen angel: trees uptorn,
Darkness, and worms, and shrouds, and sepulchres
Delight it; for it feeds upon the burrs,
245 And thorns of life; forgetting the great end
Of poesy, that it should be a friend
To sooth the cares, and lift the thoughts of man.

    Yet I rejoice: a myrtle fairer than
E'er grew in Paphos, from the bitter weeds
250 Lifts its sweet head into the air, and feeds
A silent space with ever sprouting green.

All tenderest birds there find a pleasant screen,
Creep through the shade with jaunty fluttering,
Nibble the little cupped flowers and sing.
255 Then let us clear away the choaking thorns
From round its gentle stem; let the young fawns,
Yeaned in after times, when we are flown,
Find a fresh sward beneath it, overgrown
With simple flowers: let there nothing be
260 More boisterous than a lover's bended knee;
Nought more ungentle than the placid look
Of one who leans upon a closed book;
Nought more untranquil than the grassy slopes
Between two hills. All hail delightful hopes!
265 As she was wont, th' imagination
Into most lovely labyrinths will be gone,
And they shall be accounted poet kings
Who simply tell the most heart-easing things.
O may these joys be ripe before I die.

270 Will not some say that I presumptuously
Have spoken? that from hastening disgrace
'Twere better far to hide my foolish face?
That whining boyhood should with reverence bow
Ere the dread thunderbolt could reach? How!
275 If I do hide myself, it sure shall be
In the very fane, the light of Poesy:
If I do fall, at least I will be laid
Beneath the silence of a poplar shade;
And over me the grass shall be smooth shaven;
280 And there shall be a kind memorial graven.
But off, Despondence! miserable bane!
They should not know thee, who, athirst to gain
A noble end, are thirsty every hour.
What though I am not wealthy in the dower
285 Of spanning wisdom; though I do not know
The shiftings of the mighty winds that blow
Hither and thither all the changing thoughts
Of man: though no great minist'ring reason sorts
Out the dark mysteries of human souls
290 To clear conceiving: yet there ever rolls
A vast idea before me, and I glean
Therefrom my liberty; thence too I've seen
The end and aim of Poesy. 'Tis clear

As any thing most true; as that the year
295   Is made of the four seasons—manifest
As a large cross, some old cathedral's crest,
Lifted to the white clouds. Therefore should I
Be but the essence of deformity,
A coward, did my very eye-lids wink
300   At speaking out what I have dared to think.
Ah! rather let me like a madman run
Over some precipice; let the hot sun
Melt my Dedalian wings, and drive me down
Convuls'd and headlong! Stay! an inward frown
305   Of conscience bids me be more calm awhile.
An ocean dim, sprinkled with many an isle,
Spreads awfully before me. How much toil!
How many days! what desperate turmoil!
Ere I can have explored its widenesses.
310   Ah, what a task! upon my bended knees,
I could unsay those—no, impossible!
Impossible!

           For sweet relief I'll dwell
On humbler thoughts, and let this strange assay
Begun in gentleness die so away.
315   E'en now all tumult from my bosom fades:
I turn full hearted to the friendly aids
That smooth the path of honour; brotherhood,
And friendliness, the nurse of mutual good;
The hearty grasp that sends a pleasant sonnet
320   Into the brain ere one can think upon it;
The silence when some rhymes are coming out;
And when they're come, the very pleasant rout:
The message certain to be done to-morrow—
'Tis perhaps as well that it should be to borrow
325   Some precious book from out its snug retreat,
To cluster round it when we next shall meet.
Scarce can I scribble on; for lovely airs
Are fluttering round the room like doves in pairs;
Many delights of that glad day recalling,
330   When first my senses caught their tender falling.
And with these airs come forms of elegance
Stooping their shoulders o'er a horse's prance,
Careless, and grand—fingers soft and round
Parting luxuriant curls;—and the swift bound

335   Of Bacchus from his chariot, when his eye
       Made Ariadne's cheek look blushingly.
       Thus I remember all the pleasant flow
       Of words at opening a portfolio.

         Things such as these are ever harbingers
340   To trains of peaceful images: the stirs
       Of a swan's neck unseen among the rushes:
       A linnet starting all about the bushes:
       A butterfly, with golden wings broad parted,
       Nestling a rose, convuls'd as though it smarted
345   With over pleasure—many, many more,
       Might I indulge at large in all my store
       Of luxuries: yet I must not forget
       Sleep, quiet with his poppy coronet:
       For what there may be worthy in these rhymes
350   I partly owe to him: and thus, the chimes
       Of friendly voices had just given place
       To as sweet a silence, when I 'gan retrace
       The pleasant day, upon a couch at ease.
       It was a poet's house who keeps the keys
355   Of pleasure's temple. Round about were hung
       The glorious features of the bards who sung
       In other ages—cold and sacred busts
       Smiled at each other. Happy he who trusts
       To clear futurity his darling fame!
360   Then there were fauns and satyrs taking aim
       At swelling apples with a frisky leap
       And reaching fingers, 'mid a luscious heap
       Of vine leaves. Then there rose to view a fane
       Of liny marble, and thereto a train
365   Of nymphs approaching fairly o'er the sward:
       One, loveliest, holding her white hand toward
       The dazzling sun-rise: two sisters sweet
       Bending their graceful figures till they meet
       Over the trippings of a little child:
370   And some are hearing, eagerly, the wild
       Thrilling liquidity of dewy piping.
       See, in another picture, nymphs are wiping
       Cherishingly Diana's timorous limbs;—
       A fold of lawny mantle dabbling swims
375   At the bath's edge, and keeps a gentle motion
       With the subsiding crystal: as when ocean

Heaves calmly its broad swelling smoothness o'er
Its rocky marge, and balances once more
The patient weeds, that now unshent by foam
380   Feel all about their undulating home.

Sappho's meek head was there half smiling down
At nothing; just as though the earnest frown
Of over thinking had that moment gone
From off her brow, and left her all alone.

385   Great Alfred's too, with anxious, pitying eyes,
As if he always listened to the sighs
Of the goaded world; and Kosciusko's worn
By horrid suffrance—mightily forlorn.

Petrarch, outstepping from the shady green,
390   Starts at the sight of Laura; nor can wean
His eyes from her sweet face. Most happy they!
For over them was seen a free display
Of out-spread wings, and from between them shone
The face of Poesy: from off her throne
395   She overlook'd things that I scarce could tell.
The very sense of where I was might well
Keep Sleep aloof: but more than that there came
Thought after thought to nourish up the flame
Within my breast; so that the morning light
400   Surprised me even from a sleepless night;
And up I rose refresh'd, and glad, and gay,
Resolving to begin that very day
These lines; and howsoever they be done,
I leave them as a father does his son.

I stood tip-toe upon a little hill

"Places of nestling green for Poets made."
Story of Rimini

I stood tip-toe upon a little hill,
The air was cooling, and so very still,
That the sweet buds which with a modest pride
Pull droopingly, in slanting curve aside,

5   Their scantly leaved, and finely tapering stems,
       Had not yet lost those starry diadems
       Caught from the early sobbing of the morn.
       The clouds were pure and white as flocks new shorn,
       And fresh from the clear brook; sweetly they slept
10   On the blue fields of heaven, and then there crept
       A little noiseless noise among the leaves,
       Born of the very sigh that silence heaves:
       For not the faintest motion could be seen
       Of all the shades that slanted o'er the green.
15   There was wide wand'ring for the greediest eye,
       To peer about upon variety;
       Far round the horizon's crystal air to skim,
       And trace the dwindled edgings of its brim;
       To picture out the quaint, and curious bending
20   Of a fresh woodland alley, never ending;
       Or by the bowery clefts, and leafy shelves,
       Guess where the jaunty streams refresh themselves.
       I gazed awhile, and felt as light, and free
       As though the fanning wings of Mercury
25   Had played upon my heels: I was light-hearted,
       And many pleasures to my vision started;
       So I straightway began to pluck a posey
       Of luxuries bright, milky, soft and rosy.

       A bush of May flowers with the bees about them;
30   Ah, sure no tasteful nook would be without them;
       And let a lush laburnum oversweep them,
       And let long grass grow round the roots to keep them
       Moist, cool and green; and shade the violets,
       That they may bind the moss in leafy nets.

35   A filbert hedge with wild briar overtwined,
       And clumps of woodbine taking the soft wind
       Upon their summer thrones; there too should be
       The frequent chequer of a youngling tree,
       That with a score of light green brethren shoots
40   From the quaint mossiness of aged roots:
       Round which is heard a spring-head of clear waters
       Babbling so wildly of its lovely daughters
       The spreading blue bells: it may haply mourn
       That such fair clusters should be rudely torn
45   From their fresh beds, and scattered thoughtlessly
       By infant hands, left on the path to die.

Open afresh your round of starry folds,
Ye ardent marigolds!
Dry up the moisture from your golden lids,
50 For great Apollo bids
That in these days your praises should be sung
On many harps, which he has lately strung;
And when again your dewiness he kisses,
Tell him, I have you in my world of blisses:
55 So haply when I rove in some far vale,
His mighty voice may come upon the gale.

Here are sweet peas, on tip-toe for a flight:
With wings of gentle flush o'er delicate white,
And taper fingers catching at all things,
60 To bind them all about with tiny rings.

Linger awhile upon some bending planks
That lean against a streamlet's rushy banks,
And watch intently Nature's gentle doings:
They will be found softer than ring-dove's cooings.
65 How silent comes the water round that bend;
Not the minutest whisper does it send
To the o'erhanging sallows: blades of grass
Slowly across the chequer'd shadows pass.
Why, you might read two sonnets, ere they reach
70 To where the hurrying freshnesses aye preach
A natural sermon o'er their pebbly beds;
Where swarms of minnows show their little heads,
Staying their wavy bodies 'gainst the streams,
To taste the luxury of sunny beams
75 Temper'd with coolness. How they ever wrestle
With their own sweet delight, and ever nestle
Their silver bellies on the pebbly sand.
If you but scantily hold out the hand,
That very instant not one will remain;
80 But turn your eye, and they are there again.
The ripples seem right glad to reach those cresses,
And cool themselves among the em'rald tresses;
The while they cool themselves, they freshness give,
And moisture, that the bowery green may live:
85 So keeping up an interchange of favours,
Like good men in the truth of their behaviours.
Sometimes goldfinches one by one will drop
From low hung branches; little space they stop;

But sip, and twitter, and their feathers sleek;
90   Then off at once, as in a wanton freak:
Or perhaps, to show their black, and golden wings,
Pausing upon their yellow flutterings.
Were I in such a place, I sure should pray
That nought less sweet might call my thoughts away,
95   Than the soft rustle of a maiden's gown
Fanning away the dandelion's down;
Than the light music of her nimble toes
Patting against the sorrel as she goes.
How she would start, and blush, thus to be caught
100   Playing in all her innocence of thought.
O let me lead her gently o'er the brook,
Watch her half-smiling lips, and downward look;
O let me for one moment touch her wrist;
Let me one moment to her breathing list;
105   And as she leaves me may she often turn
Her fair eyes looking through her locks aubùrne.

What next? A tuft of evening primroses,
O'er which the mind may hover till it dozes;
O'er which it well might take a pleasant sleep,
110   But that 'tis ever startled by the leap
Of buds into ripe flowers; or by the flitting
Of diverse moths, that aye their rest are quitting;
Or by the moon lifting her silver rim
Above a cloud, and with a gradual swim
115   Coming into the blue with all her light.
O Maker of sweet poets, dear delight
Of this fair world, and all its gentle livers;
Spangler of clouds, halo of crystal rivers,
Mingler with leaves, and dew and tumbling streams,
120   Closer of lovely eyes to lovely dreams,
Lover of loneliness, and wandering,
Of upcast eye, and tender pondering!
Thee must I praise above all other glories
That smile us on to tell delightful stories.
125   For what has made the sage or poet write
But the fair paradise of Nature's light?
In the calm grandeur of a sober line,
We see the waving of the mountain pine;
And when a tale is beautifully staid,
130   We feel the safety of a hawthorn glade:

When it is moving on luxurious wings,
The soul is lost in pleasant smotherings:
Fair dewy roses brush against our faces,
And flowering laurels spring from diamond vases;
135   O'er head we see the jasmine and sweet briar,
And bloomy grapes laughing from green attire;
While at our feet, the voice of crystal bubbles
Charms us at once away from all our troubles:
So that we feel uplifted from the world,
140   Walking upon the white clouds wreath'd and curl'd.
So felt he, who first told, how Psyche went
On the smooth wind to realms of wonderment;
What Psyche felt, and Love, when their full lips
First touch'd; what amorous, and fondling nips
145   They gave each other's cheeks; with all their sighs,
And how they kist each other's tremulous eyes:
The silver lamp,—the ravishment,—the wonder—
The darkness,—loneliness,—the fearful thunder;
Their woes gone by, and both to heaven upflown,
150   To bow for gratitude before Jove's throne.
So did he feel, who pull'd the boughs aside,
That we might look into a forest wide,
To catch a glimpse of Fauns, and Dryades
Coming with softest rustle through the trees;
155   And garlands woven of flowers wild, and sweet,
Upheld on ivory wrists, or sporting feet:
Telling us how fair, trembling Syrinx fled
Arcadian Pan, with such a fearful dread.
Poor nymph,—poor Pan,—how he did weep to find
160   Nought but a lovely sighing of the wind
Along the reedy stream; a half heard strain,
Full of sweet desolation—balmy pain.

What first inspired a bard of old to sing
Narcissus pining o'er the untainted spring?
165   In some delicious ramble, he had found
A little space, with boughs all woven round;
And in the midst of all, a clearer pool
Than e'er reflected in its pleasant cool
The blue sky here, and there, serenely peeping
170   Through tendril wreaths fantastically creeping.
And on the bank a lonely flower he spied,
A meek and forlorn flower, with naught of pride,

Drooping its beauty o'er the watery clearness,
To woo its own sad image into nearness:
175   Deaf to light Zephyrus it would not move;
But still would seem to droop, to pine, to love.
So while the Poet stood in this sweet spot,
Some fainter gleamings o'er his fancy shot;
Nor was it long ere he had told the tale
180   Of young Narcissus, and sad Echo's bale.

Where had he been, from whose warm head out-flew
That sweetest of all songs, that ever new,
That aye refreshing, pure deliciousness,
Coming ever to bless
185   The wanderer by moonlight? to him bringing
Shapes from the invisible world, unearthly singing
From out the middle air, from flowery nests,
And from the pillowy silkiness that rests
Full in the speculation of the stars.
190   Ah! surely he had burst our mortal bars;
Into some wond'rous region he had gone,
To search for thee, divine Endymion!

He was a Poet, sure a lover too,
Who stood on Latmus' top, what time there blew
195   Soft breezes from the myrtle vale below;
And brought in faintness solemn, sweet, and slow
A hymn from Dian's temple; while upswelling,
The incense went to her own starry dwelling.
But though her face was clear as infant's eyes,
200   Though she stood smiling o'er the sacrifice,
The Poet wept at her so piteous fate,
Wept that such beauty should be desolate:
So in fine wrath some golden sounds he won,
And gave meek Cynthia her Endymion.

205   Queen of the wide air; thou most lovely queen
Of all the brightness that mine eyes have seen!
As thou exceedest all things in thy shine,
So every tale, does this sweet tale of thine.
O for three words of honey, that I might
210   Tell but one wonder of thy bridal night!

Where distant ships do seem to show their keels,

Phœbus awhile delayed his mighty wheels,
And turned to smile upon thy bashful eyes,
Ere he his unseen pomp would solemnize.
215   The evening weather was so bright, and clear,
That men of health were of unusual cheer;
Stepping like Homer at the trumpet's call,
Or young Apollo on the pedestal:
And lovely women were as fair and warm,
220   As Venus looking sideways in alarm.
The breezes were ethereal, and pure,
And crept through half closed lattices to cure
The languid sick; it cool'd their fever'd sleep,
And soothed them into slumbers full and deep.
225   Soon they awoke clear eyed: nor burnt with thirsting,
Nor with hot fingers, nor with temples bursting:
And springing up, they met the wond'ring sight
Of their dear friends, nigh foolish with delight;
Who feel their arms, and breasts, and kiss and stare,
230   And on their placid foreheads part the hair.
Young men, and maidens at each other gaz'd
With hands held back, and motionless, amaz'd
To see the brightness in each other's eyes;
And so they stood, fill'd with a sweet surprise,
235   Until their tongues were loos'd in poesy.
Therefore no lover did of anguish die:
But the soft numbers, in that moment spoken,
Made silken ties, that never may be broken.
Cynthia! I cannot tell the greater blisses,
240   That follow'd thine, and thy dear shepherd's kisses:
Was there a Poet born?—but now no more,
My wand'ring spirit must no further soar.—

Written in Disgust of Vulgar Superstition

The church bells toll a melancholy round,
   Calling the people to some other prayers,
   Some other gloominess, more dreadful cares,
More heark'ning to the sermon's horrid sound.
5   Surely the mind of man is closely bound
   In some black spell; seeing that each one tears
   Himself from fireside joys, and Lydian airs,
And converse high of those with glory crown'd.

Still, still they toll, and I should feel a damp,
10   A chill as from a tomb, did I not know
That they are dying like an outburnt lamp;
    That 'tis their sighing, wailing ere they go
    Into oblivion;—that fresh flowers will grow,
And many glories of immortal stamp.

On the Grasshopper and Cricket

The poetry of earth is never dead:
    When all the birds are faint with the hot sun,
    And hide in cooling trees, a voice will run
From hedge to hedge about the new-mown mead;
5   That is the Grasshopper's—he takes the lead
    In summer luxury,—he has never done
    With his delights; for when tired out with fun
He rests at ease beneath some pleasant weed.
The poetry of earth is ceasing never:
10   On a lone winter evening, when the frost
        Has wrought a silence, from the stove there shrills
The Cricket's song, in warmth increasing ever,
    And seems to one in drowsiness half lost,
    The Grasshopper's among some grassy hills.

December 30, 1816

After dark vapours have oppressed our plains

After dark vapours have oppressed our plains
    For a long dreary season, comes a day
    Born of the gentle south, and clears away
From the sick heavens all unseemly stains.
5   The anxious month, relieving from its pains,
    Takes as a long lost right the feel of May,
    The eyelids with the passing coolness play,
Like rose-leaves with the drip of summer rains.
And calmest thoughts come round us—as, of leaves
10   Budding—fruit ripening in stillness—autumn suns
Smiling at eve upon the quiet sheaves—
        Sweet Sappho's cheek—a sleeping infant's breath—
        The gradual sand that through an hour glass runs—
        A woodland rivulet—a poet's death.

To a Young Lady Who Sent Me a Laurel Crown

Fresh morning gusts have blown away all fear
　From my glad bosom—now from gloominess
　I mount for ever—not an atom less
Than the proud laurel shall content my bier.
5　No! by the eternal stars! or why sit here
　In the sun's eye, and 'gainst my temples press
　Apollo's very leaves—woven to bless
By thy white fingers, and thy spirit clear.
Lo! who dares say, "Do this"?—Who dares call down
10　My will from its own purpose? who say, "Stand,"
Or "Go"? This very moment I would frown
　On abject Cæsars—not the stoutest band
Of mailed heroes should tear off my crown:—
　Yet would I kneel and kiss thy gentle hand!

On Receiving a Laurel Crown from Leigh Hunt

Minutes are flying swiftly; and as yet
　Nothing unearthly has enticed my brain
　Into a delphic labyrinth. I would fain
Catch an immortal thought to pay the debt
5　I owe to the kind poet who has set
　Upon my ambitious head a glorious gain—
　Two bending laurel sprigs—'tis nearly pain
To be conscious of such a coronet.
Still time is fleeting, and no dream arises
10　Gorgeous as I would have it—only I see
A trampling down of what the world most prizes,
　Turbans and crowns, and blank regality;
And then I run into most wild surmises
　Of all the many glories that may be.

To the Ladies Who Saw Me Crown'd

What is there in the universal earth
　More lovely than a wreath from the bay tree?
　Haply a halo round the moon—a glee
Circling from three sweet pair of lips in mirth;
5　And haply you will say the dewy birth
　Of morning roses—riplings tenderly

Spread by the halcyon's breast upon the sea—
But these comparisons are nothing worth.
Then is there nothing in the world so fair?
10   The silvery tears of April?—Youth of May?
         Or June that breathes out life for butterflies?
No—none of these can from my favorite bear
   Away the palm; yet shall it ever pay
   Due reverence to your most sovereign eyes.

God of the golden bow

God of the golden bow,
   And of the golden lyre,
And of the golden hair,
   And of the golden fire,
5   Charioteer
         Round the patient year—
      Where, where slept thine ire,
When like a blank ideot I put on thy wreath—
      Thy laurel, thy glory,
10   The light of thy story?
Or was I a worm too low-creeping for death,
      O Delphic Apollo?

The Thunderer grasp'd and grasp'd,
   The Thunderer frown'd and frown'd;
15   The eagle's feathery mane
      For wrath became stiffened; the sound
         Of breeding thunder
         Went drowsily under,
      Muttering to be unbound.
20 O why didst thou pity and beg for a worm?
         Why touch thy soft lute
         Till the thunder was mute?
Why was I not crush'd—such a pitiful germ?
         O Delphic Apollo!

25   The Pleiades were up,
         Watching the silent air;
      The seeds and roots in earth
         Were swelling for summer fare;
         The ocean, its neighbour,

30 Was at his old labor,
When—who, who did dare
To tie for a moment thy plant round his brow,
And grin and look proudly,
And blaspheme so loudly,
35 And live for that honor to stoop to thee now,
O Delphic Apollo?

This pleasant tale is like a little copse

This pleasant tale is like a little copse:
The honied lines do freshly interlace,
To keep the reader in so sweet a place,
So that he here and there full hearted stops;
5 And oftentimes he feels the dewy drops
Come cool and suddenly against his face,
And by the wandering melody may trace
Which way the tender-legged linnet hops.
Oh! what a power has white simplicity!
10 What mighty power has this gentle story!
I, that do ever feel athirst for glory,
Could at this moment be content to lie
Meekly upon the grass, as those whose sobbings
Were heard of none beside the mournful robbins.

To Leigh Hunt, Esq.

Glory and loveliness have passed away;
For if we wander out in early morn,
No wreathed incense do we see upborne
Into the east, to meet the smiling day:
5 No crowd of nymphs soft voic'd and young, and gay,
In woven baskets bringing ears of corn,
Roses, and pinks, and violets, to adorn
The shrine of Flora in her early May.
But there are left delights as high as these,
10 And I shall ever bless my destiny,
That in a time, when under pleasant trees
Pan is no longer sought, I feel a free,
A leafy luxury, seeing I could please
With these poor offerings, a man like thee.

On Seeing the Elgin Marbles

My spirit is too weak—mortality
　Weighs heavily on me like unwilling sleep,
　And each imagined pinnacle and steep
Of godlike hardship tells me I must die
5　Like a sick eagle looking at the sky.
　Yet 'tis a gentle luxury to weep
　That I have not the cloudy winds to keep
Fresh for the opening of the morning's eye.
Such dim-conceived glories of the brain
10　Bring round the heart an undescribable feud;
So do these wonders a most dizzy pain,
　That mingles Grecian grandeur with the rude
Wasting of old time—with a billowy main—
　A sun—a shadow of a magnitude.

To Haydon with a Sonnet
Written on Seeing the Elgin Marbles

Forgive me, Haydon, that I cannot speak
　Definitively on these mighty things;
　Forgive me that I have not eagle's wings—
That what I want I know not where to seek:
5　And think that I would not be overmeek
　In rolling out upfollow'd thunderings,
　Even to the steep of Heliconian springs,
Were I of ample strength for such a freak.
Think too that all those numbers should be thine;
10　Whose else? In this who touch thy vesture's hem?
For when men star'd at what was most divine
　With browless idiotism—o'erweening phlegm—
Thou hadst beheld the Hesperean shine
　Of their star in the east and gone to worship them.

On a Leander Which Miss Reynolds,
My Kind Friend, Gave Me

Come hither all sweet maidens, soberly
　Down-looking—aye, and with a chastened light
　Hid in the fringes of your eyelids white—

And meekly let your fair hands joined be.
5 So gentle are ye that ye could not see,
      Untouch'd, a victim of your beauty bright—
      Sinking away to his young spirit's night,
Sinking bewilder'd mid the dreary sea:
'Tis young Leander toiling to his death.
10   Nigh swooning, he doth purse his weary lips
         For Hero's cheek and smiles against her smile.
      O horrid dream—see how his body dips
         Dead heavy—arms and shoulders gleam awhile:
He's gone—up bubbles all his amorous breath.

On The Story of Rimini

Who loves to peer up at the morning sun,
   With half-shut eyes and comfortable cheek,
   Let him with this sweet tale full often seek
For meadows where the little rivers run.
5 Who loves to linger with that brightest one
      Of heaven, Hesperus—let him lowly speak
      These numbers to the night and starlight meek,
Or moon, if that her hunting be begun.
He who knows these delights, and, too, is prone
10   To moralize upon a smile or tear,
Will find at once a region of his own,
      A bower for his spirit, and will steer
To alleys where the fir-tree drops its cone,
      Where robins hop, and fallen leaves are sere.

On the Sea

It keeps eternal whisperings around
   Desolate shores, and with its mighty swell
   Gluts twice ten thousand caverns; till the spell
Of Hecate leaves them their old shadowy sound.
5 Often 'tis in such gentle temper found
      That scarcely will the very smallest shell
      Be moved for days from whence it sometime fell,
When last the winds of heaven were unbound.
O ye who have your eyeballs vext and tir'd,
10   Feast them upon the wideness of the sea;

O ye whose ears are dinned with uproar rude,
Or fed too much with cloying melody—
   Sit ye near some old cavern's mouth and brood
Until ye start, as if the sea nymphs quired.

Unfelt, unheard, unseen

   Unfelt, unheard, unseen,
   I've left my little queen,
Her languid arms in silver slumber dying:
   Ah! through their nestling touch,
5   Who, who could tell how much
There is for madness—cruel or complying?

   Those faery lids how sleek,
   Those lips how moist—they speak,
In ripest quiet, shadows of sweet sounds;
10   Into my fancy's ear
   Melting a burden dear,
How "love doth know no fulness nor no bounds."

   True tender monitors,
   I bend unto your laws:
15 This sweetest day for dalliance was born;
   So, without more ado,
   I'll feel my heaven anew,
For all the blushing of the hasty morn.

Hither, hither, love

Hither, hither, love,
  'Tis a shady mead;
Hither, hither, love,
  Let us feed and feed.

5 Hither, hither, sweet,
  'Tis a cowslip bed;
Hither, hither, sweet,
  'Tis with dew bespread.

Hither, hither, dear,
10 By the breath of life,

Hither, hither, dear,
　　Be the summer's wife.

Though one moment's pleasure
　　In one moment flies,
15　Though the passion's treasure
　　In one moment dies;

Yet it has not pass'd—
　　Think how near, how near;
And while it doth last,
20　Think how dear, how dear.

Hither, hither, hither,
　　Love this boon has sent;
If I die and wither
　　I shall die content.

You say you love; but with a voice

You say you love; but with a voice
　　Chaster than a nun's, who singeth
The soft vespers to herself
　　While the chime-bell ringeth—
5　　　O love me truly!

You say you love; but with a smile
　　Cold as sunrise in September,
As you were Saint Cupid's nun,
　　And kept his weeks of Ember—
10　　　O love me truly!

You say you love; but then your lips
　　Coral tinted teach no blisses,
More than coral in the sea—
　　They never pout for kisses—
15　　　O love me truly!

You say you love; but then your hand
　　No soft squeeze for squeeze returneth;
It is like a statue's, dead,—
　　While mine for passion burneth—
20　　　O love me truly!

O breathe a word or two of fire!
   Smile, as if those words should burn me,
Squeeze as lovers should—O kiss
   And in thy heart inurn me—
25   O love me truly!

Before he went to live with owls and bats

Before he went to live with owls and bats,
   Nebuchadnezzar had an ugly dream,
   Worse than a housewife's, when she thinks her cream
Made a naumachia for mice and rats:
5 So scared, he sent for that "good king of cats,"
   Young Daniel, who did straightway pluck the beam
   From out his eye, and said—"I do not deem
Your sceptre worth a straw, your cushions old door mats."
A horrid nightmare, similar somewhat,
10   Of late has haunted a most valiant crew
     Of loggerheads and chapmen;—we are told
That any Daniel, though he be a sot,
   Can make their lying lips turn pale of hue,
     By drawling out—"Ye are that head of gold!"

The Gothic looks solemn

1

   The Gothic looks solemn,
   The plain Doric column
Supports an old bishop and crosier;
   The mouldering arch,
5   Shaded o'er by a larch,
Stands next door to Wilson the Hosier.

2

   Vicè—that is, by turns,—
   O'er pale faces mourns
The black tassell'd trencher and common hat;
10   The chantry boy sings,
   The steeple-bell rings,
And as for the Chancellor—*dominat.*

3

There are plenty of trees,
And plenty of ease,
15 And plenty of fat deer for parsons;
And when it is venison,
Short is the benison,—
Then each on a leg or thigh fastens.

O grant that like to Peter I

O grant that like to Peter I
May like to Peter B.
And tell me lovely Jesus Y
Old Jonah went to C.

Think not of it, sweet one, so

Think not of it, sweet one, so;
    Give it not a tear;
Sigh thou mayest, but bid it go
    Any, any where.

5 Do not look so sad, sweet one,
    Sad and fadingly:
Shed one drop then—It is gone—
    Oh! 'twas born to die.

Still so pale?—then, dearest, weep;
10   Weep! I'll count the tears:
And each one shall be a bliss
    For thee in after years.

Brighter has it left thine eyes
    Than a sunny hill:
15 And thy whispering melodies
    Are tenderer still.

Yet, as all things mourn awhile
    At fleeting blisses,
Let us too!—but be our dirge
20   A dirge of kisses.

Endymion:
A Poetic Romance

"The stretched metre of an antique song"

INSCRIBED TO THE MEMORY OF THOMAS CHATTERTON

Preface

Knowing within myself the manner in which this Poem has been produced, it is not without a feeling of regret that I make it public.

What manner I mean, will be quite clear to the reader, who must soon perceive great inexperience, immaturity, and every error denoting a feverish attempt, rather than a deed accomplished. The two first books, and indeed the two last, I feel sensible are not of such completion as to warrant their passing the press; nor should they if I thought a year's castigation would do them any good;—it will not: the foundations are too sandy. It is just that this youngster should die away: a sad thought for me, if I had not some hope that while it is dwindling I may be plotting, and fitting myself for verses fit to live.

This may be speaking too presumptuously, and may deserve a punishment: but no feeling man will be forward to inflict it: he will leave me alone, with the conviction that there is not a fiercer hell than the failure in a great object. This is not written with the least atom of purpose to forestall criticisms of course, but from the desire I have to conciliate men who are competent to look, and who do look with a zealous eye, to the honour of English literature.

The imagination of a boy is healthy, and the mature imagination of a man is healthy; but there is a space of life between, in which the soul is in a ferment, the character undecided, the way of life uncertain, the ambition thick-sighted: thence proceeds mawkishness, and all the thousand bitters which those men I speak of must necessarily taste in going over the following pages.

I hope I have not in too late a day touched the beautiful mythology of Greece, and dulled its brightness: for I wish to try once more, before I bid it farewel.

Teignmouth, April 10, 1818

BOOK I

A thing of beauty is a joy for ever:
Its loveliness increases; it will never
Pass into nothingness; but still will keep
A bower quiet for us, and a sleep
5   Full of sweet dreams, and health, and quiet breathing.
Therefore, on every morrow, are we wreathing
A flowery band to bind us to the earth,
Spite of despondence, of the inhuman dearth
Of noble natures, of the gloomy days,
10   Of all the unhealthy and o'er-darkened ways
Made for our searching: yes, in spite of all,
Some shape of beauty moves away the pall
From our dark spirits. Such the sun, the moon,
Trees old, and young sprouting a shady boon
15   For simple sheep; and such are daffodils
With the green world they live in; and clear rills
That for themselves a cooling covert make
'Gainst the hot season; the mid forest brake,
Rich with a sprinkling of fair musk-rose blooms:
20   And such too is the grandeur of the dooms
We have imagined for the mighty dead;
All lovely tales that we have heard or read:
An endless fountain of immortal drink,
Pouring unto us from the heaven's brink.

25   Nor do we merely feel these essences
For one short hour; no, even as the trees
That whisper round a temple become soon
Dear as the temple's self, so does the moon,
The passion poesy, glories infinite,
30   Haunt us till they become a cheering light
Unto our souls, and bound to us so fast,
That, whether there be shine, or gloom o'ercast,
They alway must be with us, or we die.

Therefore, 'tis with full happiness that I
35   Will trace the story of Endymion.
The very music of the name has gone
Into my being, and each pleasant scene
Is growing fresh before me as the green
Of our own vallies: so I will begin

40   Now while I cannot hear the city's din;
      Now while the early budders are just new,
      And run in mazes of the youngest hue
      About old forests; while the willow trails
      Its delicate amber; and the dairy pails
45   Bring home increase of milk. And, as the year
      Grows lush in juicy stalks, I'll smoothly steer
      My little boat, for many quiet hours,
      With streams that deepen freshly into bowers.
      Many and many a verse I hope to write,
50   Before the daisies, vermeil rimm'd and white,
      Hide in deep herbage; and ere yet the bees
      Hum about globes of clover and sweet peas,
      I must be near the middle of my story.
      O may no wintry season, bare and hoary,
55   See it half finished: but let autumn bold,
      With universal tinge of sober gold,
      Be all about me when I make an end.
      And now at once, adventuresome, I send
      My herald thought into a wilderness:
60   There let its trumpet blow, and quickly dress
      My uncertain path with green, that I may speed
      Easily onward, thorough flowers and weed.

          Upon the sides of Latmos was outspread
      A mighty forest; for the moist earth fed
65   So plenteously all weed-hidden roots
      Into o'er-hanging boughs, and precious fruits.
      And it had gloomy shades, sequestered deep,
      Where no man went; and if from shepherd's keep
      A lamb strayed far a-down those inmost glens,
70   Never again saw he the happy pens
      Whither his brethren, bleating with content,
      Over the hills at every nightfall went.
      Among the shepherds, 'twas believed ever,
      That not one fleecy lamb which thus did sever
75   From the white flock, but pass'd unworried
      By angry wolf, or pard with prying head,
      Until it came to some unfooted plains
      Where fed the herds of Pan: ay great his gains
      Who thus one lamb did lose. Paths there were many,
80   Winding through palmy fern, and rushes fenny,
      And ivy banks; all leading pleasantly
      To a wide lawn, whence one could only see

Stems thronging all around between the swell
Of turf and slanting branches: who could tell
85   The freshness of the space of heaven above,
Edg'd round with dark tree tops? through which a dove
Would often beat its wings, and often too
A little cloud would move across the blue.

    Full in the middle of this pleasantness
90   There stood a marble altar, with a tress
Of flowers budded newly; and the dew
Had taken fairy phantasies to strew
Daisies upon the sacred sward last eve,
And so the dawned light in pomp receive.
95   For 'twas the morn: Apollo's upward fire
Made every eastern cloud a silvery pyre
Of brightness so unsullied, that therein
A melancholy spirit well might win
Oblivion, and melt out his essence fine
100   Into the winds: rain-scented eglantine
Gave temperate sweets to that well-wooing sun;
The lark was lost in him; cold springs had run
To warm their chilliest bubbles in the grass;
Man's voice was on the mountains; and the mass
105   Of nature's lives and wonders puls'd tenfold,
To feel this sun-rise and its glories old.

    Now while the silent workings of the dawn
Were busiest, into that self-same lawn
All suddenly, with joyful cries, there sped
110   A troop of little children garlanded;
Who gathering round the altar, seemed to pry
Earnestly round as wishing to espy
Some folk of holiday: nor had they waited
For many moments, ere their ears were sated
115   With a faint breath of music, which ev'n then
Fill'd out its voice, and died away again.
Within a little space again it gave
Its airy swellings, with a gentle wave,
To light-hung leaves, in smoothest echoes breaking
120   Through copse-clad vallies,—ere their death, o'ertaking
The surgy murmurs of the lonely sea.

    And now, as deep into the wood as we
Might mark a lynx's eye, there glimmered light

Fair faces and a rush of garments white,
125   Plainer and plainer shewing, till at last
Into the widest alley they all past,
Making directly for the woodland altar.
O kindly muse! let not my weak tongue faulter
In telling of this goodly company,
130   Of their old piety, and of their glee:
But let a portion of ethereal dew
Fall on my head, and presently unmew
My soul; that I may dare, in wayfaring,
To stammer where old Chaucer used to sing.

135   Leading the way, young damsels danced along,
Bearing the burden of a shepherd song;
Each having a white wicker over brimm'd
With April's tender younglings: next, well trimm'd,
A crowd of shepherds with as sunburnt looks
140   As may be read of in Arcadian books;
Such as sat listening round Apollo's pipe,
When the great deity, for earth too ripe,
Let his divinity o'er-flowing die
In music, through the vales of Thessaly:
145   Some idly trailed their sheep-hooks on the ground,
And some kept up a shrilly mellow sound
With ebon-tipped flutes: close after these,
Now coming from beneath the forest trees,
A venerable priest full soberly,
150   Begirt with ministring looks: alway his eye
Stedfast upon the matted turf he kept,
And after him his sacred vestments swept.
From his right hand there swung a vase, milk-white,
Of mingled wine, out-sparkling generous light;
155   And in his left he held a basket full
Of all sweet herbs that searching eye could cull:
Wild thyme, and valley-lilies whiter still
Than Leda's love, and cresses from the rill.
His aged head, crowned with beechen wreath,
160   Seem'd like a poll of ivy in the teeth
Of winter hoar. Then came another crowd
Of shepherds, lifting in due time aloud
Their share of the ditty. After them appear'd,
Up-followed by a multitude that rear'd
165   Their voices to the clouds, a fair wrought car,

Easily rolling so as scarce to mar
The freedom of three steeds of dapple brown:
Who stood therein did seem of great renown
Among the throng. His youth was fully blown,
170 Shewing like Ganymede to manhood grown;
And, for those simple times, his garments were
A chieftain king's: beneath his breast, half bare,
Was hung a silver bugle, and between
His nervy knees there lay a boar-spear keen.
175 A smile was on his countenance; he seem'd,
To common lookers on, like one who dream'd
Of idleness in groves Elysian:
But there were some who feelingly could scan
A lurking trouble in his nether lip,
180 And see that oftentimes the reins would slip
Through his forgotten hands: then would they sigh,
And think of yellow leaves, of owlet's cry,
Of logs piled solemnly.—Ah, well-a-day,
Why should our young Endymion pine away!

185   Soon the assembly, in a circle rang'd,
Stood silent round the shrine: each look was chang'd
To sudden veneration: women meek
Beckon'd their sons to silence; while each cheek
Of virgin bloom paled gently for slight fear.
190 Endymion too, without a forest peer,
Stood, wan, and pale, and with an awed face,
Among his brothers of the mountain chase.
In midst of all, the venerable priest
Eyed them with joy from greatest to the least,
195 And, after lifting up his aged hands,
Thus spake he: "Men of Latmos! shepherd bands!
Whose care it is to guard a thousand flocks:
Whether descended from beneath the rocks
That overtop your mountains; whether come
200 From vallies where the pipe is never dumb;
Or from your swelling downs, where sweet air stirs
Blue hare-bells lightly, and where prickly furze
Buds lavish gold; or ye, whose precious charge
Nibble their fill at ocean's very marge,
205 Whose mellow reeds are touch'd with sounds forlorn
By the dim echoes of old Triton's horn:
Mothers and wives! who day by day prepare

The scrip, with needments, for the mountain air;
And all ye gentle girls who foster up
210 Udderless lambs, and in a little cup
Will put choice honey for a favoured youth:
Yea, every one attend! for in good truth
Our vows are wanting to our great god Pan.
Are not our lowing heifers sleeker than
215 Night-swollen mushrooms? Are not our wide plains
Speckled with countless fleeces? Have not rains
Green'd over April's lap? No howling sad
Sickens our fearful ewes; and we have had
Great bounty from Endymion our lord.
220 The earth is glad: the merry lark has pour'd
His early song against yon breezy sky,
That spreads so clear o'er our solemnity."

Thus ending, on the shrine he heap'd a spire
Of teeming sweets, enkindling sacred fire;
225 Anon he stain'd the thick and spongy sod
With wine, in honour of the shepherd-god.
Now while the earth was drinking it, and while
Bay leaves were crackling in the fragrant pile,
And gummy frankincense was sparkling bright
230 'Neath smothering parsley, and a hazy light
Spread greyly eastward, thus a chorus sang:

"O thou, whose mighty palace roof doth hang
From jagged trunks, and overshadoweth
Eternal whispers, glooms, the birth, life, death
235 Of unseen flowers in heavy peacefulness;
Who lov'st to see the hamadryads dress
Their ruffled locks where meeting hazels darken;
And through whole solemn hours dost sit, and hearken
The dreary melody of bedded reeds—
240 In desolate places, where dank moisture breeds
The pipy hemlock to strange overgrowth;
Bethinking thee, how melancholy loth
Thou wast to lose fair Syrinx—do thou now,
By thy love's milky brow!
245 By all the trembling mazes that she ran,
Hear us, great Pan!

"O thou, for whose soul-soothing quiet, turtles
Passion their voices cooingly 'mong myrtles,

What time thou wanderest at eventide
250 Through sunny meadows, that outskirt the side
Of thine enmossed realms: O thou, to whom
Broad leaved fig trees even now foredoom
Their ripen'd fruitage; yellow girted bees
Their golden honeycombs; our village leas
255 Their fairest blossom'd beans and poppied corn;
The chuckling linnet its five young unborn,
To sing for thee; low creeping strawberries
Their summer coolness; pent up butterflies
Their freckled wings; yea, the fresh budding year
260 All its completions—be quickly near,
By every wind that nods the mountain pine,
O forester divine!

"Thou, to whom every faun and satyr flies
For willing service; whether to surprise
265 The squatted hare while in half sleeping fit;
Or upward ragged precipices flit
To save poor lambkins from the eagle's maw;
Or by mysterious enticement draw
Bewildered shepherds to their path again;
270 Or to tread breathless round the frothy main,
And gather up all fancifullest shells
For thee to tumble into Naiads' cells,
And, being hidden, laugh at their out-peeping;
Or to delight thee with fantastic leaping,
275 The while they pelt each other on the crown
With silvery oak apples, and fir cones brown—
By all the echoes that about thee ring,
Hear us, O satyr king!

"O Hearkener to the loud clapping shears,
280 While ever and anon to his shorn peers
A ram goes bleating: Winder of the horn,
When snouted wild-boars routing tender corn
Anger our huntsmen: Breather round our farms,
To keep off mildews, and all weather harms:
285 Strange ministrant of undescribed sounds,
That come a swooning over hollow grounds,
And wither drearily on barren moors:
Dread opener of the mysterious doors
Leading to universal knowledge—see,
290 Great son of Dryope,

The many that are come to pay their vows
With leaves about their brows!

"Be still the unimaginable lodge
For solitary thinkings; such as dodge
295   Conception to the very bourne of heaven,
Then leave the naked brain: be still the leaven,
That spreading in this dull and clodded earth
Gives it a touch ethereal—a new birth:
Be still a symbol of immensity;
300   A firmament reflected in a sea;
An element filling the space between;
An unknown—but no more: we humbly screen
With uplift hands our foreheads, lowly bending,
And giving out a shout most heaven rending,
305   Conjure thee to receive our humble pæan,
Upon thy Mount Lycean!"

Even while they brought the burden to a close,
A shout from the whole multitude arose,
That lingered in the air like dying rolls
310   Of abrupt thunder, when Ionian shoals
Of dolphins bob their noses through the brine.
Meantime, on shady levels, mossy fine,
Young companies nimbly began dancing
To the swift treble pipe, and humming string.
315   Aye, those fair living forms swam heavenly
To tunes forgotten—out of memory:
Fair creatures! whose young children's children bred
Thermopylæ its heroes—not yet dead,
But in old marbles ever beautiful.
320   High genitors, unconscious did they cull
Time's sweet first-fruits—they danc'd to weariness,
And then in quiet circles did they press
The hillock turf, and caught the latter end
Of some strange history, potent to send
325   A young mind from its bodily tenement.
Or they might watch the quoit-pitchers, intent
On either side; pitying the sad death
Of Hyacinthus, when the cruel breath
Of Zephyr slew him,—Zephyr penitent,
330   Who now, ere Phœbus mounts the firmament,
Fondles the flower amid the sobbing rain.

The archers too, upon a wider plain,
Beside the feathery whizzing of the shaft,
And the dull twanging bowstring, and the raft
335 Branch down sweeping from a tall ash top,
Call'd up a thousand thoughts to envelope
Those who would watch. Perhaps, the trembling knee
And frantic gape of lonely Niobe,
Poor, lonely Niobe! when her lovely young
340 Were dead and gone, and her caressing tongue
Lay a lost thing upon her paly lip,
And very, very deadliness did nip
Her motherly cheeks. Arous'd from this sad mood
By one, who at a distance loud halloo'd,
345 Uplifting his strong bow into the air,
Many might after brighter visions stare:
After the Argonauts, in blind amaze
Tossing about on Neptune's restless ways,
Until, from the horizon's vaulted side,
350 There shot a golden splendour far and wide,
Spangling those million poutings of the brine
With quivering ore: 'twas even an awful shine
From the exaltation of Apollo's bow;
A heavenly beacon in their dreary woe.
355 Who thus were ripe for high contemplating
Might turn their steps towards the sober ring
Where sat Endymion and the aged priest
'Mong shepherds gone in eld, whose looks increas'd
The silvery setting of their mortal star.
360 There they discours'd upon the fragile bar
That keeps us from our homes ethereal;
And what our duties there: to nightly call
Vesper, the beauty-crest of summer weather;
To summon all the downiest clouds together
365 For the sun's purple couch; to emulate
In ministring the potent rule of fate
With speed of fire-tailed exhalations;
To tint her pallid cheek with bloom, who cons
Sweet poesy by moonlight: besides these,
370 A world of other unguess'd offices.
Anon they wander'd, by divine converse,
Into Elysium; vieing to rehearse
Each one his own anticipated bliss.
One felt heart-certain that he could not miss

375 His quick gone love, among fair blossom'd boughs,
Where every zephyr-sigh pouts, and endows
Her lips with music for the welcoming.
Another wish'd, mid that eternal spring,
To meet his rosy child, with feathery sails,
380 Sweeping, eye-earnestly, through almond vales:
Who, suddenly, should stoop through the smooth wind,
And with the balmiest leaves his temples bind;
And, ever after, through those regions be
His messenger, his little Mercury.
385 Some were athirst in soul to see again
Their fellow huntsmen o'er the wide champaign
In times long past; to sit with them, and talk
Of all the chances in their earthly walk;
Comparing, joyfully, their plenteous stores
390 Of happiness, to when upon the moors,
Benighted, close they huddled from the cold,
And shar'd their famish'd scrips. Thus all out-told
Their fond imaginations,—saving him
Whose eyelids curtain'd up their jewels dim,
395 Endymion: yet hourly had he striven
To hide the cankering venom, that had riven
His fainting recollections. Now indeed
His senses had swoon'd off: he did not heed
The sudden silence, or the whispers low,
400 Or the old eyes dissolving at his woe,
Or anxious calls, or close of trembling palms,
Or maiden's sigh, that grief itself embalms:
But in the self-same fixed trance he kept,
Like one who on the earth had never stept—
405 Aye, even as dead-still as a marble man,
Frozen in that old tale Arabian.

    Who whispers him so pantingly and close?
Peona, his sweet sister: of all those,
His friends, the dearest. Hushing signs she made,
410 And breath'd a sister's sorrow to persuade
A yielding up, a cradling on her care.
Her eloquence did breathe away the curse:
She led him, like some midnight spirit nurse
Of happy changes in emphatic dreams,
415 Along a path between two little streams,—
Guarding his forehead, with her round elbow,
From low-grown branches, and his footsteps slow

From stumbling over stumps and hillocks small;
Until they came to where these streamlets fall,
420 With mingled bubblings and a gentle rush,
Into a river, clear, brimful, and flush
With crystal mocking of the trees and sky.
A little shallop, floating there hard by,
Pointed its beak over the fringed bank;
425 And soon it lightly dipt, and rose, and sank,
And dipt again, with the young couple's weight,—
Peona guiding, through the water straight,
Towards a bowery island opposite;
Which gaining presently, she steered light
430 Into a shady, fresh, and ripply cove,
Where nested was an arbour, overwove
By many a summer's silent fingering;
To whose cool bosom she was used to bring
Her playmates, with their needle broidery,
435 And minstrel memories of times gone by.

So she was gently glad to see him laid
Under her favourite bower's quiet shade,
On her own couch, new made of flower leaves,
Dried carefully on the cooler side of sheaves
440 When last the sun his autumn tresses shook,
And the tann'd harvesters rich armfuls took.
Soon was he quieted to slumbrous rest:
But, ere it crept upon him, he had prest
Peona's busy hand against his lips,
445 And still, a sleeping, held her finger-tips
In tender pressure. And as a willow keeps
A patient watch over the stream that creeps
Windingly by it, so the quiet maid
Held her in peace: so that a whispering blade
450 Of grass, a wailful gnat, a bee bustling
Down in the blue-bells, or a wren light rustling
Among sere leaves and twigs, might all be heard.

O magic sleep! O comfortable bird,
That broodest o'er the troubled sea of the mind
455 Till it is hush'd and smooth! O unconfin'd
Restraint! imprisoned liberty! great key
To golden palaces, strange minstrelsy,
Fountains grotesque, new trees, bespangled caves,
Echoing grottos, full of tumbling waves

460 And moonlight; aye, to all the mazy world
Of silvery enchantment!—who, upfurl'd
Beneath thy drowsy wing a triple hour,
But renovates and lives?—Thus, in the bower,
Endymion was calm'd to life again.
465 Opening his eyelids with a healthier brain,
He said: "I feel this thine endearing love
All through my bosom: thou art as a dove
Trembling its closed eyes and sleeked wings
About me; and the pearliest dew not brings
470 Such morning incense from the fields of May,
As do those brighter drops that twinkling stray
From those kind eyes,—the very home and haunt
Of sisterly affection. Can I want
Aught else, aught nearer heaven, than such tears?
475 Yet dry them up, in bidding hence all fears
That, any longer, I will pass my days
Alone and sad. No, I will once more raise
My voice upon the mountain-heights; once more
Make my horn parley from their foreheads hoar:
480 Again my trooping hounds their tongues shall loll
Around the breathed boar: again I'll poll
The fair-grown yew tree, for a chosen bow:
And, when the pleasant sun is getting low,
Again I'll linger in a sloping mead
485 To hear the speckled thrushes, and see feed
Our idle sheep. So be thou cheered, sweet,
And, if thy lute is here, softly intreat
My soul to keep in its resolved course."

Hereat Peona, in their silver source,
490 Shut her pure sorrow drops with glad exclaim,
And took a lute, from which there pulsing came
A lively prelude, fashioning the way
In which her voice should wander. 'Twas a lay
More subtle cadenced, more forest wild
495 Than Dryope's lone lulling of her child;
And nothing since has floated in the air
So mournful strange. Surely some influence rare
Went, spiritual, through the damsel's hand;
For still, with Delphic emphasis, she spann'd
500 The quick invisible strings, even though she saw
Endymion's spirit melt away and thaw

Before the deep intoxication.
But soon she came, with sudden burst, upon
Her self-possession—swung the lute aside,
505   And earnestly said: "Brother, 'tis vain to hide
That thou dost know of things mysterious,
Immortal, starry; such alone could thus
Weigh down thy nature. Hast thou sinn'd in aught
Offensive to the heavenly powers? Caught
510   A Paphian dove upon a message sent?
Thy deathful bow against some deer-herd bent,
Sacred to Dian? Haply, thou hast seen
Her naked limbs among the alders green;
And that, alas! is death. No, I can trace
515   Something more high perplexing in thy face!"

    Endymion look'd at her, and press'd her hand,
And said, "Art thou so pale, who wast so bland
And merry in our meadows? How is this?
Tell me thine ailment: tell me all amiss!—
520   Ah! thou hast been unhappy at the change
Wrought suddenly in me. What indeed more strange?
Or more complete to overwhelm surmise?
Ambition is no sluggard: 'tis no prize,
That toiling years would put within my grasp,
525   That I have sigh'd for: with so deadly gasp
No man e'er panted for a mortal love.
So all have set my heavier grief above
These things which happen. Rightly have they done:
I, who still saw the horizontal sun
530   Heave his broad shoulder o'er the edge of the world,
Out-facing Lucifer, and then had hurl'd
My spear aloft, as signal for the chace—
I, who, for very sport of heart, would race
With my own steed from Araby; pluck down
535   A vulture from his towery perching; frown
A lion into growling, loth retire—
To lose, at once, all my toil breeding fire,
And sink thus low! but I will ease my breast
Of secret grief, here in this bowery nest.

540   "This river does not see the naked sky,
Till it begins to progress silverly
Around the western border of the wood,

Whence, from a certain spot, its winding flood
Seems at the distance like a crescent moon:
545   And in that nook, the very pride of June,
Had I been used to pass my weary eves;
The rather for the sun unwilling leaves
So dear a picture of his sovereign power,
And I could witness his most kingly hour,
550   When he doth tighten up the golden reins,
And paces leisurely down amber plains
His snorting four. Now when his chariot last
Its beams against the zodiac-lion cast,
There blossom'd suddenly a magic bed
555   Of sacred ditamy, and poppies red:
At which I wondered greatly, knowing well
That but one night had wrought this flowery spell;
And, sitting down close by, began to muse
What it might mean. Perhaps, thought I, Morpheus,
560   In passing here, his owlet pinions shook;
Or, it may be, ere matron Night uptook
Her ebon urn, young Mercury, by stealth,
Had dipt his rod in it: such garland wealth
Came not by common growth. Thus on I thought,
565   Until my head was dizzy and distraught.
Moreover, through the dancing poppies stole
A breeze, most softly lulling to my soul;
And shaping visions all about my sight
Of colours, wings, and bursts of spangly light;
570   The which became more strange, and strange, and dim,
And then were gulph'd in a tumultuous swim:
And then I fell asleep. Ah, can I tell
The enchantment that afterwards befel?
Yet it was but a dream: yet such a dream
575   That never tongue, although it overteem
With mellow utterance, like a cavern spring,
Could figure out and to conception bring
All I beheld and felt. Methought I lay
Watching the zenith, where the milky way
580   Among the stars in virgin splendour pours;
And travelling my eye, until the doors
Of heaven appear'd to open for my flight,
I became loth and fearful to alight
From such high soaring by a downward glance:
585   So kept me stedfast in that airy trance,

Spreading imaginary pinions wide.
When, presently, the stars began to glide,
And faint away, before my eager view:
At which I sigh'd that I could not pursue,
590 And dropt my vision to the horizon's verge;
And lo! from opening clouds, I saw emerge
The loveliest moon, that ever silver'd o'er
A shell for Neptune's goblet: she did soar
So passionately bright, my dazzled soul
595 Commingling with her argent spheres did roll
Through clear and cloudy, even when she went
At last into a dark and vapoury tent—
Whereat, methought, the lidless-eyed train
Of planets all were in the blue again.
600 To commune with those orbs, once more I rais'd
My sight right upward: but it was quite dazed
By a bright something, sailing down apace,
Making me quickly veil my eyes and face:
Again I look'd, and, O ye deities,
605 Who from Olympus watch our destinies!
Whence that completed form of all completeness?
Whence came that high perfection of all sweetness?
Speak, stubborn earth, and tell me where, O where
Hast thou a symbol of her golden hair?
610 Not oat-sheaves drooping in the western sun;
Not—thy soft hand, fair sister! let me shun
Such follying before thee—yet she had,
Indeed, locks bright enough to make me mad;
And they were simply gordian'd up and braided,
615 Leaving, in naked comeliness, unshaded,
Her pearl round ears, white neck, and orbed brow;
The which were blended in, I know not how,
With such a paradise of lips and eyes,
Blush-tinted cheeks, half smiles, and faintest sighs,
620 That, when I think thereon, my spirit clings
And plays about its fancy, till the stings
Of human neighbourhood envenom all.
Unto what awful power shall I call?
To what high fane?—Ah! see her hovering feet,
625 More bluely vein'd, more soft, more whitely sweet
Than those of sea-born Venus, when she rose
From out her cradle shell. The wind out-blows
Her scarf into a fluttering pavilion;

'Tis blue, and over-spangled with a million
630   Of little eyes, as though thou wert to shed,
Over the darkest, lushest blue-bell bed,
Handfuls of daisies."—"Endymion, how strange!
Dream within dream!"—"She took an airy range,
And then, towards me, like a very maid,
635   Came blushing, waning, willing, and afraid,
And press'd me by the hand: Ah! 'twas too much;
Methought I fainted at the charmed touch,
Yet held my recollection, even as one
Who dives three fathoms where the waters run
640   Gurgling in beds of coral: for anon,
I felt upmounted in that region
Where falling stars dart their artillery forth,
And eagles struggle with the buffeting north
That balances the heavy meteor-stone;—
645   Felt too, I was not fearful, nor alone,
But lapp'd and lull'd along the dangerous sky.
Soon, as it seem'd, we left our journeying high,
And straightway into frightful eddies swoop'd;
Such as ay muster where grey time has scoop'd
650   Huge dens and caverns in a mountain's side:
There hollow sounds arous'd me, and I sigh'd
To faint once more by looking on my bliss—
I was distracted; madly did I kiss
The wooing arms which held me, and did give
655   My eyes at once to death: but 'twas to live,
To take in draughts of life from the gold fount
Of kind and passionate looks; to count, and count
The moments, by some greedy help that seem'd
A second self, that each might be redeem'd
660   And plunder'd of its load of blessedness.
Ah, desperate mortal! I ev'n dar'd to press
Her very cheek against my crowned lip,
And, at that moment, felt my body dip
Into a warmer air: a moment more,
665   Our feet were soft in flowers. There was store
Of newest joys upon that alp. Sometimes
A scent of violets, and blossoming limes,
Loiter'd around us; then of honey cells,
Made delicate from all white-flower bells;
670   And once, above the edges of our nest,
An arch face peep'd,—an Oread as I guess'd.

"Why did I dream that sleep o'er-power'd me
In midst of all this heaven? Why not see,
Far off, the shadows of his pinions dark,
675 And stare them from me? But no, like a spark
That needs must die, although its little beam
Reflects upon a diamond, my sweet dream
Fell into nothing—into stupid sleep.
And so it was, until a gentle creep,
680 A careful moving, caught my waking ears,
And up I started: Ah! my sighs, my tears,
My clenched hands;—for lo! the poppies hung
Dew-dabbled on their stalks, the ouzel sung
A heavy ditty, and the sullen day
685 Had chidden herald Hesperus away,
With leaden looks: the solitary breeze
Bluster'd, and slept, and its wild self did teaze
With wayward melancholy; and I thought,
Mark me, Peona! that sometimes it brought
690 Faint fare-thee-wells, and sigh-shrilled adieus!—
Away I wander'd—all the pleasant hues
Of heaven and earth had faded: deepest shades
Were deepest dungeons; heaths and sunny glades
Were full of pestilent light; our taintless rills
695 Seem'd sooty, and o'er-spread with upturn'd gills
Of dying fish; the vermeil rose had blown
In frightful scarlet, and its thorns out-grown
Like spiked aloe. If an innocent bird
Before my heedless footsteps stirr'd, and stirr'd
700 In little journeys, I beheld in it
A disguis'd demon, missioned to knit
My soul with under darkness; to entice
My stumblings down some monstrous precipice:
Therefore I eager followed, and did curse
705 The disappointment. Time, that aged nurse,
Rock'd me to patience. Now, thank gentle heaven!
These things, with all their comfortings, are given
To my down-sunken hours, and with thee,
Sweet sister, help to stem the ebbing sea
Of weary life."

710   Thus ended he, and both
Sat silent: for the maid was very loth
To answer; feeling well that breathed words

Would all be lost, unheard, and vain as swords
Against the enchased crocodile, or leaps
715 Of grasshoppers against the sun. She weeps,
And wonders; struggles to devise some blame;
To put on such a look as would say, *Shame
On this poor weakness!* but, for all her strife,
She could as soon have crush'd away the life
720 From a sick dove. At length, to break the pause,
She said with trembling chance: "Is this the cause?
This all? Yet it is strange, and sad, alas!
That one who through this middle earth should pass
Most like a sojourning demi-god, and leave
725 His name upon the harp-string, should achieve
No higher bard than simple maidenhood,
Singing alone, and fearfully,—how the blood
Left his young cheek; and how he used to stray
He knew not where; and how he would say, *nay,*
730 If any said 'twas love: and yet 'twas love;
What could it be but love? How a ring-dove
Let fall a sprig of yew tree in his path;
And how he died: and then, that love doth scathe
The gentle heart, as northern blasts do roses;
735 And then the ballad of his sad life closes
With sighs, and an alas!—Endymion!
Be rather in the trumpet's mouth,—anon
Among the winds at large—that all may hearken!
Although, before the crystal heavens darken,
740 I watch and dote upon the silver lakes
Pictur'd in western cloudiness, that takes
The semblance of gold rocks and bright gold sands,
Islands, and creeks, and amber-fretted strands
With horses prancing o'er them, palaces
745 And towers of amethyst,—would I so tease
My pleasant days, because I could not mount
Into those regions? The Morphean fount
Of that fine element that visions, dreams,
And fitful whims of sleep are made of, streams
750 Into its airy channels with so subtle,
So thin a breathing, not the spider's shuttle,
Circled a million times within the space
Of a swallow's nest-door, could delay a trace,
A tinting of its quality: how light
755 Must dreams themselves be; seeing they're more slight

Than the mere nothing that engenders them!
Then wherefore sully the entrusted gem
Of high and noble life with thoughts so sick?
Why pierce high-fronted honour to the quick
760   For nothing but a dream?" Hereat the youth
Look'd up: a conflicting of shame and ruth
Was in his plaited brow: yet, his eyelids
Widened a little, as when Zephyr bids
A little breeze to creep between the fans
765   Of careless butterflies: amid his pains
He seem'd to taste a drop of manna-dew,
Full palatable; and a colour grew
Upon his cheek, while thus he lifeful spake.

"Peona! ever have I long'd to slake
770   My thirst for the world's praises: nothing base,
No merely slumberous phantasm, could unlace
The stubborn canvas for my voyage prepar'd—
Though now 'tis tatter'd; leaving my bark bar'd
And sullenly drifting: yet my higher hope
775   Is of too wide, too rainbow-large a scope,
To fret at myriads of earthly wrecks.
Wherein lies happiness? In that which becks
Our ready minds to fellowship divine,
A fellowship with essence; till we shine,
780   Full alchemiz'd, and free of space. Behold
The clear religion of heaven! Fold
A rose leaf round thy finger's taperness,
And soothe thy lips: hist, when the airy stress
Of music's kiss impregnates the free winds,
785   And with a sympathetic touch unbinds
Eolian magic from their lucid wombs:
Then old songs waken from enclouded tombs;
Old ditties sigh above their father's grave;
Ghosts of melodious prophecyings rave
790   Round every spot where trod Apollo's foot;
Bronze clarions awake, and faintly bruit,
Where long ago a giant battle was;
And, from the turf, a lullaby doth pass
In every place where infant Orpheus slept.
795   Feel we these things?—that moment have we stept
Into a sort of oneness, and our state
Is like a floating spirit's. But there are

Richer entanglements, enthralments far
More self-destroying, leading, by degrees,
800   To the chief intensity: the crown of these
Is made of love and friendship, and sits high
Upon the forehead of humanity.
All its more ponderous and bulky worth
Is friendship, whence there ever issues forth
805   A steady splendour; but at the tip-top,
There hangs by unseen film, an orbed drop
Of light, and that is love: its influence,
Thrown in our eyes, genders a novel sense,
At which we start and fret; till in the end,
810   Melting into its radiance, we blend,
Mingle, and so become a part of it,—
Nor with aught else can our souls interknit
So wingedly: when we combine therewith,
Life's self is nourish'd by its proper pith,
815   And we are nurtured like a pelican brood.
Aye, so delicious is the unsating food,
That men, who might have tower'd in the van
Of all the congregated world, to fan
And winnow from the coming step of time
820   All chaff of custom, wipe away all slime
Left by men-slugs and human serpentry,
Have been content to let occasion die,
Whilst they did sleep in love's elysium.
And, truly, I would rather be struck dumb,
825   Than speak against this ardent listlessness:
For I have ever thought that it might bless
The world with benefits unknowingly;
As does the nightingale, upperched high,
And cloister'd among cool and bunched leaves—
830   She sings but to her love, nor e'er conceives
How tiptoe Night holds back her dark-grey hood.
Just so may love, although 'tis understood
The mere commingling of passionate breath,
Produce more than our searching witnesseth:
835   What I know not: but who, of men, can tell
That flowers would bloom, or that green fruit would swell
To melting pulp, that fish would have bright mail,
The earth its dower of river, wood, and vale,
The meadows runnels, runnels pebble-stones,
840   The seed its harvest, or the lute its tones,

Tones ravishment, or ravishment its sweet,
If human souls did never kiss and greet?

"Now, if this earthly love has power to make
Men's being mortal, immortal; to shake
845   Ambition from their memories, and brim
Their measure of content; what merest whim,
Seems all this poor endeavour after fame,
To one, who keeps within his stedfast aim
A love immortal, an immortal too.
850   Look not so wilder'd; for these things are true,
And never can be born of atomies
That buzz about our slumbers, like brain-flies,
Leaving us fancy-sick. No, no, I'm sure,
My restless spirit never could endure
855   To brood so long upon one luxury,
Unless it did, though fearfully, espy
A hope beyond the shadow of a dream.
My sayings will the less obscured seem,
When I have told thee how my waking sight
860   Has made me scruple whether that same night
Was pass'd in dreaming. Hearken, sweet Peona!
Beyond the matron-temple of Latona,
Which we should see but for these darkening boughs,
Lies a deep hollow, from whose ragged brows
865   Bushes and trees do lean all round athwart,
And meet so nearly, that with wings outraught,
And spreaded tail, a vulture could not glide
Past them, but he must brush on every side.
Some moulder'd steps lead into this cool cell,
870   Far as the slabbed margin of a well,
Whose patient level peeps its crystal eye
Right upward, through the bushes, to the sky.
Oft have I brought thee flowers, on their stalks set
Like vestal primroses, but dark velvet
875   Edges them round, and they have golden pits:
'Twas there I got them, from the gaps and slits
In a mossy stone, that sometimes was my seat,
When all above was faint with mid-day heat.
And there in strife no burning thoughts to heed,
880   I'd bubble up the water through a reed;
So reaching back to boy-hood: make me ships
Of moulted feathers, touchwood, alder chips,

With leaves stuck in them; and the Neptune be
Of their petty ocean. Oftener, heavily,
885   When love-lorn hours had left me less a child,
I sat contemplating the figures wild
Of o'er-head clouds melting the mirror through.
Upon a day, while thus I watch'd, by flew
A cloudy Cupid, with his bow and quiver;
890   So plainly character'd, no breeze would shiver
The happy chance: so happy, I was fain
To follow it upon the open plain,
And, therefore, was just going; when, behold!
A wonder, fair as any I have told—
895   The same bright face I tasted in my sleep,
Smiling in the clear well. My heart did leap
Through the cool depth.—It moved as if to flee—
I started up, when lo! refreshfully,
There came upon my face, in plenteous showers,
900   Dew-drops, and dewy buds, and leaves, and flowers,
Wrapping all objects from my smothered sight,
Bathing my spirit in a new delight.
Aye, such a breathless honey-feel of bliss
Alone preserved me from the drear abyss
905   Of death, for the fair form had gone again.
Pleasure is oft a visitant; but pain
Clings cruelly to us, like the gnawing sloth
On the deer's tender haunches: late, and loth,
'Tis scar'd away by slow returning pleasure.
910   How sickening, how dark the dreadful leisure
Of weary days, made deeper exquisite,
By a fore-knowledge of unslumbrous night!
Like sorrow came upon me, heavier still,
Than when I wander'd from the poppy hill:
915   And a whole age of lingering moments crept
Sluggishly by, ere more contentment swept
Away at once the deadly yellow spleen.
Yes, thrice have I this fair enchantment seen;
Once more been tortured with renewed life.
920   When last the wintry gusts gave over strife
With the conquering sun of spring, and left the skies
Warm and serene, but yet with moistened eyes
In pity of the shatter'd infant buds,—
That time thou didst adorn, with amber studs,
925   My hunting cap, because I laugh'd and smil'd,

Chatted with thee, and many days exil'd
All torment from my breast;—'twas even then,
Straying about, yet, coop'd up in the den
Of helpless discontent,—hurling my lance
930 From place to place, and following at chance,
At last, by hap, through some young trees it struck,
And, plashing among bedded pebbles, stuck
In the middle of a brook,—whose silver ramble
Down twenty little falls, through reeds and bramble,
935 Tracing along, it brought me to a cave,
Whence it ran brightly forth, and white did lave
The nether sides of mossy stones and rock,—
'Mong which it gurgled blythe adieus, to mock
Its own sweet grief at parting. Overhead,
940 Hung a lush screen of drooping weeds, and spread
Thick, as to curtain up some wood-nymph's home.
'Ah! impious mortal, whither do I roam?'
Said I, low voic'd: 'Ah, whither! 'Tis the grot
Of Proserpine, when Hell, obscure and hot,
945 Doth her resign; and where her tender hands
She dabbles, on the cool and sluicy sands:
Or 'tis the cell of Echo, where she sits,
And babbles thorough silence, till her wits
Are gone in tender madness, and anon,
950 Faints into sleep, with many a dying tone
Of sadness. O that she would take my vows,
And breathe them sighingly among the boughs,
To sue her gentle ears for whose fair head,
Daily, I pluck sweet flowerets from their bed,
955 And weave them dyingly—send honey-whispers
Round every leaf, that all those gentle lispers
May sigh my love unto her pitying!
O charitable Echo! hear, and sing
This ditty to her!—tell her'—so I stay'd
960 My foolish tongue, and listening, half afraid,
Stood stupefied with my own empty folly,
And blushing for the freaks of melancholy.
Salt tears were coming, when I heard my name
Most fondly lipp'd, and then these accents came:
965 'Endymion! the cave is secreter
Than the isle of Delos. Echo hence shall stir
No sighs but sigh-warm kisses, or light noise
Of thy combing hand, the while it travelling cloys

And trembles through my labyrinthine hair.'
970   At that oppress'd I hurried in.—Ah! where
Are those swift moments? Whither are they fled?
I'll smile no more, Peona; nor will wed
Sorrow the way to death; but patiently
Bear up against it: so farewel, sad sigh;
975   And come instead demurest meditation,
To occupy me wholly, and to fashion
My pilgrimage for the world's dusky brink.
No more will I count over, link by link,
My chain of grief: no longer strive to find
980   A half-forgetfulness in mountain wind
Blustering about my ears: aye, thou shalt see,
Dearest of sisters, what my life shall be;
What a calm round of hours shall make my days.
There is a paly flame of hope that plays
985   Where'er I look: but yet, I'll say 'tis naught—
And here I bid it die. Have not I caught,
Already, a more healthy countenance?
By this the sun is setting; we may chance
Meet some of our near-dwellers with my car."

990   This said, he rose, faint-smiling like a star
Through autumn mists, and took Peona's hand:
They stept into the boat, and launch'd from land.

BOOK II

O sovereign power of love! O grief! O balm!
All records, saving thine, come cool, and calm,
And shadowy, through the mist of passed years:
For others, good or bad, hatred and tears
5   Have become indolent; but touching thine,
One sigh doth echo, one poor sob doth pine,
One kiss brings honey-dew from buried days.
The woes of Troy, towers smothering o'er their blaze,
Stiff-holden shields, far-piercing spears, keen blades,
10   Struggling, and blood, and shrieks—all dimly fades
Into some backward corner of the brain;
Yet, in our very souls, we feel amain
The close of Troilus and Cressid sweet.
Hence, pageant history! hence, gilded cheat!

15 Swart planet in the universe of deeds!
Wide sea, that one continuous murmur breeds
Along the pebbled shore of memory!
Many old rotten-timber'd boats there be
Upon thy vaporous bosom, magnified
20 To goodly vessels; many a sail of pride,
And golden keel'd, is left unlaunch'd and dry.
But wherefore this? What care, though owl did fly
About the great Athenian admiral's mast?
What care, though striding Alexander past
25 The Indus with his Macedonian numbers?
Though old Ulysses tortured from his slumbers
The glutted Cyclops, what care?—Juliet leaning
Amid her window-flowers,—sighing,—weaning
Tenderly her fancy from its maiden snow,
30 Doth more avail than these: the silver flow
Of Hero's tears, the swoon of Imogen,
Fair Pastorella in the bandit's den,
Are things to brood on with more ardency
Than the death-day of empires. Fearfully
35 Must such conviction come upon his head,
Who, thus far, discontent, has dared to tread,
Without one muse's smile, or kind behest,
The path of love and poesy. But rest,
In chafing restlessness, is yet more drear
40 Than to be crush'd, in striving to uprear
Love's standard on the battlements of song.
So once more days and nights aid me along,
Like legion'd soldiers.

                              Brain-sick shepherd prince,
What promise hast thou faithful guarded since
45 The day of sacrifice? Or, have new sorrows
Come with the constant dawn upon thy morrows?
Alas! 'tis his old grief. For many days,
Has he been wandering in uncertain ways:
Through wilderness, and woods of mossed oaks;
50 Counting his woe-worn minutes, by the strokes
Of the lone woodcutter; and listening still,
Hour after hour, to each lush-leav'd rill.
Now he is sitting by a shady spring,
And elbow-deep with feverous fingering
55 Stems the upbursting cold: a wild rose tree

Pavilions him in bloom, and he doth see
A bud which snares his fancy: lo! but now
He plucks it, dips its stalk in the water: how!
It swells, it buds, it flowers beneath his sight;
60   And, in the middle, there is softly pight
A golden butterfly; upon whose wings
There must be surely character'd strange things,
For with wide eye he wonders, and smiles oft.

Lightly this little herald flew aloft,
65   Follow'd by glad Endymion's clasped hands:
Onward it flies. From languor's sullen bands
His limbs are loos'd, and eager, on he hies
Dazzled to trace it in the sunny skies.
It seem'd he flew, the way so easy was;
70   And like a new-born spirit did he pass
Through the green evening quiet in the sun,
O'er many a heath, through many a woodland dun,
Through buried paths, where sleepy twilight dreams
The summer time away. One track unseams
75   A wooded cleft, and, far away, the blue
Of ocean fades upon him; then, anew,
He sinks adown a solitary glen,
Where there was never sound of mortal men,
Saving, perhaps, some snow-light cadences
80   Melting to silence, when upon the breeze
Some holy bark let forth an anthem sweet,
To cheer itself to Delphi. Still his feet
Went swift beneath the merry-winged guide,
Until it reached a splashing fountain's side
85   That, near a cavern's mouth, for ever pour'd
Unto the temperate air: then high it soar'd,
And, downward, suddenly began to dip,
As if, athirst with so much toil, 'twould sip
The crystal spout-head: so it did, with touch
90   Most delicate, as though afraid to smutch
Even with mealy gold the waters clear.
But, at that very touch, to disappear
So fairy-quick, was strange! Bewildered,
Endymion sought around, and shook each bed
95   Of covert flowers in vain; and then he flung
Himself along the grass. What gentle tongue,
What whisperer disturb'd his gloomy rest?
It was a nymph uprisen to the breast

In the fountain's pebbly margin, and she stood
100 'Mong lilies, like the youngest of the brood.
To him her dripping hand she softly kist,
And anxiously began to plait and twist
Her ringlets round her fingers, saying: "Youth!
Too long, alas, hast thou starv'd on the ruth,
105 The bitterness of love: too long indeed,
Seeing thou art so gentle. Could I weed
Thy soul of care, by heavens, I would offer
All the bright riches of my crystal coffer
To Amphitrite; all my clear-eyed fish,
110 Golden, or rainbow-sided, or purplish,
Vermilion-tail'd, or finn'd with silvery gauze;
Yea, or my veined pebble-floor, that draws
A virgin light to the deep; my grotto-sands
Tawny and gold, ooz'd slowly from far lands
115 By my diligent springs; my level lilies, shells,
My charming rod, my potent river spells;
Yes, every thing, even to the pearly cup
Meander gave me,—for I bubbled up
To fainting creatures in a desert wild.
120 But woe is me, I am but as a child
To gladden thee; and all I dare to say,
Is, that I pity thee; that on this day
I've been thy guide; that thou must wander far
In other regions, past the scanty bar
125 To mortal steps, before thou canst be ta'en
From every wasting sigh, from every pain,
Into the gentle bosom of thy love.
Why it is thus, one knows in heaven above:
But, a poor Naiad, I guess not. Farewel!
130 I have a ditty for my hollow cell."

Hereat, she vanished from Endymion's gaze,
Who brooded o'er the water in amaze:
The dashing fount pour'd on, and where its pool
Lay, half asleep, in grass and rushes cool,
135 Quick waterflies and gnats were sporting still,
And fish were dimpling, as if good nor ill
Had fallen out that hour. The wanderer,
Holding his forehead, to keep off the burr
Of smothering fancies, patiently sat down;
140 And, while beneath the evening's sleepy frown
Glow-worms began to trim their starry lamps,

Thus breath'd he to himself: "Whoso encamps
To take a fancied city of delight,
O what a wretch is he! and when 'tis his,
145   After long toil and travelling, to miss
The kernel of his hopes, how more than vile:
Yet, for him there's refreshment even in toil;
Another city doth he set about,
Free from the smallest pebble-bead of doubt
150   That he will seize on trickling honey-combs:
Alas, he finds them dry; and then he foams,
And onward to another city speeds.
But this is human life: the war, the deeds,
The disappointment, the anxiety,
155   Imagination's struggles, far and nigh,
All human; bearing in themselves this good,
That they are still the air, the subtle food,
To make us feel existence, and to shew
How quiet death is. Where soil is men grow,
160   Whether to weeds or flowers; but for me,
There is no depth to strike in: I can see
Nought earthly worth my compassing; so stand
Upon a misty, jutting head of land—
Alone? No, no; and by the Orphean lute,
165   When mad Eurydice is listening to't;
I'd rather stand upon this misty peak,
With not a thing to sigh for, or to seek,
But the soft shadow of my thrice-seen love,
Than be—I care not what. O meekest dove
170   Of heaven! O Cynthia, ten-times bright and fair!
From thy blue throne, now filling all the air,
Glance but one little beam of temper'd light
Into my bosom, that the dreadful might
And tyranny of love be somewhat scar'd!
175   Yet do not so, sweet queen; one torment spar'd
Would give a pang to jealous misery,
Worse than the torment's self: but rather tie
Large wings upon my shoulders, and point out
My love's far dwelling. Though the playful rout
180   Of Cupids shun thee, too divine art thou,
Too keen in beauty, for thy silver prow
Not to have dipp'd in love's most gentle stream.
O be propitious, nor severely deem
My madness impious; for, by all the stars

185   That tend thy bidding, I do think the bars
       That kept my spirit in are burst—that I
       Am sailing with thee through the dizzy sky!
       How beautiful thou art! The world how deep!
       How tremulous-dazzlingly the wheels sweep
190   Around their axle! Then these gleaming reins,
       How lithe! When this thy chariot attains
       Its airy goal, haply some bower veils
       Those twilight eyes? Those eyes!—my spirit fails—
       Dear goddess, help! or the wide-gaping air
195   Will gulph me—help!"—At this with madden'd stare,
       And lifted hands, and trembling lips he stood;
       Like old Deucalion mountain'd o'er the flood,
       Or blind Orion hungry for the morn.
       And, but from the deep cavern there was borne
200   A voice, he had been froze to senseless stone;
       Nor sigh of his, nor plaint, nor passion'd moan
       Had more been heard. Thus swell'd it forth: "Descend,
       Young mountaineer! descend where alleys bend
       Into the sparry hollows of the world!
205   Oft hast thou seen bolts of the thunder hurl'd
       As from thy threshold; day by day hast been
       A little lower than the chilly sheen
       Of icy pinnacles, and dipp'dst thine arms
       Into the deadening ether that still charms
210   Their marble being: now, as deep profound
       As those are high, descend! He ne'er is crown'd
       With immortality, who fears to follow
       Where airy voices lead: so through the hollow,
       The silent mysteries of earth, descend!"

215   He heard but the last words, nor could contend
       One moment in reflection: for he fled
       Into the fearful deep, to hide his head
       From the clear moon, the trees, and coming madness.

       'Twas far too strange, and wonderful for sadness;
220   Sharpening, by degrees, his appetite
       To dive into the deepest. Dark, nor light,
       The region; nor bright, nor sombre wholly,
       But mingled up; a gleaming melancholy;
       A dusky empire and its diadems;
225   One faint eternal eventide of gems.

Aye, millions sparkled on a vein of gold,
Along whose track the prince quick footsteps told,
With all its lines abrupt and angular:
Out-shooting sometimes, like a meteor-star,
230   Through a vast antre; then the metal woof,
Like Vulcan's rainbow, with some monstrous roof
Curves hugely: now, far in the deep abyss,
It seems an angry lightning, and doth hiss
Fancy into belief: anon it leads
235   Through winding passages, where sameness breeds
Vexing conceptions of some sudden change;
Whether to silver grots, or giant range
Of sapphire columns, or fantastic bridge
Athwart a flood of crystal. On a ridge
240   Now fareth he, that o'er the vast beneath
Towers like an ocean-cliff, and whence he seeth
A hundred waterfalls, whose voices come
But as the murmuring surge. Chilly and numb
His bosom grew, when first he, far away,
245   Descried an orbed diamond, set to fray
Old darkness from his throne: 'twas like the sun
Uprisen o'er chaos: and with such a stun
Came the amazement, that, absorb'd in it,
He saw not fiercer wonders—past the wit
250   Of any spirit to tell, but one of those
Who, when this planet's sphering time doth close,
Will be its high remembrancers: who they?
The mighty ones who have made eternal day
For Greece and England. While astonishment
255   With deep-drawn sighs was quieting, he went
Into a marble gallery, passing through
A mimic temple, so complete and true
In sacred custom, that he well nigh fear'd
To search it inwards; whence far off appear'd,
260   Through a long pillar'd vista, a fair shrine,
And, just beyond, on light tiptoe divine,
A quiver'd Dian. Stepping awfully,
The youth approach'd; oft turning his veil'd eye
Down sidelong aisles, and into niches old.
265   And when, more near against the marble cold
He had touch'd his forehead, he began to thread
All courts and passages, where silence dead
Rous'd by his whispering footsteps murmured faint:

And long he travers'd to and fro, to acquaint
270 Himself with every mystery, and awe;
Till, weary, he sat down before the maw
Of a wide outlet, fathomless and dim,
To wild uncertainty and shadows grim.
There, when new wonders ceas'd to float before,
275 And thoughts of self came on, how crude and sore
The journey homeward to habitual self!
A mad-pursuing of the fog-born elf,
Whose flitting lantern, through rude nettle-briar,
Cheats us into a swamp, into a fire,
280 Into the bosom of a hated thing.

What misery most drowningly doth sing
In lone Endymion's ear, now he has raught
The goal of consciousness? Ah, 'tis the thought,
The deadly feel of solitude: for lo!
285 He cannot see the heavens, nor the flow
Of rivers, nor hill-flowers running wild
In pink and purple chequer, nor, up-pil'd,
The cloudy rack slow journeying in the west,
Like herded elephants; nor felt, nor prest
290 Cool grass, nor tasted the fresh slumberous air;
But far from such companionship to wear
An unknown time, surcharg'd with grief, away,
Was now his lot. And must he patient stay,
Tracing fantastic figures with his spear?
295 "No!" exclaimed he, "why should I tarry here?"
No! loudly echoed times innumerable.
At which he straightway started, and 'gan tell
His paces back into the temple's chief;
Warming and glowing strong in the belief
300 Of help from Dian: so that when again
He caught her airy form, thus did he plain,
Moving more near the while. "O Haunter chaste
Of river sides, and woods, and heathy waste,
Where with thy silver bow and arrows keen
305 Art thou now forested? O woodland Queen,
What smoothest air thy smoother forehead woos?
Where dost thou listen to the wide halloos
Of thy disparted nymphs? Through what dark tree
Glimmers thy crescent? Wheresoe'er it be,
310 'Tis in the breath of heaven: thou dost taste

Freedom as none can taste it, nor dost waste
Thy loveliness in dismal elements;
But, finding in our green earth sweet contents,
There livest blissfully. Ah, if to thee
315   It feels Elysian, how rich to me,
An exil'd mortal, sounds its pleasant name!
Within my breast there lives a choking flame—
O let me cool it the zephyr-boughs among!
A homeward fever parches up my tongue—
320   O let me slake it at the running springs!
Upon my ear a noisy nothing rings—
O let me once more hear the linnet's note!
Before mine eyes thick films and shadows float—
O let me 'noint them with the heaven's light!
325   Dost thou now lave thy feet and ankles white?
O think how sweet to me the freshening sluice!
Dost thou now please thy thirst with berry-juice?
O think how this dry palate would rejoice!
If in soft slumber thou dost hear my voice,
330   O think how I should love a bed of flowers!—
Young goddess! let me see my native bowers!
Deliver me from this rapacious deep!"

    Thus ending loudly, as he would o'erleap
His destiny, alert he stood: but when
335   Obstinate silence came heavily again,
Feeling about for its old couch of space
And airy cradle, lowly bow'd his face
Desponding, o'er the marble floor's cold thrill.
But 'twas not long; for, sweeter than the rill
340   To its old channel, or a swollen tide
To margin sallows, were the leaves he spied,
And flowers, and wreaths, and ready myrtle crowns
Up heaping through the slab: refreshment drowns
Itself, and strives its own delights to hide—
345   Nor in one spot alone; the floral pride
In a long whispering birth enchanted grew
Before his footsteps; as when heav'd anew
Old ocean rolls a lengthened wave to the shore,
Down whose green back the short-liv'd foam, all hoar,
350   Bursts gradual, with a wayward indolence.

    Increasing still in heart, and pleasant sense,
Upon his fairy journey on he hastes;

So anxious for the end, he scarcely wastes
One moment with his hand among the sweets:
355   Onward he goes—he stops—his bosom beats
As plainly in his ear, as the faint charm
Of which the throbs were born. This still alarm,
This sleepy music, forc'd him walk tiptoe:
For it came more softly than the east could blow
360   Arion's magic to the Atlantic isles;
Or than the west, made jealous by the smiles
Of thron'd Apollo, could breathe back the lyre
To seas Ionian and Tyrian.

    O did he ever live, that lonely man,
365   Who lov'd—and music slew not? 'Tis the pest
Of love, that fairest joys give most unrest;
That things of delicate and tenderest worth
Are swallow'd all, and made a seared dearth,
By one consuming flame: it doth immerse
370   And suffocate true blessings in a curse.
Half-happy, by comparison of bliss,
Is miserable. 'Twas even so with this
Dew-dropping melody, in the Carian's ear;
First heaven, then hell, and then forgotten clear,
375   Vanish'd in elemental passion.

    And down some swart abysm he had gone,
Had not a heavenly guide benignant led
To where thick myrtle branches, 'gainst his head
Brushing, awakened: then the sounds again
380   Went noiseless as a passing noontide rain
Over a bower, where little space he stood;
For, as the sunset peeps into a wood,
So saw he panting light, and towards it went
Through winding alleys; and lo, wonderment!
385   Upon soft verdure saw, one here, one there,
Cupids a slumbering on their pinions fair.

    After a thousand mazes overgone,
At last, with sudden step, he came upon
A chamber, myrtle wall'd, embowered high,
390   Full of light, incense, tender minstrelsy,
And more of beautiful and strange beside:
For on a silken couch of rosy pride,
In midst of all, there lay a sleeping youth

Of fondest beauty; fonder, in fair sooth,
395   Than sighs could fathom, or contentment reach:
And coverlids gold-tinted like the peach,
Or ripe October's faded marigolds,
Fell sleek about him in a thousand folds—
Not hiding up an Apollonian curve
400   Of neck and shoulder, nor the tenting swerve
Of knee from knee, nor ankles pointing light;
But rather, giving them to the filled sight
Officiously. Sideway his face repos'd
On one white arm, and tenderly unclos'd,
405   By tenderest pressure, a faint damask mouth
To slumbery pout; just as the morning south
Disparts a dew-lipp'd rose. Above his head,
Four lily stalks did their white honours wed
To make a coronal; and round him grew
410   All tendrils green, of every bloom and hue,
Together intertwin'd and trammel'd fresh:
The vine of glossy sprout; the ivy mesh,
Shading its Ethiop berries; and woodbine,
Of velvet leaves and bugle-blooms divine;
415   Convolvulus in streaked vases flush;
The creeper, mellowing for an autumn blush;
And virgin's bower, trailing airily;
With others of the sisterhood. Hard by,
Stood serene Cupids watching silently.
420   One, kneeling to a lyre, touch'd the strings,
Muffling to death the pathos with his wings;
And, ever and anon, uprose to look
At the youth's slumber; while another took
A willow-bough, distilling odorous dew,
425   And shook it on his hair; another flew
In through the woven roof, and fluttering-wise
Rain'd violets upon his sleeping eyes.

At these enchantments, and yet many more,
The breathless Latmian wonder'd o'er and o'er;
430   Until, impatient in embarrassment,
He forthright pass'd, and lightly treading went
To that same feather'd lyrist, who straightway,
Smiling, thus whisper'd: "Though from upper day
Thou art a wanderer, and thy presence here
435   Might seem unholy, be of happy cheer!

For 'tis the nicest touch of human honour,
When some ethereal and high-favouring donor
Presents immortal bowers to mortal sense;
As now 'tis done to thee, Endymion. Hence
440 Was I in no wise startled. So recline
Upon these living flowers. Here is wine,
Alive with sparkles—never, I aver,
Since Ariadne was a vintager,
So cool a purple: taste these juicy pears,
445 Sent me by sad Vertumnus, when his fears
Were high about Pomona: here is cream,
Deepening to richness from a snowy gleam;
Sweeter than that nurse Amalthea skimm'd
For the boy Jupiter: and here, undimm'd
450 By any touch, a bunch of blooming plums
Ready to melt between an infant's gums:
And here is manna pick'd from Syrian trees,
In starlight, by the three Hesperides.
Feast on, and meanwhile I will let thee know
455 Of all these things around us." He did so,
Still brooding o'er the cadence of his lyre;
And thus: "I need not any hearing tire
By telling how the sea-born goddess pin'd
For a mortal youth, and how she strove to bind
460 Him all in all unto her doting self.
Who would not be so prison'd? but, fond elf,
He was content to let her amorous plea
Faint through his careless arms; content to see
An unseiz'd heaven dying at his feet;
465 Content, O fool! to make a cold retreat,
When on the pleasant grass such love, lovelorn,
Lay sorrowing; when every tear was born
Of diverse passion; when her lips and eyes
Were clos'd in sullen moisture, and quick sighs
470 Came vex'd and pettish through her nostrils small.
Hush! no exclaim—yet, justly mightst thou call
Curses upon his head.—I was half glad,
But my poor mistress went distract and mad,
When the boar tusk'd him: so away she flew
475 To Jove's high throne, and by her plainings drew
Immortal tear-drops down the thunderer's beard;
Whereon, it was decreed he should be rear'd
Each summer time to life. Lo! this is he,

That same Adonis, safe in the privacy
480 Of this still region all his winter-sleep.
Aye, sleep; for when our love-sick queen did weep
Over his waned corse, the tremulous shower
Heal'd up the wound, and, with a balmy power,
Medicined death to a lengthened drowsiness:
485 The which she fills with visions, and doth dress
In all this quiet luxury; and hath set
Us young immortals, without any let,
To watch his slumber through. 'Tis well nigh pass'd,
Even to a moment's filling up, and fast
490 She scuds with summer breezes, to pant through
The first long kiss, warm firstling, to renew
Embower'd sports in Cytherea's isle.
Look! how those winged listeners all this while
Stand anxious: see! behold!"—This clamant word
495 Broke through the careful silence; for they heard
A rustling noise of leaves, and out there flutter'd
Pigeons and doves: Adonis something mutter'd,
The while one hand, that erst upon his thigh
Lay dormant, mov'd convuls'd and gradually
500 Up to his forehead. Then there was a hum
Of sudden voices, echoing, "Come! come!
Arise! awake! Clear summer has forth walk'd
Unto the clover-sward, and she has talk'd
Full soothingly to every nested finch:
505 Rise, Cupids! or we'll give the blue-bell pinch
To your dimpled arms. Once more sweet life begin!"
At this, from every side they hurried in,
Rubbing their sleepy eyes with lazy wrists,
And doubling over head their little fists
510 In backward yawns. But all were soon alive:
For as delicious wine doth, sparkling, dive
In nectar'd clouds and curls through water fair,
So from the arbour roof down swell'd an air
Odorous and enlivening; making all
515 To laugh, and play, and sing, and loudly call
For their sweet queen: when lo! the wreathed green
Disparted, and far upward could be seen
Blue heaven, and a silver car, air-borne,
Whose silent wheels, fresh wet from clouds of morn,
520 Spun off a drizzling dew,—which falling chill
On soft Adonis' shoulders, made him still

Nestle and turn uneasily about.
Soon were the white doves plain, with necks stretch'd out,
And silken traces tighten'd in descent;
525 And soon, returning from love's banishment,
Queen Venus leaning downward open arm'd:
Her shadow fell upon his breast, and charm'd
A tumult to his heart, and a new life
Into his eyes. Ah, miserable strife,
530 But for her comforting! unhappy sight,
But meeting her blue orbs! Who, who can write
Of these first minutes? The unchariest muse
To embracements warm as theirs makes coy excuse.

O it has ruffled every spirit there,
535 Saving Love's self, who stands superb to share
The general gladness: awfully he stands;
A sovereign quell is in his waving hands;
No sight can bear the lightning of his bow;
His quiver is mysterious, none can know
540 What themselves think of it; from forth his eyes
There darts strange light of varied hues and dyes:
A scowl is sometimes on his brow, but who
Look full upon it feel anon the blue
Of his fair eyes run liquid through their souls.
545 Endymion feels it, and no more controls
The burning prayer within him; so, bent low,
He had begun a plaining of his woe.
But Venus, bending forward, said: "My child,
Favour this gentle youth; his days are wild
550 With love—he—but alas! too well I see
Thou know'st the deepness of his misery.
Ah, smile not so, my son: I tell thee true,
That when through heavy hours I used to rue
The endless sleep of this new-born Adon',
555 This stranger ay I pitied. For upon
A dreary morning once I fled away
Into the breezy clouds, to weep and pray
For this my love: for vexing Mars had teaz'd
Me even to tears: thence, when a little eas'd,
560 Down-looking, vacant, through a hazy wood,
I saw this youth as he despairing stood:
Those same dark curls blown vagrant in the wind;
Those same full fringed lids a constant blind

Over his sullen eyes: I saw him throw
565   Himself on wither'd leaves, even as though
Death had come sudden; for no jot he mov'd,
Yet mutter'd wildly. I could hear he lov'd
Some fair immortal, and that his embrace
Had zoned her through the night. There is no trace
570   Of this in heaven: I have mark'd each cheek,
And find it is the vainest thing to seek;
And that of all things 'tis kept secretest.
Endymion! one day thou wilt be blest:
So still obey the guiding hand that fends
575   Thee safely through these wonders for sweet ends.
'Tis a concealment needful in extreme;
And if I guess'd not so, the sunny beam
Thou shouldst mount up to with me. Now adieu!
Here must we leave thee."—At these words up flew
580   The impatient doves, up rose the floating car,
Up went the hum celestial. High afar
The Latmian saw them minish into nought;
And, when all were clear vanish'd, still he caught
A vivid lightning from that dreadful bow.
585   When all was darkened, with Etnean throe
The earth clos'd—gave a solitary moan—
And left him once again in twilight lone.

He did not rave, he did not stare aghast,
For all those visions were o'ergone, and past,
590   And he in loneliness: he felt assur'd
Of happy times, when all he had endur'd
Would seem a feather to the mighty prize.
So, with unusual gladness, on he hies
Through caves, and palaces of mottled ore,
595   Gold dome, and crystal wall, and turquois floor,
Black polish'd porticos of awful shade,
And, at the last, a diamond balustrade,
Leading afar past wild magnificence,
Spiral through ruggedest loopholes, and thence
600   Stretching across a void, then guiding o'er
Enormous chasms, where, all foam and roar,
Streams subterranean tease their granite beds,
Then heighten'd just above the silvery heads
Of a thousand fountains, so that he could dash

605   The waters with his spear; but at the splash,
      Done heedlessly, those spouting columns rose
      Sudden a poplar's height, and 'gan to enclose
      His diamond path with fretwork, streaming round
      Alive, and dazzling cool, and with a sound,
610   Haply, like dolphin tumults, when sweet shells
      Welcome the float of Thetis. Long he dwells
      On this delight; for, every minute's space,
      The streams with changed magic interlace:
      Sometimes like delicatest lattices,
615   Cover'd with crystal vines; then weeping trees,
      Moving about as in a gentle wind,
      Which, in a wink, to watery gauze refin'd,
      Pour'd into shapes of curtain'd canopies,
      Spangled, and rich with liquid broideries
620   Of flowers, peacocks, swans, and naiads fair.
      Swifter than lightning went these wonders rare;
      And then the water, into stubborn streams
      Collecting, mimick'd the wrought oaken beams,
      Pillars, and frieze, and high fantastic roof,
625   Of those dusk places in times far aloof
      Cathedrals call'd. He bade a loth farewel
      To these founts Protean, passing gulph, and dell,
      And torrent, and ten thousand jutting shapes,
      Half seen through deepest gloom, and griesly gapes,
630   Blackening on every side, and overhead
      A vaulted dome like heaven's, far bespread
      With starlight gems: aye, all so huge and strange,
      The solitary felt a hurried change
      Working within him into something dreary,—
635   Vex'd like a morning eagle, lost, and weary,
      And purblind amid foggy, midnight wolds.
      But he revives at once: for who beholds
      New sudden things, nor casts his mental slough?
      Forth from a rugged arch, in the dusk below,
640   Came mother Cybele! alone—alone—
      In sombre chariot; dark foldings thrown
      About her majesty, and front death-pale,
      With turrets crown'd. Four maned lions hale
      The sluggish wheels; solemn their toothed maws,
645   Their surly eyes brow-hidden, heavy paws
      Uplifted drowsily, and nervy tails

Cowering their tawny brushes. Silent sails
This shadowy queen athwart, and faints away
In another gloomy arch.

                            Wherefore delay,
650   Young traveller, in such a mournful place?
Art thou wayworn, or canst not further trace
The diamond path? And does it indeed end
Abrupt in middle air? Yet earthward bend
Thy forehead, and to Jupiter cloud-borne
655   Call ardently! He was indeed wayworn;
Abrupt, in middle air, his way was lost;
To cloud-borne Jove he bowed, and there crost
Towards him a large eagle, 'twixt whose wings,
Without one impious word, himself he flings,
660   Committed to the darkness and the gloom:
Down, down, uncertain to what pleasant doom,
Swift as a fathoming plummet down he fell
Through unknown things; till exhaled asphodel,
And rose, with spicy fannings interbreath'd,
665   Came swelling forth where little caves were wreath'd
So thick with leaves and mosses, that they seem'd
Large honey-combs of green, and freshly teem'd
With airs delicious. In the greenest nook
The eagle landed him, and farewel took.

670   It was a jasmine bower, all bestrown
With golden moss. His every sense had grown
Ethereal for pleasure; 'bove his head
Flew a delight half-graspable; his tread
Was Hesperean; to his capable ears
675   Silence was music from the holy spheres;
A dewy luxury was in his eyes;
The little flowers felt his pleasant sighs
And stirr'd them faintly. Verdant cave and cell
He wander'd through, oft wondering at such swell
680   Of sudden exaltation: but, "Alas!"
Said he, "will all this gush of feeling pass
Away in solitude? And must they wane,
Like melodies upon a sandy plain,
Without an echo? Then shall I be left
685   So sad, so melancholy, so bereft!
Yet still I feel immortal! O my love,

My breath of life, where art thou? High above,
Dancing before the morning gates of heaven?
Or keeping watch among those starry seven,
690 Old Atlas' children? Art a maid of the waters,
One of shell-winding Triton's bright-hair'd daughters?
Or art, impossible! a nymph of Dian's,
Weaving a coronal of tender scions
For very idleness? Where'er thou art,
695 Methinks it now is at my will to start
Into thine arms; to scare Aurora's train,
And snatch thee from the morning; o'er the main
To scud like a wild bird, and take thee off
From thy sea-foamy cradle; or to doff
700 Thy shepherd vest, and woo thee mid fresh leaves.
No, no, too eagerly my soul deceives
Its powerless self: I know this cannot be.
O let me then by some sweet dreaming flee
To her entrancements: hither, sleep, awhile!
705 Hither, most gentle sleep! and soothing foil
For some few hours the coming solitude."

     Thus spake he, and that moment felt endued
With power to dream deliciously; so wound
Through a dim passage, searching till he found
710 The smoothest mossy bed and deepest, where
He threw himself, and just into the air
Stretching his indolent arms, he took, O bliss!
A naked waist: "Fair Cupid, whence is this?"
A well-known voice sigh'd, "Sweetest, here am I!"
715 At which soft ravishment, with doating cry
They trembled to each other.—Helicon!
O fountain'd hill! Old Homer's Helicon!
That thou wouldst spout a little streamlet o'er
These sorry pages; then the verse would soar
720 And sing above this gentle pair, like lark
Over his nested young: but all is dark
Around thine aged top, and thy clear fount
Exhales in mists to heaven. Aye, the count
Of mighty Poets is made up; the scroll
725 Is folded by the Muses; the bright roll
Is in Apollo's hand: our dazed eyes
Have seen a new tinge in the western skies:
The world has done its duty. Yet, oh yet,

Although the sun of poesy is set,
730 These lovers did embrace, and we must weep
That there is no old power left to steep
A quill immortal in their joyous tears.
Long time in silence did their anxious fears
Question that thus it was; long time they lay
735 Fondling and kissing every doubt away;
Long time ere soft caressing sobs began
To mellow into words, and then there ran
Two bubbling springs of talk from their sweet lips.
"O known Unknown! from whom my being sips
740 Such darling essence, wherefore may I not
Be ever in these arms? in this sweet spot
Pillow my chin for ever? ever press
These toying hands and kiss their smooth excess?
Why not for ever and for ever feel
745 That breath about my eyes? Ah, thou wilt steal
Away from me again, indeed, indeed—
Thou wilt be gone away, and wilt not heed
My lonely madness. Speak, delicious fair!
Is—is it to be so? No! Who will dare
750 To pluck thee from me? And, of thine own will,
Full well I feel thou wouldst not leave me. Still
Let me entwine thee surer, surer—now
How can we part? Elysium! who art thou?
Who, that thou canst not be for ever here,
755 Or lift me with thee to some starry sphere?
Enchantress! tell me by this soft embrace,
By the most soft completion of thy face,
Those lips, O slippery blisses, twinkling eyes,
And by these tenderest, milky sovereignties—
760 These tenderest, and by the nectar-wine,
The passion"——"O dov'd Ida the divine!
Endymion! dearest! Ah, unhappy me!
His soul will 'scape us—O felicity!
How he does love me! His poor temples beat
765 To the very tune of love—how sweet, sweet, sweet.
Revive, dear youth, or I shall faint and die;
Revive, or these soft hours will hurry by
In tranced dulness; speak, and let that spell
Affright this lethargy! I cannot quell
770 Its heavy pressure, and will press at least
My lips to thine, that they may richly feast

Until we taste the life of love again.
What! dost thou move? dost kiss? O bliss! O pain!
I love thee, youth, more than I can conceive;
775   And so long absence from thee doth bereave
My soul of any rest: yet must I hence:
Yet, can I not to starry eminence
Uplift thee; nor for very shame can own
Myself to thee. Ah, dearest, do not groan
780   Or thou wilt force me from this secrecy,
And I must blush in heaven. O that I
Had done't already; that the dreadful smiles
At my lost brightness, my impassion'd wiles,
Had waned from Olympus' solemn height,
785   And from all serious Gods; that our delight
Was quite forgotten, save of us alone!
And wherefore so ashamed? 'Tis but to atone
For endless pleasure, by some coward blushes:
Yet must I be a coward!—Horror rushes
790   Too palpable before me—the sad look
Of Jove—Minerva's start—no bosom shook
With awe of purity—no Cupid pinion
In reverence vailed—my crystalline dominion
Half lost, and all old hymns made nullity!
795   But what is this to love? O I could fly
With thee into the ken of heavenly powers,
So thou wouldst thus, for many sequent hours,
Press me so sweetly. Now I swear at once
That I am wise, that Pallas is a dunce—
800   Perhaps her love like mine is but unknown—
O I do think that I have been alone
In chastity: yes, Pallas has been sighing,
While every eve saw me my hair uptying
With fingers cool as aspen leaves. Sweet love,
805   I was as vague as solitary dove,
Nor knew that nests were built. Now a soft kiss—
Aye, by that kiss, I vow an endless bliss,
An immortality of passion's thine:
Ere long I will exalt thee to the shine
810   Of heaven ambrosial; and we will shade
Ourselves whole summers by a river glade;
And I will tell thee stories of the sky,
And breathe thee whispers of its minstrelsy.
My happy love will overwing all bounds!

815 O let me melt into thee; let the sounds .
    Of our close voices marry at their birth;
    Let us entwine hoveringly—O dearth
    Of human words! roughness of mortal speech!
    Lispings empyrean will I sometime teach
820 Thine honied tongue—lute-breathings, which I gasp
    To have thee understand, now while I clasp
    Thee thus, and weep for fondness—I am pain'd,
    Endymion: woe! woe! is grief contain'd
    In the very deeps of pleasure, my sole life?"—
825 Hereat, with many sobs, her gentle strife
    Melted into a languor. He return'd
    Entranced vows and tears.

                 Ye who have yearn'd
    With too much passion, will here stay and pity,
    For the mere sake of truth; as 'tis a ditty
830 Not of these days, but long ago 'twas told
    By a cavern wind unto a forest old;
    And then the forest told it in a dream
    To a sleeping lake, whose cool and level gleam
    A poet caught as he was journeying
835 To Phœbus' shrine; and in it he did fling
    His weary limbs, bathing an hour's space,
    And after, straight in that inspired place
    He sang the story up into the air,
    Giving it universal freedom. There
840 Has it been ever sounding for those ears
    Whose tips are glowing hot. The legend cheers
    Yon centinel stars; and he who listens to it
    Must surely be self-doomed or he will rue it:
    For quenchless burnings come upon the heart,
845 Made fiercer by a fear lest any part
    Should be engulphed in the eddying wind.
    As much as here is penn'd doth always find
    A resting place, thus much comes clear and plain;
    Anon the strange voice is upon the wane—
850 And 'tis but echo'd from departing sound,
    That the fair visitant at last unwound
    Her gentle limbs, and left the youth asleep.—
    Thus the tradition of the gusty deep.

    Now turn we to our former chroniclers.—
855 Endymion awoke, that grief of hers

Sweet paining on his ear: he sickly guess'd
How lone he was once more, and sadly press'd
His empty arms together, hung his head,
And most forlorn upon that widow'd bed
860 Sat silently. Love's madness he had known:
Often with more than tortured lion's groan
Moanings had burst from him; but now that rage
Had pass'd away: no longer did he wage
A rough-voic'd war against the dooming stars.
865 No, he had felt too much for such harsh jars:
The lyre of his soul Eolian tun'd
Forgot all violence, and but commun'd
With melancholy thought: O he had swoon'd
Drunken from pleasure's nipple; and his love
870 Henceforth was dove-like.—Loth was he to move
From the imprinted couch, and when he did,
'Twas with slow, languid paces, and face hid
In muffling hands. So temper'd, out he stray'd
Half seeing visions that might have dismay'd
875 Alecto's serpents; ravishments more keen
Than Hermes' pipe, when anxious he did lean
Over eclipsing eyes: and at the last
It was a sounding grotto, vaulted, vast,
O'er studded with a thousand, thousand pearls,
880 And crimson mouthed shells with stubborn curls,
Of every shape and size, even to the bulk
In which whales harbour close, to brood and sulk
Against an endless storm. Moreover too,
Fish-semblances, of green and azure hue,
885 Ready to snort their streams. In this cool wonder
Endymion sat down, and 'gan to ponder
On all his life: his youth, up to the day
When 'mid acclaim, and feasts, and garlands gay,
He stept upon his shepherd throne: the look
890 Of his white palace in wild forest nook,
And all the revels he had lorded there:
Each tender maiden whom he once thought fair,
With every friend and fellow-woodlander—
Pass'd like a dream before him. Then the spur
895 Of the old bards to mighty deeds: his plans
To nurse the golden age 'mong shepherd clans:
That wondrous night: the great Pan-festival:
His sister's sorrow; and his wanderings all,
Until into the earth's deep maw he rush'd:

900 Then all its buried magic, till it flush'd
  High with excessive love. "And now," thought he,
  "How long must I remain in jeopardy
  Of blank amazements that amaze no more?
  Now I have tasted her sweet soul to the core
905 All other depths are shallow: essences,
  Once spiritual, are like muddy lees,
  Meant but to fertilize my earthly root,
  And make my branches lift a golden fruit
  Into the bloom of heaven: other light,
910 Though it be quick and sharp enough to blight
  The Olympian eagle's vision, is dark,
  Dark as the parentage of chaos. Hark!
  My silent thoughts are echoing from these shells;
  Or they are but the ghosts, the dying swells
915 Of noises far away?—list!"—Hereupon
  He kept an anxious ear. The humming tone
  Came louder, and behold, there as he lay,
  On either side outgush'd, with misty spray,
  A copious spring; and both together dash'd
920 Swift, mad, fantastic round the rocks, and lash'd
  Among the conchs and shells of the lofty grot,
  Leaving a trickling dew. At last they shot
  Down from the ceiling's height, pouring a noise
  As of some breathless racers whose hopes poize
925 Upon the last few steps, and with spent force
  Along the ground they took a winding course.
  Endymion follow'd—for it seem'd that one
  Ever pursued, the other strove to shun—
  Follow'd their languid mazes, till well nigh
930 He had left thinking of the mystery,—
  And was now rapt in tender hoverings
  Over the vanish'd bliss. Ah! what is it sings
  His dream away? What melodies are these?
  They sound as through the whispering of trees,
935 Not native in such barren vaults. Give ear!

   "O Arethusa, peerless nymph! why fear
  Such tenderness as mine? Great Dian, why,
  Why didst thou hear her prayer? O that I
  Were rippling round her dainty fairness now,
940 Circling about her waist, and striving how
  To entice her to a dive! then stealing in

Between her luscious lips and eyelids thin.
O that her shining hair was in the sun,
And I distilling from it thence to run
945   In amorous rillets down her shrinking form!
To linger on her lily shoulders, warm
Between her kissing breasts, and every charm
Touch raptur'd!—See how painfully I flow:
Fair maid, be pitiful to my great woe.
950   Stay, stay thy weary course, and let me lead,
A happy wooer, to the flowery mead
Where all that beauty snar'd me."—"Cruel god,
Desist! or my offended mistress' nod
Will stagnate all thy fountains:—tease me not
955   With syren words—Ah, have I really got
Such power to madden thee? And is it true—
Away, away, or I shall dearly rue
My very thoughts: in mercy then away,
Kindest Alpheus, for should I obey
960   My own dear will, 'twould be a deadly bane.
O, Oread-Queen! would that thou hadst a pain
Like this of mine, then would I fearless turn
And be a criminal. Alas, I burn,
I shudder—gentle river, get thee hence.
965   Alpheus! thou enchanter! every sense
Of mine was once made perfect in these woods.
Fresh breezes, bowery lawns, and innocent floods,
Ripe fruits, and lonely couch, contentment gave;
But ever since I heedlessly did lave
970   In thy deceitful stream, a panting glow
Grew strong within me: wherefore serve me so,
And call it love? Alas, 'twas cruelty.
Not once more did I close my happy eye
Amid the thrush's song. Away! Avaunt!
975   O 'twas a cruel thing."—"Now thou dost taunt
So softly, Arethusa, that I think
If thou wast playing on my shady brink,
Thou wouldst bathe once again. Innocent maid!
Stifle thine heart no more;—nor be afraid
980   Of angry powers: there are deities
Will shade us with their wings. Those fitful sighs
'Tis almost death to hear: O let me pour
A dewy balm upon them!—fear no more,
Sweet Arethusa! Dian's self must feel

985 Sometimes these very pangs. Dear maiden, steal
Blushing into my soul, and let us fly
These dreary caverns for the open sky.
I will delight thee all my winding course,
From the green sea up to my hidden source
990 About Arcadian forests; and will shew
The channels where my coolest waters flow
Through mossy rocks; where, 'mid exuberant green,
I roam in pleasant darkness, more unseen
Than Saturn in his exile; where I brim
995 Round flowery islands, and take thence a skim
Of mealy sweets, which myriads of bees
Buzz from their honied wings: and thou shouldst please
Thyself to choose the richest, where we might
Be incense-pillow'd every summer night.
1000 Doff all sad fears, thou white deliciousness,
And let us be thus comforted; unless
Thou couldst rejoice to see my hopeless stream
Hurry distracted from Sol's temperate beam,
And pour to death along some hungry sands."—
1005 "What can I do, Alpheus? Dian stands
Severe before me: persecuting fate!
Unhappy Arethusa! thou wast late
A huntress free in"—At this, sudden fell
Those two sad streams adown a fearful dell.
1010 The Latmian listen'd, but he heard no more,
Save echo, faint repeating o'er and o'er
The name of Arethusa. On the verge
Of that dark gulph he wept, and said: "I urge
Thee, gentle Goddess of my pilgrimage,
1015 By our eternal hopes, to soothe, to assuage,
If thou art powerful, these lovers' pains;
And make them happy in some happy plains."

He turn'd—there was a whelming sound—he stept,
There was a cooler light; and so he kept
1020 Towards it by a sandy path, and lo!
More suddenly than doth a moment go,
The visions of the earth were gone and fled—
He saw the giant sea above his head.

BOOK III

There are who lord it o'er their fellow-men
With most prevailing tinsel: who unpen
Their baaing vanities, to browse away
The comfortable green and juicy hay
5   From human pastures; or, O torturing fact!
Who, through an idiot blink, will see unpack'd
Fire-branded foxes to sear up and singe
Our gold and ripe-ear'd hopes. With not one tinge
Of sanctuary splendour, not a sight
10   Able to face an owl's, they still are dight
By the blear-eyed nations in empurpled vests,
And crowns, and turbans. With unladen breasts,
Save of blown self-applause, they proudly mount
To their spirit's perch, their being's high account,
15   Their tiptop nothings, their dull skies, their thrones—
Amid the fierce intoxicating tones
Of trumpets, shoutings, and belabour'd drums,
And sudden cannon. Ah! how all this hums,
In wakeful ears, like uproar past and gone—
20   Like thunder clouds that spake to Babylon,
And set those old Chaldeans to their tasks.—
Are then regalities all gilded masks?
No, there are throned seats unscalable
But by a patient wing, a constant spell,
25   Or by ethereal things that, unconfin'd,
Can make a ladder of the eternal wind,
And poise about in cloudy thunder-tents
To watch the abysm-birth of elements.
Aye, 'bove the withering of old-lipp'd Fate
30   A thousand Powers keep religious state,
In water, fiery realm, and airy bourne;
And, silent as a consecrated urn,
Hold sphery sessions for a season due.
Yet few of these far majesties, ah, few!
35   Have bared their operations to this globe—
Few, who with gorgeous pageantry enrobe
Our piece of heaven—whose benevolence
Shakes hand with our own Ceres; every sense
Filling with spiritual sweets to plenitude,
40   As bees gorge full their cells. And, by the feud
'Twixt Nothing and Creation, I here swear,

Eterne Apollo! that thy Sister fair
Is of all these the gentlier-mightiest.
When thy gold breath is misting in the west,
45   She unobserved steals unto her throne,
And there she sits most meek and most alone;
As if she had not pomp subservient;
As if thine eye, high Poet! was not bent
Towards her with the Muses in thine heart;
50   As if the ministring stars kept not apart,
Waiting for silver-footed messages.
O Moon! the oldest shades 'mong oldest trees
Feel palpitations when thou lookest in:
O Moon! old boughs lisp forth a holier din
55   The while they feel thine airy fellowship.
Thou dost bless every where, with silver lip
Kissing dead things to life. The sleeping kine,
Couched in thy brightness, dream of fields divine:
Innumerable mountains rise, and rise,
60   Ambitious for the hallowing of thine eyes;
And yet thy benediction passeth not
One obscure hiding-place, one little spot
Where pleasure may be sent: the nested wren
Has thy fair face within its tranquil ken,
65   And from beneath a sheltering ivy leaf
Takes glimpses of thee; thou art a relief
To the poor patient oyster, where it sleeps
Within its pearly house.—The mighty deeps,
The monstrous sea is thine—the myriad sea!
70   O Moon! far-spooming Ocean bows to thee,
And Tellus feels his forehead's cumbrous load.

Cynthia! where art thou now? What far abode
Of green or silvery bower doth enshrine
Such utmost beauty? Alas, thou dost pine
75   For one as sorrowful: thy cheek is pale
For one whose cheek is pale: thou dost bewail
His tears, who weeps for thee. Where dost thou sigh?
Ah! surely that light peeps from Vesper's eye,
Or what a thing is love! 'Tis She, but lo!
80   How chang'd, how full of ache, how gone in woe!
She dies at the thinnest cloud; her loveliness
Is wan on Neptune's blue: yet there's a stress
Of love-spangles, just off yon cape of trees,

Dancing upon the waves, as if to please
85   The curly foam with amorous influence.
O, not so idle: for down-glancing thence
She fathoms eddies, and runs wild about
O'erwhelming water-courses; scaring out
The thorny sharks from hiding-holes, and fright'ning
90   Their savage eyes with unaccustomed lightning.
Where will the splendor be content to reach?
O love! how potent hast thou been to teach
Strange journeyings! Wherever beauty dwells,
In gulf or aerie, mountains or deep dells,
95   In light, in gloom, in star or blazing sun,
Thou pointest out the way, and straight 'tis won.
Amid his toil thou gav'st Leander breath;
Thou leddest Orpheus through the gleams of death;
Thou madest Pluto bear thin element;
100   And now, O winged Chieftain! thou hast sent
A moon-beam to the deep, deep water-world,
To find Endymion.

         On gold sand impearl'd
With lily shells, and pebbles milky white,
Poor Cynthia greeted him, and sooth'd her light
105   Against his pallid face: he felt the charm
To breathlessness, and suddenly a warm
Of his heart's blood: 'twas very sweet; he stay'd
His wandering steps, and half-entranced laid
His head upon a tuft of straggling weeds,
110   To taste the gentle moon, and freshening beads,
Lashed from the crystal roof by fishes' tails.
And so he kept, until the rosy veils
Mantling the east, by Aurora's peering hand
Were lifted from the water's breast, and fann'd
115   Into sweet air; and sober'd morning came
Meekly through billows:—when like taper-flame
Left sudden by a dallying breath of air,
He rose in silence, and once more 'gan fare
Along his fated way.

         Far had he roam'd,
120   With nothing save the hollow vast, that foam'd
Above, around, and at his feet; save things
More dead than Morpheus' imaginings:

Old rusted anchors, helmets, breast-plates large
Of gone sea-warriors; brazen beaks and targe;
125   Rudders that for a hundred years had lost
The sway of human hand; gold vase emboss'd
With long-forgotten story, and wherein
No reveller had ever dipp'd a chin
But those of Saturn's vintage; mouldering scrolls,
130   Writ in the tongue of heaven, by those souls
Who first were on the earth; and sculptures rude
In ponderous stone, developing the mood
Of ancient Nox;—then skeletons of man,
Of beast, behemoth, and leviathan,
135   And elephant, and eagle, and huge jaw
Of nameless monster. A cold leaden awe
These secrets struck into him; and unless
Dian had chaced away that heaviness,
He might have died: but now, with cheered feel,
140   He onward kept; wooing these thoughts to steal
About the labyrinth in his soul of love.

"What is there in thee, Moon! that thou shouldst move
My heart so potently? When yet a child
I oft have dried my tears when thou hast smil'd.
145   Thou seem'dst my sister: hand in hand we went
From eve to morn across the firmament.
No apples would I gather from the tree,
Till thou hadst cool'd their cheeks deliciously:
No tumbling water ever spake romance,
150   But when my eyes with thine thereon could dance:
No woods were green enough, no bower divine,
Until thou liftedst up thine eyelids fine:
In sowing time ne'er would I dibble take,
Or drop a seed, till thou wast wide awake;
155   And, in the summer tide of blossoming,
No one but thee hath heard me blithely sing
And mesh my dewy flowers all the night.
No melody was like a passing spright
If it went not to solemnize thy reign.
160   Yes, in my boyhood, every joy and pain
By thee were fashion'd to the self-same end;
And as I grew in years, still didst thou blend
With all my ardours: thou wast the deep glen;
Thou wast the mountain-top—the sage's pen—

165   The poet's harp—the voice of friends—the sun;
         Thou wast the river—thou wast glory won;
         Thou wast my clarion's blast—thou wast my steed—
         My goblet full of wine—my topmost deed:—
         Thou wast the charm of women, lovely Moon!
170   O what a wild and harmonized tune
         My spirit struck from all the beautiful!
         On some bright essence could I lean, and lull
         Myself to immortality: I prest
         Nature's soft pillow in a wakeful rest.
175   But, gentle Orb! there came a nearer bliss—
         My strange love came—Felicity's abyss!
         She came, and thou didst fade, and fade away—
         Yet not entirely; no, thy starry sway
         Has been an under-passion to this hour.
180   Now I begin to feel thine orby power
         Is coming fresh upon me: O be kind,
         Keep back thine influence, and do not blind
         My sovereign vision.—Dearest love, forgive
         That I can think away from thee and live!—
185   Pardon me, airy planet, that I prize
         One thought beyond thine argent luxuries!
         How far beyond!" At this a surpris'd start
         Frosted the springing verdure of his heart;
         For as he lifted up his eyes to swear
190   How his own goddess was past all things fair,
         He saw far in the concave green of the sea
         An old man sitting calm and peacefully.
         Upon a weeded rock this old man sat,
         And his white hair was awful, and a mat
195   Of weeds were cold beneath his cold thin feet;
         And, ample as the largest winding-sheet,
         A cloak of blue wrapp'd up his aged bones,
         O'erwrought with symbols by the deepest groans
         Of ambitious magic: every ocean-form
200   Was woven in with black distinctness; storm,
         And calm, and whispering, and hideous roar,
         Quicksand and whirlpool, and deserted shore
         Were emblem'd in the woof; with every shape
         That skims, or dives, or sleeps, 'twixt cape and cape.
205   The gulphing whale was like a dot in the spell,
         Yet look upon it, and 'twould size and swell
         To its huge self; and the minutest fish

Would pass the very hardest gazer's wish,
And shew his little eye's anatomy.
210 Then there was pictur'd the regality
Of Neptune; and the sea nymphs round his state,
In beauteous vassalage, look up and wait.
Beside this old man lay a pearly wand,
And in his lap a book, the which he conn'd
215 So stedfastly, that the new denizen
Had time to keep him in amazed ken,
To mark these shadowings, and stand in awe.

The old man rais'd his hoary head and saw
The wilder'd stranger—seeming not to see,
220 His features were so lifeless. Suddenly
He woke as from a trance; his snow-white brows
Went arching up, and like two magic ploughs
Furrow'd deep wrinkles in his forehead large,
Which kept as fixedly as rocky marge,
225 Till round his wither'd lips had gone a smile.
Then up he rose, like one whose tedious toil
Had watch'd for years in forlorn hermitage,
Who had not from mid-life to utmost age
Eas'd in one accent his o'er-burden'd soul,
230 Even to the trees. He rose: he grasp'd his stole,
With convuls'd clenches waving it abroad,
And in a voice of solemn joy, that aw'd
Echo into oblivion, he said:—

"Thou art the man! Now shall I lay my head
235 In peace upon my watery pillow: now
Sleep will come smoothly to my weary brow.
O Jove! I shall be young again, be young!
O shell-borne Neptune, I am pierc'd and stung
With new-born life! What shall I do? Where go,
240 When I have cast this serpent-skin of woe?—
I'll swim to the syrens, and one moment listen
Their melodies, and see their long hair glisten;
Anon upon that giant's arm I'll be,
That writhes about the roots of Sicily:
245 To northern seas I'll in a twinkling sail,
And mount upon the snortings of a whale
To some black cloud; thence down I'll madly sweep

On forked lightning, to the deepest deep,
Where through some sucking pool I will be hurl'd
250 With rapture to the other side of the world!
O, I am full of gladness! Sisters three,
I bow full hearted to your old decree!
Yes, every god be thank'd, and power benign,
For I no more shall wither, droop, and pine.
255 Thou art the man!" Endymion started back
Dismay'd; and, like a wretch from whom the rack
Tortures hot breath, and speech of agony,
Mutter'd: "What lonely death am I to die
In this cold region? Will he let me freeze,
260 And float my brittle limbs o'er polar seas?
Or will he touch me with his searing hand,
And leave a black memorial on the sand?
Or tear me piece-meal with a bony saw,
And keep me as a chosen food to draw
265 His magian fish through hated fire and flame?
O misery of hell! resistless, tame,
Am I to be burnt up? No, I will shout,
Until the gods through heaven's blue look out!—
O Tartarus! but some few days agone
270 Her soft arms were entwining me, and on
Her voice I hung like fruit among green leaves:
Her lips were all my own, and—ah, ripe sheaves
Of happiness! ye on the stubble droop,
But never may be garner'd. I must stoop
275 My head, and kiss death's foot. Love! love, farewel!
Is there no hope from thee? This horrid spell
Would melt at thy sweet breath.—By Dian's hind
Feeding from her white fingers, on the wind
I see thy streaming hair! and now, by Pan,
280 I care not for this old mysterious man!"

He spake, and walking to that aged form,
Look'd high defiance. Lo! his heart 'gan warm
With pity, for the grey-hair'd creature wept.
Had he then wrong'd a heart where sorrow kept?
285 Had he, though blindly contumelious, brought
Rheum to kind eyes, a sting to humane thought,
Convulsion to a mouth of many years?
He had in truth; and he was ripe for tears.

The penitent shower fell, as down he knelt
290   Before that care-worn sage, who trembling felt
About his large dark locks, and faultering spake:

"Arise, good youth, for sacred Phœbus' sake!
I know thine inmost bosom, and I feel
A very brother's yearning for thee steal
295   Into mine own: for why? thou openest
The prison gates that have so long opprest
My weary watching. Though thou know'st it not,
Thou art commission'd to this fated spot
For great enfranchisement. O weep no more;
300   I am a friend to love, to loves of yore:
Aye, hadst thou never lov'd an unknown power,
I had been grieving at this joyous hour.
But even now most miserable old,
I saw thee, and my blood no longer cold
305   Gave mighty pulses: in this tottering case
Grew a new heart, which at this moment plays
As dancingly as thine. Be not afraid,
For thou shalt hear this secret all display'd,
Now as we speed towards our joyous task."

310   So saying, this young soul in age's mask
Went forward with the Carian side by side:
Resuming quickly thus; while ocean's tide
Hung swollen at their backs, and jewel'd sands
Took silently their foot-prints.

"My soul stands
315   Now past the midway from mortality,
And so I can prepare without a sigh
To tell thee briefly all my joy and pain.
I was a fisher once, upon this main,
And my boat danc'd in every creek and bay;
320   Rough billows were my home by night and day,—
The sea-gulls not more constant; for I had
No housing from the storm and tempests mad,
But hollow rocks,—and they were palaces
Of silent happiness, of slumberous ease:
325   Long years of misery have told me so.
Aye, thus it was one thousand years ago.
One thousand years!—Is it then possible

To look so plainly through them? to dispel
A thousand years with backward glance sublime?
330   To breathe away as 'twere all scummy slime
From off a crystal pool, to see its deep,
And one's own image from the bottom peep?
Yes: now I am no longer wretched thrall,
My long captivity and moanings all
335   Are but a slime, a thin pervading scum,
The which I breathe away, and thronging come
Like things of yesterday my youthful pleasures.

"I touch'd no lute, I sang not, trod no measures:
I was a lonely youth on desert shores.
340   My sports were lonely, 'mid continuous roars,
And craggy isles, and sea-mew's plaintive cry
Plaining discrepant between sea and sky.
Dolphins were still my playmates; shapes unseen
Would let me feel their scales of gold and green,
345   Nor be my desolation; and, full oft,
When a dread waterspout had rear'd aloft
Its hungry hugeness, seeming ready ripe
To burst with hoarsest thunderings, and wipe
My life away like a vast sponge of fate,
350   Some friendly monster, pitying my sad state,
Has dived to its foundations, gulph'd it down,
And left me tossing safely. But the crown
Of all my life was utmost quietude:
More did I love to lie in cavern rude,
355   Keeping in wait whole days for Neptune's voice,
And if it came at last, hark, and rejoice!
There blush'd no summer eve but I would steer
My skiff along green shelving coasts, to hear
The shepherd's pipe come clear from airy steep,
360   Mingled with ceaseless bleatings of his sheep:
And never was a day of summer shine,
But I beheld its birth upon the brine:
For I would watch all night to see unfold
Heaven's gates, and Æthon snort his morning gold
365   Wide o'er the swelling streams: and constantly
At brim of day-tide, on some grassy lea,
My nets would be spread out, and I at rest.
The poor folk of the sea-country I blest
With daily boon of fish most delicate:

370   They knew not whence this bounty, and elate
        Would strew sweet flowers on a sterile beach.

            "Why was I not contented? Wherefore reach
        At things which, but for thee, O Latmian!
        Had been my dreary death? Fool! I began
375   To feel distemper'd longings: to desire
        The utmost privilege that ocean's sire
        Could grant in benediction: to be free
        Of all his kingdom. Long in misery
        I wasted, ere in one extremest fit
380   I plung'd for life or death. To interknit
        One's senses with so dense a breathing stuff
        Might seem a work of pain; so not enough
        Can I admire how crystal-smooth it felt,
        And buoyant round my limbs. At first I dwelt
385   Whole days and days in sheer astonishment;
        Forgetful utterly of self-intent;
        Moving but with the mighty ebb and flow.
        Then, like a new fledg'd bird that first doth shew
        His spreaded feathers to the morrow chill,
390   I tried in fear the pinions of my will.
        'Twas freedom! and at once I visited
        The ceaseless wonders of this ocean-bed.
        No need to tell thee of them, for I see
        That thou hast been a witness—it must be—
395   For these I know thou canst not feel a drouth,
        By the melancholy corners of that mouth.
        So I will in my story straightway pass
        To more immediate matter. Woe, alas!
        That love should be my bane! Ah, Scylla fair!
400   Why did poor Glaucus ever—ever dare
        To sue thee to his heart? Kind stranger-youth!
        I lov'd her to the very white of truth,
        And she would not conceive it. Timid thing!
        She fled me swift as sea-bird on the wing,
405   Round every isle, and point, and promontory,
        From where large Hercules wound up his story
        Far as Egyptian Nile. My passion grew
        The more, the more I saw her dainty hue
        Gleam delicately through the azure clear:
410   Until 'twas too fierce agony to bear;

And in that agony, across my grief
It flash'd, that Circe might find some relief—
Cruel enchantress! So above the water
I rear'd my head, and look'd for Phœbus' daughter.
415 Æææ's isle was wondering at the moon:—
It seem'd to whirl around me, and a swoon
Left me dead-drifting to that fatal power.

"When I awoke, 'twas in a twilight bower;
Just when the light of morn, with hum of bees,
420 Stole through its verdurous matting of fresh trees.
How sweet, and sweeter! for I heard a lyre,
And over it a sighing voice expire.
It ceased—I caught light footsteps; and anon
The fairest face that morn e'er look'd upon
425 Push'd through a screen of roses. Starry Jove!
With tears, and smiles, and honey-words she wove
A net whose thraldom was more bliss than all
The range of flower'd Elysium. Thus did fall
The dew of her rich speech: 'Ah! Art awake?
430 O let me hear thee speak, for Cupid's sake!
I am so oppress'd with joy! Why, I have shed
An urn of tears, as though thou wert cold dead;
And now I find thee living, I will pour
From these devoted eyes their silver store,
435 Until exhausted of the latest drop,
So it will pleasure thee, and force thee stop
Here, that I too may live: but if beyond
Such cool and sorrowful offerings, thou art fond
Of soothing warmth, of dalliance supreme;
440 If thou art ripe to taste a long love dream;
If smiles, if dimples, tongues for ardour mute,
Hang in thy vision like a tempting fruit,
O let me pluck it for thee.' Thus she link'd
Her charming syllables, till indistinct
445 Their music came to my o'er-sweeten'd soul;
And then she hover'd over me, and stole
So near, that if no nearer it had been
This furrow'd visage thou hadst never seen.

"Young man of Latmos! thus particular
450 Am I, that thou may'st plainly see how far

This fierce temptation went: and thou may'st not
Exclaim, How then, was Scylla quite forgot?

    "Who could resist? Who in this universe?
She did so breathe ambrosia; so immerse
455   My fine existence in a golden clime.
She took me like a child of suckling time,
And cradled me in roses. Thus condemn'd,
The current of my former life was stemm'd,
And to this arbitrary queen of sense
460   I bow'd a tranced vassal: nor would thence
Have mov'd, even though Amphion's harp had woo'd
Me back to Scylla o'er the billows rude.
For as Apollo each eve doth devise
A new appareling for western skies;
465   So every eve, nay every spendthrift hour
Shed balmy consciousness within that bower.
And I was free of haunts umbrageous;
Could wander in the mazy forest-house
Of squirrels, foxes shy, and antler'd deer,
470   And birds from coverts innermost and drear
Warbling for very joy mellifluous sorrow—
To me new born delights!

                   "Now let me borrow,
For moments few, a temperament as stern
As Pluto's sceptre, that my words not burn
475   These uttering lips, while I in calm speech tell
How specious heaven was changed to real hell.

    "One morn she left me sleeping: half awake
I sought for her smooth arms and lips, to slake
My greedy thirst with nectarous camel-draughts;
480   But she was gone. Whereat the barbed shafts
Of disappointment stuck in me so sore,
That out I ran and search'd the forest o'er.
Wandering about in pine and cedar gloom
Damp awe assail'd me; for there 'gan to boom
485   A sound of moan, an agony of sound,
Sepulchral from the distance all around.
Then came a conquering earth-thunder, and rumbled
That fierce complain to silence: while I stumbled
Down a precipitous path, as if impell'd.

490 I came to a dark valley.—Groanings swell'd
     Poisonous about my ears, and louder grew,
     The nearer I approach'd a flame's gaunt blue,
     That glar'd before me through a thorny brake.
     This fire, like the eye of gordian snake,
495 Bewitch'd me towards; and I soon was near
     A sight too fearful for the feel of fear:
     In thicket hid I curs'd the haggard scene—
     The banquet of my arms, my arbour queen,
     Seated upon an uptorn forest root;
500 And all around her shapes, wizard and brute,
     Laughing, and wailing, groveling, serpenting,
     Shewing tooth, tusk, and venom-bag, and sting!
     O such deformities! Old Charon's self,
     Should he give up awhile his penny pelf,
505 And take a dream 'mong rushes Stygian,
     It could not be so phantasied. Fierce, wan,
     And tyrannizing was the lady's look,
     As over them a gnarled staff she shook.
     Oft-times upon the sudden she laugh'd out,
510 And from a basket emptied to the rout
     Clusters of grapes, the which they raven'd quick
     And roar'd for more; with many a hungry lick
     About their shaggy jaws. Avenging, slow,
     Anon she took a branch of mistletoe,
515 And emptied on't a black dull-gurgling phial:
     Groan'd one and all, as if some piercing trial
     Was sharpening for their pitiable bones.
     She lifted up the charm: appealing groans
     From their poor breasts went sueing to her ear
520 In vain; remorseless as an infant's bier
     She whisk'd against their eyes the sooty oil.
     Whereat was heard a noise of painful toil,
     Increasing gradual to a tempest rage,
     Shrieks, yells, and groans of torture-pilgrimage;
525 Until their grieved bodies 'gan to bloat
     And puff from the tail's end to stifled throat:
     Then was appalling silence: then a sight
     More wildering than all that hoarse affright;
     For the whole herd, as by a whirlwind writhen,
530 Went through the dismal air like one huge Python
     Antagonizing Boreas,—and so vanish'd.
     Yet there was not a breath of wind: she banish'd

These phantoms with a nod. Lo! from the dark
Came waggish fauns, and nymphs, and satyrs stark,
535   With dancing and loud revelry,—and went
Swifter than centaurs after rapine bent.—
Sighing, an elephant appear'd and bow'd
Before the fierce witch, speaking thus aloud
In human accent: 'Potent goddess! chief
540   Of pains resistless! make my being brief,
Or let me from this heavy prison fly:
Or give me to the air, or let me die!
I sue not for my happy crown again;
I sue not for my phalanx on the plain;
545   I sue not for my lone, my widow'd wife;
I sue not for my ruddy drops of life,
My children fair, my lovely girls and boys!
I will forget them; I will pass these joys;
Ask nought so heavenward, so too—too high:
550   Only I pray, as fairest boon, to die,
Or be deliver'd from this cumbrous flesh,
From this gross, detestable, filthy mesh,
And merely given to the cold bleak air.
Have mercy, Goddess! Circe, feel my prayer!'

555   "That curst magician's name fell icy numb
Upon my wild conjecturing: truth had come
Naked and sabre-like against my heart.
I saw a fury whetting a death-dart;
And my slain spirit, overwrought with fright,
560   Fainted away in that dark lair of night.
Think, my deliverer, how desolate
My waking must have been! disgust, and hate,
And terrors manifold divided me
A spoil amongst them. I prepar'd to flee
565   Into the dungeon core of that wild wood:
I fled three days—when lo! before me stood
Glaring the angry witch. O Dis, even now,
A clammy dew is beading on my brow,
At mere remembering her pale laugh, and curse.
570   'Ha! ha! Sir Dainty! there must be a nurse
Made of rose leaves and thistledown, express,
To cradle thee, my sweet, and lull thee: yes,
I am too flinty-hard for thy nice touch:
My tenderest squeeze is but a giant's clutch.

575 So, fairy-thing, it shall have lullabies
Unheard of yet; and it shall still its cries
Upon some breast more lily-feminine.
Oh, no—it shall not pine, and pine, and pine
More than one pretty, trifling thousand years;
580 And then 'twere pity, but fate's gentle shears
Cut short its immortality. Sea-flirt!
Young dove of the waters! truly I'll not hurt
One hair of thine: see how I weep and sigh,
That our heart-broken parting is so nigh.
585 And must we part? Ah, yes, it must be so.
Yet ere thou leavest me in utter woe,
Let me sob over thee my last adieus,
And speak a blessing: Mark me! Thou hast thews
Immortal, for thou art of heavenly race:
590 But such a love is mine, that here I chase
Eternally away from thee all bloom
Of youth, and destine thee towards a tomb.
Hence shalt thou quickly to the watery vast;
And there, ere many days be overpast,
595 Disabled age shall seize thee; and even then
Thou shalt not go the way of aged men;
But live and wither, cripple and still breathe
Ten hundred years: which gone, I then bequeath
Thy fragile bones to unknown burial.
600 Adieu, sweet love, adieu!'—As shot stars fall,
She fled ere I could groan for mercy. Stung
And poisoned was my spirit: despair sung
A war-song of defiance 'gainst all hell.
A hand was at my shoulder to compel
605 My sullen steps; another 'fore my eyes
Moved on with pointed finger. In this guise
Enforced, at the last by ocean's foam
I found me; by my fresh, my native home.
Its tempering coolness, to my life akin,
610 Came salutary as I waded in;
And, with a blind voluptuous rage, I gave
Battle to the swollen billow-ridge, and drave
Large froth before me, while there yet remain'd
Hale strength, nor from my bones all marrow drain'd.

615   "Young lover, I must weep—such hellish spite
With dry cheek who can tell? While thus my might

Proving upon this element, dismay'd,
Upon a dead thing's face my hand I laid;
I look'd—'twas Scylla! Cursed, cursed Circe!
620 O vulture-witch, hast never heard of mercy?
Could not thy harshest vengeance be content,
But thou must nip this tender innocent
Because I lov'd her?—Cold, O cold indeed
Were her fair limbs, and like a common weed
625 The sea-swell took her hair. Dead as she was
I clung about her waist, nor ceas'd to pass
Fleet as an arrow through unfathom'd brine,
Until there shone a fabric crystalline,
Ribb'd and inlaid with coral, pebble, and pearl.
630 Headlong I darted; at one eager swirl
Gain'd its bright portal, enter'd, and behold!
'Twas vast, and desolate, and icy-cold;
And all around—But wherefore this to thee
Who in few minutes more thyself shalt see?—
635 I left poor Scylla in a niche and fled.
My fever'd parchings up, my scathing dread
Met palsy half way: soon these limbs became
Gaunt, wither'd, sapless, feeble, cramp'd, and lame.

"Now let me pass a cruel, cruel space,
640 Without one hope, without one faintest trace
Of mitigation, or redeeming bubble
Of colour'd phantasy; for I fear 'twould trouble
Thy brain to loss of reason: and next tell
How a restoring chance came down to quell
One half of the witch in me.

645   "On a day,
Sitting upon a rock above the spray,
I saw grow up from the horizon's brink
A gallant vessel: soon she seem'd to sink
Away from me again, as though her course
650 Had been resum'd in spite of hindering force—
So vanish'd: and not long, before arose
Dark clouds, and muttering of winds morose.
Old Eolus would stifle his mad spleen,
But could not: therefore all the billows green
655 Toss'd up the silver spume against the clouds.
The tempest came: I saw that vessel's shrouds

In perilous bustle; while upon the deck
Stood trembling creatures. I beheld the wreck;
The final gulphing; the poor struggling souls:
660   I heard their cries amid loud thunder-rolls.
O they had all been sav'd but crazed eld
Annull'd my vigorous cravings: and thus quell'd
And curb'd, think on't, O Latmian! did I sit
Writhing with pity, and a cursing fit
665   Against that hell-born Circe. The crew had gone,
By one and one, to pale oblivion;
And I was gazing on the surges prone,
With many a scalding tear and many a groan,
When at my feet emerg'd an old man's hand,
670   Grasping this scroll, and this same slender wand.
I knelt with pain—reached out my hand—had grasp'd
These treasures—touch'd the knuckles—they unclasp'd—
I caught a finger: but the downward weight
O'erpowered me—it sank. Then 'gan abate
675   The storm, and through chill aguish gloom outburst
The comfortable sun. I was athirst
To search the book, and in the warming air
Parted its dripping leaves with eager care.
Strange matters did it treat of, and drew on
680   My soul page after page, till well-nigh won
Into forgetfulness; when, stupefied,
I read these words, and read again, and tried
My eyes against the heavens, and read again.
O what a load of misery and pain
685   Each Atlas-line bore off!—a shine of hope
Came gold around me, cheering me to cope
Strenuous with hellish tyranny. Attend!
For thou hast brought their promise to an end.

    "In the wide sea there lives a forlorn wretch,
690   *Doom'd with enfeebled carcase to outstretch*
His loath'd existence through ten centuries,
And then to die alone. Who can devise
A total opposition? No one. So
One million times ocean must ebb and flow,
695   *And he oppressed. Yet he shall not die,*
These things accomplish'd:—If he utterly
Scans all the depths of magic, and expounds
The meanings of all motions, shapes, and sounds;

If he explores all forms and substances
700   *Straight homeward to their symbol-essences;*
He shall not die. Moreover, and in chief,
He must pursue this task of joy and grief
Most piously;—all lovers tempest-tost,
And in the savage overwhelming lost,
705   *He shall deposit side by side, until*
Time's creeping shall the dreary space fulfil:
Which done, and all these labours ripened,
A youth, by heavenly power lov'd and led,
Shall stand before him; whom he shall direct
710   *How to consummate all. The youth elect*
Must do the thing, or both will be destroy'd."—

"Then," cried the young Endymion, overjoy'd,
"We are twin brothers in this destiny!
Say, I intreat thee, what achievement high
715   Is, in this restless world, for me reserv'd.
What! if from thee my wandering feet had swerv'd,
Had we both perish'd?"—"Look!" the sage replied,
"Dost thou not mark a gleaming through the tide,
Of divers brilliances? 'tis the edifice
720   I told thee of, where lovely Scylla lies;
And where I have enshrined piously
All lovers, whom fell storms have doom'd to die
Throughout my bondage." Thus discoursing, on
They went till unobscur'd the porches shone;
725   Which hurryingly they gain'd, and enter'd straight.
Sure never since king Neptune held his state
Was seen such wonder underneath the stars.
Turn to some level plain where haughty Mars
Has legion'd all his battle; and behold
730   How every soldier, with firm foot, doth hold
His even breast: see, many steeled squares,
And rigid ranks of iron—whence who dares
One step? Imagine further, line by line,
These warrior thousands on the field supine:—
735   So in that crystal place, in silent rows,
Poor lovers lay at rest from joys and woes.—
The stranger from the mountains, breathless, trac'd
Such thousands of shut eyes in order plac'd;
Such ranges of white feet, and patient lips
740   All ruddy,—for here death no blossom nips.

He mark'd their brows and foreheads; saw their hair
Put sleekly on one side with nicest care;
And each one's gentle wrists, with reverence,
Put cross-wise to its heart.

                              "Let us commence,"
745   Whisper'd the guide, stuttering with joy, "even now."
He spake, and, trembling like an aspen-bough,
Began to tear his scroll in pieces small,
Uttering the while some mumblings funeral.
He tore it into pieces small as snow
750   That drifts unfeather'd when bleak northerns blow;
And having done it, took his dark blue cloak
And bound it round Endymion: then struck
His wand against the empty air times nine.—
"What more there is to do, young man, is thine:
755   But first a little patience; first undo
This tangled thread, and wind it to a clue.
Ah, gentle! 'tis as weak as spider's skein;
And shouldst thou break it—What, is it done so clean?
A power overshadows thee! Oh, brave!
760   The spite of hell is tumbling to its grave.
Here is a shell; 'tis pearly blank to me,
Nor mark'd with any sign or charactery—
Canst thou read aught? O read for pity's sake!
Olympus! we are safe! Now, Carian, break
765   This wand against yon lyre on the pedestal."

      'Twas done: and straight with sudden swell and fall
Sweet music breath'd her soul away, and sigh'd
A lullaby to silence.—"Youth! now strew
These minced leaves on me, and passing through
770   Those files of dead, scatter the same around,
And thou wilt see the issue."—'Mid the sound
Of flutes and viols, ravishing his heart,
Endymion from Glaucus stood apart,
And scatter'd in his face some fragments light.
775   How lightning-swift the change! a youthful wight
Smiling beneath a coral diadem,
Out-sparkling sudden like an upturn'd gem,
Appear'd, and, stepping to a beauteous corse,
Kneel'd down beside it, and with tenderest force
780   Press'd its cold hand, and wept,—and Scylla sigh'd!

Endymion, with quick hand, the charm applied—
The nymph arose: he left them to their joy,
And onward went upon his high employ,
Showering those powerful fragments on the dead.
785 And, as he pass'd, each lifted up its head,
As doth a flower at Apollo's touch.
Death felt it to his inwards: 'twas too much:
Death fell a weeping in his charnel-house.
The Latmian persever'd along, and thus
790 All were re-animated. There arose
A noise of harmony, pulses and throes
Of gladness in the air—while many, who
Had died in mutual arms devout and true,
Sprang to each other madly; and the rest
795 Felt a high certainty of being blest.
They gaz'd upon Endymion. Enchantment
Grew drunken, and would have its head and bent.
Delicious symphonies, like airy flowers,
Budded, and swell'd, and, full-blown, shed full showers
800 Of light, soft, unseen leaves of sounds divine.
The two deliverers tasted a pure wine
Of happiness, from fairy-press ooz'd out.
Speechless they eyed each other, and about
The fair assembly wander'd to and fro,
805 Distracted with the richest overflow
Of joy that ever pour'd from heaven.

                                   ——"Away!"
Shouted the new born god; "Follow, and pay
Our piety to Neptunus supreme!"—
Then Scylla, blushing sweetly from her dream,
810 They led on first, bent to her meek surprise,
Through portal columns of a giant size,
Into the vaulted, boundless emerald.
Joyous all follow'd, as the leader call'd,
Down marble steps; pouring as easily
815 As hour-glass sand,—and fast, as you might see
Swallows obeying the south summer's call,
Or swans upon a gentle waterfall.

    Thus went that beautiful multitude, nor far,
Ere from among some rocks of glittering spar,
820 Just within ken, they saw descending thick

Another multitude. Whereat more quick
Moved either host. On a wide sand they met,
And of those numbers every eye was wet;
For each their old love found. A murmuring rose,
825   Like what was never heard in all the throes
Of wind and waters: 'tis past human wit
To tell; 'tis dizziness to think of it.

This mighty consummation made, the host
Mov'd on for many a league; and gain'd, and lost
830   Huge sea-marks; vanward swelling in array,
And from the rear diminishing away,—
Till a faint dawn surpris'd them. Glaucus cried,
"Behold! behold, the palace of his pride!
God Neptune's palaces!" With noise increas'd,
835   They shoulder'd on towards that brightening east.
At every onward step proud domes arose
In prospect,—diamond gleams, and golden glows
Of amber 'gainst their faces levelling.
Joyous, and many as the leaves in spring,
840   Still onward; still the splendour gradual swell'd.
Rich opal domes were seen, on high upheld
By jasper pillars, letting through their shafts
A blush of coral. Copious wonder-draughts
Each gazer drank; and deeper drank more near:
845   For what poor mortals fragment up, as mere
As marble was there lavish, to the vast
Of one fair palace, that far far surpass'd,
Even for common bulk, those olden three,
Memphis, and Babylon, and Nineveh.

850   As large, as bright, as colour'd as the bow
Of Iris, when unfading it doth shew
Beyond a silvery shower, was the arch
Through which this Paphian army took its march,
Into the outer courts of Neptune's state:
855   Whence could be seen, direct, a golden gate,
To which the leaders sped; but not half raught
Ere it burst open swift as fairy thought,
And made those dazzled thousands veil their eyes
Like callow eagles at the first sunrise.
860   Soon with an eagle nativeness their gaze
Ripe from hue-golden swoons took all the blaze,

And then, behold! large Neptune on his throne
Of emerald deep: yet not exalt alone;
At his right hand stood winged Love, and on
865   His left sat smiling Beauty's paragon.

Far as the mariner on highest mast
Can see all round upon the calmed vast,
So wide was Neptune's hall: and as the blue
Doth vault the waters, so the waters drew
870   Their doming curtains, high, magnificent,
Aw'd from the throne aloof;—and when storm-rent
Disclos'd the thunder-gloomings in Jove's air;
But sooth'd as now, flash'd sudden everywhere,
Noiseless, sub-marine cloudlets, glittering
875   Death to a human eye: for there did spring
From natural west, and east, and south, and north,
A light as of four sunsets, blazing forth
A gold-green zenith 'bove the Sea-God's head.
Of lucid depth the floor, and far outspread
880   As breezeless lake, on which the slim canoe
Of feather'd Indian darts about, as through
The delicatest air: air verily,
But for the portraiture of clouds and sky:
This palace floor breath-air,—but for the amaze
885   Of deep-seen wonders motionless,—and blaze
Of the dome pomp, reflected in extremes,
Globing a golden sphere.

They stood in dreams
Till Triton blew his horn. The palace rang;
The Nereids danc'd; the Syrens faintly sang;
890   And the great Sea-King bow'd his dripping head.
Then Love took wing, and from his pinions shed
On all the multitude a nectarous dew.
The ooze-born Goddess beckoned and drew
Fair Scylla and her guides to conference;
895   And when they reach'd the throned eminence
She kist the sea-nymph's cheek,—who sat her down
A toying with the doves. Then,—"Mighty crown
And sceptre of this kingdom!" Venus said,
"Thy vows were on a time to Nais paid:
900   Behold!"—Two copious tear-drops instant fell
From the God's large eyes; he smil'd delectable,

And over Glaucus held his blessing hands.—
"Endymion! Ah! still wandering in the bands
Of love? Now this is cruel. Since the hour
905   I met thee in earth's bosom, all my power
Have I put forth to serve thee. What, not yet
Escap'd from dull mortality's harsh net?
A little patience, youth! 'twill not be long,
Or I am skilless quite: an idle tongue,
910   A humid eye, and steps luxurious,
Where these are new and strange, are ominous.
Aye, I have seen these signs in one of heaven,
When others were all blind; and were I given
To utter secrets, haply I might say
915   Some pleasant words:—but Love will have his day.
So wait awhile expectant. Pr'ythee soon,
Even in the passing of thine honey-moon,
Visit my Cytherea: thou wilt find
Cupid well-natured, my Adonis kind;
920   And pray persuade with thee—Ah, I have done,
All blisses be upon thee, my sweet son!"—
Thus the fair goddess: while Endymion
Knelt to receive those accents halcyon.

      Meantime a glorious revelry began
925   Before the Water-Monarch. Nectar ran
In courteous fountains to all cups outreach'd;
And plunder'd vines, teeming exhaustless, pleach'd
New growth about each shell and pendent lyre;
The which, in disentangling for their fire,
930   Pull'd down fresh foliage and coverture
For dainty toying. Cupid, empire-sure,
Flutter'd and laugh'd, and oft-times through the throng
Made a delighted way. Then dance, and song,
And garlanding grew wild; and pleasure reign'd.
935   In harmless tendril they each other chain'd,
And strove who should be smother'd deepest in
Fresh crush of leaves.

            O 'tis a very sin
For one so weak to venture his poor verse
In such a place as this. O do not curse,
940   High Muses! let him hurry to the ending.

All suddenly were silent. A soft blending
Of dulcet instruments came charmingly;
And then a hymn.

"King of the stormy sea!
Brother of Jove, and co-inheritor
945   Of elements! Eternally before
Thee the waves awful bow. Fast, stubborn rock,
At thy fear'd trident shrinking, doth unlock
Its deep foundations, hissing into foam.
All mountain-rivers lost in the wide home
950   Of thy capacious bosom ever flow.
Thou frownest, and old Eolus thy foe
Skulks to his cavern, 'mid the gruff complaint
Of all his rebel tempests. Dark clouds faint
When, from thy diadem, a silver gleam
955   Slants over blue dominion. Thy bright team
Gulphs in the morning light, and scuds along
To bring thee nearer to that golden song
Apollo singeth, while his chariot
Waits at the doors of heaven. Thou art not
960   For scenes like this: an empire stern hast thou;
And it hath furrow'd that large front: yet now,
As newly come of heaven, dost thou sit
To blend and interknit
Subdued majesty with this glad time.
965   O shell-borne King sublime!
We lay our hearts before thee evermore—
We sing, and we adore!

"Breathe softly, flutes;
Be tender of your strings, ye soothing lutes;
970   Nor be the trumpet heard! O vain, O vain;
Not flowers budding in an April rain,
Nor breath of sleeping dove, nor river's flow,—
No, nor the Eolian twang of Love's own bow,
Can mingle music fit for the soft ear
975   Of goddess Cytherea!
Yet deign, white Queen of Beauty, thy fair eyes
On our souls' sacrifice.

"Bright-winged Child!
Who has another care when thou hast smil'd?

980 Unfortunates on earth, we see at last
All death-shadows, and glooms that overcast
Our spirits, fann'd away by thy light pinions.
O sweetest essence! sweetest of all minions!
God of warm pulses, and dishevell'd hair,
985 And panting bosoms bare!
Dear unseen light in darkness! eclipser
Of light in light! delicious poisoner!
Thy venom'd goblet will we quaff until
We fill—we fill!
And by thy Mother's lips——"

990   Was heard no more
For clamour, when the golden palace door
Opened again, and from without, in shone
A new magnificence. On oozy throne
Smooth-moving came Oceanus the old,
995 To take a latest glimpse at his sheep-fold,   ·
Before he went into his quiet cave
To muse for ever—Then a lucid wave,
Scoop'd from its trembling sisters of mid-sea,
Afloat, and pillowing up the majesty
1000 Of Doris, and the Egean seer, her spouse—
Next, on a dolphin, clad in laurel boughs,
Theban Amphion leaning on his lute:
His fingers went across it—All were mute
To gaze on Amphitrite, queen of pearls,
And Thetis pearly too.—

1005   The palace whirls
Around giddy Endymion; seeing he
Was there far strayed from mortality.
He could not bear it—shut his eyes in vain;
Imagination gave a dizzier pain.
1010 "O I shall die! sweet Venus, be my stay!
Where is my lovely mistress? Well-away!
I die—I hear her voice—I feel my wing—"
At Neptune's feet he sank. A sudden ring
Of Nereids were about him, in kind strife
1015 To usher back his spirit into life:
But still he slept. At last they interwove
Their cradling arms, and purpos'd to convey
Towards a crystal bower far away.

Lo! while slow carried through the pitying crowd,
1020 To his inward senses these words spake aloud;
Written in star-light on the dark above:
Dearest Endymion! my entire love!
How have I dwelt in fear of fate: 'tis done—
Immortal bliss for me too hast thou won.
1025 *Arise then! for the hen-dove shall not hatch*
Her ready eggs, before I'll kissing snatch
Thee into endless heaven. Awake! awake!

The youth at once arose: a placid lake
Came quiet to his eyes; and forest green,
1030 Cooler than all the wonders he had seen,
Lull'd with its simple song his fluttering breast.
How happy once again in grassy nest!

BOOK IV

Muse of my native land! loftiest Muse!
O first-born on the mountains! by the hues
Of heaven on the spiritual air begot:
Long didst thou sit alone in northern grot,
5 While yet our England was a wolfish den;
Before our forests heard the talk of men;
Before the first of Druids was a child;—
Long didst thou sit amid our regions wild
Rapt in a deep prophetic solitude.
10 There came an eastern voice of solemn mood:—
Yet wast thou patient. Then sang forth the Nine,
Apollo's garland:—yet didst thou divine
Such home-bred glory, that they cry'd in vain,
"Come hither, Sister of the Island!" Plain
15 Spake fair Ausonia; and once more she spake
A higher summons:—still didst thou betake
Thee to thy native hopes. O thou hast won
A full accomplishment! The thing is done,
Which undone, these our latter days had risen
20 On barren souls. Great Muse, thou know'st what prison,
Of flesh and bone, curbs, and confines, and frets
Our spirit's wings: despondency besets
Our pillows; and the fresh to-morrow morn
Seems to give forth its light in very scorn

25   Of our dull, uninspired, snail-paced lives.
      Long have I said, how happy he who shrives
      To thee! But then I thought on poets gone,
      And could not pray:—nor can I now—so on
      I move to the end in lowliness of heart.——

30   "Ah, woe is me! that I should fondly part
      From my dear native land! Ah, foolish maid!
      Glad was the hour, when, with thee, myriads bade
      Adieu to Ganges and their pleasant fields!
      To one so friendless the clear freshet yields
35   A bitter coolness; the ripe grape is sour:
      Yet I would have, great gods! but one short hour
      Of native air—let me but die at home."

        Endymion to heaven's airy dome
      Was offering up a hecatomb of vows,
40   When these words reach'd him. Whereupon he bows
      His head through thorny-green entanglement
      Of underwood, and to the sound is bent,
      Anxious as hind towards her hidden fawn.

        "Is no one near to help me? No fair dawn
45   Of life from charitable voice? No sweet saying
      To set my dull and sadden'd spirit playing?
      No hand to toy with mine? No lips so sweet
      That I may worship them? No eyelids meet
      To twinkle on my bosom? No one dies
50   Before me, till from these enslaving eyes
      Redemption sparkles!—I am sad and lost."

        Thou, Carian lord, hadst better have been tost
      Into a whirlpool. Vanish into air,
      Warm mountaineer! for canst thou only bear
55   A woman's sigh alone and in distress?
      See not her charms! Is Phœbe passionless?
      Phœbe is fairer far—O gaze no more:—
      Yet if thou wilt behold all beauty's store,
      Behold her panting in the forest grass!
60   Do not those curls of glossy jet surpass
      For tenderness the arms so idly lain
      Amongst them? Feelest not a kindred pain,
      To see such lovely eyes in swimming search

After some warm delight, that seems to perch
65   Dovelike in the dim cell lying beyond
Their upper lids?—Hist!

                              "O for Hermes' wand,
To touch this flower into human shape!
That woodland Hyacinthus could escape
From his green prison, and here kneeling down
70   Call me his queen, his second life's fair crown!
Ah me, how I could love!—My soul doth melt
For the unhappy youth—Love! I have felt
So faint a kindness, such a meek surrender
To what my own full thoughts had made too tender,
75   That but for tears my life had fled away!—
Ye deaf and senseless minutes of the day,
And thou, old forest, hold ye this for true,
There is no lightning, no authentic dew
But in the eye of love: there's not a sound,
80   Melodious howsoever, can confound
The heavens and earth in one to such a death
As doth the voice of love: there's not a breath
Will mingle kindly with the meadow air,
Till it has panted round, and stolen a share
Of passion from the heart!"—

85   Upon a bough
He leant, wretched. He surely cannot now
Thirst for another love: O impious,
That he can even dream upon it thus!—
Thought he, "Why am I not as are the dead,
90   Since to a woe like this I have been led
Through the dark earth, and through the wondrous sea?
Goddess! I love thee not the less: from thee
By Juno's smile I turn not—no, no, no—
While the great waters are at ebb and flow.—
95   I have a triple soul! O fond pretence—
For both, for both my love is so immense,
I feel my heart is cut for them in twain."

And so he groan'd, as one by beauty slain.
The lady's heart beat quick, and he could see
100   Her gentle bosom heave tumultuously.

He sprang from his green covert: there she lay,
Sweet as a muskrose upon new-made hay;
With all her limbs on tremble, and her eyes
Shut softly up alive. To speak he tries.
105 "Fair damsel, pity me! forgive that I
Thus violate thy bower's sanctity!
O pardon me, for I am full of grief—
Grief born of thee, young angel! fairest thief!
Who stolen hast away the wings wherewith
110 I was to top the heavens. Dear maid, sith
Thou art my executioner, and I feel
Loving and hatred, misery and weal,
Will in a few short hours be nothing to me,
And all my story that much passion slew me;
115 Do smile upon the evening of my days:
And, for my tortur'd brain begins to craze,
Be thou my nurse; and let me understand
How dying I shall kiss that lily hand.—
Dost weep for me? Then should I be content.
120 Scowl on, ye fates! until the firmament
Outblackens Erebus, and the full-cavern'd earth
Crumbles into itself. By the cloud girth
Of Jove, those tears have given me a thirst
To meet oblivion."—As her heart would burst
125 The maiden sobb'd awhile, and then replied:
"Why must such desolation betide
As that thou speakest of? Are not these green nooks
Empty of all misfortune? Do the brooks
Utter a gorgon voice? Does yonder thrush,
130 Schooling its half-fledg'd little ones to brush
About the dewy forest, whisper tales?—
Speak not of grief, young stranger, or cold snails
Will slime the rose to night. Though if thou wilt,
Methinks 'twould be a guilt—a very guilt—
135 Not to companion thee, and sigh away
The light—the dusk—the dark—till break of day!"
"Dear lady," said Endymion, "'tis past:
I love thee! and my days can never last.
That I may pass in patience still speak:
140 Let me have music dying, and I seek
No more delight—I bid adieu to all.
Didst thou not after other climates call,

And murmur about Indian streams?"—Then she,
Sitting beneath the midmost forest tree,
145   For pity sang this roundelay——

        "O Sorrow,
          Why dost borrow
    The natural hue of health, from vermeil lips?—
          To give maiden blushes
150   To the white rose bushes?
    Or is't thy dewy hand the daisy tips?

        "O Sorrow,
          Why dost borrow
    The lustrous passion from a falcon-eye?—
155   To give the glow-worm light?
          Or, on a moonless night,
    To tinge, on syren shores, the salt sea-spry?

        "O Sorrow,
          Why dost borrow
160   The mellow ditties from a mourning tongue?—
          To give at evening pale
          Unto the nightingale,
    That thou mayst listen the cold dews among?

        "O Sorrow,
165   Why dost borrow
    Heart's lightness from the merriment of May?—
          A lover would not tread
          A cowslip on the head,
    Though he should dance from eve till peep of day—
170   Nor any drooping flower
          Held sacred for thy bower,
    Wherever he may sport himself and play.

        "To Sorrow,
          I bade good-morrow,
175   And thought to leave her far away behind;
          But cheerly, cheerly,
          She loves me dearly;
    She is so constant to me, and so kind:
          I would deceive her

180   And so leave her,
   But ah! she is so constant and so kind.

   "Beneath my palm trees, by the river side,
   I sat a weeping: in the whole world wide
   There was no one to ask me why I wept,—
185   And so I kept
   Brimming the water-lily cups with tears
      Cold as my fears.

   "Beneath my palm trees, by the river side,
   I sat a weeping: what enamour'd bride,
190   Cheated by shadowy wooer from the clouds,
      But hides and shrouds
   Beneath dark palm trees by a river side?

   "And as I sat, over the light blue hills
   There came a noise of revellers: the rills
195   Into the wide stream came of purple hue—
      'Twas Bacchus and his crew!
   The earnest trumpet spake, and silver thrills
   From kissing cymbals made a merry din—
      'Twas Bacchus and his kin!
200   Like to a moving vintage down they came,
   Crown'd with green leaves, and faces all on flame;
   All madly dancing through the pleasant valley,
      To scare thee, Melancholy!
   O then, O then, thou wast a simple name!
205   And I forgot thee, as the berried holly
   By shepherds is forgotten, when, in June,
   Tall chesnuts keep away the sun and moon:—
      I rush'd into the folly!

   "Within his car, aloft, young Bacchus stood,
210   Trifling his ivy-dart, in dancing mood,
      With sidelong laughing;
   And little rills of crimson wine imbrued
   His plump white arms, and shoulders, enough white
      For Venus' pearly bite:
215   And near him rode Silenus on his ass,
   Pelted with flowers as he on did pass
      Tipsily quaffing.

"Whence came ye, merry Damsels! whence came ye!
So many, and so many, and such glee?
220   Why have ye left your bowers desolate,
        Your lutes, and gentler fate?—
'We follow Bacchus! Bacchus on the wing,
        A conquering!
Bacchus, young Bacchus! good or ill betide,
225   We dance before him thorough kingdoms wide:—
Come hither, lady fair, and joined be
        To our wild minstrelsy!'

"Whence came ye, jolly Satyrs! whence came ye!
So many, and so many, and such glee?
230   Why have ye left your forest haunts, why left
        Your nuts in oak-tree cleft?—
'For wine, for wine we left our kernel tree;
For wine we left our heath, and yellow brooms,
        And cold mushrooms;
235   For wine we follow Bacchus through the earth;
Great God of breathless cups and chirping mirth!—
Come hither, lady fair, and joined be
        To our mad minstrelsy!'

"Over wide streams and mountains great we went,
240   And, save when Bacchus kept his ivy tent,
Onward the tiger and the leopard pants,
        With Asian elephants:
Onward these myriads—with song and dance,
With zebras striped, and sleek Arabians' prance,
245   Web-footed alligators, crocodiles,
Bearing upon their scaly backs, in files,
Plump infant laughers mimicking the coil
Of seamen, and stout galley-rowers' toil:
With toying oars and silken sails they glide,
250   Nor care for wind and tide.

"Mounted on panthers' furs and lions' manes,
From rear to van they scour about the plains;
A three days' journey in a moment done:
And always, at the rising of the sun,
255   About the wilds they hunt with spear and horn,
        On spleenful unicorn.

        "I saw Osirian Egypt kneel adown
              Before the vine-wreath crown!
        I saw parch'd Abyssinia rouse and sing
260   To the silver cymbals' ring!
        I saw the whelming vintage hotly pierce
              Old Tartary the fierce!
        The kings of Inde their jewel-sceptres vail,
        And from their treasures scatter pearled hail;
265   Great Brahma from his mystic heaven groans,
              And all his priesthood moans;
        Before young Bacchus' eye-wink turning pale.—
        Into these regions came I following him,
        Sick hearted, weary—so I took a whim
270   To stray away into these forests drear
              Alone, without a peer:
        And I have told thee all thou mayest hear.

              "Young stranger!
              I've been a ranger
275   In search of pleasure throughout every clime:
              Alas, 'tis not for me!
              Bewitch'd I sure must be,
        To lose in grieving all my maiden prime.

              "Come then, Sorrow!
280   Sweetest Sorrow!
        Like an own babe I nurse thee on my breast:
              I thought to leave thee
              And deceive thee,
        But now of all the world I love thee best.

285   "There is not one,
              No, no, not one
        But thee to comfort a poor lonely maid;
              Thou art her mother,
              And her brother,
290   Her playmate, and her wooer in the shade."

       O what a sigh she gave in finishing,
        And look, quite dead to every worldly thing!
        Endymion could not speak, but gazed on her;
        And listened to the wind that now did stir

295   About the crisped oaks full drearily,
       Yet with as sweet a softness as might be
       Remember'd from its velvet summer song.
       At last he said: "Poor lady, how thus long
       Have I been able to endure that voice?
300   Fair Melody! kind Syren! I've no choice;
       I must be thy sad servant evermore:
       I cannot choose but kneel here and adore.
       Alas, I must not think—by Phœbe, no!
       Let me not think, soft Angel! shall it be so?
305   Say, beautifullest, shall I never think?
       O thou could'st foster me beyond the brink
       Of recollection! make my watchful care
       Close up its bloodshot eyes, nor see despair!
       Do gently murder half my soul, and I
310   Shall feel the other half so utterly!—
       I'm giddy at that cheek so fair and smooth;
       O let it blush so ever! let it soothe
       My madness! let it mantle rosy-warm
       With the tinge of love, panting in safe alarm.—
315   This cannot be thy hand, and yet it is;
       And this is sure thine other softling—this
       Thine own fair bosom, and I am so near!
       Wilt fall asleep? O let me sip that tear!
       And whisper one sweet word that I may know
320   This is this world—sweet dewy blossom!"—*Woe!*
       Woe! Woe to that Endymion! Where is he?—
       Even these words went echoing dismally
       Through the wide forest—a most fearful tone,
       Like one repenting in his latest moan;
325   And while it died away a shade pass'd by,
       As of a thunder cloud. When arrows fly
       Through the thick branches, poor ring-doves sleek forth
       Their timid necks and tremble; so these both
       Leant to each other trembling, and sat so
330   Waiting for some destruction—when lo,
       Foot-feather'd Mercury appear'd sublime
       Beyond the tall tree tops; and in less time
       Than shoots the slanted hail-storm, down he dropt
       Towards the ground; but rested not, nor stopt
335   One moment from his home: only the sward
       He with his wand light touch'd, and heavenward
       Swifter than sight was gone—even before

The teeming earth a sudden witness bore
Of his swift magic. Diving swans appear
340   Above the crystal circlings white and clear;
And catch the cheated eye in wide surprise,
How they can dive in sight and unseen rise—
So from the turf outsprang two steeds jet-black,
Each with large dark blue wings upon his back.
345   The youth of Caria plac'd the lovely dame
On one, and felt himself in spleen to tame
The other's fierceness. Through the air they flew,
High as the eagles. Like two drops of dew
Exhal'd to Phœbus' lips, away they are gone,
350   Far from the earth away—unseen, alone,
Among cool clouds and winds, but that the free,
The buoyant life of song can floating be
Above their heads, and follow them untir'd.—
Muse of my native land, am I inspir'd?
355   This is the giddy air, and I must spread
Wide pinions to keep here; nor do I dread
Or height, or depth, or width, or any chance
Precipitous: I have beneath my glance
Those towering horses and their mournful freight.
360   Could I thus sail, and see, and thus await
Fearless for power of thought, without thine aid?—

      There is a sleepy dusk, an odorous shade
From some approaching wonder, and behold
Those winged steeds, with snorting nostrils bold
365   Snuff at its faint extreme, and seem to tire,
Dying to embers from their native fire!

      There curl'd a purple mist around them; soon,
It seem'd as when around the pale new moon
Sad Zephyr droops the clouds like weeping willow:
370   'Twas Sleep slow journeying with head on pillow.
For the first time, since he came nigh dead born
From the old womb of night, his cave forlorn
Had he left more forlorn; for the first time,
He felt aloof the day and morning's prime—
375   Because into his depth Cimmerian
There came a dream, shewing how a young man,
Ere a lean bat could plump its wintery skin,
Would at high Jove's empyreal footstool win

An immortality, and how espouse
380 Jove's daughter, and be reckon'd of his house.
     Now was he slumbering towards heaven's gate,
     That he might at the threshold one hour wait
     To hear the marriage melodies, and then
     Sink downward to his dusky cave again.
385 His litter of smooth semilucent mist,
     Diversely ting'd with rose and amethyst,
     Puzzled those eyes that for the centre sought;
     And scarcely for one moment could be caught
     His sluggish form reposing motionless.
390 Those two on winged steeds, with all the stress
     Of vision search'd for him, as one would look
     Athwart the sallows of a river nook
     To catch a glance at silver throated eels,—
     Or from old Skiddaw's top, when fog conceals
395 His rugged forehead in a mantle pale,
     With an eye-guess towards some pleasant vale
     Descry a favourite hamlet faint and far.

         These raven horses, though they foster'd are
     Of earth's splenetic fire, dully drop
400 Their full-veined ears, nostrils blood wide, and stop;
     Upon the spiritless mist have they outspread
     Their ample feathers, are in slumber dead,—
     And on those pinions, level in mid air,
     Endymion sleepeth and the lady fair.
405 Slowly they sail, slowly as icy isle
     Upon a calm sea drifting: and meanwhile
     The mournful wanderer dreams. Behold! he walks
     On heaven's pavement; brotherly he talks
     To divine powers: from his hand full fain
410 Juno's proud birds are pecking pearly grain:
     He tries the nerve of Phœbus' golden bow,
     And asketh where the golden apples grow:
     Upon his arm he braces Pallas' shield,
     And strives in vain to unsettle and wield
415 A Jovian thunderbolt: arch Hebe brings
     A full-brimm'd goblet, dances lightly, sings
     And tantalizes long; at last he drinks,
     And lost in pleasure at her feet he sinks,
     Touching with dazzled lips her starlight hand.
420 He blows a bugle,—an ethereal band
     Are visible above: the Seasons four,—

Green-kyrtled Spring, flush Summer, golden store
In Autumn's sickle, Winter frosty hoar,
Join dance with shadowy Hours; while still the blast,
425   In swells unmitigated, still doth last
To sway their floating morris. "Whose is this?
Whose bugle?" he inquires: they smile—"O Dis!
Why is this mortal here? Dost thou not know
Its mistress' lips? Not thou?—'Tis Dian's: lo!
430   She rises crescented!" He looks, 'tis she,
His very goddess: good-bye earth, and sea,
And air, and pains, and care, and suffering;
Good-bye to all but love! Then doth he spring
Towards her, and awakes—and, strange, o'erhead,
435   Of those same fragrant exhalations bred,
Beheld awake his very dream: the gods
Stood smiling; merry Hebe laughs and nods;
And Phœbe bends towards him crescented.
O state perplexing! On the pinion bed,
440   Too well awake, he feels the panting side
Of his delicious lady. He who died
For soaring too audacious in the sun,
When that same treacherous wax began to run,
Felt not more tongue-tied than Endymion.
445   His heart leapt up as to its rightful throne,
To that fair shadow'd passion puls'd its way—
Ah, what perplexity! Ah, well a day!
So fond, so beauteous was his bed-fellow,
He could not help but kiss her: then he grew
450   Awhile forgetful of all beauty save
Young Phœbe's, golden hair'd; and so 'gan crave
Forgiveness: yet he turn'd once more to look
At the sweet sleeper,—all his soul was shook,—
She press'd his hand in slumber; so once more
455   He could not help but kiss her and adore.
At this the shadow wept, melting away.
The Latmian started up: "Bright goddess, stay!
Search my most hidden breast! By truth's own tongue,
I have no dædale heart: why is it wrung
460   To desperation? Is there nought for me,
Upon the bourne of bliss, but misery?"

These words awoke the stranger of dark tresses:
Her dawning love-look rapt Endymion blesses
With 'haviour soft. Sleep yawned from underneath.

465 "Thou swan of Ganges, let us no more breathe
    This murky phantasm! thou contented seem'st
    Pillow'd in lovely idleness, nor dream'st
    What horrors may discomfort thee and me.
    Ah, shouldst thou die from my heart-treachery!—
470 Yet did she merely weep—her gentle soul
    Hath no revenge in it: as it is whole
    In tenderness, would I were whole in love!
    Can I prize thee, fair maid, all price above,
    Even when I feel as true as innocence?
475 I do, I do.—What is this soul then? Whence
    Came it? It does not seem my own, and I
    Have no self-passion or identity.
    Some fearful end must be: where, where is it?
    By Nemesis, I see my spirit flit
480 Alone about the dark—Forgive me, sweet:
    Shall we away?" He rous'd the steeds: they beat
    Their wings chivalrous into the clear air,
    Leaving old Sleep within his vapoury lair.

        The good-night blush of eve was waning slow,
485 And Vesper, risen star, began to throe
    In the dusk heavens silverly, when they
    Thus sprang direct towards the Galaxy.
    Nor did speed hinder converse soft and strange—
    Eternal oaths and vows they interchange,
490 In such wise, in such temper, so aloof
    Up in the winds, beneath a starry roof,
    So witless of their doom, that verily
    'Tis well nigh past man's search their hearts to see;
    Whether they wept, or laugh'd, or griev'd, or toy'd—
495 Most like with joy gone mad, with sorrow cloy'd.

        Full facing their swift flight, from ebon streak,
    The moon put forth a little diamond peak,
    No bigger than an unobserved star,
    Or tiny point of fairy scymetar;
500 Bright signal that she only stoop'd to tie
    Her silver sandals, ere deliciously
    She bow'd into the heavens her timid head.
    Slowly she rose, as though she would have fled,
    While to his lady meek the Carian turn'd,
505 To mark if her dark eyes had yet discern'd

This beauty in its birth—Despair! despair!
He saw her body fading gaunt and spare
In the cold moonshine. Straight he seiz'd her wrist;
It melted from his grasp: her hand he kiss'd,
510   And, horror! kiss'd his own—he was alone.
Her steed a little higher soar'd, and then
Dropt hawkwise to the earth.

               There lies a den,
Beyond the seeming confines of the space
Made for the soul to wander in and trace
515   Its own existence, of remotest glooms.
Dark regions are around it, where the tombs
Of buried griefs the spirit sees, but scarce
One hour doth linger weeping, for the pierce
Of new-born woe it feels more inly smart:
520   And in these regions many a venom'd dart
At random flies; they are the proper home
Of every ill: the man is yet to come
Who hath not journeyed in this native hell.
But few have ever felt how calm and well
525   Sleep may be had in that deep den of all.
There anguish does not sting; nor pleasure pall:
Woe-hurricanes beat ever at the gate,
Yet all is still within and desolate.
Beset with plainful gusts, within ye hear
530   No sound so loud as when on curtain'd bier
The death-watch tick is stifled. Enter none
Who strive therefore: on the sudden it is won.
Just when the sufferer begins to burn,
Then it is free to him; and from an urn,
535   Still fed by melting ice, he takes a draught—
Young Semele such richness never quaft
In her maternal longing! Happy gloom!
Dark paradise! where pale becomes the bloom
Of health by due; where silence dreariest
540   Is most articulate; where hopes infest;
Where those eyes are the brightest far that keep
Their lids shut longest in a dreamless sleep.
O happy spirit-home! O wondrous soul!
Pregnant with such a den to save the whole
545   In thine own depth. Hail, gentle Carian!
For, never since thy griefs and woes began,

Hast thou felt so content: a grievous feud
Hath led thee to this Cave of Quietude.
Aye, his lull'd soul was there, although upborne
550 With dangerous speed: and so he did not mourn
Because he knew not whither he was going.
So happy was he, not the aerial blowing
Of trumpets at clear parley from the east
Could rouse from that fine relish, that high feast.
555 They stung the feather'd horse: with fierce alarm
He flapp'd towards the sound. Alas, no charm
Could lift Endymion's head, or he had view'd
A skyey masque, a pinion'd multitude,—
And silvery was its passing: voices sweet
560 Warbling the while as if to lull and greet
The wanderer in his path. Thus warbled they,
While past the vision went in bright array.

"Who, who from Dian's feast would be away?
For all the golden bowers of the day
565 Are empty left? Who, who away would be
From Cynthia's wedding and festivity?
Not Hesperus: lo! upon his silver wings
He leans away for highest heaven and sings,
Snapping his lucid fingers merrily!—
570 Ah, Zephyrus! art here, and Flora too!
Ye tender bibbers of the rain and dew,
Young playmates of the rose and daffodil,
Be careful, ere ye enter in, to fill
   Your baskets high
575 With fennel green, and balm, and golden pines,
Savory, latter-mint, and columbines,
Cool parsley, basil sweet, and sunny thyme;
Yea, every flower and leaf of every clime,
All gather'd in the dewy morning: hie
580   Away! fly, fly!—
Crystalline brother of the belt of heaven,
Aquarius! to whom king Jove has given
Two liquid pulse streams 'stead of feather'd wings,
Two fan-like fountains,—thine illuminings
585   For Dian play:
Dissolve the frozen purity of air;
Let thy white shoulders silvery and bare
Shew cold through watery pinions; make more bright

The Star-Queen's crescent on her marriage night:
590   Haste, haste away!—
Castor has tamed the planet Lion, see!
And of the Bear has Pollux mastery:
A third is in the race! who is the third,
Speeding away swift as the eagle bird?
595   The ramping Centaur!
The Lion's mane's on end: the Bear how fierce!
The Centaur's arrow ready seems to pierce
Some enemy: far forth his bow is bent
Into the blue of heaven. He'll be shent,
600   Pale unrelentor,
When he shall hear the wedding lutes a playing.—
Andromeda! sweet woman! why delaying
So timidly among the stars: come hither!
Join this bright throng, and nimbly follow whither
605   They all are going.
Danae's Son, before Jove newly bow'd,
Has wept for thee, calling to Jove aloud.
Thee, gentle lady, did he disenthral:
Ye shall for ever live and love, for all
610   Thy tears are flowing.—
By Daphne's fright, behold Apollo!—"

                      More
Endymion heard not: down his steed him bore,
Prone to the green head of a misty hill.

    His first touch of the earth went nigh to kill.
615 "Alas!" said he, "were I but always borne
Through dangerous winds, had but my footsteps worn
A path in hell, for ever would I bless
Horrors which nourish an uneasiness
For my own sullen conquering: to him
620 Who lives beyond earth's boundary, grief is dim,
Sorrow is but a shadow: now I see
The grass; I feel the solid ground—Ah, me!
It is thy voice—divinest! Where?—who? who
Left thee so quiet on this bed of dew?
625 Behold upon this happy earth we are;
Let us ay love each other; let us fare
On forest-fruits, and never, never go
Among the abodes of mortals here below,

Or be by phantoms duped. O destiny!
630   Into a labyrinth now my soul would fly,
But with thy beauty will I deaden it.
Where didst thou melt to? By thee will I sit
For ever: let our fate stop here—a kid
I on this spot will offer: Pan will bid
635   Us live in peace, in love and peace among
His forest wildernesses. I have clung
To nothing, lov'd a nothing, nothing seen
Or felt but a great dream! O I have been
Presumptuous against love, against the sky,
640   Against all elements, against the tie
Of mortals each to each, against the blooms
Of flowers, rush of rivers, and the tombs
Of heroes gone! Against his proper glory
Has my own soul conspired: so my story
645   Will I to children utter, and repent.
There never liv'd a mortal man, who bent
His appetite beyond his natural sphere,
But starv'd and died. My sweetest Indian, here,
Here will I kneel, for thou redeemed hast
650   My life from too thin breathing: gone and past
Are cloudy phantasms. Caverns lone, farewel!
And air of visions, and the monstrous swell
Of visionary seas! No, never more
Shall airy voices cheat me to the shore
655   Of tangled wonder, breathless and aghast.
Adieu, my daintiest Dream! although so vast
My love is still for thee. The hour may come
When we shall meet in pure elysium.
On earth I may not love thee; and therefore
660   Doves will I offer up, and sweetest store
All through the teeming year: so thou wilt shine
On me, and on this damsel fair of mine,
And bless our simple lives. My Indian bliss!
My river-lily bud! one human kiss!
665   One sigh of real breath—one gentle squeeze,
Warm as a dove's nest among summer trees,
And warm with dew at ooze from living blood!
Whither didst melt? Ah, what of that!—all good
We'll talk about—no more of dreaming.—Now,
670   Where shall our dwelling be? Under the brow
Of some steep mossy hill, where ivy dun

Would hide us up, although spring leaves were none;
And where dark yew trees, as we rustle through,
Will drop their scarlet berry cups of dew?
675   O thou wouldst joy to live in such a place;
Dusk for our loves, yet light enough to grace
Those gentle limbs on mossy bed reclin'd:
For by one step the blue sky shouldst thou find,
And by another, in deep dell below,
680   See, through the trees, a little river go
All in its mid-day gold and glimmering.
Honey from out the gnarled hive I'll bring,
And apples, wan with sweetness, gather thee,—
Cresses that grow where no man may them see,
685   And sorrel untorn by the dew-claw'd stag:
Pipes will I fashion of the syrinx flag,
That thou mayst always know whither I roam,
When it shall please thee in our quiet home
To listen and think of love. Still let me speak;
690   Still let me dive into the joy I seek,—
For yet the past doth prison me. The rill,
Thou haply mayst delight in, will I fill
With fairy fishes from the mountain tarn,
And thou shalt feed them from the squirrel's barn.
695   Its bottom will I strew with amber shells,
And pebbles blue from deep enchanted wells.
Its sides I'll plant with dew-sweet eglantine,
And honeysuckles full of clear bee-wine.
I will entice this crystal rill to trace
700   Love's silver name upon the meadow's face.
I'll kneel to Vesta, for a flame of fire;
And to god Phœbus, for a golden lyre;
To Empress Dian, for a hunting spear;
To Vesper, for a taper silver-clear,
705   That I may see thy beauty through the night;
To Flora, and a nightingale shall light
Tame on thy finger; to the River-gods,
And they shall bring thee taper fishing-rods
Of gold, and lines of Naiads' long bright tress.
710   Heaven shield thee for thine utter loveliness!
Thy mossy footstool shall the altar be
'Fore which I'll bend, bending, dear love, to thee:
Those lips shall be my Delphos, and shall speak
Laws to my footsteps, colour to my cheek,

715   Trembling or stedfastness to this same voice,
       And of three sweetest pleasurings the choice:
       And that affectionate light, those diamond things,
       Those eyes, those passions, those supreme pearl springs,
       Shall be my grief, or twinkle me to pleasure.
720   Say, is not bliss within our perfect seisure?
       O that I could not doubt!"

                            The mountaineer
       Thus strove by fancies vain and crude to clear
       His briar'd path to some tranquillity.
       It gave bright gladness to his lady's eye,
725   And yet the tears she wept were tears of sorrow;
       Answering thus, just as the golden morrow
       Beam'd upward from the vallies of the east:
       "O that the flutter of this heart had ceas'd,
       Or the sweet name of love had pass'd away.
730   Young feather'd tyrant! by a swift decay
       Wilt thou devote this body to the earth:
       And I do think that at my very birth
       I lisp'd thy blooming titles inwardly;
       For at the first, first dawn and thought of thee,
735   With uplift hands I blest the stars of heaven.
       Art thou not cruel? Ever have I striven
       To think thee kind, but ah, it will not do!
       When yet a child, I heard that kisses drew
       Favour from thee, and so I kisses gave
740   To the void air, bidding them find out love:
       But when I came to feel how far above
       All fancy, pride, and fickle maidenhood,
       All earthly pleasure, all imagin'd good,
       Was the warm tremble of a devout kiss,—
745   Even then, that moment, at the thought of this,
       Fainting I fell into a bed of flowers,
       And languish'd there three days. Ye milder powers,
       Am I not cruelly wrong'd? Believe, believe
       Me, dear Endymion, were I to weave
750   With my own fancies garlands of sweet life,
       Thou shouldst be one of all. Ah, bitter strife!
       I may not be thy love: I am forbidden—
       Indeed I am—thwarted, affrighted, chidden,
       By things I trembled at, and gorgon wrath.
755   Twice hast thou ask'd whither I went: henceforth

Ask me no more! I may not utter it,
Nor may I be thy love. We might commit
Ourselves at once to vengeance; we might die;
We might embrace and die: voluptuous thought!
760 Enlarge not to my hunger, or I'm caught
In trammels of perverse deliciousness.
No, no, that shall not be: thee will I bless,
And bid a long adieu."

      The Carian
No word return'd: both lovelorn, silent, wan,
765 Into the vallies green together went.
Far wandering, they were perforce content
To sit beneath a fair lone beechen tree;
Nor at each other gaz'd, but heavily
Por'd on its hazle cirque of shedded leaves.

770 Endymion! unhappy! it nigh grieves
Me to behold thee thus in last extreme:
Ensky'd ere this, but truly that I deem
Truth the best music in a first-born song.
Thy lute-voic'd brother will I sing ere long,
775 And thou shalt aid—hast thou not aided me?
Yes, moonlight Emperor! felicity
Has been thy meed for many thousand years;
Yet often have I, on the brink of tears,
Mourn'd as if yet thou wert a forester;—
Forgetting the old tale.

780   He did not stir
His eyes from the dead leaves, or one small pulse
Of joy he might have felt. The spirit culls
Unfaded amaranth, when wild it strays
Through the old garden-ground of boyish days.
785 A little onward ran the very stream
By which he took his first soft poppy dream;
And on the very bark 'gainst which he leant
A crescent he had carv'd, and round it spent
His skill in little stars. The teeming tree
790 Had swollen and green'd the pious charactery,
But not ta'en out. Why, there was not a slope
Up which he had not fear'd the antelope;
And not a tree, beneath whose rooty shade

He had not with his tamed leopards play'd:
795   Nor could an arrow light, or javelin,
Fly in the air where his had never been—
And yet he knew it not.

O treachery!
Why does his lady smile, pleasing her eye
With all his sorrowing? He sees her not.
800   But who so stares on him? His sister sure!
Peona of the woods!—Can she endure—
Impossible—how dearly they embrace!
His lady smiles; delight is in her face;
It is no treachery.

"Dear brother mine!
805   Endymion, weep not so! Why shouldst thou pine
When all great Latmos so exalt will be?
Thank the great gods, and look not bitterly;
And speak not one pale word, and sigh no more.
Sure I will not believe thou hast such store
810   Of grief, to last thee to my kiss again.
Thou surely canst not bear a mind in pain,
Come hand in hand with one so beautiful.
Be happy both of you! for I will pull
The flowers of autumn for your coronals.
815   Pan's holy priest for young Endymion calls;
And when he is restor'd, thou, fairest dame,
Shalt be our queen. Now, is it not a shame
To see ye thus,—not very, very sad?
Perhaps ye are too happy to be glad:
820   O feel as if it were a common day;
Free-voic'd as one who never was away.
No tongue shall ask, whence come ye? but ye shall
Be gods of your own rest imperial.
Not even I, for one whole month, will pry
825   Into the hours that have pass'd us by,
Since in my arbour I did sing to thee.
O Hermes! on this very night will be
A hymning up to Cynthia, queen of light;
For the soothsayers old saw yesternight
830   Good visions in the air,—whence will befal,
As say these sages, health perpetual
To shepherds and their flocks; and furthermore,

In Dian's face they read the gentle lore:
Therefore for her these vesper-carols are.
835 Our friends will all be there from nigh and far.
Many upon thy death have ditties made;
And many, even now, their foreheads shade
With cypress, on a day of sacrifice.
New singing for our maids shalt thou devise,
840 And pluck the sorrow from our huntsmen's brows.
Tell me, my lady-queen, how to espouse
This wayward brother to his rightful joys!
His eyes are on thee bent, as thou didst poise
His fate most goddess-like. Help me, I pray,
845 To lure—Endymion, dear brother, say
What ails thee?" He could bear no more, and so
Bent his soul fiercely like a spiritual bow,
And twang'd it inwardly, and calmly said:
"I would have thee my only friend, sweet maid!
850 My only visitor! not ignorant though,
That those deceptions which for pleasure go
'Mong men, are pleasures real as real may be:
But there are higher ones I may not see,
If impiously an earthly realm I take.
855 Since I saw thee, I have been wide awake
Night after night, and day by day, until
Of the empyrean I have drunk my fill.
Let it content thee, sister, seeing me
More happy than betides mortality.
860 A hermit young, I'll live in mossy cave,
Where thou alone shalt come to me, and lave
Thy spirit in the wonders I shall tell.
Through me the shepherd realm shall prosper well;
For to thy tongue will I all health confide.
865 And, for my sake, let this young maid abide
With thee as a dear sister. Thou alone,
Peona, mayst return to me. I own
This may sound strangely: but when, dearest girl,
Thou seest it for my happiness, no pearl
870 Will trespass down those cheeks. Companion fair!
Wilt be content to dwell with her, to share
This sister's love with me?" Like one resign'd
And bent by circumstance, and thereby blind
In self-commitment, thus that meek unknown:
875 "Aye, but a buzzing by my ears has flown,

Of jubilee to Dian:—truth I heard?
Well then, I see there is no little bird,
Tender soever, but is Jove's own care.
Long have I sought for rest, and, unaware,
880   Behold I find it! so exalted too!
So after my own heart! I knew, I knew
There was a place untenanted in it:
In that same void white Chastity shall sit,
And monitor me nightly to lone slumber.
885   With sanest lips I vow me to the number
Of Dian's sisterhood; and, kind lady,
With thy good help, this very night shall see
My future days to her fane consecrate."

As feels a dreamer what doth most create
890   His own particular fright, so these three felt:
Or like one who, in after ages, knelt
To Lucifer or Baal, when he'd pine
After a little sleep: or when in mine
Far under-ground, a sleeper meets his friends
895   Who know him not. Each diligently bends
Towards common thoughts and things for very fear;
Striving their ghastly malady to cheer,
By thinking it a thing of yes and no,
That housewives talk of. But the spirit-blow
900   Was struck, and all were dreamers. At the last
Endymion said: "Are not our fates all cast?
Why stand we here? Adieu, ye tender pair!
Adieu!" Whereat those maidens, with wild stare,
Walk'd dizzily away. Pained and hot
905   His eyes went after them, until they got
Near to a cypress grove, whose deadly maw,
In one swift moment, would what then he saw
Engulph for ever. "Stay!" he cried, "ah, stay!
Turn, damsels! hist! one word I have to say.
910   Sweet Indian, I would see thee once again.
It is a thing I dote on: so I'd fain,
Peona, ye should hand in hand repair
Into those holy groves, that silent are
Behind great Dian's temple. I'll be yon,
915   At Vesper's earliest twinkle—they are gone—
But once, once, once again—" At this he press'd
His hands against his face, and then did rest

His head upon a mossy hillock green,
And so remain'd as he a corpse had been
920   All the long day; save when he scantly lifted
His eyes abroad, to see how shadows shifted
With the slow move of time,—sluggish and weary
Until the poplar tops, in journey dreary,
Had reach'd the river's brim. Then up he rose,
925   And, slowly as that very river flows,
Walk'd towards the temple grove with this lament:
"Why such a golden eve? The breeze is sent
Careful and soft, that not a leaf may fall
Before the serene father of them all
930   Bows down his summer head below the west.
Now am I of breath, speech, and speed possest,
But at the setting I must bid adieu
To her for the last time. Night will strew
On the damp grass myriads of lingering leaves,
935   And with them shall I die; nor much it grieves
To die, when summer dies on the cold sward.
Why, I have been a butterfly, a lord
Of flowers, garlands, love-knots, silly posies,
Groves, meadows, melodies, and arbour roses;
940   My kingdom's at its death, and just it is
That I should die with it: so in all this
We miscal grief, bale, sorrow, heartbreak, woe,
What is there to plain of? By Titan's foe
I am but rightly serv'd." So saying, he
945   Tripp'd lightly on, in sort of deathful glee;
Laughing at the clear stream and setting sun,
As though they jests had been: nor had he done
His laugh at nature's holy countenance,
Until that grove appear'd, as if perchance,
950   And then his tongue with sober seemlihed
Gave utterance as he entered: "Ha! I said,
King of the butterflies; but by this gloom,
And by old Rhadamanthus' tongue of doom,
This dusk religion, pomp of solitude,
955   And the Promethean clay by thief endued,
By old Saturnus' forelock, by his head
Shook with eternal palsy, I did wed
Myself to things of light from infancy;
And thus to be cast out, thus lorn to die,
960   Is sure enough to make a mortal man

Grow impious." So he inwardly began
On things for which no wording can be found;
Deeper and deeper sinking, until drown'd
Beyond the reach of music: for the choir
965   Of Cynthia he heard not, though rough briar
Nor muffling thicket interpos'd to dull
The vesper hymn, far swollen, soft and full,
Through the dark pillars of those sylvan aisles.
He saw not the two maidens, nor their smiles,
970   Wan as primroses gather'd at midnight
By chilly finger'd spring. "Unhappy wight!
Endymion!" said Peona, "we are here!
What wouldst thou ere we all are laid on bier?"
Then he embrac'd her, and his lady's hand
975   Press'd, saying: "Sister, I would have command,
If it were heaven's will, on our sad fate."
At which that dark-eyed stranger stood elate
And said, in a new voice, but sweet as love,
To Endymion's amaze: "By Cupid's dove,
980   And so thou shalt! and by the lily truth
Of my own breast thou shalt, beloved youth!"
And as she spake, into her face there came
Light, as reflected from a silver flame:
Her long black hair swell'd ampler, in display
985   Full golden; in her eyes a brighter day
Dawn'd blue and full of love. Aye, he beheld
Phœbe, his passion! joyous she upheld
Her lucid bow, continuing thus: "Drear, drear
Has our delaying been; but foolish fear
990   Withheld me first; and then decrees of fate;
And then 'twas fit that from this mortal state
Thou shouldst, my love, by some unlook'd for change
Be spiritualiz'd. Peona, we shall range
These forests, and to thee they safe shall be
995   As was thy cradle; hither shalt thou flee
To meet us many a time." Next Cynthia bright
Peona kiss'd, and bless'd with fair good night:
Her brother kiss'd her too, and knelt adown
Before his goddess, in a blissful swoon.
1000   She gave her fair hands to him, and behold,
Before three swiftest kisses he had told,
They vanish'd far away!—Peona went
Home through the gloomy wood in wonderment.

In drear nighted December

In drear nighted December,
   Too happy, happy tree,
Thy branches ne'er remember
   Their green felicity—
5   The north cannot undo them
With a sleety whistle through them,
Nor frozen thawings glue them
   From budding at the prime.

In drear nighted December,
10   Too happy, happy brook,
Thy bubblings ne'er remember
   Apollo's summer look;
But with a sweet forgetting
They stay their crystal fretting,
15   Never, never petting
   About the frozen time.

Ah! would 'twere so with many
   A gentle girl and boy—
But were there ever any
20   Writh'd not of passed joy?
The feel of not to feel it,
When there is none to heal it,
Nor numbed sense to steel it,
   Was never said in rhyme.

Apollo to the Graces

APOLLO

   Which of the fairest three
   To-day will ride with me?
My steeds are all pawing on the thresholds of morn:
   Which of the fairest three
5   To-day will ride with me
Across the gold autumn's whole kingdoms of corn?

THE GRACES *all answer*

    I will, I—I—I—
O young Apollo, let me fly along with thee;
    I will, I—I—I—
10   The many, many wonders see,
      I—I—I—I—
And thy lyre shall never have a slacken'd string;
      I—I—I—I—
Through the golden day will sing.

To Mrs. Reynolds's Cat

Cat! who hast past thy grand climacteric,
    How many mice and rats hast in thy days
    Destroy'd?—how many tit bits stolen? Gaze
With those bright languid segments green and prick
5   Those velvet ears—but prythee do not stick
    Thy latent talons in me—and upraise
    Thy gentle mew—and tell me all thy frays
Of fish and mice and rats and tender chick.
Nay, look not down, nor lick thy dainty wrists—
10   For all the wheezy asthma—and for all
Thy tail's tip is nicked off—and though the fists
    Of many a maid have given thee many a maul,
Still is that fur as soft as when the lists
    In youth thou enter'dst on glass bottled wall.

Lines on Seeing a Lock of Milton's Hair

    Chief of organic numbers!
      Old scholar of the spheres!
    Thy spirit never slumbers,
      But rolls about our ears
5   For ever, and for ever:
    O, what a mad endeavour
      Worketh he,
Who, to thy sacred and ennobled hearse,
Would offer a burnt sacrifice of verse
10   And melody.

How heavenward thou soundedst,
  Live temple of sweet noise;
And discord unconfoundedst,—
  Giving delight new joys,
15   And pleasure nobler pinions—
  O, where are thy dominions?
      Lend thine ear,
To a young Delian oath—aye, by thy soul,
By all that from thy mortal lips did roll;
20 And by the kernel of thine earthly love,
Beauty, in things on earth and things above;
  When every childish fashion
    Has vanish'd from my rhyme,
  Will I, grey-gone in passion,
25   Leave to an after time
      Hymning and harmony
Of thee, and of thy works, and of thy life;
But vain is now the burning, and the strife,
Pangs are in vain—until I grow high-rife
30   With old philosophy;
And mad with glimpses at futurity!

For many years my offerings must be hush'd.
  When I do speak, I'll think upon this hour,
Because I feel my forehead hot and flush'd—
35 Even at the simplest vassal of thy power;
    A lock of thy bright hair—
    Sudden it came,
And I was startled, when I caught thy name
    Coupled so unaware;
40 Yet at the moment, temperate was my blood—
Methought I had beheld it from the Flood.

On Sitting Down to Read King Lear *Once Again*

O golden-tongued Romance, with serene lute!
  Fair plumed syren, queen of far-away!
  Leave melodizing on this wintry day,
Shut up thine olden pages, and be mute.
5 Adieu! for, once again, the fierce dispute
  Betwixt damnation and impassion'd clay

Must I burn through; once more humbly assay
The bitter-sweet of this Shaksperean fruit.
Chief Poet! and ye clouds of Albion,
10   Begetters of our deep eternal theme!
When through the old oak forest I am gone,
    Let me not wander in a barren dream:
But, when I am consumed in the fire,
Give me new phœnix wings to fly at my desire.

When I have fears that I may cease to be

When I have fears that I may cease to be
    Before my pen has glean'd my teeming brain,
Before high piled books, in charactry,
    Hold like rich garners the full ripen'd grain;
5   When I behold, upon the night's starr'd face,
    Huge cloudy symbols of a high romance,
And think that I may never live to trace
    Their shadows, with the magic hand of chance;
And when I feel, fair creature of an hour,
10   That I shall never look upon thee more,
Never have relish in the fairy power
    Of unreflecting love;—then on the shore
Of the wide world I stand alone, and think
Till love and fame to nothingness do sink.

Lines on the Mermaid Tavern

Souls of poets dead and gone,
What elysium have ye known,
Happy field or mossy cavern,
Choicer than the Mermaid Tavern?
5   Have ye tippled drink more fine
Than mine host's Canary wine?
Or are fruits of Paradise
Sweeter than those dainty pies
Of venison? O generous food!
10   Drest as though bold Robin Hood
Would, with his maid Marian,
Sup and bowse from horn and can.

I have heard that on a day
Mine host's sign-board flew away,
15   Nobody knew whither, till
An astrologer's old quill
To a sheepskin gave the story,
Said he saw you in your glory,
Underneath a new old sign
20   Sipping beverage divine,
And pledging with contented smack
The Mermaid in the zodiac.

Souls of poets dead and gone,
What elysium have ye known,
25   Happy field or mossy cavern,
Choicer than the Mermaid Tavern?

O blush not so! O blush not so

1

O blush not so! O blush not so!
    Or I shall think you knowing;
And if you smile, the blushing while,
    Then maidenheads are going.

2

5   There's a blush for won't, and a blush for shan't,
    And a blush for having done it;
There's a blush for thought, and a blush for nought,
    And a blush for just begun it.

3

O sigh not so! O sigh not so!
10   For it sounds of Eve's sweet pippin;
By those loosen'd hips, you have tasted the pips,
    And fought in an amorous nipping.

4

Will you play once more, at nice cut-core,
    For it only will last our youth out;
15   And we have the prime of the kissing time,
    We have not one sweet tooth out.

5

There's a sigh for yes, and a sigh for no,
　And a sigh for I can't bear it!
O what can be done? Shall we stay or run?
20　　O cut the sweet apple and share it!

Hence burgundy, claret, and port

Hence burgundy, claret, and port,
　Away with old hock and madeira!
Too earthly ye are for my sport;
　There's a beverage brighter and clearer!
5　Instead of a pitiful rummer,
My wine overbrims a whole summer;
　　My bowl is the sky,
　　And I drink at my eye,
　　Till I feel in the brain
10　　A Delphian pain—
Then follow, my Caius, then follow!
　　On the green of the hill,
　　We will drink our fill
　　Of golden sunshine,
15　　Till our brains intertwine
With the glory and grace of Apollo!

God of the meridian

God of the meridian!
　And of the east and west!
To thee my soul is flown,
　And my body is earthward press'd:
5　It is an awful mission,
A terrible division,
And leaves a gulf austere
To be fill'd with worldly fear.
Aye, when the soul is fled
10　Too high above our head,
Affrighted do we gaze
After its airy maze—
As doth a mother wild

When her young infant child
15   Is in an eagle's claws.
And is not this the cause
Of madness?—God of Song,
Thou bearest me along
Through sights I scarce can bear;
20   O let me, let me share
With the hot lyre and thee
The staid philosophy.
Temper my lonely hours
And let me see thy bowers
25   More unalarmed!   *   *   *

Robin Hood

TO A FRIEND

No! those days are gone away,
And their hours are old and gray,
And their minutes buried all
Under the down-trodden pall
5   Of the leaves of many years:
Many times have winter's shears,
Frozen north, and chilling east,
Sounded tempests to the feast
Of the forest's whispering fleeces,
10   Since men knew nor rent nor leases.

No, the bugle sounds no more,
And the twanging bow no more;
Silent is the ivory shrill
Past the heath and up the hill;
15   There is no mid-forest laugh,
Where lone Echo gives the half
To some wight, amaz'd to hear
Jesting, deep in forest drear.

On the fairest time of June
20   You may go, with sun or moon,
Or the seven stars to light you,
Or the polar ray to right you;
But you never may behold

Little John, or Robin bold;
25   Never one, of all the clan,
Thrumming on an empty can
Some old hunting ditty, while
He doth his green way beguile
To fair hostess Merriment,
30   Down beside the pasture Trent;
For he left the merry tale
Messenger for spicy ale.

Gone, the merry morris din;
Gone, the song of Gamelyn;
35   Gone, the tough-belted outlaw
Idling in the "grenè shawe";
All are gone away and past!
And if Robin should be cast
Sudden from his turfed grave,
40   And if Marian should have
Once again her forest days,
She would weep, and he would craze:
He would swear, for all his oaks,
Fall'n beneath the dockyard strokes,
45   Have rotted on the briny seas;
She would weep that her wild bees
Sang not to her—strange! that honey
Can't be got without hard money!

So it is: yet let us sing,
50   Honour to the old bow-string!
Honour to the bugle-horn!
Honour to the woods unshorn!
Honour to the Lincoln green!
Honour to the archer keen!
55   Honour to tight little John,
And the horse he rode upon!
Honour to bold Robin Hood,
Sleeping in the underwood!
Honour to maid Marian,
60   And to all the Sherwood-clan!
Though their days have hurried by
Let us two a burden try.

Welcome joy, and welcome sorrow

"Under the flag
Of each his faction, they to battle bring
Their embryo atoms."

Milton

Welcome joy, and welcome sorrow,
  Lethe's weed, and Hermes' feather,
Come to-day, and come to-morrow,
  I do love you both together!
5   I love to mark sad faces in fair weather,
And hear a merry laugh amid the thunder;
  Fair and foul I love together;
Meadows sweet where flames burn under;
And a giggle at a wonder;
10 Visage sage at pantomime;
Funeral and steeple-chime;
Infant playing with a skull;
Morning fair and storm-wreck'd hull;
Night-shade with the woodbine kissing;
15 Serpents in red roses hissing;
Cleopatra, regal drest,
With the aspics at her breast;
Dancing music, music sad,
Both together, sane and mad;
20 Muses bright and Muses pale;
Sombre Saturn, Momus hale,
Laugh and sigh, and laugh again,
Oh! the sweetness of the pain!
Muses bright and Muses pale,
25 Bare your faces of the veil,
Let me see, and let me write
Of the day, and of the night,
Both together,—let me slake
All my thirst for sweet heart-ache!
30 Let my bower be of yew,
Interwreath'd with myrtles new,
Pines, and lime-trees full in bloom,
And my couch a low grass tomb.

Time's sea hath been five years at its slow ebb

Time's sea hath been five years at its slow ebb;
  Long hours have to and fro let creep the sand,
Since I was tangled in thy beauty's web,
  And snared by the ungloving of thy hand:
5 And yet I never look on midnight sky,
  But I behold thine eyes' well-memoried light;
I cannot look upon the rose's dye,
  But to thy cheek my soul doth take its flight:
I cannot look on any budding flower,
10 But my fond ear, in fancy at thy lips,
And hearkening for a love-sound, doth devour
  Its sweets in the wrong sense.—Thou dost eclipse
Every delight with sweet remembering,
And grief unto my darling joys dost bring.

To the Nile

Son of the old moon-mountains African!
  Chief of the pyramid and crocodile!
  We call thee fruitful, and, that very while,
A desert fills our seeing's inward span;
5 Nurse of swart nations since the world began,
  Art thou so fruitful? or dost thou beguile
  Such men to honor thee, who, worn with toil,
Rest for a space 'twixt Cairo and Decan?
O may dark fancies err! they surely do;
10 'Tis ignorance that makes a barren waste
Of all beyond itself: thou dost bedew
  Green rushes like our rivers, and dost taste
The pleasant sun-rise; green isles hast thou too,
  And to the sea as happily dost haste.

Spenser, a jealous honorer of thine

Spenser, a jealous honorer of thine,
  A forester deep in thy midmost trees,
Did last eve ask my promise to refine
  Some English that might strive thine ear to please.
5 But Elfin-Poet, 'tis impossible

For an inhabitant of wintry earth
To rise like Phœbus with a golden quell,
    Fire-wing'd, and make a morning in his mirth:
    It is impossible to escape from toil
10   O' the sudden, and receive thy spiriting:—
    The flower must drink the nature of the soil
        Before it can put forth its blossoming.
    Be with me in the summer days, and I
    Will for thine honor and his pleasure try.

Blue!—'Tis the life of heaven—the domain

Blue!—'Tis the life of heaven—the domain
    Of Cynthia:—the wide palace of the sun;
The tent of Hesperus and all his train;
    The bosomer of clouds gold, grey, and dun.
5   Blue!—'Tis the life of waters—Ocean,
    And all its vassal streams, pools numberless,
May rage, and foam, and fret, but never can
    Subside, if not to dark blue nativeness.
Blue!—gentle cousin to the forest green,
10   Married to green in all the sweetest flowers—
Forget-me-not—the blue-bell—and, that queen
    Of secrecy, the violet:—What strange powers
Hast thou, as a mere shadow?—But how great,
When in an eye thou art, alive with fate!

O thou whose face hath felt the winter's wind

O thou whose face hath felt the winter's wind,
Whose eye has seen the snow clouds hung in mist,
And the black-elm tops 'mong the freezing stars,
To thee the spring will be a harvest-time.
5   O thou whose only book has been the light
Of supreme darkness which thou feddest on
Night after night, when Phœbus was away,
To thee the spring shall be a tripple morn.
O fret not after knowledge—I have none,
10   And yet my song comes native with the warmth;
O fret not after knowledge—I have none,

And yet the evening listens. He who saddens
At thought of idleness cannot be idle,
And he's awake who thinks himself asleep.

Extracts from an Opera

O were I one of the Olympian twelve,
Their godships should pass this into a law;
That when a man doth set himself in toil
After some beauty veiled far-away,
5   Each step he took should make his lady's hand
More soft, more white, and her fair cheek more fair;
And for each briar-berry he might eat,
A kiss should bud upon the tree of love,
And pulp, and ripen, richer every hour,
10   To melt away upon the traveller's lips.

* * * * * * *

DAISY'S SONG

1

The sun, with his great eye,
Sees not so much as I;
And the moon, all silver proud,
Might as well be in a cloud.

2

5   And O the spring—the spring!
I lead the life of a king!
Couch'd in the teeming grass,
I spy each pretty lass.

3

I look where no one dares,
10   And I stare where no one stares,
And when the night is nigh,
Lambs bleat my lullaby.

* * * * * * *

FOLLY'S SONG

When wedding fiddles are a playing,
    Huzza for folly O!
And when maidens go a maying,
    Huzza etc.
5   When a milk-pail is upset,
    Huzza etc.
And the clothes left in the wet,
    Huzza etc.
When the barrel's set abroach,
10   Huzza etc.
When Kate Eyebrow keeps a coach,
    Huzza etc.
When the pig is overroasted,
    Huzza etc.
15 And the cheese is overtoasted,
    Huzza etc.
When Sir Snap is with his lawyer,
    Huzza etc.
And Miss Chip has kiss'd the sawyer,
20   Huzza etc.

      * * * * * * *

O, I am frighten'd with most hateful thoughts!
Perhaps her voice is not a nightingale's,
Perhaps her teeth are not the fairest pearl;
Her eye-lashes may be, for ought I know,
5   Not longer than the May-fly's small fan-horns;
There may not be one dimple on her hand,
And freckles many; ah! a careless nurse,
In haste to teach the little thing to walk,
May have crumpt up a pair of Dian's legs,
10 And warpt the ivory of a Juno's neck.

      * * * * * * *

SONG

1

The stranger lighted from his steed,
    And ere he spake a word,

He seiz'd my lady's lily hand,
   And kiss'd it all unheard.

2

5   The stranger walk'd into the hall,
   And ere he spake a word,
He kiss'd my lady's cherry lips,
   And kiss'd 'em all unheard.

3

The stranger walk'd into the bower,—
10   But my lady first did go,—
Aye hand in hand into the bower,
   Where my lord's roses blow.

4

My lady's maid had a silken scarf,
   And a golden ring had she,
15 And a kiss from the stranger as off he went
   Again on his fair palfrey.

* * * * * * *

Asleep! O sleep a little while, white pearl,
And let me kneel, and let me pray to thee,
And let me call heaven's blessing on thine eyes,
And let me breathe into the happy air,
5   That doth enfold and touch thee all about,
Vows of my slavery, my giving up,
My sudden adoration, my great love!

Four seasons fill the measure of the year

Four seasons fill the measure of the year;
   Four seasons are there in the mind of man.
He hath his lusty spring, when fancy clear
   Takes in all beauty with an easy span:
5   He hath his summer, when luxuriously
   He chews the honied cud of fair spring thoughts,
Till, in his soul dissolv'd, they come to be
   Part of himself. He hath his autumn ports

And havens of repose, when his tired wings
10   Are folded up, and he content to look
On mists in idleness: to let fair things
   Pass by unheeded as a threshold brook.
He hath his winter too of pale misfeature,
Or else he would forget his mortal nature.

For there's Bishop's Teign

1

For there's Bishop's Teign
And King's Teign
And Coomb at the clear Teign head—
Where close by the stream
5 You may have your cream
All spread upon barley bread.

2

There's Arch Brook
And there's Larch Brook,
Both turning many a mill,
10 And cooling the drouth
Of the salmon's mouth,
And fattening his silver gill.

3

There is Wild Wood,
A mild hood
15 To the sheep on the lea o' the down,
Where the golden furze
With its green thin spurs
Doth catch at the maiden's gown.

4

There is Newton Marsh
20 With its spear grass harsh—
A pleasant summer level
Where the maidens sweet
Of the Market Street
Do meet in the dusk to revel.

5

25   There's the barton rich
With dyke and ditch
And hedge for the thrush to live in,
And the hollow tree
For the buzzing bee,
30   And a bank for the wasp to hive in.

6

And O, and O
The daisies blow,
And the primroses are waken'd,
And the violet white
35   Sits in silver plight,
And the green bud's as long as the spike end.

7

Then who would go
Into dark Soho
And chatter with dack'd hair'd critics,
40   When he can stay
For the new mown hay
And startle the dappled prickets?

Where be ye going, you Devon maid

1

Where be ye going, you Devon maid,
    And what have ye there i' the basket?
Ye tight little fairy, just fresh from the dairy,
    Will ye give me some cream if I ask it?

2

5   I love your meads and I love your flowers,
    And I love your junkets mainly;
But 'hind the door, I love kissing more—
    O look not so disdainly!

3

I love your hills and I love your dales,
10   And I love your flocks a bleating—

But O on the hether to lie together
　　With both our hearts a beating.

4

I'll put your basket all safe in a nook
　　And your shawl I hang up on this willow,
15　　And we will sigh in the daisy's eye
　　And kiss on a grass green pillow.

Over the hill and over the dale

Over the hill and over the dale,
　　And over the bourn to Dawlish—
Where gingerbread wives have a scanty sale,
　　And gingerbread nuts are smallish.

5　Rantipole Betty she ran down a hill,
　　And kick'd up her petticoats fairly.
Says I, I'll be Jack if you will be Gill—
　　So she sat on the grass debonnairly.

Here's somebody coming, here's somebody coming!
10　　Says I, 'tis the wind at a parley.
So without any fuss, any hawing and humming,
　　She lay on the grass debonnairly.

Here's somebody here and here's somebody there!
　　Says I, hold your tongue, you young gipsey.
15　So she held her tongue and lay plump and fair
　　And dead as a venus tipsy.

O who wouldn't hie to Dawlish fair,
　　O who wouldn't stop in a meadow?
O who would not rumple the daisies there,
20　　And make the wild fern for a bed do?

Dear Reynolds, as last night I lay in bed

Dear Reynolds, as last night I lay in bed,
There came before my eyes that wonted thread
Of shapes, and shadows, and remembrances,

That every other minute vex and please:
5 Things all disjointed come from north and south,
Two witch's eyes above a cherub's mouth,
Voltaire with casque and shield and habergeon,
And Alexander with his night-cap on—
Old Socrates a tying his cravat;
10 And Hazlitt playing with Miss Edgeworth's cat;
And Junius Brutus pretty well so so,
Making the best of 's way towards Soho.

 Few are there who escape these visitings—
P'rhaps one or two, whose lives have patient wings,
15 And through whose curtains peeps no hellish nose,
No wild boar tushes, and no mermaid's toes:
But flowers bursting out with lusty pride,
And young Æolian harps personified,
Some, Titian colours touch'd into real life.
20 The sacrifice goes on; the pontif knife
Gleams in the sun, the milk-white heifer lows,
The pipes go shrilly, the libation flows:
A white sail shews above the green-head cliff,
Moves round the point, and throws her anchor stiff.
25 The mariners join hymn with those on land.
You know the Enchanted Castle—it doth stand
Upon a rock on the border of a lake
Nested in trees, which all do seem to shake
From some old magic like Urganda's sword.
30 O Phœbus, that I had thy sacred word
To shew this castle in fair dreaming wise
Unto my friend, while sick and ill he lies.

 You know it well enough, where it doth seem
A mossy place, a Merlin's hall, a dream.
35 You know the clear lake, and the little isles,
The mountains blue, and cold near neighbour rills—
All which elsewhere are but half animate,
Here do they look alive to love and hate,
To smiles and frowns; they seem a lifted mound
40 Above some giant, pulsing underground.

 Part of the building was a chosen see
Built by a banish'd santon of Chaldee:
The other part two thousand years from him

Was built by Cuthbert de Saint Aldebrim;
45   Then there's a little wing, far from the sun,
Built by a Lapland witch turn'd maudlin nun—
And many other juts of aged stone
Founded with many a mason-devil's groan.

The doors all look as if they oped themselves,
50   The windows as if latch'd by fays and elves—
And from them comes a silver flash of light
As from the westward of a summer's night;
Or like a beauteous woman's large blue eyes
Gone mad through olden songs and poesies.

55   See what is coming from the distance dim!
A golden galley all in silken trim!
Three rows of oars are lightening moment-whiles
Into the verdurous bosoms of those isles.
Towards the shade under the castle wall
60   It comes in silence—now 'tis hidden all.
The clarion sounds; and from a postern grate
An echo of sweet music doth create
A fear in the poor herdsman who doth bring
His beasts to trouble the enchanted spring:
65   He tells of the sweet music and the spot
To all his friends, and they believe him not.

O that our dreamings all of sleep or wake
Would all their colours from the sunset take:
From something of material sublime,
70   Rather than shadow our own soul's daytime
In the dark void of night. For in the world
We jostle—but my flag is not unfurl'd
On the admiral staff—and to philosophize
I dare not yet!—Oh never will the prize,
75   High reason, and the lore of good and ill,
Be my award. Things cannot to the will
Be settled, but they tease us out of thought.
Or is it that imagination brought
Beyond its proper bound, yet still confined,—
80   Lost in a sort of purgatory blind,
Cannot refer to any standard law
Of either earth or heaven?—It is a flaw
In happiness to see beyond our bourn—

It forces us in summer skies to mourn:
85   It spoils the singing of the nightingale.

Dear Reynolds, I have a mysterious tale
And cannot speak it. The first page I read
Upon a lampit rock of green sea weed
Among the breakers.—'Twas a quiet eve;
90   The rocks were silent—the wide sea did weave
An untumultuous fringe of silver foam
Along the flat brown sand. I was at home,
And should have been most happy—but I saw
Too far into the sea; where every maw
95   The greater on the less feeds evermore:—
But I saw too distinct into the core
Of an eternal fierce destruction,
And so from happiness I far was gone.
Still am I sick of it: and though to-day
100   I've gathered young spring-leaves, and flowers gay
Of periwinkle and wild strawberry,
Still do I that most fierce destruction see,
The shark at savage prey—the hawk at pounce,
The gentle robin, like a pard or ounce,
105   Ravening a worm.—Away ye horrid moods,
Moods of one's mind! You know I hate them well,
You know I'd sooner be a clapping bell
To some Kamschatkan missionary church,
Than with these horrid moods be left in lurch.
110   Do you get health—and Tom the same—I'll dance,
And from detested moods in new romance
Take refuge.—Of bad lines a centaine dose
Is sure enough—and so "here follows prose."

To J. R.

O that a week could be an age, and we
    Felt parting and warm meeting every week;
Then one poor year a thousand years would be,
    The flush of welcome ever on the cheek.
5   So could we live long life in little space;
    So time itself would be annihilate;
So a day's journey, in oblivious haze
    To serve our joys, would lengthen and dilate.

O to arrive each Monday morn from Ind,
10   To land each Tuesday from the rich Levant,
In little time a host of joys to bind,
    And keep our souls in one eternal pant!
This morn, my friend, and yester evening taught
Me how to harbour such a happy thought.

Isabella;
or,
The Pot of Basil

A STORY FROM BOCCACCIO

1

Fair Isabel, poor simple Isabel!
  Lorenzo, a young palmer in Love's eye!
They could not in the self-same mansion dwell
  Without some stir of heart, some malady;
They could not sit at meals but feel how well
  It soothed each to be the other by;
They could not, sure, beneath the same roof sleep
But to each other dream, and nightly weep.

2

With every morn their love grew tenderer,
  With every eve deeper and tenderer still;
He might not in house, field, or garden stir,
  But her full shape would all his seeing fill;
And his continual voice was pleasanter
  To her, than noise of trees or hidden rill;
Her lute-string gave an echo of his name,
She spoilt her half-done broidery with the same.

3

He knew whose gentle hand was at the latch,
  Before the door had given her to his eyes;
And from her chamber-window he would catch
  Her beauty farther than the falcon spies;
And constant as her vespers would he watch,
  Because her face was turn'd to the same skies;
And with sick longing all the night outwear,
To hear her morning-step upon the stair.

4

A whole long month of May in this sad plight
  Made their cheeks paler by the break of June:
"To-morrow will I bow to my delight,
  To-morrow will I ask my lady's boon."—

"O may I never see another night,
30   Lorenzo, if thy lips breathe not love's tune."—
So spake they to their pillows; but, alas,
Honeyless days and days did he let pass;

5

Until sweet Isabella's untouch'd cheek
      Fell sick within the rose's just domain,
35   Fell thin as a young mother's, who doth seek
      By every lull to cool her infant's pain:
"How ill she is," said he, "I may not speak,
      And yet I will, and tell my love all plain:
If looks speak love-laws, I will drink her tears,
40   And at the least 'twill startle off her cares."

6

So said he one fair morning, and all day
      His heart beat awfully against his side;
And to his heart he inwardly did pray
      For power to speak; but still the ruddy tide
45   Stifled his voice, and puls'd resolve away—
      Fever'd his high conceit of such a bride,
Yet brought him to the meekness of a child:
Alas! when passion is both meek and wild!

7

So once more he had wak'd and anguished
50   A dreary night of love and misery,
If Isabel's quick eye had not been wed
      To every symbol on his forehead high;
She saw it waxing very pale and dead,
      And straight all flush'd; so, lisped tenderly,
55   "Lorenzo!"—here she ceas'd her timid quest,
But in her tone and look he read the rest.

8

"O Isabella, I can half perceive
      That I may speak my grief into thine ear;
If thou didst ever any thing believe,
60   Believe how I love thee, believe how near
My soul is to its doom: I would not grieve

Thy hand by unwelcome pressing, would not fear
Thine eyes by gazing; but I cannot live
Another night, and not my passion shrive.

9

65   "Love! thou art leading me from wintry cold,
Lady! thou leadest me to summer clime,
And I must taste the blossoms that unfold
In its ripe warmth this gracious morning time."
So said, his erewhile timid lips grew bold,
70   And poesied with hers in dewy rhyme:
Great bliss was with them, and great happiness
Grew, like a lusty flower in June's caress.

10

Parting they seem'd to tread upon the air,
Twin roses by the zephyr blown apart
75   Only to meet again more close, and share
The inward fragrance of each other's heart.
She, to her chamber gone, a ditty fair
Sang, of delicious love and honey'd dart;
He with light steps went up a western hill,
80   And bade the sun farewell, and joy'd his fill.

11

All close they met again, before the dusk
Had taken from the stars its pleasant veil,
All close they met, all eves, before the dusk
Had taken from the stars its pleasant veil,
85   Close in a bower of hyacinth and musk,
Unknown of any, free from whispering tale.
Ah! better had it been for ever so,
Than idle ears should pleasure in their woe.

12

Were they unhappy then?—It cannot be—
90   Too many tears for lovers have been shed,
Too many sighs give we to them in fee,
Too much of pity after they are dead,
Too many doleful stories do we see,
Whose matter in bright gold were best be read;

95   Except in such a page where Theseus' spouse
      Over the pathless waves towards him bows.

13

    But, for the general award of love,
      The little sweet doth kill much bitterness;
    Though Dido silent is in under-grove,
100   And Isabella's was a great distress,
    Though young Lorenzo in warm Indian clove
      Was not embalm'd, this truth is not the less—
    Even bees, the little almsmen of spring-bowers,
    Know there is richest juice in poison-flowers.

14

105   With her two brothers this fair lady dwelt,
      Enriched from ancestral merchandize,
    And for them many a weary hand did swelt
      In torched mines and noisy factories,
    And many once proud-quiver'd loins did melt
110   In blood from stinging whip;—with hollow eyes
    Many all day in dazzling river stood,
    To take the rich-ored driftings of the flood.

15

    For them the Ceylon diver held his breath,
      And went all naked to the hungry shark;
115   For them his ears gush'd blood; for them in death
      The seal on the cold ice with piteous bark
    Lay full of darts; for them alone did seethe
      A thousand men in troubles wide and dark:
    Half-ignorant, they turn'd an easy wheel,
120   That set sharp racks at work, to pinch and peel.

16

    Why were they proud? Because their marble founts
      Gush'd with more pride than do a wretch's tears?—
    Why were they proud? Because fair orange-mounts
      Were of more soft ascent than lazar stairs?—
125   Why were they proud? Because red-lin'd accounts
      Were richer than the songs of Grecian years?—
    Why were they proud? again we ask aloud,
    Why in the name of Glory were they proud?

17

₁₃₀

Yet were these Florentines as self-retired
    In hungry pride and gainful cowardice,
As two close Hebrews in that land inspired,
    Paled in and vineyarded from beggar-spies;
The hawks of ship-mast forests—the untired
    And pannier'd mules for ducats and old lies—
Quick cat's-paws on the generous stray-away,—
Great wits in Spanish, Tuscan, and Malay.

₁₃₅

18

₁₄₀

How was it these same ledger-men could spy
    Fair Isabella in her downy nest?
How could they find out in Lorenzo's eye
    A straying from his toil? Hot Egypt's pest
Into their vision covetous and sly!
    How could these money-bags see east and west?—
Yet so they did—and every dealer fair
Must see behind, as doth the hunted hare.

19

₁₄₅

O eloquent and famed Boccaccio!
    Of thee we now should ask forgiving boon,
And of thy spicy myrtles as they blow,
    And of thy roses amorous of the moon,
And of thy lilies, that do paler grow
    Now they can no more hear thy ghittern's tune,
For venturing syllables that ill beseem
The quiet glooms of such a piteous theme.

₁₅₀

20

₁₅₅

Grant thou a pardon here, and then the tale
    Shall move on soberly, as it is meet;
There is no other crime, no mad assail
    To make old prose in modern rhyme more sweet:
But it is done—succeed the verse or fail—
    To honour thee, and thy gone spirit greet;
To stead thee as a verse in English tongue,
An echo of thee in the north-wind sung.

₁₆₀

21

These brethren having found by many signs
    What love Lorenzo for their sister had,

And how she lov'd him too, each unconfines
   His bitter thoughts to other, well nigh mad
165 That he, the servant of their trade designs,
   Should in their sister's love be blithe and glad,
When 'twas their plan to coax her by degrees
To some high noble and his olive-trees.

22

And many a jealous conference had they,
170   And many times they bit their lips alone,
Before they fix'd upon a surest way
   To make the youngster for his crime atone;
And at the last, these men of cruel clay
   Cut Mercy with a sharp knife to the bone;
175 For they resolved in some forest dim
To kill Lorenzo, and there bury him.

23

So on a pleasant morning, as he leant
   Into the sun-rise, o'er the balustrade
Of the garden-terrace, towards him they bent
180   Their footing through the dews; and to him said,
"You seem there in the quiet of content,
   Lorenzo, and we are most loth to invade
Calm speculation; but if you are wise,
Bestride your steed while cold is in the skies.

24

185 "To-day we purpose, ay, this hour we mount
   To spur three leagues towards the Apennine;
Come down, we pray thee, ere the hot sun count
   His dewy rosary on the eglantine."
Lorenzo, courteously as he was wont,
190   Bow'd a fair greeting to these serpents' whine;
And went in haste, to get in readiness,
With belt, and spur, and bracing huntsman's dress.

25

And as he to the court-yard pass'd along,
   Each third step did he pause, and listen'd oft
195 If he could hear his lady's matin-song,
   Or the light whisper of her footstep soft;

And as he thus over his passion hung,
   He heard a laugh full musical aloft;
When, looking up, he saw her features bright
200   Smile through an in-door lattice, all delight.

26

"Love, Isabel!" said he, "I was in pain
   Lest I should miss to bid thee a good morrow:
Ah! what if I should lose thee, when so fain
   I am to stifle all the heavy sorrow
205 Of a poor three hours' absence? but we'll gain
   Out of the amorous dark what day doth borrow.
Good bye! I'll soon be back."—"Good bye!" said she:—
And as he went she chanted merrily.

27

So the two brothers and their murder'd man
210 Rode past fair Florence, to where Arno's stream
Gurgles through straiten'd banks, and still doth fan
   Itself with dancing bulrush, and the bream
Keeps head against the freshets. Sick and wan
   The brothers' faces in the ford did seem,
215 Lorenzo's flush with love.—They pass'd the water
Into a forest quiet for the slaughter.

28

There was Lorenzo slain and buried in,
   There in that forest did his great love cease;
Ah! when a soul doth thus its freedom win,
220   It aches in loneliness—is ill at peace
As the break-covert blood-hounds of such sin:
   They dipp'd their swords in the water, and did tease
Their horses homeward, with convulsed spur,
Each richer by his being a murderer.

29

225 They told their sister how, with sudden speed,
   Lorenzo had ta'en ship for foreign lands,
Because of some great urgency and need
   In their affairs, requiring trusty hands.
Poor Girl! put on thy stifling widow's weed,
230   And 'scape at once from Hope's accursed bands;

To-day thou wilt not see him, nor to-morrow,
And the next day will be a day of sorrow.

30

She weeps alone for pleasures not to be;
   Sorely she wept until the night came on,
235   And then, instead of love, O misery!
      She brooded o'er the luxury alone:
His image in the dusk she seem'd to see,
   And to the silence made a gentle moan,
Spreading her perfect arms upon the air,
240   And on her couch low murmuring "Where? O where?"

31

But Selfishness, Love's cousin, held not long
   Its fiery vigil in her single breast;
She fretted for the golden hour, and hung
   Upon the time with feverish unrest—
245   Not long—for soon into her heart a throng
      Of higher occupants, a richer zest,
Came tragic; passion not to be subdued,
And sorrow for her love in travels rude.

32

In the mid days of autumn, on their eves
250   The breath of Winter comes from far away,
And the sick west continually bereaves
   Of some gold tinge, and plays a roundelay
Of death among the bushes and the leaves,
   To make all bare before he dares to stray
255   From his north cavern. So sweet Isabel
By gradual decay from beauty fell,

33

Because Lorenzo came not. Oftentimes
   She ask'd her brothers, with an eye all pale,
Striving to be itself, what dungeon climes
260   Could keep him off so long? They spake a tale
Time after time, to quiet her. Their crimes
   Came on them, like a smoke from Hinnom's vale;
And every night in dreams they groan'd aloud,
To see their sister in her snowy shroud.

34

265 And she had died in drowsy ignorance,
But for a thing more deadly dark than all;
It came like a fierce potion, drunk by chance,
Which saves a sick man from the feather'd pall
For some few gasping moments; like a lance,
270 Waking an Indian from his cloudy hall
With cruel pierce, and bringing him again
Sense of the gnawing fire at heart and brain.

35

It was a vision.—In the drowsy gloom,
The dull of midnight, at her couch's foot
275 Lorenzo stood, and wept: the forest tomb
Had marr'd his glossy hair which once could shoot
Lustre into the sun, and put cold doom
Upon his lips, and taken the soft lute
From his lorn voice, and past his loamed ears
280 Had made a miry channel for his tears.

36

Strange sound it was, when the pale shadow spake;
For there was striving, in its piteous tongue,
To speak as when on earth it was awake,
And Isabella on its music hung:
285 Languor there was in it, and tremulous shake,
As in a palsied Druid's harp unstrung;
And through it moan'd a ghostly under-song,
Like hoarse night-gusts sepulchral briars among.

37

Its eyes, though wild, were still all dewy bright
290 With love, and kept all phantom fear aloof
From the poor girl by magic of their light,
The while it did unthread the horrid woof
Of the late darken'd time,—the murderous spite
Of pride and avarice,—the dark pine roof
295 In the forest,—and the sodden turfed dell,
Where, without any word, from stabs he fell.

38

Saying moreover, "Isabel, my sweet!
Red whortle-berries droop above my head,

And a large flint-stone weighs upon my feet;
300   Around me beeches and high chestnuts shed
Their leaves and prickly nuts; a sheep-fold bleat
        Comes from beyond the river to my bed:
Go, shed one tear upon my heather-bloom,
And it shall comfort me within the tomb.

39

305   "I am a shadow now, alas! alas!
        Upon the skirts of human-nature dwelling
Alone: I chant alone the holy mass,
        While little sounds of life are round me knelling,
And glossy bees at noon do fieldward pass,
310   And many a chapel bell the hour is telling,
Paining me through: those sounds grow strange to me,
And thou art distant in Humanity.

40

"I know what was, I feel full well what is,
        And I should rage, if spirits could go mad;
315   Though I forget the taste of earthly bliss,
        That paleness warms my grave, as though I had
A Seraph chosen from the bright abyss
        To be my spouse: thy paleness makes me glad;
Thy beauty grows upon me, and I feel
320   A greater love through all my essence steal."

41

The Spirit mourn'd "Adieu!"—dissolv'd, and left
        The atom darkness in a slow turmoil;
As when of healthful midnight sleep bereft,
        Thinking on rugged hours and fruitless toil,
325   We put our eyes into a pillowy cleft,
        And see the spangly gloom froth up and boil:
It made sad Isabella's eyelids ache,
And in the dawn she started up awake;

42

"Ha! ha!" said she, "I knew not this hard life,
330   I thought the worst was simple misery;
I thought some Fate with pleasure or with strife
        Portion'd us—happy days, or else to die;
But there is crime—a brother's bloody knife!

Sweet Spirit, thou hast school'd my infancy:
335   I'll visit thee for this, and kiss thine eyes,
And greet thee morn and even in the skies."

43

When the full morning came, she had devised
    How she might secret to the forest hie;
How she might find the clay, so dearly prized,
340   And sing to it one latest lullaby;
How her short absence might be unsurmised,
    While she the inmost of the dream would try.
Resolv'd, she took with her an aged nurse,
And went into that dismal forest-hearse.

44

345   See, as they creep along the river side,
    How she doth whisper to that aged Dame,
And, after looking round the champaign wide,
    Shows her a knife.—"What feverous hectic flame
Burns in thee, child?—What good can thee betide,
350   That thou should'st smile again?"—The evening came,
And they had found Lorenzo's earthy bed;
The flint was there, the berries at his head.

45

Who hath not loiter'd in a green church-yard,
    And let his spirit, like a demon-mole,
355   Work through the clayey soil and gravel hard,
    To see scull, coffin'd bones, and funeral stole;
Pitying each form that hungry Death hath marr'd,
    And filling it once more with human soul?
Ah! this is holiday to what was felt
360   When Isabella by Lorenzo knelt.

46

She gaz'd into the fresh-thrown mould, as though
    One glance did fully all its secrets tell;
Clearly she saw, as other eyes would know
    Pale limbs at bottom of a crystal well;
365   Upon the murderous spot she seem'd to grow,
    Like to a native lily of the dell:
Then with her knife, all sudden, she began
To dig more fervently than misers can.

47

Soon she turn'd up a soiled glove, whereon
370   Her silk had play'd in purple phantasies,
She kiss'd it with a lip more chill than stone,
      And put it in her bosom, where it dries
And freezes utterly unto the bone
      Those dainties made to still an infant's cries:
375   Then 'gan she work again; nor stay'd her care,
But to throw back at times her veiling hair.

48

That old nurse stood beside her wondering,
      Until her heart felt pity to the core
At sight of such a dismal labouring,
380   And so she kneeled, with her locks all hoar,
And put her lean hands to the horrid thing:
      Three hours they labour'd at this travail sore;
At last they felt the kernel of the grave,
And Isabella did not stamp and rave.

49

385   Ah! wherefore all this wormy circumstance?
      Why linger at the yawning tomb so long?
O for the gentleness of old Romance,
      The simple plaining of a minstrel's song!
Fair reader, at the old tale take a glance,
390   For here, in truth, it doth not well belong
To speak:—O turn thee to the very tale,
And taste the music of that vision pale.

50

With duller steel than the Perséan sword
      They cut away no formless monster's head,
395   But one, whose gentleness did well accord
      With death, as life. The ancient harps have said,
Love never dies, but lives, immortal Lord:
      If Love impersonate was ever dead,
Pale Isabella kiss'd it, and low moan'd.
400   'Twas love; cold,—dead indeed, but not dethroned.

51

In anxious secrecy they took it home,
      And then the prize was all for Isabel:

She calm'd its wild hair with a golden comb,
　　And all around each eye's sepulchral cell
405 Pointed each fringed lash; the smeared loam
　　With tears, as chilly as a dripping well,
She drench'd away:—and still she comb'd, and kept
Sighing all day—and still she kiss'd, and wept.

52

Then in a silken scarf,—sweet with the dews
410 　　Of precious flowers pluck'd in Araby,
And divine liquids come with odorous ooze
　　Through the cold serpent-pipe refreshfully,—
She wrapp'd it up; and for its tomb did choose
　　A garden-pot, wherein she laid it by,
415 And cover'd it with mould, and o'er it set
Sweet basil, which her tears kept ever wet.

53

And she forgot the stars, the moon, and sun,
　　And she forgot the blue above the trees,
And she forgot the dells where waters run,
420 　　And she forgot the chilly autumn breeze;
She had no knowledge when the day was done,
　　And the new morn she saw not: but in peace
Hung over her sweet basil evermore,
And moisten'd it with tears unto the core.

54

425 And so she ever fed it with thin tears,
　　Whence thick, and green, and beautiful it grew,
So that it smelt more balmy than its peers
　　Of basil-tufts in Florence; for it drew
Nurture besides, and life, from human fears,
430 　　From the fast mouldering head there shut from view:
So that the jewel, safely casketed,
Came forth, and in perfumed leafits spread.

55

O Melancholy, linger here awhile!
　　O Music, Music, breathe despondingly!
435 O Echo, Echo, from some sombre isle,
　　Unknown, Lethean, sigh to us—O sigh!

Spirits in grief, lift up your heads, and smile;
   Lift up your heads, sweet Spirits, heavily,
And make a pale light in your cypress glooms,
440   Tinting with silver wan your marble tombs.

56

Moan hither, all ye syllables of woe,
   From the deep throat of sad Melpomene!
Through bronzed lyre in tragic order go,
   And touch the strings into a mystery;
445   Sound mournfully upon the winds and low;
   For simple Isabel is soon to be
Among the dead: She withers, like a palm
Cut by an Indian for its juicy balm.

57

O leave the palm to wither by itself;
450   Let not quick Winter chill its dying hour!—
It may not be—those Baälites of pelf,
   Her brethren, noted the continual shower
From her dead eyes; and many a curious elf,
   Among her kindred, wonder'd that such dower
455   Of youth and beauty should be thrown aside
By one mark'd out to be a noble's bride.

58

And, furthermore, her brethren wonder'd much
   Why she sat drooping by the basil green,
And why it flourish'd, as by magic touch;
460   Greatly they wonder'd what the thing might mean:
They could not surely give belief, that such
   A very nothing would have power to wean
Her from her own fair youth, and pleasures gay,
And even remembrance of her love's delay.

59

465   Therefore they watch'd a time when they might sift
   This hidden whim; and long they watch'd in vain;
For seldom did she go to chapel-shrift,
   And seldom felt she any hunger-pain;
And when she left, she hurried back, as swift
470   As bird on wing to breast its eggs again;

And, patient as a hen-bird, sat her there
Beside her basil, weeping through her hair.

60

Yet they contriv'd to steal the basil-pot,
    And to examine it in secret place:
475   The thing was vile with green and livid spot,
    And yet they knew it was Lorenzo's face:
The guerdon of their murder they had got,
    And so left Florence in a moment's space,
Never to turn again.—Away they went,
480   With blood upon their heads, to banishment.

61

O Melancholy, turn thine eyes away!
    O Music, Music, breathe despondingly!
O Echo, Echo, on some other day,
    From isles Lethean, sigh to us—O sigh!
485   Spirits of grief, sing not your "Well-a-way!"
    For Isabel, sweet Isabel, will die;
Will die a death too lone and incomplete,
Now they have ta'en away her basil sweet.

62

Piteous she look'd on dead and senseless things,
490   Asking for her lost basil amorously;
And with melodious chuckle in the strings
    Of her lorn voice, she oftentimes would cry
After the pilgrim in his wanderings,
    To ask him where her basil was; and why
495   'Twas hid from her: "For cruel 'tis," said she,
"To steal my basil-pot away from me."

63

And so she pined, and so she died forlorn,
    Imploring for her basil to the last.
No heart was there in Florence but did mourn
500   In pity of her love, so overcast.
And a sad ditty of this story born
    From mouth to mouth through all the country pass'd:
Still is the burthen sung—"O cruelty,
To steal my basil-pot away from me!"

Mother of Hermes! and still youthful Maia

Mother of Hermes! and still youthful Maia!
    May I sing to thee
As thou wast hymned on the shores of Baiæ?
    Or may I woo thee
5   In earlier Sicilian? or thy smiles
Seek, as they once were sought, in Grecian isles,
By bards who died content in pleasant sward,
    Leaving great verse unto a little clan?
O give me their old vigour, and unheard,
10   Save of the quiet primrose, and the span
    Of heaven, and few ears
Rounded by thee, my song should die away,
    Content as theirs,
Rich in the simple worship of a day.

To Homer

Standing aloof in giant ignorance,
    Of thee I hear and of the Cyclades,
As one who sits ashore and longs perchance
    To visit dolphin-coral in deep seas.
5   So wast thou blind;—but then the veil was rent,
    For Jove uncurtain'd heaven to let thee live,
And Neptune made for thee a spumy tent,
    And Pan made sing for thee his forest-hive;
Aye on the shores of darkness there is light,
10   And precipices show untrodden green,
There is a budding morrow in midnight,
    There is a triple sight in blindness keen;
Such seeing hadst thou, as it once befel
To Dian, Queen of Earth, and Heaven, and Hell.

Give me your patience, sister, while I frame

Give me your patience, sister, while I frame
Exact in capitals your golden name:
Or sue the fair Apollo and he will

Rouse from his heavy slumber and instill
5   Great love in me for thee and Poesy.
Imagine not that greatest mastery
And kingdom over all the realms of verse
Nears more to heaven in aught than when we nurse
And surety give to love and brotherhood.

10   Anthropophagi in Othello's mood,
Ulysses stormed, and his enchanted belt
Glow with the muse, but they are never felt
Unbosom'd so and so eternal made,
Such tender incense in their laurel shade,
15   To all the regent sisters of the Nine,
As this poor offering to you, sister mine.

Kind sister! aye, this third name says you are;
Enchanted has it been the Lord knows where.
And may it taste to you like good old wine,
20   Take you to real happiness and give
Sons, daughters, and a home like honied hive.

Sweet, sweet is the greeting of eyes

Sweet, sweet is the greeting of eyes,
And sweet is the voice in its greeting,
When adieux have grown old and goodbyes
Fade away where old time is retreating.

5   Warm the nerve of a welcoming hand,
And earnest a kiss on the brow,
When we meet over sea and o'er land
Where furrows are new to the plough.

On Visiting the Tomb of Burns

The town, the churchyard, and the setting sun,
  The clouds, the trees, the rounded hills all seem,
    Though beautiful, cold—strange—as in a dream

I dreamed long ago. Now new begun,
5   The short-lived, paly summer is but won
From winter's ague, for one hour's gleam;
Though saphire warm, their stars do never beam;
All is cold beauty; pain is never done
For who has mind to relish, Minos-wise,
10   The real of beauty, free from that dead hue
Sickly imagination and sick pride
Cast wan upon it! Burns! with honour due
I have oft honoured thee. Great shadow, hide
Thy face—I sin against thy native skies.

Old Meg she was a gipsey

Old Meg she was a gipsey,
And liv'd upon the moors;
Her bed it was the brown heath turf,
And her house was out of doors.

5   Her apples were swart blackberries,
Her currants pods o' broom,
Her wine was dew o' the wild white rose,
Her book a churchyard tomb.

Her brothers were the craggy hills,
10   Her sisters larchen trees—
Alone with her great family
She liv'd as she did please.

No breakfast had she many a morn,
No dinner many a noon,
15   And 'stead of supper she would stare
Full hard against the moon.

But every morn of woodbine fresh
She made her garlanding,
And every night the dark glen yew
20   She wove and she would sing.

And with her fingers old and brown
She plaited mats o' rushes,

And gave them to the cottagers
  She met among the bushes.

25 Old Meg was brave as Margaret Queen
  And tall as Amazon:
An old red blanket cloak she wore;
  A chip hat had she on.
God rest her aged bones somewhere—
30 She died full long agone!

There was a naughty boy

There was a naughty boy
  A naughty boy was he
He would not stop at home
  He could not quiet be—
5   He took
    In his knapsack
    A book
    Full of vowels
    And a shirt
10   With some towels—
    A slight cap
    For night cap—
    A hair brush
    Comb ditto
15   New stockings
    For old ones
    Would split O!
    This knapsack
    Tight at 's back
20   He rivetted close
    And follow'd his nose
    To the north
    To the north
    And follow'd his nose
25   To the north—

There was a naughty boy
  And a naughty boy was he

For nothing would he do
But scribble poetry—
30   He took
An inkstand
In his hand
And a pen
Big as ten
35   In the other
And away
In a pother
He ran
To the mountains
40   And fountains
And ghostes
And postes
And witches
And ditches
45   And wrote
In his coat
When the weather
Was cool
Fear of gout
50   And without
When the weather
Was warm—
Och the charm
When we choose
55   To follow one's nose
To the north
To the north
To follow one's nose to the north!

There was a naughty boy
60   And a naughty boy was he
He kept little fishes
In washing tubs three
In spite
Of the might
65   Of the maid
Nor afraid
Of his granny-good—
He often would
Hurly burly

70   Get up early
      And go
      By hook or crook
      To the brook
      And bring home
75   Miller's thumb
      Tittlebat
      Not over fat
      Minnows small
      As the stall
80   Of a glove
      Not above
      The size
      Of a nice
      Little baby's
85   Little finger—
      O he made
      'Twas his trade
      Of fish a pretty kettle
      A kettle—a kettle
90   Of fish a pretty kettle
      A kettle!

      There was a naughty boy
        And a naughty boy was he
      He ran away to Scotland
95   The people for to see—
      There he found
      That the ground
      Was as hard
      That a yard
100   Was as long,
      That a song
      Was as merry,
      That a cherry
      Was as red—
105   That lead
      Was as weighty
      That fourscore
      Was as eighty
      That a door
110   Was as wooden
      As in England—

So he stood in
His shoes
And he wonder'd
115   He wonder'd
He stood in his
Shoes and he wonder'd—

Ah! ken ye what I met the day

Ah! ken ye what I met the day
    Out owre the mountains,
A coming down by craggis grey
    An' mossie fountains?
5   Ah goud hair'd Marie, yeve I pray
    Ane minute's guessing—
For that I met upon the way
    Is past expressing.
As I stood where a rocky brig
10   A torrent crosses,
I spied upon a misty rig
    A troup o' horses—
And as they trotted down the glen
    I sped to meet them,
15   To see if I might know the men,
    To stop and greet them.
First Willie on his sleek mare came
    At canting gallop—
His long hair rustled like a flame
20   On board a shallop.
Then came his brother Rab and then
    Young Peggy's mither,
And Peggy too—adown the glen
    They went togither.
25   I saw her wrappit in her hood
    Fra wind and raining—
Her cheek was flush wi' timid blood
    'Twixt growth and waning.
She turn'd her dazed head full oft,
30   For thence her brithers
Came riding with her bridegroom soft
    An' mony ithers.

Young Tam came up an' eyed me quick
   With reddened cheek—
35   Braw Tam was daffed like a chick,
   He coud na speak.
Ah Marie, they are all gane hame
   Through blustring weather,
An' every heart is full on flame
40   An' light as feather.
Ah! Marie, they are all gone hame
   Fra happy wedding,
Whilst I—Ah is it not a shame?
   Sad tears am shedding.

To Ailsa Rock

Hearken, thou craggy ocean pyramid,
   Give answer by thy voice, the sea fowls' screams!
   When were thy shoulders mantled in huge streams?
When from the sun was thy broad forehead hid?
5   How long is't since the mighty power bid
   Thee heave to airy sleep from fathom dreams—
   Sleep in the lap of thunder or sunbeams,
Or when grey clouds are thy cold coverlid?
Thou answer'st not, for thou art dead asleep;
10   Thy life is but two dead eternities,
The last in air, the former in the deep—
   First with the whales, last with the eagle skies;
Drown'd wast thou till an earthquake made thee steep—
   Another cannot wake thy giant size!

This mortal body of a thousand days

This mortal body of a thousand days
   Now fills, O Burns, a space in thine own room,
Where thou didst dream alone on budded bays,
   Happy and thoughtless of thy day of doom!
5   My pulse is warm with thine old barley-bree,
   My head is light with pledging a great soul,
My eyes are wandering, and I cannot see,
   Fancy is dead and drunken at its goal;

Yet can I stamp my foot upon thy floor,
10   Yet can I ope thy window-sash to find
The meadow thou hast tramped o'er and o'er,—
    Yet can I think of thee till thought is blind,—
Yet can I gulp a bumper to thy name,—
O smile among the shades, for this is fame!

All gentle folks who owe a grudge

All gentle folks who owe a grudge
    To any living thing,
Open your ears and stay your trudge
    Whilst I in dudgeon sing.

5   The gadfly he hath stung me sore—
    O may he ne'er sting you!
But we have many a horrid bore
    He may sting black and blue.

Has any here an old grey mare
10   With three legs all her store?
O put it to her buttocks bare
    And straight she'll run on four.

Has any here a lawyer suit
    Of 1743?
15 Take lawyer's nose and put it to't
    And you the end will see.

Is there a man in Parliament
    Dumfounder'd in his speech?
O let his neighbour make a rent
20   And put one in his breech.

O Lowther, how much better thou
    Hadst figur'd t' other day,
When to the folks thou mad'st a bow
    And hadst no more to say,

25 If lucky gadfly had but ta'en
    His seat upon thine a—e,

And put thee to a little pain
  To save thee from a worse.

Better than Southey it had been,
30   Better than Mr. D——,
Better than Wordsworth too, I ween,
  Better than Mr. V——.

Forgive me pray, good people all,
  For deviating so;
35 In spirit sure I had a call—
  And now I on will go.

Has any here a daughter fair
  Too fond of reading novels,
Too apt to fall in love with care
40   And charming Mister Lovels?

O put a gadfly to that thing
  She keeps so white and pert—
I mean the finger for the ring—
  And it will breed a wert.

45 Has any here a pious spouse
  Who seven times a day
Scolds as King David pray'd, to chouse
  And have her holy way?

O let a gadfly's little sting
50   Persuade her sacred tongue
That noises are a common thing
  But that her bell has rung.

And as this is the summum bo-
  Num of all conquering,
55 I leave withouten wordes mo
  The gadfly's little sting.

Of late two dainties were before me plac'd

Of late two dainties were before me plac'd,
  Sweet, holy, pure, sacred, and innocent,

From the ninth sphere to me benignly sent
That gods might know my own particular taste.
5   First the soft bag-pipe mourn'd with zealous haste;
   The Stranger next with head on bosom bent
   Sigh'd; rueful again the piteous bag-pipe went;
Again the Stranger sighings fresh did waste.
O bag-pipe, thou didst steal my heart away;
10   O Stranger, thou my nerves from pipe didst charm;
   O bag-pipe, thou didst reassert thy sway;
   Again thou Stranger gav'st me fresh alarm—
Alas! I could not choose. Ah! my poor heart,
Mumchance art thou with both obliged to part.

There is a joy in footing slow across a silent plain

There is a joy in footing slow across a silent plain,
Where patriot battle has been fought, when glory had the
   gain;
There is a pleasure on the heath where Druids old have been,
Where mantles grey have rustled by and swept the nettles
   green:
5   There is a joy in every spot made known by times of old,
New to the feet, although the tale a hundred times be told:
There is a deeper joy than all, more solemn in the heart,
More parching to the tongue than all, of more divine a smart,
When weary feet forget themselves upon a pleasant turf,
10   Upon hot sand, or flinty road, or sea shore iron scurf,
Toward the castle or the cot where long ago was born
One who was great through mortal days and died of fame
   unshorn.
Light hether-bells may tremble then, but they are far away;
Woodlark may sing from sandy fern,—the sun may hear his
   lay;
15   Runnels may kiss the grass on shelves and shallows clear,
But their low voices are not heard, though come on travels
   drear;
Blood-red the sun may set behind black mountain peaks;
Blue tides may sluice and drench their time in caves and
   weedy creeks;
Eagles may seem to sleep wing-wide upon the air;
20   Ring doves may fly convuls'd across to some high cedar'd lair;
But the forgotten eye is still fast wedded to the ground—

As palmer's that with weariness mid-desert shrine hath found.
At such a time the soul's a child, in childhood is the brain;
Forgotten is the worldly heart—alone, it beats in vain.
25   Aye, if a madman could have leave to pass a healthful day,
To tell his forehead's swoon and faint when first began decay,
He might make tremble many a man whose spirit had gone
         forth
To find a bard's low cradle place about the silent north.
Scanty the hour and few the steps beyond the bourn of care,
30   Beyond the sweet and bitter world—beyond it unaware;
Scanty the hour and few the steps, because a longer stay
Would bar return and make a man forget his mortal way.
O horrible! to lose the sight of well remember'd face,
Of brother's eyes, of sister's brow, constant to every place;
35   Filling the air, as on we move, with portraiture intense,
More warm than those heroic tints that fill a painter's sense,
When shapes of old come striding by and visages of old,
Locks shining black, hair scanty grey, and passions manifold.
No, no, that horror cannot be—for at the cable's length
40   Man feels the gentle anchor pull and gladdens in its strength.
One hour, half ideot, he stands by mossy waterfall,
But in the very next he reads his soul's memorial:
He reads it on the mountain's height, where chance he may sit
         down
Upon rough marble diadem, that hill's eternal crown.
45   Yet be the anchor e'er so fast, room is there for a prayer
That man may never lose his mind on mountains bleak and
         bare;
That he may stray league after league some great birthplace
         to find,
And keep his vision clear from speck, his inward sight un-
         blind.

Not Aladdin magian

Not Aladdin magian
Ever such a work began;
Not the Wizard of the Dee
Ever such a dream could see;
5   Not St. John in Patmos' isle,
In the passion of his toil,
When he saw the churches seven,

Golden aisled, built up in heaven,
Gazed at such a rugged wonder.
10   As I stood its roofing under,
Lo! I saw one sleeping there
On the marble cold and bare,
While the surges washed his feet
And his garments white did beat
15   Drench'd about the sombre rocks;
On his neck his well-grown locks,
Lifted dry above the main,
Were upon the curl again.
"What is this and what art thou?"
20   Whisper'd I and touch'd his brow.
"What art thou and what is this?"
Whisper'd I and strove to kiss
The spirit's hand to wake his eyes.
Up he started in a trice.
25   "I am Lycidas," said he,
"Fam'd in funeral minstrelsy.
This was architected thus
By the great Oceanus;
Here his mighty waters play
30   Hollow organs all the day;
Here by turns his dolphins all,
Finny palmers great and small,
Come to pay devotion due—
Each a mouth of pearls must strew.
35   Many a mortal of these days
Dares to pass our sacred ways,
Dares to touch audaciously
This cathedral of the sea.
I have been the pontif priest
40   Where the waters never rest,
Where a fledgy sea bird choir
Soars for ever; holy fire
I have hid from mortal man;
Proteus is my sacristan.
45   But the stupid eye of mortal
Hath pass'd beyond the rocky portal;
So for ever will I leave
Such a taint, and soon unweave
All the magic of the place.
50   'Tis now free to stupid face,

To cutters and to fashion boats,
To cravats and to petticoats.
The great sea shall war it down,
For its fame shall not be blown
55   At every farthing quadrille dance."
So saying with a spirit's glance
He dived—

Read me a lesson, Muse, and speak it loud

Read me a lesson, Muse, and speak it loud
   Upon the top of Nevis, blind in mist!
I look into the chasms, and a shroud
   Vaprous doth hide them; just so much I wist
5   Mankind do know of hell: I look o'erhead,
   And there is sullen mist; even so much
Mankind can tell of heaven: mist is spread
   Before the earth beneath me; even such,
Even so vague is man's sight of himself.
10   Here are the craggy stones beneath my feet;
Thus much I know, that, a poor witless elf,
   I tread on them; that all my eye doth meet
Is mist and crag—not only on this height,
But in the world of thought and mental might.

Upon my life, Sir Nevis, I am piqu'd

MRS. C——

Upon my life, Sir Nevis, I am piqu'd
That I have so far panted, tugg'd, and reek'd
To do an honor to your old bald pate
And now am sitting on you just to bate,
5   Without your paying me one compliment.
Alas, 'tis so with all, when our intent
Is plain, and in the eye of all mankind
We fair ones show a preference, too blind!
You gentlemen immediately turn tail—
10   O let me then my hapless fate bewail!
Ungrateful baldpate, have I not disdain'd

The pleasant valleys—have I not, mad brain'd,
Deserted all my pickles and preserves,
My china closet too—with wretched nerves
15   To boot—say, wretched ingrate, have I not
Left my soft cushion chair and caudle pot?
'Tis true I had no corns—no! thank the fates,
My shoemaker was always Mr. Bates.
And if not Mr. Bates, why I'm not old!
20   Still dumb, ungrateful Nevis—still so cold!

(Here the lady took some more whiskey and was putting even
more to her lips when she dashed it to the ground, for the
mountain began to grumble; which continued for a few minutes
before he thus began,)

BEN NEVIS

What whining bit of tongue and mouth thus dares
Disturb my slumber of a thousand years?
Even so long my sleep has been secure,
And to be so awaked I'll not endure.
25   Oh pain—for since the eagle's earliest scream
I've had a damn'd confounded ugly dream,
A nightmare sure—What, madam, was it you?
It cannot be! My old eyes are not true!
Red-Crag,* my spectacles! Now let me see!
30   Good heavens, lady, how the gemini
Did you get here? O I shall split my sides!
I shall earthquake——

MRS. C——

Sweet Nevis, do not quake, for though I love
Your honest countenance all things above,
35   Truly I should not like to be convey'd
So far into your bosom—gentle maid
Loves not too rough a treatment, gentle sir;
Pray thee be calm and do not quake nor stir,
No, not a stone, or I shall go in fits—

* A domestic of Ben's.

BEN NEVIS

40   I must—I shall—I meet not such tit bits,
I meet not such sweet creatures every day.
By my old night cap, night cap night and day,
I must have one sweet buss—I must and shall!
Red-Crag!—What, madam, can you then repent
45   Of all the toil and vigour you have spent
To see Ben Nevis and to touch his nose?
Red-Crag, I say! O I must have you close!
Red-Crag, there lies beneath my farthest toe
A vein of sulphur—go, dear Red-Crag, go—
50   And rub your flinty back against it—budge!
Dear madam, I must kiss you, faith I must!
I must embrace you with my dearest gust!
Blockhead,* d'ye hear—Blockhead, I'll make her feel.
There lies beneath my east leg's northern heel
55   A cave of young earth dragons—well, my boy,
Go thither quick and so complete my joy.
Take you a bundle of the largest pines,
And where the sun on fiercest phosphor shines
Fire them and ram them in the dragons' nest;
60   Then will the dragons fry and fizz their best,
Until ten thousand now no bigger than
Poor alligators, poor things of one span,
Will each one swell to twice ten times the size
Of northern whale; then for the tender prize—
65   The moment then—for then will Red-Crag rub
His flinty back, and I shall kiss and snub
And press my dainty morsel to my breast.
Blockhead, make haste!

                              O Muses, weep the rest—
The lady fainted and he thought her dead,
70   So pulled the clouds again about his head
And went to sleep again. Soon she was rous'd
By her affrighted servants. Next day, hous'd
Safe on the lowly ground, she bless'd her fate
That fainting fit was not delayed too late.

* Another domestic of Ben's.

On Some Skulls in Beauley Abbey, near Inverness

> "I shed no tears;
> Deep thought, or awful vision, I had none;
> By thousand petty fancies I was crossed."
> >   Wordsworth

> "And mock'd the dead bones that lay scatter'd by."
> >   Shakspeare

1

In silent barren synod met
Within these roofless walls, where yet
The shafted arch and carved fret
    Cling to the ruin,
5   The brethren's skulls mourn, dewy wet,
    Their creed's undoing.

2

The mitred ones of Nice and Trent
Were not so tongue-tied,—no, they went
Hot to their Councils, scarce content
10   With orthodoxy;
But ye, poor tongueless things, were meant
    To speak by proxy.

3

Your chronicles no more exist,
Since Knox, the revolutionist,
15   Destroy'd the work of every fist
    That scrawl'd black letter;
Well! I'm a craniologist,
    And may do better.

4

This skull-cap wore the cowl from sloth,
20   Or discontent, perhaps from both;
And yet one day, against his oath,
    He tried escaping,
For men, though idle, may be loth
    To live on gaping.

5

25 A toper this! he plied his glass
More strictly than he said the mass,
And lov'd to see a tempting lass
      Come to confession,
Letting her absolution pass
30   O'er fresh transgression.

6

This crawl'd through life in feebleness,
Boasting he never knew excess,
Cursing those crimes he scarce could guess,
      Or feel but faintly,
35 With prayers that heaven would cease to bless
      Men so unsaintly.

7

Here's a true churchman! he'd affect
Much charity, and ne'er neglect
To pray for mercy on th' elect,
40   But thought no evil
In sending heathen, Turk, and sect
      All to the devil!

8

Poor skull, thy fingers set ablaze,
With silver saint in golden rays,
45 The holy missal; thou didst craze
      'Mid bead and spangle,
While others pass'd their idle days
      In coil and wrangle.

9

Long time this sconce a helmet wore,
50 But sickness smites the conscience sore;
He broke his sword, and hither bore
      His gear and plunder,
Took to the cowl,—then rav'd and swore
      At his damn'd blunder!

10

55   This lily colour'd skull, with all
The teeth complete, so white and small,
Belong'd to one whose early pall
    A lover shaded;
He died ere superstition's gall
60   His heart invaded.

11

Ha! here is "undivulged crime"!
Despair forbad his soul to climb
Beyond this world, this mortal time
    Of fever'd sadness,
65   Until their monkish pantomime
        Dazzled his madness!

12

A younger brother this! a man
Aspiring as a Tartar khan,
But, curb'd and baffled, he began
70   The trade of frightening;
It smack'd of power!—and here he ran
    To deal heaven's lightning.

13

This ideot-skull belong'd to one,
A buried miser's only son,
75   Who, penitent ere he'd begun
    To taste of pleasure,
And hoping heaven's dread wrath to shun,
    Gave hell his treasure.

14

Here is the forehead of an ape,
80   A robber's mark,—and near the nape
That bone, fie on't, bears just the shape
    Of carnal passion;
Ah! he was one for theft and rape,
    In monkish fashion!

15

85   This was the porter!—he could sing,
    Or dance, or play, do any thing,
    And what the friars bade him bring,
        They ne'er were balk'd of;
    Matters not worth remembering,
90   And seldom talk'd of.

16

    Enough! why need I further pore?
    This corner holds at least a score,
    And yonder twice as many more
        Of reverend brothers;
95   'Tis the same story o'er and o'er,—
        They're like the others!

Nature withheld Cassandra in the skies

Nature withheld Cassandra in the skies
    For meet adornment a full thousand years;
She took their cream of beauty, fairest dyes,
    And shaped and tinted her above all peers.
5   Love meanwhile held her dearly with his wings,
    And underneath their shadow charm'd her eyes
To such a richness, that the cloudy kings
    Of high Olympus utter'd slavish sighs.
When I beheld her on the earth descend,
10   My heart began to burn—and only pains,
They were my pleasures, they my sad life's end;
    Love pour'd her beauty into my warm veins.

Fragment of Castle-builder

CASTLE-BUILDER

*   *   *   *   *   *   *

In short, convince you that however wise
You may have grown from convent libraries,
I have, by many yards at least, been carding
A longer skein of wit in Convent Garden.

BERNADINE

5   A very Eden that same place must be!
Pray what demesne? Whose lordship's legacy?
What, have you convents in that Gothic isle?
Pray pardon me, I cannot help but smile—

*   *   *   *   *   *   *

CASTLE-BUILDER

Sir, Convent Garden is a monstrous beast;
10   From morning, four o'clock, to twelve at noon,
It swallows cabbages without a spoon,
And then, from twelve till two, this Eden made is
A promenade for cooks and ancient ladies;
And then for supper, 'stead of soup and poaches,
15   It swallows chairmen, damns, and hackney coaches.
In short, sir, 'tis a very place for monks,
For it containeth twenty thousand punks,
Which any man may number for his sport,
By following fat elbows up a court.

*   *   *   *   *   *   *

20   In such like nonsense would I pass an hour
With random friar, or rake upon his tour,
Or one of few of that imperial host
Who came unmaimed from the Russian frost.
To-night I'll have my friar,—let me think
25   About my room,—I'll have it in the pink;
It should be rich and sombre, and the moon,
Just in its mid-life in the midst of June,
Should look through four large windows, and display
Clear, but for golden fishes in the way,
30   Their glassy diamonding on Turkish floor;
The tapers keep aside an hour and more,
To see what else the moon alone can shew;
While the night breeze doth softly let us know
My terrace is well bowered with oranges.
35   Upon the floor the dullest spirit sees
A guitar-ribband—and a lady's glove
Beside a crumple-leaved tale of love;
A tambour frame, with Venus sleeping there,
All finish'd but some ringlets of her hair;

40   A viol, bow strings torn, cross-wise upon
      A glorious folio of Anacreon;
      A skull upon a mat of roses lying,
      Ink'd purple with a song concerning dying;
      An hour glass on the turn, amid the trails
45   Of passion-flower;—just in time there sails
      A cloud across the moon,—the lights bring in!
      And see what more my phantasy can win.
      It is a gorgeous room, but somewhat sad;
      The draperies are so as though they had
50   Been made for Cleopatra's winding sheet;
      And opposite the stedfast eye doth meet
      A spacious looking-glass, upon whose face,
      In letters raven-sombre, you may trace
      Old "Mene, Mene, Tekel, Upharsin."
55   Greek busts and statuary have ever been
      Held by the finest spirits fitter far
      Than vase grotesque and Siamesian jar;
      Therefore 'tis sure a want of Attic taste,
      That I should rather love a Gothic waste
60   Of eye-sight on cinque coloured potter's clay
      Than on the marble fairness of old Greece.
      My table coverlets of Jason's fleece
      And black Numidian sheep wool should be wrought,
      Gold, black, and heavy, from the lama brought.
65   My ebon sofa should delicious be
      With down from Leda's cygnet progeny:
      My pictures all Salvator's, save a few
      Of Titian's portraiture, and one, though new,
      Of Haydon's in its fresh magnificence.
70   My wine—O good! 'tis here at my desire,
      And I must sit to supper with my friar.

                    *   *   *   *   *   *   *

      And what is Love?—It is a doll dress'd up

      And what is Love?—It is a doll dress'd up
      For idleness to cosset, nurse, and dandle;
      A thing of soft misnomers, so divine
      That silly youth doth think to make itself
5   Divine by loving, and so goes on
      Yawning and doating a whole summer long,

Till Miss's comb is made a pearl tiara,
And common Wellingtons turn Romeo boots;
Till Cleopatra lives at Number Seven,
10   And Anthony resides in Brunswick Square.
Fools! if some passions high have warm'd the world,
If queens and soldiers have play'd high for hearts,
It is no reason why such agonies
Should be more common than the growth of weeds.
15   Fools! make me whole again that weighty pearl
The Queen of Egypt melted, and I'll say
That ye may love in spite of beaver hats.

’Tis the *“witching time of night”*

'Tis the "witching time of night"—
Orbed is the moon and bright,
And the stars they glisten, glisten,
Seeming with bright eyes to listen.
5   For what listen they?
For a song and for a charm—
See they glisten in alarm,
And the moon is waxing warm
To hear what I shall say.
10   Moon, keep wide thy golden ears;
Hearken, stars, and hearken, spheres;
Hearken, thou eternal sky—
I sing an infant's lullaby,
A pretty lullaby!
15   Listen, listen, listen, listen,
Glisten, glisten, glisten, glisten,
And hear my lullaby!
Though the rushes that will make
Its cradle still are in the lake;
20   Though the linnen then that will be
Its swathe is on the cotton tree;
Though the woollen that will keep
It warm is on the silly sheep;
Listen, stars' light, listen, listen,
25   Glisten, glisten, glisten, glisten,
And hear my lullaby!
Child, I see thee! Child, I've found thee,
Midst of the quiet all around thee!

Child, I see thee! Child, I spy thee,
30   And thy mother sweet is nigh thee!
Child, I know thee! Child no more,
But a Poet *evermore*.
See, see the lyre, the lyre,
In a flame of fire,
35   Upon the little cradle's top
Flaring, flaring, flaring,
Past the eyesight's bearing—
Awake it from its sleep,
And see if it can keep
40   Its eyes upon the blaze.
Amaze, amaze!
It stares, it stares, it stares;
It dares what no one dares;
It lifts its little hand into the flame
45   Unharm'd, and on the strings
Paddles a little tune and sings
With dumb endeavour sweetly!
Bard art thou completely!
Little child
50   O' the western wild,
Bard art thou completely!—
Sweetly, with dumb endeavour,
A Poet now or never!
Little child
55   O' the western wild,
A Poet now or never!

Where's the Poet? Show him! show him

Where's the Poet? Show him! show him!
Muses nine, that I may know him!
'Tis the man who with a man
Is an equal, be he king,
5   Or poorest of the beggar-clan,
Or any other wondrous thing
A man may be 'twixt ape and Plato;
'Tis the man who with a bird,
Wren or eagle, finds his way to
10   All its instincts;—he hath heard
The lion's roaring, and can tell

What his horny throat expresseth;
And to him the tiger's yell
   Comes articulate, and presseth
15 On his ear like mother-tongue;
    *   *   *   *   *   *   *   *

Fancy

Ever let the Fancy roam,
Pleasure never is at home:
At a touch sweet Pleasure melteth,
Like to bubbles when rain pelteth;
5 Then let winged Fancy wander
Through the thought still spread beyond her:
Open wide the mind's cage-door,
She'll dart forth, and cloudward soar.
O sweet Fancy! let her loose;
10 Summer's joys are spoilt by use,
And the enjoying of the spring
Fades as does its blossoming;
Autumn's red-lipp'd fruitage too,
Blushing through the mist and dew,
15 Cloys with tasting: What do then?
Sit thee by the ingle, when
The sear faggot blazes bright,
Spirit of a winter's night;
When the soundless earth is muffled,
20 And the caked snow is shuffled
From the ploughboy's heavy shoon;
When the Night doth meet the Noon
In a dark conspiracy
To banish Even from her sky.
25 Sit thee there, and send abroad,
With a mind self-overaw'd,
Fancy, high-commission'd:—send her!
She has vassals to attend her:
She will bring, in spite of frost,
30 Beauties that the earth hath lost;
She will bring thee, all together,
All delights of summer weather;
All the buds and bells of May,
From dewy sward or thorny spray;

35 All the heaped autumn's wealth,
With a still, mysterious stealth:
She will mix these pleasures up
Like three fit wines in a cup,
And thou shalt quaff it:—thou shalt hear
40 Distant harvest-carols clear;
Rustle of the reaped corn;
Sweet birds antheming the morn:
And, in the same moment—hark!
'Tis the early April lark,
45 Or the rooks, with busy caw,
Foraging for sticks and straw.
Thou shalt, at one glance, behold
The daisy and the marigold;
White-plum'd lilies, and the first
50 Hedge-grown primrose that hath burst;
Shaded hyacinth, alway
Sapphire queen of the mid-May;
And every leaf, and every flower
Pearled with the self-same shower.
55 Thou shalt see the field-mouse peep
Meagre from its celled sleep;
And the snake all winter-thin
Cast on sunny bank its skin;
Freckled nest-eggs thou shalt see
60 Hatching in the hawthorn-tree,
When the hen-bird's wing doth rest
Quiet on her mossy nest;
Then the hurry and alarm
When the bee-hive casts its swarm;
65 Acorns ripe down-pattering,
While the autumn breezes sing.

Oh, sweet Fancy! let her loose;
Every thing is spoilt by use:
Where's the cheek that doth not fade,
70 Too much gaz'd at? Where's the maid
Whose lip mature is ever new?
Where's the eye, however blue,
Doth not weary? Where's the face
One would meet in every place?
75 Where's the voice, however soft,
One would hear so very oft?

At a touch sweet Pleasure melteth
Like to bubbles when rain pelteth.
Let, then, winged Fancy find
80　Thee a mistress to thy mind:
Dulcet-eyed as Ceres' daughter,
Ere the God of Torment taught her
How to frown and how to chide;
With a waist and with a side
85　White as Hebe's, when her zone
Slipt its golden clasp, and down
Fell her kirtle to her feet,
While she held the goblet sweet,
And Jove grew languid.—Break the mesh
90　Of the Fancy's silken leash;
Quickly break her prison-string
And such joys as these she'll bring.—
Let the winged Fancy roam,
Pleasure never is at home.

Bards of passion and of mirth

Bards of passion and of mirth,
Ye have left your souls on earth!
Have ye souls in heaven too,
Double-lived in regions new?
5　Yes, and those of heaven commune
With the spheres of sun and moon;
With the noise of fountains wond'rous,
And the parle of voices thund'rous;
With the whisper of heaven's trees
10　And one another, in soft ease
Seated on Elysian lawns
Brows'd by none but Dian's fawns;
Underneath large blue-bells tented,
Where the daisies are rose-scented,
15　And the rose herself has got
Perfume which on earth is not;
Where the nightingale doth sing
Not a senseless, tranced thing,
But divine melodious truth;
20　Philosophic numbers smooth;

Tales and golden histories
Of heaven and its mysteries.

Thus ye live on high, and then
On the earth ye live again;
25   And the souls ye left behind you
Teach us, here, the way to find you,
Where your other souls are joying,
Never slumber'd, never cloying.
Here, your earth-born souls still speak
30   To mortals, of their little week;
Of their sorrows and delights;
Of their passions and their spites;
Of their glory and their shame;
What doth strengthen and what maim.
35   Thus ye teach us, every day,
Wisdom, though fled far away.

Bards of passion and of mirth,
Ye have left your souls on earth!
Ye have souls in heaven too,
40   Double-lived in regions new!

Spirit here that reignest

Spirit here that reignest!
Spirit here that painest!
Spirit here that burneth!
Spirit here that mourneth!
5   Spirit! I bow
My forehead low,
Enshaded with thy pinions!
Spirit! I look,
All passion struck,
10   Into thy pale dominions!

Spirit here that laughest!
Spirit here that quaffest!
Spirit here that danceth!
Noble soul that pranceth!
15   Spirit! with thee
I join in the glee,

While nudging the elbow of Momus!
  Spirit! I flush
With a Bacchanal blush,
20   Just fresh from the banquet of Comus!

I had a dove, and the sweet dove died

I had a dove, and the sweet dove died,
  And I have thought it died of grieving;
O what could it grieve for? Its feet were tied
  With a silken thread of my own hand's weaving:
5   Sweet little red feet! why would you die?
    Why would you leave me, sweet bird, why?
You liv'd alone on the forest tree,
Why, pretty thing, could you not live with me?
  I kiss'd you oft, and gave you white pease;
10   Why not live sweetly as in the green trees?

Hush, hush, tread softly, hush, hush, my dear

1

Hush, hush, tread softly, hush, hush, my dear,
  All the house is asleep, but we know very well
That the jealous, the jealous old baldpate may hear,
  Though you've padded his night-cap, O sweet Isabel.
5   Though your feet are more light than a fairy's feet,
    Who dances on bubbles where brooklets meet—
Hush, hush, tread softly, hush, hush, my dear,
For less than a nothing the jealous can hear.

2

No leaf doth tremble, no ripple is there
10   On the river—all's still, and the night's sleepy eye
Closes up, and forgets all its Lethean care,
  Charmed to death by the drone of the humming may fly.
    And the moon, whether prudish or complaisant,
    Hath fled to her bower, well knowing I want
15 No light in the darkness, no torch in the gloom,
But my Isabel's eyes and her lips pulped with bloom.

3

Lift the latch, ah gently! ah tenderly, sweet,
  We are dead if that latchet gives one little chink.
Well done—now those lips and a flowery seat:
20   The old man may sleep, and the planets may wink;
     The shut rose shall dream of our loves and awake
     Full blown, and such warmth for the morning take;
The stockdove shall hatch her soft brace and shall coo,
While I kiss to the melody, aching all through.

Ah! woe is me! poor Silver-wing

Ah! woe is me! poor Silver-wing!
  That I must chaunt thy lady's dirge,
And death to this fair haunt of spring,
  Of melody, and streams of flowery verge,—
5   Poor Silver-wing! Ah! woe is me!
    That I must see
These blossoms snow upon thy lady's pall!
  Go, pretty page, and in her ear
  Whisper that the hour is near!
10   Softly tell her not to fear
Such calm favonian burial!
  Go, pretty page, and soothly tell,—
  The blossoms hang by a melting spell,
    And fall they must, ere a star wink thrice
15   Upon her closed eyes,
That now in vain are weeping their last tears,
  At sweet life leaving, and these arbours green,—
Rich dowry from the spirit of the spheres,—
    Alas! poor queen!

The Eve of St. Agnes

1

St. Agnes' Eve—Ah, bitter chill it was!
The owl, for all his feathers, was a-cold;
The hare limp'd trembling through the frozen grass,
And silent was the flock in woolly fold:
5 Numb were the Beadsman's fingers, while he told
His rosary, and while his frosted breath,
Like pious incense from a censer old,
Seem'd taking flight for heaven, without a death,
Past the sweet Virgin's picture, while his prayer he saith.

2

10 His prayer he saith, this patient, holy man;
Then takes his lamp, and riseth from his knees,
And back returneth, meagre, barefoot, wan,
Along the chapel aisle by slow degrees:
The sculptur'd dead, on each side, seem to freeze,
15 Emprison'd in black, purgatorial rails:
Knights, ladies, praying in dumb orat'ries,
He passeth by; and his weak spirit fails
To think how they may ache in icy hoods and mails.

3

Northward he turneth through a little door,
20 And scarce three steps, ere Music's golden tongue
Flatter'd to tears this aged man and poor;
But no—already had his deathbell rung;
The joys of all his life were said and sung:
His was harsh penance on St. Agnes' Eve:
25 Another way he went, and soon among
Rough ashes sat he for his soul's reprieve,
And all night kept awake, for sinners' sake to grieve.

4

That ancient Beadsman heard the prelude soft;
And so it chanc'd, for many a door was wide,
30 From hurry to and fro. Soon, up aloft,
The silver, snarling trumpets 'gan to chide:
The level chambers, ready with their pride,
Were glowing to receive a thousand guests:

The carved angels, ever eager-eyed,
35   Star'd, where upon their heads the cornice rests,
With hair blown back, and wings put cross-wise on their
        breasts.

5

At length burst in the argent revelry,
With plume, tiara, and all rich array,
Numerous as shadows haunting fairily
40   The brain, new stuff'd, in youth, with triumphs gay
Of old romance. These let us wish away,
And turn, sole-thoughted, to one Lady there,
Whose heart had brooded, all that wintry day,
On love, and wing'd St. Agnes' saintly care,
45   As she had heard old dames full many times declare.

6

They told her how, upon St. Agnes' Eve,
Young virgins might have visions of delight,
And soft adorings from their loves receive
Upon the honey'd middle of the night,
50   If ceremonies due they did aright;
As, supperless to bed they must retire,
And couch supine their beauties, lily white;
Nor look behind, nor sideways, but require
Of heaven with upward eyes for all that they desire.

7

55   Full of this whim was thoughtful Madeline:
The music, yearning like a god in pain,
She scarcely heard: her maiden eyes divine,
Fix'd on the floor, saw many a sweeping train
Pass by—she heeded not at all: in vain
60   Came many a tiptoe, amorous cavalier,
And back retir'd, not cool'd by high disdain;
But she saw not: her heart was otherwhere:
She sigh'd for Agnes' dreams, the sweetest of the year.

8

She danc'd along with vague, regardless eyes,
65   Anxious her lips, her breathing quick and short:
The hallow'd hour was near at hand: she sighs
Amid the timbrels, and the throng'd resort

Of whisperers in anger, or in sport;
'Mid looks of love, defiance, hate, and scorn,
70   Hoodwink'd with faery fancy; all amort,
Save to St. Agnes and her lambs unshorn,
And all the bliss to be before to-morrow morn.

9

So, purposing each moment to retire,
She linger'd still. Meantime, across the moors,
75   Had come young Porphyro, with heart on fire
For Madeline. Beside the portal doors,
Buttress'd from moonlight, stands he, and implores
All saints to give him sight of Madeline,
But for one moment in the tedious hours,
80   That he might gaze and worship all unseen;
Perchance speak, kneel, touch, kiss—in sooth such things have
     been.

10

He ventures in: let no buzz'd whisper tell:
All eyes be muffled, or a hundred swords
Will storm his heart, Love's fev'rous citadel:
85   For him, those chambers held barbarian hordes,
Hyena foemen, and hot-blooded lords,
Whose very dogs would execrations howl
Against his lineage: not one breast affords
Him any mercy, in that mansion foul,
90   Save one old beldame, weak in body and in soul.

11

Ah, happy chance! the aged creature came,
Shuffling along with ivory-headed wand,
To where he stood, hid from the torch's flame,
Behind a broad hall-pillar, far beyond
95   The sound of merriment and chorus bland:
He startled her; but soon she knew his face,
And grasp'd his fingers in her palsied hand,
Saying, "Mercy, Porphyro! hie thee from this place;
They are all here to-night, the whole blood-thirsty race!

12

100   "Get hence! get hence! there's dwarfish Hildebrand;
He had a fever late, and in the fit

He cursed thee and thine, both house and land:
Then there's that old Lord Maurice, not a whit
More tame for his gray hairs—Alas me! flit!
105   Flit like a ghost away."—"Ah, Gossip dear,
We're safe enough; here in this arm-chair sit,
And tell me how"—"Good Saints! not here, not here;
Follow me, child, or else these stones will be thy bier."

13

He follow'd through a lowly arched way,
110   Brushing the cobwebs with his lofty plume,
And as she mutter'd "Well-a—well-a-day!"
He found him in a little moonlight room,
Pale, lattic'd, chill, and silent as a tomb.
"Now tell me where is Madeline," said he,
115   "O tell me, Angela, by the holy loom
Which none but secret sisterhood may see,
When they St. Agnes' wool are weaving piously."

14

"St. Agnes! Ah! it is St. Agnes' Eve—
Yet men will murder upon holy days:
120   Thou must hold water in a witch's sieve,
And be liege-lord of all the Elves and Fays,
To venture so: it fills me with amaze
To see thee, Porphyro!—St. Agnes' Eve!
God's help! my lady fair the conjuror plays
125   This very night: good angels her deceive!
But let me laugh awhile, I've mickle time to grieve."

15

Feebly she laugheth in the languid moon,
While Porphyro upon her face doth look,
Like puzzled urchin on an aged crone
130   Who keepeth clos'd a wond'rous riddle-book,
As spectacled she sits in chimney nook.
But soon his eyes grew brilliant, when she told
His lady's purpose; and he scarce could brook
Tears, at the thought of those enchantments cold,
135   And Madeline asleep in lap of legends old.

16

Sudden a thought came like a full-blown rose,
Flushing his brow, and in his pained heart
Made purple riot: then doth he propose
A stratagem, that makes the beldame start:
140   "A cruel man and impious thou art:
Sweet lady, let her pray, and sleep, and dream
Alone with her good angels, far apart
From wicked men like thee. Go, go!—I deem
Thou canst not surely be the same that thou didst seem."

17

145   "I will not harm her, by all saints I swear,"
Quoth Porphyro: "O may I ne'er find grace
When my weak voice shall whisper its last prayer,
If one of her soft ringlets I displace,
Or look with ruffian passion in her face:
150   Good Angela, believe me by these tears;
Or I will, even in a moment's space,
Awake, with horrid shout, my foemen's ears,
And beard them, though they be more fang'd than wolves
    and bears."

18

"Ah! why wilt thou affright a feeble soul?
155   A poor, weak, palsy-stricken, churchyard thing,
Whose passing-bell may ere the midnight toll;
Whose prayers for thee, each morn and evening,
Were never miss'd."—Thus plaining, doth she bring
A gentler speech from burning Porphyro;
160   So woful, and of such deep sorrowing,
That Angela gives promise she will do
Whatever he shall wish, betide her weal or woe.

19

Which was, to lead him, in close secrecy,
Even to Madeline's chamber, and there hide
165   Him in a closet, of such privacy
That he might see her beauty unespied,
And win perhaps that night a peerless bride,
While legion'd fairies pac'd the coverlet,
And pale enchantment held her sleepy-eyed.

170   Never on such a night have lovers met,
       Since Merlin paid his Demon all the monstrous debt.

20

       "It shall be as thou wishest," said the Dame:
       "All cates and dainties shall be stored there
       Quickly on this feast-night: by the tambour frame
175   Her own lute thou wilt see: no time to spare,
       For I am slow and feeble, and scarce dare
       On such a catering trust my dizzy head.
       Wait here, my child, with patience; kneel in prayer
       The while: Ah! thou must needs the lady wed,
180   Or may I never leave my grave among the dead."

21

       So saying, she hobbled off with busy fear.
       The lover's endless minutes slowly pass'd;
       The dame return'd, and whisper'd in his ear
       To follow her; with aged eyes aghast
185   From fright of dim espial. Safe at last,
       Through many a dusky gallery, they gain
       The maiden's chamber, silken, hush'd, and chaste;
       Where Porphyro took covert, pleas'd amain.
   His poor guide hurried back with agues in her brain.

22

190   Her falt'ring hand upon the balustrade,
       Old Angela was feeling for the stair,
       When Madeline, St. Agnes' charmed maid,
       Rose, like a mission'd spirit, unaware:
       With silver taper's light, and pious care,
195   She turn'd, and down the aged gossip led
       To a safe level matting. Now prepare,
       Young Porphyro, for gazing on that bed;
   She comes, she comes again, like ring-dove fray'd and fled.

23

       Out went the taper as she hurried in;
200   Its little smoke, in pallid moonshine, died:
       She clos'd the door, she panted, all akin
       To spirits of the air, and visions wide:
       No uttered syllable, or, woe betide!

But to her heart, her heart was voluble,
205   Paining with eloquence her balmy side;
As though a tongueless nightingale should swell
Her throat in vain, and die, heart-stifled, in her dell.

24

A casement high and triple-arch'd there was,
All garlanded with carven imag'ries
210   Of fruits, and flowers, and bunches of knot-grass,
And diamonded with panes of quaint device,
Innumerable of stains and splendid dyes,
As are the tiger-moth's deep-damask'd wings;
And in the midst, 'mong thousand heraldries,
215   And twilight saints, and dim emblazonings,
A shielded scutcheon blush'd with blood of queens and kings.

25

Full on this casement shone the wintry moon,
And threw warm gules on Madeline's fair breast,
As down she knelt for heaven's grace and boon;
220   Rose-bloom fell on her hands, together prest,
And on her silver cross soft amethyst,
And on her hair a glory, like a saint:
She seem'd a splendid angel, newly drest,
Save wings, for heaven:—Porphyro grew faint:
225   She knelt, so pure a thing, so free from mortal taint.

26

Anon his heart revives: her vespers done,
Of all its wreathed pearls her hair she frees;
Unclasps her warmed jewels one by one;
Loosens her fragrant boddice; by degrees
230   Her rich attire creeps rustling to her knees:
Half-hidden, like a mermaid in sea-weed,
Pensive awhile she dreams awake, and sees,
In fancy, fair St. Agnes in her bed,
But dares not look behind, or all the charm is fled.

27

235   Soon, trembling in her soft and chilly nest,
In sort of wakeful swoon, perplex'd she lay,
Until the poppied warmth of sleep oppress'd

Her soothed limbs, and soul fatigued away;
Flown, like a thought, until the morrow-day;
240   Blissfully haven'd both from joy and pain;
Clasp'd like a missal where swart Paynims pray;
Blinded alike from sunshine and from rain,
As though a rose should shut, and be a bud again.

28

Stol'n to this paradise, and so entranced,
245   Porphyro gazed upon her empty dress,
And listen'd to her breathing, if it chanced
To wake into a slumberous tenderness;
Which when he heard, that minute did he bless,
And breath'd himself: then from the closet crept,
250   Noiseless as fear in a wide wilderness,
And over the hush'd carpet, silent, stept,
And 'tween the curtains peep'd, where, lo!—how fast she
slept.

29

Then by the bed-side, where the faded moon
Made a dim, silver twilight, soft he set
255   A table, and, half anguish'd, threw thereon
A cloth of woven crimson, gold, and jet:—
O for some drowsy Morphean amulet!
The boisterous, midnight, festive clarion,
The kettle-drum, and far-heard clarionet,
260   Affray his ears, though but in dying tone:—
The hall door shuts again, and all the noise is gone.

30

And still she slept an azure-lidded sleep,
In blanched linen, smooth, and lavender'd,
While he from forth the closet brought a heap
265   Of candied apple, quince, and plum, and gourd;
With jellies soother than the creamy curd,
And lucent syrops, tinct with cinnamon;
Manna and dates, in argosy transferr'd
From Fez; and spiced dainties, every one,
270   From silken Samarcand to cedar'd Lebanon.

31

These delicates he heap'd with glowing hand
On golden dishes and in baskets bright

Of wreathed silver: sumptuous they stand
In the retired quiet of the night,
275 Filling the chilly room with perfume light.—
"And now, my love, my seraph fair, awake!
Thou art my heaven, and I thine eremite:
Open thine eyes, for meek St. Agnes' sake,
Or I shall drowse beside thee, so my soul doth ache."

32

280 Thus whispering, his warm, unnerved arm
Sank in her pillow. Shaded was her dream
By the dusk curtains:—'twas a midnight charm
Impossible to melt as iced stream:
The lustrous salvers in the moonlight gleam;
285 Broad golden fringe upon the carpet lies:
It seem'd he never, never could redeem
From such a stedfast spell his lady's eyes;
So mus'd awhile, entoil'd in woofed phantasies.

33

Awakening up, he took her hollow lute,—
290 Tumultuous,—and, in chords that tenderest be,
He play'd an ancient ditty, long since mute,
In Provence call'd, "La belle dame sans mercy":
Close to her ear touching the melody;—
Wherewith disturb'd, she utter'd a soft moan:
295 He ceased—she panted quick—and suddenly
Her blue affrayed eyes wide open shone:
Upon his knees he sank, pale as smooth-sculptured stone.

34

Her eyes were open, but she still beheld,
Now wide awake, the vision of her sleep:
300 There was a painful change, that nigh expell'd
The blisses of her dream so pure and deep:
At which fair Madeline began to weep,
And moan forth witless words with many a sigh;
While still her gaze on Porphyro would keep;
305 Who knelt, with joined hands and piteous eye,
Fearing to move or speak, she look'd so dreamingly.

35

"Ah, Porphyro!" said she, "but even now
Thy voice was at sweet tremble in mine ear,

Made tuneable with every sweetest vow;
310   And those sad eyes were spiritual and clear:
How chang'd thou art! how pallid, chill, and drear!
Give me that voice again, my Porphyro,
Those looks immortal, those complainings dear!
Oh leave me not in this eternal woe,
315   For if thou diest, my love, I know not where to go."

36

Beyond a mortal man impassion'd far
At these voluptuous accents, he arose,
Ethereal, flush'd, and like a throbbing star
Seen mid the sapphire heaven's deep repose;
320   Into her dream he melted, as the rose
Blendeth its odour with the violet,—
Solution sweet: meantime the frost-wind blows
Like Love's alarum pattering the sharp sleet
Against the window-panes; St. Agnes' moon hath set.

37

325   'Tis dark: quick pattereth the flaw-blown sleet:
"This is no dream, my bride, my Madeline!"
'Tis dark: the iced gusts still rave and beat:
"No dream, alas! alas! and woe is mine!
Porphyro will leave me here to fade and pine.—
330   Cruel! what traitor could thee hither bring?
I curse not, for my heart is lost in thine,
Though thou forsakest a deceived thing;—
A dove forlorn and lost with sick unpruned wing."

38

"My Madeline! sweet dreamer! lovely bride!
335   Say, may I be for aye thy vassal blest?
Thy beauty's shield, heart-shap'd and vermeil dyed?
Ah, silver shrine, here will I take my rest
After so many hours of toil and quest,
A famish'd pilgrim,—saved by miracle.
340   Though I have found, I will not rob thy nest
Saving of thy sweet self; if thou think'st well
To trust, fair Madeline, to no rude infidel.

39

"Hark! 'tis an elfin-storm from faery land,
Of haggard seeming, but a boon indeed:

345   Arise—arise! the morning is at hand;—
       The bloated wassaillers will never heed:—
       Let us away, my love, with happy speed;
       There are no ears to hear, or eyes to see,—
       Drown'd all in Rhenish and the sleepy mead:
350   Awake! arise! my love, and fearless be,
For o'er the southern moors I have a home for thee."

40

       She hurried at his words, beset with fears,
       For there were sleeping dragons all around,
       At glaring watch, perhaps, with ready spears—
355   Down the wide stairs a darkling way they found.—
       In all the house was heard no human sound.
       A chain-droop'd lamp was flickering by each door;
       The arras, rich with horseman, hawk, and hound,
       Flutter'd in the besieging wind's uproar;
360   And the long carpets rose along the gusty floor.

41

       They glide, like phantoms, into the wide hall;
       Like phantoms, to the iron porch, they glide;
       Where lay the Porter, in uneasy sprawl,
       With a huge empty flaggon by his side:
365   The wakeful bloodhound rose, and shook his hide,
       But his sagacious eye an inmate owns:
       By one, and one, the bolts full easy slide:—
       The chains lie silent on the footworn stones;—
The key turns, and the door upon its hinges groans.

42

370   And they are gone: ay, ages long ago
       These lovers fled away into the storm.
       That night the Baron dreamt of many a woe,
       And all his warrior-guests, with shade and form
       Of witch, and demon, and large coffin-worm,
375   Were long be-nightmar'd. Angela the old
       Died palsy-twitch'd, with meagre face deform;
       The Beadsman, after thousand aves told,
For aye unsought for slept among his ashes cold.

The Eve of St. Mark

Upon a Sabbath day it fell;
Twice holy was the Sabbath bell,
That call'd the folk to evening prayer.
The city streets were clean and fair
5   From wholesome drench of April rains,
And on the western window panes
The chilly sunset faintly told
Of unmatur'd green vallies cold,
Of the green thorny bloomless hedge,
10   Of rivers new with springtide sedge,
Of primroses by shelter'd rills,
And daisies on the aguish hills.
Twice holy was the Sabbath bell:
The silent streets were crowded well
15   With staid and pious companies,
Warm from their fireside orat'ries,
And moving with demurest air
To even song and vesper prayer.
Each arched porch and entry low
20   Was fill'd with patient folk and slow,
With whispers hush and shuffling feet,
While play'd the organs loud and sweet.

The bells had ceas'd, the prayers begun,
And Bertha had not yet half done
25   A curious volume, patch'd and torn,
That all day long, from earliest morn,
Had taken captive her two eyes
Among its golden broideries;
Perplex'd her with a thousand things—
30   The stars of heaven, and angels' wings,
Martyrs in a fiery blaze,
Azure saints mid silver rays,
Aaron's breastplate, and the seven
Candlesticks John saw in heaven,
35   The winged Lion of St. Mark,
And the Covenantal Ark,
With its many mysteries,
Cherubim and golden mice.

Bertha was a maiden fair
40   Dwelling in the old Minster Square;

From her fireside she could see
Sidelong its rich antiquity,
Far as the bishop's garden wall,
Where sycamores and elm trees tall,
45 Full leav'd, the forest had outstript,
By no sharp north wind ever nipt,
So shelter'd by the mighty pile.
Bertha arose and read awhile,
With forehead 'gainst the window pane;
50 Again she tried, and then again,
Until the dusk eve left her dark
Upon the legend of St. Mark.
From pleated lawn-frill fine and thin
She lifted up her soft warm chin,
55 With aching neck and swimming eyes,
And dazed with saintly imageries.

All was gloom, and silent all,
Save now and then the still footfall
Of one returning townwards late,
60 Past the echoing minster gate.
The clamorous daws, that all the day
Above tree tops and towers play,
Pair by pair had gone to rest,
Each in its ancient belfry nest,
65 Where asleep they fall betimes
To music of the drowsy chimes.

All was silent, all was gloom,
Abroad and in the homely room;
Down she sat, poor cheated soul,
70 And struck a lamp from the dismal coal,
Leaned forward, with bright drooping hair,
And slant book full against the glare.
Her shadow in uneasy guise
Hover'd about, a giant size,
75 On ceiling beam and old oak chair,
The parrot's cage and pannel square,
And the warm angled winter screen,
On which were many monsters seen,
Call'd doves of Siam, Lima mice,
80 And legless birds of paradise,
Macaw, and tender av'davat,
And silken furr'd Angora cat.

Untired she read; her shadow still
Glower'd about as it would fill
85 The room with wildest forms and shades,
As though some ghostly queens of spades
Had come to mock behind her back,
And dance, and ruffle their garments black.
Untir'd she read the legend page
90 Of holy Mark from youth to age;
On land, on seas, in pagan-chains,
Rejoicing for his many pains.
Sometimes the learned eremite,
With golden star, or dagger bright,
95 Referr'd to pious poesies
Written in smallest crow-quill size
Beneath the text; and thus the rhyme
Was parcel'd out from time to time:
——"Als writith he of swevenis
100 Men han beforne they wake in bliss,
Whanne thate hir friendes thinke hem bound
In crimpid shroude farre under grounde;
And how a litling child mote be
A saint er its nativitie,
105 Gif thate the modre (God her blesse)
Kepen in solitarinesse,
And kissen devoute the holy croce.
Of Goddis love and Sathan's force
He writith; and thinges many mo:
110 Of swiche thinges I may not shew;
Bot I must tellen verilie
Somdel of Saintè Cicilie;
And chieflie whate he auctorethe
Of Saintè Markis life and dethe."

115   At length her constant eyelids come
Upon the fervent martyrdom;
Then lastly to his holy shrine,
Exalt amid the tapers' shine
At Venice

Why did I laugh tonight? No voice will tell

Why did I laugh tonight? No voice will tell:
  No god, no demon of severe response,
Deigns to reply from heaven or from hell.
  Then to my human heart I turn at once—
5 Heart! thou and I are here sad and alone;
  Say, wherefore did I laugh? O mortal pain!
O darkness! darkness! ever must I moan,
  To question heaven and hell and heart in vain!
Why did I laugh? I know this being's lease—
10 My fancy to its utmost blisses spreads:
Yet could I on this very midnight cease,
  And the world's gaudy ensigns see in shreds.
Verse, fame, and beauty are intense indeed,
But death intenser—death is life's high meed.

When they were come unto the Faery's court

When they were come unto the Faery's court
They rang—no one at home—all gone to sport
And dance and kiss and love as faeries do,
For faeries be as humans, lovers true.
5 Amid the woods they were, so lone and wild,
Where even the robin feels himself exil'd,
And where the very brooks as if afraid
Hurry along to some less magic shade.
"No one at home!" the fretful Princess cry'd,
10 "And all for nothing such a dreary ride,
And all for nothing my new diamond cross,
No one to see my Persian feathers toss,
No one to see my Ape, my Dwarf, my Fool,
Or how I pace my Otaheitan mule.
15 Ape, Dwarf, and Fool, why stand you gaping there?
Burst the door open, quick—or I declare
I'll switch you soundly and in pieces tear."
The Dwarf began to tremble and the Ape
Star'd at the Fool, the Fool was all agape;
20 The Princess grasp'd her switch, but just in time
The Dwarf with piteous face began to rhyme.
"O mighty Princess, did you ne'er hear tell
What your poor servants know but too, too well?

Know you the three 'great crimes' in faery land?
25   The first, alas! poor Dwarf, I understand—
I made a whipstock of a faery's wand;
The next is snoring in their company;
The next, the last, the direst of the three,
Is making free when they are not at home.
30   I was a prince—a baby prince—my doom
You see: I made a whipstock of a wand;
My top has henceforth slept in faery land.
He was a prince, the Fool, a grown up prince,
But he has never been a king's son since
35   He fell a snoring at a faery ball.
Your poor Ape was a prince, and he, poor thing,
Picklock'd a faery's boudoir—now no king,
But ape. So pray your highness stay awhile;
'Tis sooth indeed, we know it to our sorrow—
40   Persist and *you* may be an ape tomorrow."
While the Dwarf spake the Princess all for spite
Peel'd the brown hazel twig to lilly white,
Clench'd her small teeth, and held her lips apart,
Try'd to look unconcern'd with beating heart.
45   They saw her highness had made up her mind,
A quavering like three reeds before the wind—
And they had had it, but, O happy chance,
The Ape for very fear began to dance,
And grinn'd as all his ugliness did ache.
50   She staid her vixen fingers for his sake,
He was so very ugly: then she took
Her pocket mirror and began to look
First at herself and at him and then
She smil'd at her own beauteous face again.
55   Yet for all this—for all her pretty face—
She took it in her head to see the place.
Women gain little from experience
Either in lovers, husbands, or expence.
The more the beauty, the more fortune too:
60   Beauty before the wide world never knew—
So each Fair reasons—though it oft miscarries.
She thought *her* pretty face would please the faeries.
"My darling Ape, I won't whip you to-day—
Give me the picklock, sirrah, and go play."
65   They all three wept—but counsel was as vain
As crying cup biddy to drops of rain.

Yet lingeringly did the sad Ape forth draw
The picklock from the pocket in his jaw.
The Princess took it and, dismounting straight,
70   Tripp'd in blue silver'd slippers to the gate
And touch'd the wards; the door full courteously
Opened—she enter'd with her servants three.
Again it clos'd and there was nothing seen
But the Mule grasing on the herbage green.

End of Canto xii

Canto the xiii

75   The Mule no sooner saw himself alone
Than he prick'd up his ears and said, "Well done;
At least, unhappy Prince, I may be free—
No more a princess shall side saddle me.
O king of Otaheitè—though a mule,
80   'Aye every inch a king'—though 'Fortune's fool,'
Well done—for by what Mr. Dwarfy said,
I would not give a sixpence for her head."
Even as he spake he trotted in high glee
To the knotty side of an old pollard tree
85   And rubb'd his sides against the mossed bark
Till his girths burst and left him naked stark
Except his bridle—how get rid of that,
Buckled and tied with many a twist and plait?
At last it struck him to pretend to sleep,
90   And then the thievish monkies down would creep
And filch the unpleasant trammels quite away.
No sooner thought of than adown he lay,
Shamm'd a good snore—the monkey-men descended,
And whom they thought to injure they befriended.
95   They hung his bridle on a topmost bough,
And off he went, run, trot, or any how.

As Hermes once took to his feathers light

As Hermes once took to his feathers light,
    When lulled Argus, baffled, swoon'd and slept,
So on a Delphic reed, my idle spright
    So play'd, so charm'd, so conquer'd, so bereft

5   The dragon-world of all its hundred eyes;
            And, seeing it asleep, so fled away—
        Not to pure Ida with its snow-cold skies,
            Nor unto Tempe, where Jove griev'd a day,
        But to that second circle of sad hell,
10   Where in the gust, the whirlwind, and the flaw
        Of rain and hail-stones, lovers need not tell
            Their sorrows. Pale were the sweet lips I saw,
        Pale were the lips I kiss'd, and fair the form
        I floated with, about that melancholy storm.

Character of C. B.

        He was to weet a melancholy carle,
            Thin in the waist, with bushy head of hair,
        As hath the seeded thistle, when in parle
            It holds the zephyr, ere it sendeth fair
5   Its light balloons into the summer air;
        Thereto his beard had not begun to bloom,
            No brush had touch'd his chin or razor sheer;
        No care had touch'd his cheek with mortal doom,
    But new he was and bright as scarf from Persian loom.

10   Ne cared he for wine, or half and half,
            Ne cared he for fish, or flesh, or fowl,
        And sauces held he worthless as the chaff;
            He 'sdeign'd the swine-herd at the wassel bowl,
            Ne with lewd ribbalds sat he cheek by jowl,
15   Ne with sly lemans in the scorner's chair;
        But after water-brooks this pilgrim's soul
            Panted, and all his food was woodland air,
    Though he would ofttimes feed on gillyflowers rare.

        The slang of cities in no wise he knew,
20   Tipping the wink to him was heathen Greek;
        He sipp'd no olden Tom, or ruin blue,
            Or nantz, or cherry brandy, drank full meek
        By many a damsel hoarse and rouge of cheek;
            Nor did he know each aged watchman's beat,
25   Nor in obscured purlieus would he seek
            For curled Jewesses with ancles neat,
    Who as they walk abroad make tinkling with their feet.

Bright star, would I were stedfast as thou art

Bright star, would I were stedfast as thou art—
  Not in lone splendor hung aloft the night,
And watching, with eternal lids apart,
  Like nature's patient, sleepless eremite,
5 The moving waters at their priestlike task
  Of pure ablution round earth's human shores,
Or gazing on the new soft-fallen mask
  Of snow upon the mountains and the moors;
No—yet still stedfast, still unchangeable,
10 Pillow'd upon my fair love's ripening breast,
To feel for ever its soft swell and fall,
  Awake for ever in a sweet unrest,
Still, still to hear her tender-taken breath,
And so live ever—or else swoon to death.

Hyperion:
A Fragment

BOOK I

Deep in the shady sadness of a vale
Far sunken from the healthy breath of morn,
Far from the fiery noon, and eve's one star,
Sat gray-hair'd Saturn, quiet as a stone,
5   Still as the silence round about his lair;
Forest on forest hung above his head
Like cloud on cloud. No stir of air was there,
Not so much life as on a summer's day
Robs not one light seed from the feather'd grass,
10   But where the dead leaf fell, there did it rest.
A stream went voiceless by, still deadened more
By reason of his fallen divinity
Spreading a shade: the Naiad 'mid her reeds
Press'd her cold finger closer to her lips.

15   Along the margin-sand large foot-marks went,
No further than to where his feet had stray'd,
And slept there since. Upon the sodden ground
His old right hand lay nerveless, listless, dead,
Unsceptred; and his realmless eyes were closed;
20   While his bow'd head seem'd list'ning to the Earth,
His ancient mother, for some comfort yet.

It seem'd no force could wake him from his place;
But there came one, who with a kindred hand
Touch'd his wide shoulders, after bending low
25   With reverence, though to one who knew it not.
She was a Goddess of the infant world;
By her in stature the tall Amazon
Had stood a pigmy's height: she would have ta'en
Achilles by the hair and bent his neck;
30   Or with a finger stay'd Ixion's wheel.
Her face was large as that of Memphian sphinx,
Pedestal'd haply in a palace court,
When sages look'd to Egypt for their lore.
But oh! how unlike marble was that face:
35   How beautiful, if sorrow had not made
Sorrow more beautiful than Beauty's self.

There was a listening fear in her regard,
As if calamity had but begun;
As if the vanward clouds of evil days
40 Had spent their malice, and the sullen rear
Was with its stored thunder labouring up.
One hand she press'd upon that aching spot
Where beats the human heart, as if just there,
Though an immortal, she felt cruel pain:
45 The other upon Saturn's bended neck
She laid, and to the level of his ear
Leaning with parted lips, some words she spake
In solemn tenour and deep organ tone:
Some mourning words, which in our feeble tongue
50 Would come in these like accents; O how frail
To that large utterance of the early Gods!
"Saturn, look up!—though wherefore, poor old King?
I have no comfort for thee, no not one:
I cannot say, 'O wherefore sleepest thou?'
55 For heaven is parted from thee, and the earth
Knows thee not, thus afflicted, for a God;
And ocean too, with all its solemn noise,
Has from thy sceptre pass'd; and all the air
Is emptied of thine hoary majesty.
60 Thy thunder, conscious of the new command,
Rumbles reluctant o'er our fallen house;
And thy sharp lightning in unpractised hands
Scorches and burns our once serene domain.
O aching time! O moments big as years!
65 All as ye pass swell out the monstrous truth,
And press it so upon our weary griefs
That unbelief has not a space to breathe.
Saturn, sleep on:—O thoughtless, why did I
Thus violate thy slumbrous solitude?
70 Why should I ope thy melancholy eyes?
Saturn, sleep on! while at thy feet I weep."

    As when, upon a tranced summer-night,
Those green-rob'd senators of mighty woods,
Tall oaks, branch-charmed by the earnest stars,
75 Dream, and so dream all night without a stir,
Save from one gradual solitary gust
Which comes upon the silence, and dies off,
As if the ebbing air had but one wave;

So came these words and went; the while in tears
80   She touch'd her fair large forehead to the ground,
Just where her falling hair might be outspread,
A soft and silken mat for Saturn's feet.
One moon, with alteration slow, had shed
Her silver seasons four upon the night,
85   And still these two were postured motionless,
Like natural sculpture in cathedral cavern;
The frozen God still couchant on the earth,
And the sad Goddess weeping at his feet:
Until at length old Saturn lifted up
90   His faded eyes, and saw his kingdom gone,
And all the gloom and sorrow of the place,
And that fair kneeling Goddess; and then spake,
As with a palsied tongue, and while his beard
Shook horrid with such aspen-malady:
95   "O tender spouse of gold Hyperion,
Thea, I feel thee ere I see thy face;
Look up, and let me see our doom in it;
Look up, and tell me if this feeble shape
Is Saturn's; tell me, if thou hear'st the voice
100   Of Saturn; tell me, if this wrinkling brow,
Naked and bare of its great diadem,
Peers like the front of Saturn. Who had power
To make me desolate? whence came the strength?
How was it nurtur'd to such bursting forth,
105   While Fate seem'd strangled in my nervous grasp?
But it is so; and I am smother'd up,
And buried from all godlike exercise
Of influence benign on planets pale,
Of admonitions to the winds and seas,
110   Of peaceful sway above man's harvesting,
And all those acts which Deity supreme
Doth ease its heart of love in.—I am gone
Away from my own bosom: I have left
My strong identity, my real self,
115   Somewhere between the throne, and where I sit
Here on this spot of earth. Search, Thea, search!
Open thine eyes eterne, and sphere them round
Upon all space: space starr'd, and lorn of light;
Space region'd with life-air; and barren void;
120   Spaces of fire, and all the yawn of hell.—
Search, Thea, search! and tell me, if thou seest

A certain shape or shadow, making way
With wings or chariot fierce to repossess
A heaven he lost erewhile: it must—it must
125   Be of ripe progress—Saturn must be King.
Yes, there must be a golden victory;
There must be Gods thrown down, and trumpets blown
Of triumph calm, and hymns of festival
Upon the gold clouds metropolitan,
130   Voices of soft proclaim, and silver stir
Of strings in hollow shells; and there shall be
Beautiful things made new, for the surprise
Of the sky-children; I will give command:
Thea! Thea! Thea! where is Saturn?"

135   This passion lifted him upon his feet,
And made his hands to struggle in the air,
His Druid locks to shake and ooze with sweat,
His eyes to fever out, his voice to cease.
He stood, and heard not Thea's sobbing deep;
140   A little time, and then again he snatch'd
Utterance thus.—"But cannot I create?
Cannot I form? Cannot I fashion forth
Another world, another universe,
To overbear and crumble this to nought?
145   Where is another Chaos? Where?"—That word
Found way unto Olympus, and made quake
The rebel three.—Thea was startled up,
And in her bearing was a sort of hope,
As thus she quick-voic'd spake, yet full of awe.

150   "This cheers our fallen house: come to our friends,
O Saturn! come away, and give them heart;
I know the covert, for thence came I hither."
Thus brief; then with beseeching eyes she went
With backward footing through the shade a space:
155   He follow'd, and she turn'd to lead the way
Through aged boughs, that yielded like the mist
Which eagles cleave upmounting from their nest.

Meanwhile in other realms big tears were shed,
More sorrow like to this, and such like woe,
160   Too huge for mortal tongue or pen of scribe:
The Titans fierce, self-hid, or prison-bound,

Groan'd for the old allegiance once more,
And listen'd in sharp pain for Saturn's voice.
But one of the whole mammoth-brood still kept
165   His sov'reignty, and rule, and majesty;—
Blazing Hyperion on his orbed fire
Still sat, still snuff'd the incense, teeming up
From man to the sun's God; yet unsecure:
For as among us mortals omens drear
170   Fright and perplex, so also shuddered he—
Not at dog's howl, or gloom-bird's hated screech,
Or the familiar visiting of one
Upon the first toll of his passing-bell,
Or prophesyings of the midnight lamp;
175   But horrors, portion'd to a giant nerve,
Oft made Hyperion ache. His palace bright,
Bastion'd with pyramids of glowing gold,
And touch'd with shade of bronzed obelisks,
Glar'd a blood-red through all its thousand courts,
180   Arches, and domes, and fiery galleries;
And all its curtains of Aurorian clouds
Flush'd angerly: while sometimes eagle's wings,
Unseen before by Gods or wondering men,
Darken'd the place; and neighing steeds were heard,
185   Not heard before by Gods or wondering men.
Also, when he would taste the spicy wreaths
Of incense, breath'd aloft from sacred hills,
Instead of sweets, his ample palate took
Savour of poisonous brass and metal sick:
190   And so, when harbour'd in the sleepy west,
After the full completion of fair day,—
For rest divine upon exalted couch
And slumber in the arms of melody,
He pac'd away the pleasant hours of ease
195   With stride colossal, on from hall to hall;
While far within each aisle and deep recess,
His winged minions in close clusters stood,
Amaz'd and full of fear; like anxious men
Who on wide plains gather in panting troops,
200   When earthquakes jar their battlements and towers.
Even now, while Saturn, rous'd from icy trance,
Went step for step with Thea through the woods,
Hyperion, leaving twilight in the rear,
Came slope upon the threshold of the west;

205 Then, as was wont, his palace-door flew ope
In smoothest silence, save what solemn tubes,
Blown by the serious Zephyrs, gave of sweet
And wandering sounds, slow-breathed melodies;
And like a rose in vermeil tint and shape,
210 In fragrance soft, and coolness to the eye,
That inlet to severe magnificence
Stood full blown, for the God to enter in.

He enter'd, but he enter'd full of wrath;
His flaming robes stream'd out beyond his heels,
215 And gave a roar, as if of earthly fire,
That scar'd away the meek ethereal Hours
And made their dove-wings tremble. On he flared,
From stately nave to nave, from vault to vault,
Through bowers of fragrant and enwreathed light,
220 And diamond-paved lustrous long arcades,
Until he reach'd the great main cupola;
There standing fierce beneath, he stampt his foot,
And from the basements deep to the high towers
Jarr'd his own golden region; and before
225 The quavering thunder thereupon had ceas'd,
His voice leapt out, despite of godlike curb,
To this result: "O dreams of day and night!
O monstrous forms! O effigies of pain!
O spectres busy in a cold, cold gloom!
230 O lank-eared Phantoms of black-weeded pools!
Why do I know ye? why have I seen ye? why
Is my eternal essence thus distraught
To see and to behold these horrors new?
Saturn is fallen, am I too to fall?
235 Am I to leave this haven of my rest,
This cradle of my glory, this soft clime,
This calm luxuriance of blissful light,
These crystalline pavilions, and pure fanes,
Of all my lucent empire? It is left
240 Deserted, void, nor any haunt of mine.
The blaze, the splendor, and the symmetry,
I cannot see—but darkness, death and darkness.
Even here, into my centre of repose,
The shady visions come to domineer,
245 Insult, and blind, and stifle up my pomp.—
Fall!—No, by Tellus and her briny robes!

Over the fiery frontier of my realms
I will advance a terrible right arm
Shall scare that infant thunderer, rebel Jove,
250   And bid old Saturn take his throne again."—
He spake, and ceas'd, the while a heavier threat
Held struggle with his throat but came not forth;
For as in theatres of crowded men
Hubbub increases more they call out "Hush!"
255   So at Hyperion's words the Phantoms pale
Bestirr'd themselves, thrice horrible and cold;
And from the mirror'd level where he stood
A mist arose, as from a scummy marsh.
At this, through all his bulk an agony
260   Crept gradual, from the feet unto the crown,
Like a lithe serpent vast and muscular
Making slow way, with head and neck convuls'd
From over-strained might. Releas'd, he fled
To the eastern gates, and full six dewy hours
265   Before the dawn in season due should blush,
He breath'd fierce breath against the sleepy portals,
Clear'd them of heavy vapours, burst them wide
Suddenly on the ocean's chilly streams.
The planet orb of fire, whereon he rode
270   Each day from east to west the heavens through,
Spun round in sable curtaining of clouds;
Not therefore veiled quite, blindfold, and hid,
But ever and anon the glancing spheres,
Circles, and arcs, and broad-belting colure,
275   Glow'd through, and wrought upon the muffling dark
Sweet-shaped lightnings from the nadir deep
Up to the zenith,—hieroglyphics old,
Which sages and keen-eyed astrologers
Then living on the earth, with labouring thought
280   Won from the gaze of many centuries:
Now lost, save what we find on remnants huge
Of stone, or marble swart; their import gone,
Their wisdom long since fled.—Two wings this orb
Possess'd for glory, two fair argent wings,
285   Ever exalted at the God's approach:
And now, from forth the gloom their plumes immense
Rose, one by one, till all outspreaded were;
While still the dazzling globe maintain'd eclipse,
Awaiting for Hyperion's command.

290 Fain would he have commanded, fain took throne
     And bid the day begin, if but for change.
     He might not:—No, though a primeval God:
     The sacred seasons might not be disturb'd.
     Therefore the operations of the dawn
295 Stay'd in their birth, even as here 'tis told.
     Those silver wings expanded sisterly,
     Eager to sail their orb; the porches wide
     Open'd upon the dusk demesnes of night;
     And the bright Titan, phrenzied with new woes,
300 Unus'd to bend, by hard compulsion bent
     His spirit to the sorrow of the time;
     And all along a dismal rack of clouds,
     Upon the boundaries of day and night,
     He stretch'd himself in grief and radiance faint.
305 There as he lay, the heaven with its stars
     Look'd down on him with pity, and the voice
     Of Cœlus, from the universal space,
     Thus whisper'd low and solemn in his ear.
     "O brightest of my children dear, earth-born
310 And sky-engendered, Son of Mysteries
     All unrevealed even to the powers
     Which met at thy creating; at whose joys
     And palpitations sweet, and pleasures soft,
     I, Cœlus, wonder, how they came and whence;
315 And at the fruits thereof what shapes they be,
     Distinct, and visible; symbols divine,
     Manifestations of that beauteous life
     Diffus'd unseen throughout eternal space:
     Of these new-form'd art thou, oh brightest child!
320 Of these, thy brethren and the Goddesses!
     There is sad feud among ye, and rebellion
     Of son against his sire. I saw him fall,
     I saw my first-born tumbled from his throne!
     To me his arms were spread, to me his voice
325 Found way from forth the thunders round his head!
     Pale wox I, and in vapours hid my face.
     Art thou, too, near such doom? vague fear there is:
     For I have seen my sons most unlike Gods.
     Divine ye were created, and divine
330 In sad demeanour, solemn, undisturb'd,
     Unruffled, like high Gods, ye liv'd and ruled:
     Now I behold in you fear, hope, and wrath;

Actions of rage and passion; even as
I see them, on the mortal world beneath,
335   In men who die.—This is the grief, O Son!
Sad sign of ruin, sudden dismay, and fall!
Yet do thou strive; as thou art capable,
As thou canst move about, an evident God;
And canst oppose to each malignant hour
340   Ethereal presence:—I am but a voice;
My life is but the life of winds and tides,
No more than winds and tides can I avail:—
But thou canst.—Be thou therefore in the van
Of circumstance; yea, seize the arrow's barb
345   Before the tense string murmur.—To the earth!
For there thou wilt find Saturn, and his woes.
Meantime I will keep watch on thy bright sun,
And of thy seasons be a careful nurse."—
Ere half this region-whisper had come down,
350   Hyperion arose, and on the stars
Lifted his curved lids, and kept them wide
Until it ceas'd; and still he kept them wide:
And still they were the same bright, patient stars.
Then with a slow incline of his broad breast,
355   Like to a diver in the pearly seas,
Forward he stoop'd over the airy shore,
And plung'd all noiseless into the deep night.

BOOK II

Just at the self-same beat of Time's wide wings
Hyperion slid into the rustled air,
And Saturn gain'd with Thea that sad place
Where Cybele and the bruised Titans mourn'd.
5   It was a den where no insulting light
Could glimmer on their tears; where their own groans
They felt, but heard not, for the solid roar
Of thunderous waterfalls and torrents hoarse,
Pouring a constant bulk, uncertain where.
10   Crag jutting forth to crag, and rocks that seem'd
Ever as if just rising from a sleep,
Forehead to forehead held their monstrous horns;
And thus in thousand hugest phantasies
Made a fit roofing to this nest of woe.
15   Instead of thrones, hard flint they sat upon,

Couches of rugged stone, and slaty ridge
Stubborn'd with iron. All were not assembled:
Some chain'd in torture, and some wandering.
Cœus, and Gyges, and Briareüs,
20 Typhon, and Dolor, and Porphyrion,
With many more, the brawniest in assault,
Were pent in regions of laborious breath;
Dungeon'd in opaque element, to keep
Their clenched teeth still clench'd, and all their limbs
25 Lock'd up like veins of metal, crampt and screw'd;
Without a motion, save of their big hearts
Heaving in pain, and horribly convuls'd
With sanguine feverous boiling gurge of pulse.
Mnemosyne was straying in the world;
30 Far from her moon had Phœbe wandered;
And many else were free to roam abroad,
But for the main, here found they covert drear.
Scarce images of life, one here, one there,
Lay vast and edgeways; like a dismal cirque
35 Of Druid stones, upon a forlorn moor,
When the chill rain begins at shut of eve,
In dull November, and their chancel vault,
The heaven itself, is blinded throughout night.
Each one kept shroud, nor to his neighbour gave
40 Or word, or look, or action of despair.
Creüs was one; his ponderous iron mace
Lay by him, and a shatter'd rib of rock
Told of his rage, ere he thus sank and pined.
Iäpetus another; in his grasp,
45 A serpent's plashy neck; its barbed tongue
Squeez'd from the gorge, and all its uncurl'd length
Dead; and because the creature could not spit
Its poison in the eyes of conquering Jove.
Next Cottus: prone he lay, chin uppermost,
50 As though in pain; for still upon the flint
He ground severe his skull, with open mouth
And eyes at horrid working. Nearest him
Asia, born of most enormous Caf,
Who cost her mother Tellus keener pangs,
55 Though feminine, than any of her sons:
More thought than woe was in her dusky face,
For she was prophesying of her glory;
And in her wide imagination stood

Palm-shaded temples, and high rival fanes,
60   By Oxus or in Ganges' sacred isles.
Even as Hope upon her anchor leans,
So leant she, not so fair, upon a tusk
Shed from the broadest of her elephants.
Above her, on a crag's uneasy shelve,
65   Upon his elbow rais'd, all prostrate else,
Shadow'd Enceladus; once tame and mild
As grazing ox unworried in the meads;
Now tiger-passion'd, lion-thoughted, wroth,
He meditated, plotted, and even now
70   Was hurling mountains in that second war,
Not long delay'd, that scar'd the younger Gods
To hide themselves in forms of beast and bird.
Not far hence Atlas; and beside him prone
Phorcus, the sire of Gorgons. Neighbour'd close
75   Oceanus, and Tethys, in whose lap
Sobb'd Clymene among her tangled hair.
In midst of all lay Themis, at the feet
Of Ops the queen all clouded round from sight;
No shape distinguishable, more than when
80   Thick night confounds the pine-tops with the clouds:
And many else whose names may not be told.
For when the Muse's wings are air-ward spread,
Who shall delay her flight? And she must chaunt
Of Saturn, and his guide, who now had climb'd
85   With damp and slippery footing from a depth
More horrid still. Above a sombre cliff
Their heads appear'd, and up their stature grew
Till on the level height their steps found ease:
Then Thea spread abroad her trembling arms
90   Upon the precincts of this nest of pain,
And sidelong fix'd her eye on Saturn's face:
There saw she direst strife; the supreme God
At war with all the frailty of grief,
Of rage, of fear, anxiety, revenge,
95   Remorse, spleen, hope, but most of all despair.
Against these plagues he strove in vain; for Fate
Had pour'd a mortal oil upon his head,
A disanointing poison: so that Thea,
Affrighted, kept her still, and let him pass
100   First onwards in, among the fallen tribe.

As with us mortal men, the laden heart
Is persecuted more, and fever'd more,
When it is nighing to the mournful house
Where other hearts are sick of the same bruise;
105   So Saturn, as he walk'd into the midst,
Felt faint, and would have sunk among the rest,
But that he met Enceladus's eye,
Whose mightiness, and awe of him, at once
Came like an inspiration; and he shouted,
110   "Titans, behold your God!" at which some groan'd;
Some started on their feet; some also shouted;
Some wept, some wail'd, all bow'd with reverence;
And Ops, uplifting her black folded veil,
Show'd her pale cheeks, and all her forehead wan,
115   Her eye-brows thin and jet, and hollow eyes.
There is a roaring in the bleak-grown pines
When Winter lifts his voice; there is a noise
Among immortals when a God gives sign,
With hushing finger, how he means to load
120   His tongue with the full weight of utterless thought,
With thunder, and with music, and with pomp:
Such noise is like the roar of bleak-grown pines;
Which, when it ceases in this mountain'd world,
No other sound succeeds; but ceasing here,
125   Among these fallen, Saturn's voice therefrom
Grew up like organ, that begins anew
Its strain, when other harmonies, stopt short,
Leave the dinn'd air vibrating silverly.
Thus grew it up—"Not in my own sad breast,
130   Which is its own great judge and searcher out,
Can I find reason why ye should be thus:
Not in the legends of the first of days,
Studied from that old spirit-leaved book
Which starry Uranus with finger bright
135   Sav'd from the shores of darkness, when the waves
Low-ebb'd still hid it up in shallow gloom;—
And the which book ye know I ever kept
For my firm-based footstool:—Ah, infirm!
Not there, nor in sign, symbol, or portent
140   Of element, earth, water, air, and fire,—
At war, at peace, or inter-quarreling
One against one, or two, or three, or all

Each several one against the other three,
As fire with air loud warring when rain-floods
145   Drown both, and press them both against earth's face,
Where, finding sulphur, a quadruple wrath
Unhinges the poor world;—not in that strife,
Wherefrom I take strange lore, and read it deep,
Can I find reason why ye should be thus:
150   No, no-where can unriddle, though I search,
And pore on Nature's universal scroll
Even to swooning, why ye, Divinities,
The first-born of all shap'd and palpable Gods,
Should cower beneath what, in comparison,
155   Is untremendous might. Yet ye are here,
O'erwhelm'd, and spurn'd, and batter'd, ye are here!
O Titans, shall I say 'Arise!'—Ye groan:
Shall I say 'Crouch!'—Ye groan. What can I then?
O Heaven wide! O unseen parent dear!
160   What can I? Tell me, all ye brethren Gods,
How we can war, how engine our great wrath!
O speak your counsel now, for Saturn's ear
Is all a-hunger'd. Thou, Oceanus,
Ponderest high and deep; and in thy face
165   I see, astonied, that severe content
Which comes of thought and musing: give us help!"

So ended Saturn; and the God of the Sea,
Sophist and sage, from no Athenian grove,
But cogitation in his watery shades,
170   Arose, with locks not oozy, and began,
In murmurs, which his first-endeavouring tongue
Caught infant-like from the far-foamed sands.
"O ye, whom wrath consumes! who, passion-stung,
Writhe at defeat, and nurse your agonies!
175   Shut up your senses, stifle up your ears,
My voice is not a bellows unto ire.
Yet listen, ye who will, whilst I bring proof
How ye, perforce, must be content to stoop:
And in the proof much comfort will I give,
180   If ye will take that comfort in its truth.
We fall by course of Nature's law, not force
Of thunder, or of Jove. Great Saturn, thou
Hast sifted well the atom-universe;
But for this reason, that thou art the King,

185 And only blind from sheer supremacy,
     One avenue was shaded from thine eyes,
     Through which I wandered to eternal truth.
     And first, as thou wast not the first of powers,
     So art thou not the last; it cannot be:
190 Thou art not the beginning nor the end.
     From Chaos and parental Darkness came
     Light, the first fruits of that intestine broil,
     That sullen ferment, which for wondrous ends
     Was ripening in itself. The ripe hour came,
195 And with it Light, and Light, engendering
     Upon its own producer, forthwith touch'd
     The whole enormous matter into life.
     Upon that very hour, our parentage,
     The Heavens and the Earth, were manifest:
200 Then thou first-born, and we the giant-race,
     Found ourselves ruling new and beauteous realms.
     Now comes the pain of truth, to whom 'tis pain;
     O folly! for to bear all naked truths,
     And to envisage circumstance, all calm,
205 That is the top of sovereignty. Mark well!
     As Heaven and Earth are fairer, fairer far
     Than Chaos and blank Darkness, though once chiefs;
     And as we show beyond that Heaven and Earth
     In form and shape compact and beautiful,
210 In will, in action free, companionship,
     And thousand other signs of purer life;
     So on our heels a fresh perfection treads,
     A power more strong in beauty, born of us
     And fated to excel us, as we pass
215 In glory that old Darkness: nor are we
     Thereby more conquer'd, than by us the rule
     Of shapeless Chaos. Say, doth the dull soil
     Quarrel with the proud forests it hath fed,
     And feedeth still, more comely than itself?
220 Can it deny the chiefdom of green groves?
     Or shall the tree be envious of the dove
     Because it cooeth, and hath snowy wings
     To wander wherewithal and find its joys?
     We are such forest-trees, and our fair boughs
225 Have bred forth, not pale solitary doves,
     But eagles golden-feather'd, who do tower
     Above us in their beauty, and must reign

In right thereof; for 'tis the eternal law
That first in beauty should be first in might:
230   Yea, by that law, another race may drive
Our conquerors to mourn as we do now.
Have ye beheld the young God of the Seas,
My dispossessor? Have ye seen his face?
Have ye beheld his chariot, foam'd along
235   By noble winged creatures he hath made?
I saw him on the calmed waters scud,
With such a glow of beauty in his eyes,
That it enforc'd me to bid sad farewell
To all my empire: farewell sad I took,
240   And hither came, to see how dolorous fate
Had wrought upon ye; and how I might best
Give consolation in this woe extreme.
Receive the truth, and let it be your balm."

　　　　Whether through poz'd conviction, or disdain,
245   They guarded silence, when Oceanus
Left murmuring, what deepest thought can tell?
But so it was, none answer'd for a space,
Save one whom none regarded, Clymene;
And yet she answer'd not, only complain'd,
250   With hectic lips, and eyes up-looking mild,
Thus wording timidly among the fierce:
"O Father, I am here the simplest voice,
And all my knowledge is that joy is gone,
And this thing woe crept in among our hearts,
255   There to remain for ever, as I fear:
I would not bode of evil, if I thought
So weak a creature could turn off the help
Which by just right should come of mighty Gods;
Yet let me tell my sorrow, let me tell
260   Of what I heard, and how it made me weep,
And know that we had parted from all hope.
I stood upon a shore, a pleasant shore,
Where a sweet clime was breathed from a land
Of fragrance, quietness, and trees, and flowers.
265   Full of calm joy it was, as I of grief;
Too full of joy and soft delicious warmth;
So that I felt a movement in my heart
To chide, and to reproach that solitude
With songs of misery, music of our woes;

270 And sat me down, and took a mouthed shell
     And murmur'd into it, and made melody—
     O melody no more! for while I sang,
     And with poor skill let pass into the breeze
     The dull shell's echo, from a bowery strand
275 Just opposite, an island of the sea,
     There came enchantment with the shifting wind,
     That did both drown and keep alive my ears.
     I threw my shell away upon the sand,
     And a wave fill'd it, as my sense was fill'd
280 With that new blissful golden melody.
     A living death was in each gush of sounds,
     Each family of rapturous hurried notes,
     That fell, one after one, yet all at once,
     Like pearl beads dropping sudden from their string:
285 And then another, then another strain,
     Each like a dove leaving its olive perch,
     With music wing'd instead of silent plumes,
     To hover round my head, and make me sick
     Of joy and grief at once. Grief overcame,
290 And I was stopping up my frantic ears,
     When, past all hindrance of my trembling hands,
     A voice came sweeter, sweeter than all tune,
     And still it cried, 'Apollo! young Apollo!
     The morning-bright Apollo! young Apollo!'
295 I fled, it follow'd me, and cried 'Apollo!'
     O Father, and O Brethren, had ye felt
     Those pains of mine; O Saturn, hadst thou felt,
     Ye would not call this too indulged tongue
     Presumptuous, in thus venturing to be heard."

300   So far her voice flow'd on, like timorous brook
     That, lingering along a pebbled coast,
     Doth fear to meet the sea: but sea it met,
     And shudder'd; for the overwhelming voice
     Of huge Enceladus swallow'd it in wrath:
305 The ponderous syllables, like sullen waves
     In the half-glutted hollows of reef-rocks,
     Came booming thus, while still upon his arm
     He lean'd; not rising, from supreme contempt.
     "Or shall we listen to the over-wise,
310 Or to the over-foolish, Giant-Gods?
     Not thunderbolt on thunderbolt, till all

That rebel Jove's whole armoury were spent,
Not world on world upon these shoulders piled,
Could agonize me more than baby-words
315   In midst of this dethronement horrible.
Speak! roar! shout! yell! ye sleepy Titans all.
Do ye forget the blows, the buffets vile?
Are ye not smitten by a youngling arm?
Dost thou forget, sham Monarch of the Waves,
320   Thy scalding in the seas? What, have I rous'd
Your spleens with so few simple words as these?
O joy! for now I see ye are not lost:
O joy! for now I see a thousand eyes
Wide glaring for revenge!"—As this he said,
325   He lifted up his stature vast, and stood,
Still without intermission speaking thus:
"Now ye are flames, I'll tell you how to burn,
And purge the ether of our enemies;
How to feed fierce the crooked stings of fire,
330   And singe away the swollen clouds of Jove,
Stifling that puny essence in its tent.
O let him feel the evil he hath done;
For though I scorn Oceanus's lore,
Much pain have I for more than loss of realms:
335   The days of peace and slumberous calm are fled;
Those days, all innocent of scathing war,
When all the fair Existences of heaven
Came open-eyed to guess what we would speak:—
That was before our brows were taught to frown,
340   Before our lips knew else but solemn sounds;
That was before we knew the winged thing,
Victory, might be lost, or might be won.
And be ye mindful that Hyperion,
Our brightest brother, still is undisgraced—
345   Hyperion, lo! his radiance is here!"

All eyes were on Enceladus's face,
And they beheld, while still Hyperion's name
Flew from his lips up to the vaulted rocks,
A pallid gleam across his features stern:
350   Not savage, for he saw full many a God
Wroth as himself. He look'd upon them all,
And in each face he saw a gleam of light,
But splendider in Saturn's, whose hoar locks
Shone like the bubbling foam about a keel

355   When the prow sweeps into a midnight cove.
       In pale and silver silence they remain'd,
       Till suddenly a splendour, like the morn,
       Pervaded all the beetling gloomy steeps,
       All the sad spaces of oblivion,
360   And every gulf, and every chasm old,
       And every height, and every sullen depth,
       Voiceless, or hoarse with loud tormented streams:
       And all the everlasting cataracts,
       And all the headlong torrents far and near,
365   Mantled before in darkness and huge shade,
       Now saw the light and made it terrible.
       It was Hyperion:—a granite peak
       His bright feet touch'd, and there he stay'd to view
       The misery his brilliance had betray'd
370   To the most hateful seeing of itself.
       Golden his hair of short Numidian curl,
       Regal his shape majestic, a vast shade
       In midst of his own brightness, like the bulk
       Of Memnon's image at the set of sun
375   To one who travels from the dusking east:
       Sighs, too, as mournful as that Memnon's harp
       He utter'd, while his hands contemplative
       He press'd together, and in silence stood.
       Despondence seiz'd again the fallen Gods
380   At sight of the dejected King of Day,
       And many hid their faces from the light:
       But fierce Enceladus sent forth his eyes
       Among the brotherhood; and, at their glare,
       Uprose Iäpetus, and Creüs too,
385   And Phorcus, sea-born, and together strode
       To where he towered on his eminence.
       There those four shouted forth old Saturn's name;
       Hyperion from the peak loud answered, "Saturn!"
       Saturn sat near the Mother of the Gods,
390   In whose face was no joy, though all the Gods
       Gave from their hollow throats the name of "Saturn!"

                    BOOK III

       Thus in alternate uproar and sad peace,
       Amazed were those Titans utterly.
       O leave them, Muse! O leave them to their woes;

For thou art weak to sing such tumults dire:
5   A solitary sorrow best befits
Thy lips, and antheming a lonely grief.
Leave them, O Muse! for thou anon wilt find
Many a fallen old Divinity
Wandering in vain about bewildered shores.
10   Meantime touch piously the Delphic harp,
And not a wind of heaven but will breathe
In aid soft warble from the Dorian flute;
For lo! 'tis for the Father of all verse.
Flush every thing that hath a vermeil hue,
15   Let the rose glow intense and warm the air,
And let the clouds of even and of morn
Float in voluptuous fleeces o'er the hills;
Let the red wine within the goblet boil,
Cold as a bubbling well; let faint-lipp'd shells,
20   On sands, or in great deeps, vermilion turn
Through all their labyrinths; and let the maid
Blush keenly, as with some warm kiss surpris'd.
Chief isle of the embowered Cyclades,
Rejoice, O Delos, with thine olives green,
25   And poplars, and lawn-shading palms, and beech,
In which the Zephyr breathes the loudest song,
And hazels thick, dark-stemm'd beneath the shade:
Apollo is once more the golden theme!
Where was he, when the Giant of the Sun
30   Stood bright, amid the sorrow of his peers?
Together had he left his mother fair
And his twin-sister sleeping in their bower,
And in the morning twilight wandered forth
Beside the osiers of a rivulet,
35   Full ankle-deep in lilies of the vale.
The nightingale had ceas'd, and a few stars
Were lingering in the heavens, while the thrush
Began calm-throated. Throughout all the isle
There was no covert, no retired cave
40   Unhaunted by the murmurous noise of waves,
Though scarcely heard in many a green recess.
He listen'd, and he wept, and his bright tears
Went trickling down the golden bow he held.
Thus with half-shut suffused eyes he stood,
45   While from beneath some cumbrous boughs hard by
With solemn step an awful Goddess came,

And there was purport in her looks for him,
Which he with eager guess began to read
Perplex'd, the while melodiously he said:
50   "How cam'st thou over the unfooted sea?
Or hath that antique mien and robed form
Mov'd in these vales invisible till now?
Sure I have heard those vestments sweeping o'er
The fallen leaves, when I have sat alone
55   In cool mid-forest. Surely I have traced
The rustle of those ample skirts about
These grassy solitudes, and seen the flowers
Lift up their heads, as still the whisper pass'd.
Goddess! I have beheld those eyes before,
60   And their eternal calm, and all that face,
Or I have dream'd."—"Yes," said the supreme shape,
"Thou hast dream'd of me; and awaking up
Didst find a lyre all golden by thy side,
Whose strings touch'd by thy fingers, all the vast
65   Unwearied ear of the whole universe
Listen'd in pain and pleasure at the birth
Of such new tuneful wonder. Is't not strange
That thou shouldst weep, so gifted? Tell me, youth,
What sorrow thou canst feel; for I am sad
70   When thou dost shed a tear: explain thy griefs
To one who in this lonely isle hath been
The watcher of thy sleep and hours of life,
From the young day when first thy infant hand
Pluck'd witless the weak flowers, till thine arm
75   Could bend that bow heroic to all times.
Show thy heart's secret to an ancient Power
Who hath forsaken old and sacred thrones
For prophecies of thee, and for the sake
Of loveliness new born."—Apollo then,
80   With sudden scrutiny and gloomless eyes,
Thus answer'd, while his white melodious throat
Throbb'd with the syllables.—"Mnemosyne!
Thy name is on my tongue, I know not how;
Why should I tell thee what thou so well seest?
85   Why should I strive to show what from thy lips
Would come no mystery? For me, dark, dark,
And painful vile oblivion seals my eyes:
I strive to search wherefore I am so sad,
Until a melancholy numbs my limbs;

90   And then upon the grass I sit, and moan,
      Like one who once had wings.—O why should I
      Feel curs'd and thwarted, when the liegeless air
      Yields to my step aspirant? why should I
      Spurn the green turf as hateful to my feet?
95   Goddess benign, point forth some unknown thing:
      Are there not other regions than this isle?
      What are the stars? There is the sun, the sun!
      And the most patient brilliance of the moon!
      And stars by thousands! Point me out the way
100   To any one particular beauteous star,
      And I will flit into it with my lyre,
      And make its silvery splendour pant with bliss.
      I have heard the cloudy thunder: Where is power?
      Whose hand, whose essence, what divinity
105   Makes this alarum in the elements,
      While I here idle listen on the shores
      In fearless yet in aching ignorance?
      O tell me, lonely Goddess, by thy harp,
      That waileth every morn and eventide,
110   Tell me why thus I rave, about these groves!
      Mute thou remainest—mute! yet I can read
      A wondrous lesson in thy silent face:
      Knowledge enormous makes a God of me.
      Names, deeds, gray legends, dire events, rebellions,
115   Majesties, sovran voices, agonies,
      Creations and destroyings, all at once
      Pour into the wide hollows of my brain,
      And deify me, as if some blithe wine
      Or bright elixir peerless I had drunk,
120   And so become immortal."—Thus the God,
      While his enkindled eyes, with level glance
      Beneath his white soft temples, stedfast kept
      Trembling with light upon Mnemosyne.
      Soon wild commotions shook him, and made flush
125   All the immortal fairness of his limbs;
      Most like the struggle at the gate of death;
      Or liker still to one who should take leave
      Of pale immortal death, and with a pang
      As hot as death's is chill, with fierce convulse
130   Die into life: so young Apollo anguish'd:
      His very hair, his golden tresses famed,

Kept undulation round his eager neck.
During the pain Mnemosyne upheld
Her arms as one who prophesied.—At length
135   Apollo shriek'd;—and lo! from all his limbs
Celestial *   *   *   *   *   *   *   *   *   *
        *   *   *   *   *   *   *   *   *   *   *   *   *

La Belle Dame sans Merci:
A Ballad

1

O what can ail thee, knight at arms,
    Alone and palely loitering?
The sedge has wither'd from the lake,
    And no birds sing.

2

5   O what can ail thee, knight at arms,
    So haggard and so woe-begone?
The squirrel's granary is full,
    And the harvest's done.

3

I see a lily on thy brow
10   With anguish moist and fever dew,
And on thy cheeks a fading rose
    Fast withereth too.

4

I met a lady in the meads,
    Full beautiful, a fairy's child;
15   Her hair was long, her foot was light,
    And her eyes were wild.

5

I made a garland for her head,
    And bracelets too, and fragrant zone;
She look'd at me as she did love,
20   And made sweet moan.

6

I set her on my pacing steed,
    And nothing else saw all day long,
For sidelong would she bend, and sing
    A fairy's song.

7

25   She found me roots of relish sweet,
    And honey wild, and manna dew,

And sure in language strange she said—
    I love thee true.

8

She took me to her elfin grot,
30   And there she wept, and sigh'd full sore,
And there I shut her wild wild eyes
    With kisses four.

9

And there she lulled me asleep,
    And there I dream'd—Ah! woe betide!
35   The latest dream I ever dream'd
    On the cold hill's side.

10

I saw pale kings, and princes too,
    Pale warriors, death pale were they all;
They cried—"La belle dame sans merci
40   Hath thee in thrall!"

11

I saw their starv'd lips in the gloam
    With horrid warning gaped wide,
And I awoke and found me here
    On the cold hill's side.

12

45   And this is why I sojourn here,
    Alone and palely loitering,
Though the sedge is wither'd from the lake,
    And no birds sing.

Song of Four Fairies: *Fire, Air, Earth, and Water*

SALAMANDER, ZEPHYR, DUSKETHA, AND BREAMA

SALAMANDER

Happy, happy glowing fire!

ZEPHYR

Fragrant air! Delicious light!

DUSKETHA

Let me to my glooms retire!

BREAMA

I to green-weed rivers bright!

SALAMANDER

5   Happy, happy glowing fire,
Dazzling bowers of soft retire,
Ever let my nourish'd wing,
Like a bat's, still wandering,
Nimbly fan your fiery spaces,
10   Spirit sole in deadly places;
In unhaunted roar and blaze,
Open eyes that never daze:
Let me see the myriad shapes
Of men, and beasts, and fish, and apes,
15   Portray'd in many a fiery den
And wrought by spumy bitumen
On the deep intenser roof,
Arched every way aloof;
Let me breathe upon their skies,
20   And anger their live tapestries;
Free from cold and every care
Of chilly rain, and shivering air.

ZEPHYR

Spirit of Fire—away, away!
Or your very roundelay
25   Will sear my plumage newly budded
From its quilled sheath, and studded
With the self-same dews that fell
On the May-grown asphodel.
Spirit of Fire—away, away!

30   Spirit of Fire—away, away!
      Zephyr, blue-eyed fairy, turn
      And see my cool sedge-buried urn,
      Where it rests its mossy brim
      'Mid water mint and cresses dim;
35   And the flowers in sweet troubles
      Lift their eyes above the bubbles,
      Like our Queen when she would please
      To sleep and Oberon will tease.
      Love me, blue-eyed fairy true,
40   Soothly I am sick for you.

ZEPHYR

      Gentle Breama! by the first
      Violet young nature nurst,
      I will bathe myself with thee,
      So you sometime follow me
45   To my home, far, far in west,
      Beyond the nimble-wheeled quest
      Of the golden-presenc'd sun.
      Come with me, o'er tops of trees,
      To my fragrant pallaces,
50   Where they ever floating are
      Beneath the cherish of a star
      Call'd Vesper, who with silver veil
      Ever hides his brilliance pale,
      Ever gently drows'd doth keep
55   Twilight for the fays to sleep.
      Fear not that your watry hair
      Will thirst in drouthy ringlets there;
      Clouds of stored summer rains
      Thou shalt taste, before the stains
60   From the mountain soil they take,
      And too unlucent for thee make.
      I love thee, chrystal fairy true;
      Sooth I am as sick for you!

SALAMANDER

      Out, ye aguish fairies, out!
65   Chilly lovers, what a rout

Keep ye with your frozen breath,
Colder than the mortal death.
Adder-eyed Dusketha, speak,
Shall we leave these and go seek
70   In the earth's wide entrails old
Couches warm as theirs is cold?
O for a fiery-gloom and thee,
Dusketha, so enchantingly
Freckle-wing'd and lizard-sided!

DUSKETHA

75   By thee, sprite, will I be guided!
I care not for cold or heat;
Frost or flame, or sparks, or sleet
To my essence are the same;
But I honor more the flame.
80   Sprite of Fire! I follow thee
Wheresoever it may be;
To the torrid spouts and fountains
Underneath earth-quaked mountains;
Or, at thy supreme desire,
85   Touch the very pulse of fire
With my bare unlidded eyes.

SALAMANDER

Sweet Dusketha! Paradise!
Off, ye icy spirits, fly,
Frosty creatures of the sky!

DUSKETHA

90   Breathe upon them, fiery sprite!

ZEPHYR *and* BREAMA

Away, away to our delight!

SALAMANDER

Go feed on icicles, while we
Bedded in tongued flames will be.

DUSKETHA

Lead me to those fevrous glooms,
Sprite of Fire!

BREAMA

95   Me to the blooms,
Blue-eyed Zephyr, of those flowers
Far in the west where the May-cloud lowers,
And the beams of still Vesper, when winds are all whist,
Are shed through the rain and the milder mist,
100   And twilight your floating bowers.

Sonnet to Sleep

O soft embalmer of the still midnight,
    Shutting with careful fingers and benign
Our gloom-pleas'd eyes, embower'd from the light,
    Enshaded in forgetfulness divine:
5 O soothest Sleep! if so it please thee, close,
    In midst of this thine hymn, my willing eyes,
Or wait the Amen ere thy poppy throws
    Around my bed its lulling charities.
Then save me or the passed day will shine
10   Upon my pillow, breeding many woes:
Save me from curious conscience, that still hoards
    Its strength for darkness, burrowing like the mole;
Turn the key deftly in the oiled wards,
    And seal the hushed casket of my soul.

Ode to Psyche

O Goddess! hear these tuneless numbers, wrung
    By sweet enforcement and remembrance dear,
And pardon that thy secrets should be sung
    Even into thine own soft-conched ear:
5 Surely I dreamt to-day, or did I see
    The winged Psyche with awaken'd eyes?
I wander'd in a forest thoughtlessly,
    And, on the sudden, fainting with surprise,

Saw two fair creatures, couched side by side
10   In deepest grass, beneath the whisp'ring roof
              Of leaves and trembled blossoms, where there ran
                  A brooklet, scarce espied:
          'Mid hush'd, cool-rooted flowers, fragrant-eyed,
              Blue, silver-white, and budded Tyrian,
15   They lay calm-breathing on the bedded grass;
              Their arms embraced, and their pinions too;
              Their lips touch'd not, but had not bade adieu,
          As if disjoined by soft-handed slumber,
          And ready still past kisses to outnumber
20   At tender eye-dawn of aurorean love:
                  The winged boy I knew;
              But who wast thou, O happy, happy dove?.
                  His Psyche true!

          O latest born and loveliest vision far
25   Of all Olympus' faded hierarchy!
          Fairer than Phœbe's sapphire-region'd star,
              Or Vesper, amorous glow-worm of the sky;
          Fairer than these, though temple thou hast none,
              Nor altar heap'd with flowers;
30   Nor virgin-choir to make delicious moan
                  Upon the midnight hours;
          No voice, no lute, no pipe, no incense sweet
              From chain-swung censer teeming;
          No shrine, no grove, no oracle, no heat
35   Of pale-mouth'd prophet dreaming.

          O brightest! though too late for antique vows,
              Too, too late for the fond believing lyre,
          When holy were the haunted forest boughs,
              Holy the air, the water, and the fire;
40   Yet even in these days so far retir'd
              From happy pieties, thy lucent fans,
              Fluttering among the faint Olympians,
          I see, and sing, by my own eyes inspired.
          So let me be thy choir, and make a moan
45   Upon the midnight hours;
          Thy voice, thy lute, thy pipe, thy incense sweet
              From swinged censer teeming;

Thy shrine, thy grove, thy oracle, thy heat
  Of pale-mouth'd prophet dreaming.

50 Yes, I will be thy priest, and build a fane
  In some untrodden region of my mind,
Where branched thoughts, new grown with pleasant pain,
  Instead of pines shall murmur in the wind:
Far, far around shall those dark-cluster'd trees
55   Fledge the wild-ridged mountains steep by steep;
And there by zephyrs, streams, and birds, and bees,
  The moss-lain Dryads shall be lull'd to sleep;
And in the midst of this wide quietness
A rosy sanctuary will I dress
60 With the wreath'd trellis of a working brain,
  With buds, and bells, and stars without a name,
With all the gardener Fancy e'er could feign,
  Who breeding flowers, will never breed the same:
And there shall be for thee all soft delight
65   That shadowy thought can win,
A bright torch, and a casement ope at night,
  To let the warm Love in!

On Fame

Fame, like a wayward girl, will still be coy
  To those who woo her with too slavish knees,
But makes surrender to some thoughtless boy,
  And dotes the more upon a heart at ease;
5 She is a gipsey, will not speak to those
  Who have not learnt to be content without her;
A jilt, whose ear was never whisper'd close,
  Who thinks they scandal her who talk about her;
A very gipsey is she, Nilus born,
10   Sister-in-law to jealous Potiphar;
Ye love-sick bards, repay her scorn for scorn;
  Ye artists lovelorn, madmen that ye are!
Make your best bow to her and bid adieu;
Then, if she likes it, she will follow you.

On Fame

"You cannot eat your cake and have it too."
                        Proverb

How fever'd is the man who cannot look
    Upon his mortal days with temperate blood,
Who vexes all the leaves of his life's book,
    And robs his fair name of its maidenhood;
5   It is as if the rose should pluck herself,
    Or the ripe plum finger its misty bloom,
As if a Naiad, like a meddling elf,
    Should darken her pure grot with muddy gloom;
But the rose leaves herself upon the briar,
10   For winds to kiss and grateful bees to feed,
And the ripe plum still wears its dim attire,
        The undisturbed lake has crystal space;
        Why then should man, teasing the world for grace,
    Spoil his salvation for a fierce miscreed?

If by dull rhymes our English must be chain'd

If by dull rhymes our English must be chain'd,
    And, like Andromeda, the sonnet sweet
        Fetter'd, in spite of pained loveliness;
Let us find out, if we must be constrain'd,
5   Sandals more interwoven and complete
To fit the naked foot of Poesy;
        Let us inspect the lyre, and weigh the stress
Of every chord, and see what may be gain'd
        By ear industrious, and attention meet;
10   Misers of sound and syllable, no less
Than Midas of his coinage, let us be
    Jealous of dead leaves in the bay wreath crown;
So, if we may not let the muse be free,
    She will be bound with garlands of her own.

Two or three posies

Two or three posies
With two or three simples

Two or three noses
With two or three pimples—
5   Two or three wise men
And two or three ninnies
Two or three purses
And two or three guineas
Two or three raps
10   At two or three doors
Two or three naps
Of two or three hours—
Two or three cats
And two or three mice
15   Two or three sprats
At a very great price—
Two or three sandies
And two or three tabbies
Two or three dandies—
20   And two Mrs. ——
Two or three smiles
And two or three frowns
Two or three miles
To two or three towns
25   Two or three pegs
For two or three bonnets
Two or three dove's eggs
To hatch into sonnets—

Ode to a Nightingale

1

My heart aches, and a drowsy numbness pains
   My sense, as though of hemlock I had drunk,
Or emptied some dull opiate to the drains
   One minute past, and Lethe-wards had sunk:
5   'Tis not through envy of thy happy lot,
     But being too happy in thine happiness,—
       That thou, light-winged Dryad of the trees,
        In some melodious plot
     Of beechen green, and shadows numberless,
10   Singest of summer in full-throated ease.

2

O, for a draught of vintage! that hath been
　　Cool'd a long age in the deep-delved earth,
Tasting of Flora and the country green,
　　Dance, and Provençal song, and sunburnt mirth!
15　　O for a beaker full of the warm South,
　　　　Full of the true, the blushful Hippocrene,
　　　　　With beaded bubbles winking at the brim,
　　　　　　And purple-stained mouth;
　　　That I might drink, and leave the world unseen,
20　　　　And with thee fade away into the forest dim:

3

Fade far away, dissolve, and quite forget
　　What thou among the leaves hast never known,
The weariness, the fever, and the fret
　　Here, where men sit and hear each other groan;
25　Where palsy shakes a few, sad, last gray hairs,
　　　Where youth grows pale, and spectre-thin, and dies;
　　　　Where but to think is to be full of sorrow
　　　　　And leaden-eyed despairs,
　　　Where Beauty cannot keep her lustrous eyes,
30　　　　Or new Love pine at them beyond to-morrow.

4

Away! away! for I will fly to thee,
　　Not charioted by Bacchus and his pards,
But on the viewless wings of Poesy,
　　Though the dull brain perplexes and retards:
35　Already with thee! tender is the night,
　　　And haply the Queen-Moon is on her throne,
　　　　Cluster'd around by all her starry Fays;
　　　　　But here there is no light,
　　　Save what from heaven is with the breezes blown
40　　　　Through verdurous glooms and winding mossy ways.

5

I cannot see what flowers are at my feet,
　　Nor what soft incense hangs upon the boughs,
But, in embalmed darkness, guess each sweet
　　Wherewith the seasonable month endows
45　The grass, the thicket, and the fruit-tree wild;

White hawthorn, and the pastoral eglantine;
Fast fading violets cover'd up in leaves;
And mid-May's eldest child,
The coming musk-rose, full of dewy wine,
50   The murmurous haunt of flies on summer eves.

6

Darkling I listen; and, for many a time
I have been half in love with easeful Death,
Call'd him soft names in many a mused rhyme,
To take into the air my quiet breath;
55   Now more than ever seems it rich to die,
To cease upon the midnight with no pain,
While thou art pouring forth thy soul abroad
In such an ecstasy!
Still wouldst thou sing, and I have ears in vain—
60   To thy high requiem become a sod.

7

Thou wast not born for death, immortal Bird!
No hungry generations tread thee down;
The voice I hear this passing night was heard
In ancient days by emperor and clown:
65   Perhaps the self-same song that found a path
Through the sad heart of Ruth, when, sick for home,
She stood in tears amid the alien corn;
The same that oft-times hath
Charm'd magic casements, opening on the foam
70   Of perilous seas, in faery lands forlorn.

8

Forlorn! the very word is like a bell
To toll me back from thee to my sole self!
Adieu! the fancy cannot cheat so well
As she is fam'd to do, deceiving elf.
75   Adieu! adieu! thy plaintive anthem fades
Past the near meadows, over the still stream,
Up the hill-side; and now 'tis buried deep
In the next valley-glades:
Was it a vision, or a waking dream?
80   Fled is that music:—Do I wake or sleep?

Ode on a Grecian Urn

1

Thou still unravish'd bride of quietness,
  Thou foster-child of silence and slow time,
Sylvan historian, who canst thus express
  A flowery tale more sweetly than our rhyme:
5 What leaf-fring'd legend haunts about thy shape
    Of deities or mortals, or of both,
      In Tempe or the dales of Arcady?
  What men or gods are these? What maidens loth?
What mad pursuit? What struggle to escape?
10   What pipes and timbrels? What wild ecstasy?

2

Heard melodies are sweet, but those unheard
  Are sweeter; therefore, ye soft pipes, play on;
Not to the sensual ear, but, more endear'd,
  Pipe to the spirit ditties of no tone:
15 Fair youth, beneath the trees, thou canst not leave
  Thy song, nor ever can those trees be bare;
    Bold lover, never, never canst thou kiss,
  Though winning near the goal—yet, do not grieve;
    She cannot fade, though thou hast not thy bliss,
20   For ever wilt thou love, and she be fair!

3

Ah, happy, happy boughs! that cannot shed
  Your leaves, nor ever bid the spring adieu;
And, happy melodist, unwearied,
  For ever piping songs for ever new;
25 More happy love! more happy, happy love!
    For ever warm and still to be enjoy'd,
      For ever panting, and for ever young;
All breathing human passion far above,
    That leaves a heart high-sorrowful and cloy'd,
30   A burning forehead, and a parching tongue.

4

Who are these coming to the sacrifice?
  To what green altar, O mysterious priest,
Lead'st thou that heifer lowing at the skies,

And all her silken flanks with garlands drest?
35   What little town by river or sea shore,
    Or mountain-built with peaceful citadel,
        Is emptied of this folk, this pious morn?
    And, little town, thy streets for evermore
        Will silent be; and not a soul to tell
40   Why thou art desolate, can e'er return.

5

O Attic shape! Fair attitude! with brede
    Of marble men and maidens overwrought,
With forest branches and the trodden weed;
    Thou, silent form, dost tease us out of thought
45 As doth eternity: Cold Pastoral!
    When old age shall this generation waste,
        Thou shalt remain, in midst of other woe
    Than ours, a friend to man, to whom thou say'st,
        "Beauty is truth, truth beauty,"—that is all
50   Ye know on earth, and all ye need to know.

Ode on Melancholy

1

No, no, go not to Lethe, neither twist
    Wolf's-bane, tight-rooted, for its poisonous wine;
Nor suffer thy pale forehead to be kiss'd
    By nightshade, ruby grape of Proserpine;
5 Make not your rosary of yew-berries,
    Nor let the beetle, nor the death-moth be
        Your mournful Psyche, nor the downy owl
    A partner in your sorrow's mysteries;
        For shade to shade will come too drowsily,
10   And drown the wakeful anguish of the soul.

2

But when the melancholy fit shall fall
    Sudden from heaven like a weeping cloud,
That fosters the droop-headed flowers all,
    And hides the green hill in an April shroud;
15 Then glut thy sorrow on a morning rose,
    Or on the rainbow of the salt sand-wave,

　　　　Or on the wealth of globed peonies;
　　Or if thy mistress some rich anger shows,
　　　Emprison her soft hand, and let her rave,
20　　　　And feed deep, deep upon her peerless eyes.

3

　　She dwells with Beauty—Beauty that must die;
　　　And Joy, whose hand is ever at his lips
　　Bidding adieu; and aching Pleasure nigh,
　　　Turning to poison while the bee-mouth sips:
25　　Ay, in the very temple of Delight
　　　Veil'd Melancholy has her sovran shrine,
　　　　Though seen of none save him whose strenuous tongue
　　Can burst Joy's grape against his palate fine;
　　His soul shall taste the sadness of her might,
30　　　　And be among her cloudy trophies hung.

Ode on Indolence

"They toil not, neither do they spin."

1

　　One morn before me were three figures seen,
　　　With bowed necks, and joined hands, side-faced;
　　And one behind the other stepp'd serene,
　　　In placid sandals, and in white robes graced:
5　　They pass'd, like figures on a marble urn,
　　　When shifted round to see the other side;
　　　　They came again; as when the urn once more
　　Is shifted round, the first seen shades return;
　　　And they were strange to me, as may betide
10　　　With vases, to one deep in Phidian lore.

2

　　How is it, shadows, that I knew ye not?
　　　How came ye muffled in so hush a masque?
　　Was it a silent deep-disguised plot
　　　To steal away, and leave without a task
15　　My idle days? Ripe was the drowsy hour;
　　　The blissful cloud of summer-indolence
　　　　Benumb'd my eyes; my pulse grew less and less;

Pain had no sting, and pleasure's wreath no flower.
　　O, why did ye not melt, and leave my sense
20　　　　Unhaunted quite of all but—nothingness?

3

A third time pass'd they by, and, passing, turn'd
　　Each one the face a moment whiles to me;
Then faded, and to follow them I burn'd
　　And ached for wings, because I knew the three:
25　The first was a fair maid, and Love her name;
　　　　The second was Ambition, pale of cheek,
　　　　　And ever watchful with fatigued eye;
The last, whom I love more, the more of blame
　　Is heap'd upon her, maiden most unmeek,—
30　　　　I knew to be my demon Poesy.

4

They faded, and, forsooth! I wanted wings:
　　O folly! What is Love? and where is it?
And for that poor Ambition—it springs
　　From a man's little heart's short fever-fit;
35　For Poesy!—no,—she has not a joy,—
　　　　At least for me,—so sweet as drowsy noons,
　　　　　And evenings steep'd in honied indolence;
O, for an age so shelter'd from annoy,
　　That I may never know how change the moons,
40　　　　Or hear the voice of busy common-sense!

5

A third time came they by;—alas! wherefore?
　　My sleep had been embroider'd with dim dreams;
My soul had been a lawn besprinkled o'er
　　With flowers, and stirring shades, and baffled beams:
45　The morn was clouded, but no shower fell,
　　　　Though in her lids hung the sweet tears of May;
　　　　　The open casement press'd a new-leaved vine,
　　Let in the budding warmth and throstle's lay;
O shadows! 'twas a time to bid farewell!
50　　　　Upon your skirts had fallen no tears of mine.

6

So, ye three ghosts, adieu! Ye cannot raise
　　My head cool-bedded in the flowery grass;

For I would not be dieted with praise,
    A pet-lamb in a sentimental farce!
55   Fade softly from my eyes, and be once more
      In masque-like figures on the dreamy urn;
        Farewell! I yet have visions for the night,
And for the day faint visions there is store;
        Vanish, ye phantoms, from my idle spright,
60   Into the clouds, and never more return!

Shed no tear—O shed no tear

Shed no tear—O shed no tear!
The flower will bloom another year.
Weep no more—O weep no more!
Young buds sleep in the root's white core.
5   Dry your eyes—O dry your eyes!
For I was taught in Paradise
To ease my breast of melodies—
        Shed no tear!

Over head—look over head,
10   'Mong the blossoms white and red.
Look up, look up—I flutter now
On this flush pomgranate bough.
See me—'tis this silvery bill
Ever cures the good man's ill.
15   Shed no tear—O shed no tear!
The flower will bloom another year.
Adieu—adieu—I fly, adieu!
I vanish in the heaven's blue—
        Adieu, adieu!

Otho the Great:
A Tragedy in Five Acts

Dramatis Personæ

OTHO THE GREAT, *Emperor of Germany*
LUDOLPH, *his Son*
CONRAD, *Duke of Franconia*
ALBERT, *a Knight, favoured by Otho*
SIGIFRED, *an Officer, friend of Ludolph*
THEODORE,⎱ *Officers*
GONFRID, ⎰
ETHELBERT, *an Abbot*
GERSA, *Prince of Hungary*
An Hungarian Captain
Physician
Page
Nobles, Knights, Attendants, and Soldiers

ERMINIA, *Niece of Otho*
AURANTHE, *Conrad's Sister*
Ladies and Attendants

SCENE. *The Castle of Friedburg, its vicinity,*
and the Hungarian Camp

TIME. *One Day*

ACT I

SCENE I. *An Apartment in the Castle.*

Enter CONRAD.

Conrad. So, I am safe emerged from these broils!
Amid the wreck of thousands I am whole;
For every crime I have a laurel-wreath,
For every lie a lordship. Nor yet has
5   My ship of fortune furl'd her silken sails,—
Let her glide on! This danger'd neck is saved,
By dexterous policy, from the rebel's axe;
And of my ducal palace not one stone

Is bruised by the Hungarian petards.
10   Toil hard, ye slaves, and from the miser-earth
Bring forth once more my bullion, treasured deep,
With all my jewell'd salvers, silver and gold,
And precious goblets that make rich the wine.
But why do I stand babbling to myself?
15   Where is Auranthe? I have news for her
Shall—

Enter AURANTHE.

Auranthe. Conrad! what tidings? Good, if I may guess
From your alert eyes and high-lifted brows.
What tidings of the battle? Albert? Ludolph?
20   Otho?
    Conrad. You guess aright. And, sister, slurring o'er
Our by-gone quarrels, I confess my heart
Is beating with a child's anxiety,
To make our golden fortune known to you.
    Auranthe. So serious?
25   *Conrad.*   Yes, so serious, that before
I utter even the shadow of a hint
Concerning what will make that sin-worn cheek
Blush joyous blood through every lineament,
You must make here a solemn vow to me.
30   *Auranthe.* I pr'ythee, Conrad, do not overact
The hypocrite. What vow would you impose?
    Conrad. Trust me for once. That you may be assured
'Tis not confiding in a broken reed,
A poor court-bankrupt, outwitted and lost,
35   Revolve these facts in your acutest mood,
In such a mood as now you listen to me:
A few days since, I was an open rebel,—
Against the Emperor had suborn'd his son,—
Drawn off his nobles to revolt,—and shown
40   Contented fools causes for discontent,
Fresh hatch'd in my ambition's eagle-nest;
So thrived I as a rebel,—and, behold!
Now I am Otho's favorite, his dear friend,
His right hand, his brave Conrad!
    Auranthe.   I confess
45   You have intrigued with these unsteady times
To admiration. But to be a favorite—

  Conrad. I saw my moment. The Hungarians,
Collected silently in holes and corners,
Appear'd, a sudden host, in the open day.
50 I should have perish'd in our empire's wreck;
But, calling interest loyalty, swore faith
To most believing Otho; and so help'd
His blood-stain'd ensigns to the victory
In yesterday's hard fight, that it has turn'd
55 The edge of his sharp wrath to eager kindness.
  Auranthe. So far yourself. But what is this to me
More than that I am glad? I gratulate you.
  Conrad. Yes, sister, but it does regard you greatly,
Nearly, momentously,—aye, painfully!
Make me this vow—
60 *Auranthe.* Concerning whom or what?
  Conrad. Albert!
  Auranthe. I would enquire somewhat of him:
You had a letter from me touching him?
No treason 'gainst his head in deed or word!
Surely you spared him at my earnest prayer?
65 Give me the letter—it should not exist!
  Conrad. At one pernicious charge of the enemy,
I, for a moment-whiles, was prisoner ta'en
And rifled,—stuff! the horses' hoofs have minced it!
  Auranthe. He is alive?
  Conrad. He is! but here make oath
70 To alienate him from your scheming brain,
Divorce him from your solitary thoughts,
And cloud him in such utter banishment,
That when his person meets again your eye,
Your vision shall quite lose its memory,
75 And wander past him as through vacancy.
  Auranthe. I'll not be perjured.
  Conrad. No, nor great, nor mighty;
You would not wear a crown, or rule a kingdom,
To you it is indifferent.
  Auranthe. What means this?
  Conrad. You'll not be perjured! Go to Albert then,
80 That camp-mushroom, dishonour of our house;
Go, page his dusty heels upon a march,
Furbish his jingling baldric while he sleeps,
And share his mouldy ratio in a siege.
Yet stay,—perhaps a charm may call you back,

85 And make the widening circlets of your eyes
    Sparkle with healthy fevers,—the Emperor
    Hath given consent that you should marry Ludolph!
        Auranthe. Can it be, brother? For a golden crown
    With a queen's awful lips I doubly thank you!
90 This is to wake in Paradise! farewell,
    Thou clod of yesterday—'twas not myself!
    Not till this moment did I ever feel
    My spirit's faculties! I'll flatter you
    For this, and be you ever proud of it;
95 Thou, Jove-like, struck'dst thy forehead,
    And from the teeming marrow of thy brain
    I spring complete Minerva! But the Prince—
    His Highness Ludolph—where is he?
        Conrad.   I know not:
    When, lackeying my counsel at a beck,
100 The rebel-lords, on bended knees, received
    The Emperor's pardon, Ludolph kept aloof,
    Sole,—in a stiff, fool-hardy, sulky pride;
    Yet, for all this, I never saw a father
    In such a sickly longing for his son.
105 We shall soon see him,—for the Emperor,
    He will be here this morning.
        Auranthe.   That I heard
    Among the midnight rumours from the camp.
        Conrad. You give up Albert to me?
        Auranthe.   Harm him not!
    E'en for his Highness Ludolph's sceptry hand,
110 I would not Albert suffer any wrong.
        Conrad. Have I not labour'd, plotted—?
        Auranthe.   See you spare him;
    Nor be pathetic, my kind benefactor,
    On all the many bounties of your hand,—
    'Twas for yourself you labour'd—not for me!
115 Do you not count, when I am queen, to take
    Advantage of your chance discoveries
    Of my poor secrets, and so hold a rod
    Over my life?
        Conrad.   Let not this slave—this villain—
    Be cause of feud between us. See! he comes!
120 Look, woman, look, your Albert is quite safe!
    In haste it seems. Now shall I be in the way,

And wish'd with silent curses in my grave,
Or side by side with whelmed mariners.

Enter ALBERT.

   Albert. Fair on your Graces fall this early morrow!
125 So it is like to do, without my prayers,
For your right noble names, like favorite tunes,
Have fallen full frequent from our Emperor's lips,
High commented with smiles.
   Auranthe.   Noble Albert!
   Conrad (*aside*). Noble!
130   *Auranthe.* Such salutation argues a glad heart
In our prosperity. We thank you, sir.
   Albert. Lady! O would to heaven your poor servant
Could do you better service than mere words!
But I have other greeting than mine own
135 From no less man than Otho, who has sent
This ring as pledge of dearest amity;
'Tis chosen I hear from Hymen's jewelry,
And you will prize it, lady, I doubt not,
Beyond all pleasures past, and all to come:
To you, great Duke—
140   *Conrad.*   To me! What of me, ha?
   Albert. What pleas'd your Grace to say?
   Conrad.   Your message, sir!
   Albert. You mean not this to me?
   Conrad.   Sister, this way;
For there shall be no "gentle Alberts" now,   *[Aside.*
No "sweet Auranthes"!   *[Exeunt* CONRAD *and* AURANTHE.
145   *Albert* (*solus*). The Duke is out of temper; if he knows
More than a brother of a sister ought,
I should not quarrel with his peevishness.
Auranthe—heaven preserve her always fair!—
Is in the heady, proud, ambitious vein;
150 I bicker not with her,—bid her farewell!
She has taken flight from me, then let her soar,—
He is a fool who stands at pining gaze!
But for poor Ludolph, he is food for sorrow;
No leveling bluster of my licensed thoughts,
155 No military swagger of my mind,
Can smother from myself the wrong I've done him,—

Without design indeed,—yet it is so,—
And opiate for the conscience have I none!   [*Exit.*

SCENE II. *The Court-yard of the Castle.*

Martial music. Enter, from the outer gate, OTHO, *Nobles, Knights,
and Attendants. The Soldiers halt at the gate, with banners in sight.*

Otho. Where is my noble herald?
[*Enter* CONRAD, *from the Castle, attended by two Knights and Ser-
vants.* ALBERT *following.*
                                                        Well! hast told
Auranthe our intent imperial?
Lest our rent banners, too o' the sudden shown,
Should fright her silken casements, and dismay
5   Her household to our lack of entertainment.
A victory!
    Conrad. God save illustrious Otho!
    Otho. Aye, Conrad, it will pluck out all grey hairs;
It is the best physician for the spleen;
The courtliest inviter to a feast;
10   The subtelest excuser of small faults;
And a nice judge in the age and smack of wine.
        [*Enter, from the Castle,* AURANTHE, *followed by Pages holding up
        her robes, and a train of Women. She kneels.*
Hail, my sweet hostess! I do thank the stars,
Or my good soldiers, or their ladies' eyes,
That, after such a merry battle fought,
15   I can, all safe in body and in soul,
Kiss your fair hand and lady fortune's too.
My ring! now, on my life, it doth rejoice
These lips to feel't on this soft ivory!
Keep it, my brightest daughter; it may prove
20   The little prologue to a line of kings.
I strove against thee and my hot-blood son,
Dull blockhead that I was to be so blind,
But now my sight is clear; forgive me, lady.
    Auranthe. My lord, I was a vassal to your frown,
25   And now your favour makes me but more humble;
In wintry winds the simple snow is safe,
But fadeth at the greeting of the sun:
Unto thine anger I might well have spoken,
Taking on me a woman's privilege,

30   But this so sudden kindness makes me dumb.
      Otho. What need of this? Enough, if you will be
A potent tutoress to my wayward boy,
And teach him, what it seems his nurse could not,
To say for once I thank you. Sigifred!
35   *Albert.* He has not yet return'd, my gracious liege.
      Otho. What then! No tidings of my friendly Arab?
      Conrad. None, mighty Otho.
                  [*To one of his Knights, who goes out.*
                  Send forth instantly
An hundred horsemen from my honoured gates,
To scour the plains and search the cottages.
40   Cry a reward, to him who shall first bring
News of that vanished Arabian,
A full-heaped helmet of the purest gold.
      Otho. More thanks, good Conrad; for, except my son's,
There is no face I rather would behold
45   Than that same quick-eyed pagan's. By the saints,
This coming night of banquets must not light
Her dazzling torches; nor the music breathe
Smooth, without clashing cymbal, tones of peace
And in-door melodies; nor the ruddy wine
50   Ebb spouting to the lees;—if I pledge not,
In my first cup, that Arab!
      Albert.   Mighty monarch,
I wonder not this stranger's victor-deeds
So hang upon your spirit. Twice in the fight
It was my chance to meet his olive brow,
55   Triumphant in the enemy's shatter'd rhomb;
And, to say truth, in any Christian arm
I never saw such prowess.
      Otho.   Did you ever?
O, 'tis a noble boy!—tut!—what do I say?
I mean a tripple-Saladin, whose eyes,
60   When in the glorious scuffle they met mine,
Seem'd to say—"Sleep, old man, in safety sleep;
I am the victory!"
      Conrad.   Pity he's not here.
      Otho. And my son too, pity he is not here.
Lady Auranthe, I would not make you blush,
65   But can you give a guess where Ludolph is?
Know you not of him?
      Auranthe.   Indeed, my liege, no secret—

    Otho. Nay, nay, without more words, dost know of him?
    Auranthe. I would I were so over-fortunate,
Both for his sake and mine, and to make glad
70 A father's ears with tidings of his son.
    Otho. I see 'tis like to be a tedious day.
Were Theodore and Gonfrid and the rest
Sent forth with my commands?
    Albert.   Aye, my lord.
    Otho. And no news! No news! 'Faith! 'tis very strange
75 He thus avoids us. Lady, is't not strange?
Will he be truant to you too? It is a shame.
    Conrad. Will't please your Highness enter, and accept
The unworthy welcome of your servant's house?
Leaving your cares to one whose diligence
80 May in few hours make pleasures of them all.
    Otho. Not so tedious, Conrad. No, no, no, no,—
I must see Ludolph or the—What's that shout?
    Voices without. Huzza! Huzza! Long live the Emperor!
    Other voices. Fall back! Away there!
    Otho.   Say, what noise is that?
    *Albert (advancing from the back of the stage, whither he had hastened
        on hearing the cheers of the soldiery).* It is young Gersa, the
85   Hungarian prince,
Pick'd like a red stag from the fallow herd
Of prisoners. Poor prince, forlorn he steps,
Slow, and demure, and proud in his despair.
If I may judge by his so tragic bearing,
90 His eye not downcast, and his folded arm,
He doth this moment wish himself asleep
Among his fallen captains on yon plains.

           Enter GERSA, *in chains, and guarded.*

    Otho. Well said, Sir Albert.
    Gersa.   Not a word of greeting,
No welcome to a princely visitor,
95 Most mighty Otho? Will not my great host
Vouchsafe a syllable, before he bids
His gentlemen conduct me with all care
To some securest lodging—cold perhaps!
    Otho. What mood is this? Hath fortune touch'd thy brain?
100   *Gersa.* O kings and princes of this fevrous world,
What abject things, what mockeries must ye be,

What nerveless minions of safe palaces!
When here, a monarch, whose proud foot is used
To fallen princes' necks, as to his stirrup,
105   Must needs exclaim that I am mad forsooth,
Because I cannot flatter with bent knees
My conqueror!
    Otho.   Gersa, I think you wrong me:
I think I have a better fame abroad.
    Gersa. I pr'ythee mock me not with gentle speech,
110   But, as a favour, bid me from thy presence;
Let me no longer be the wondering food
Of all these eyes; pr'ythee command me hence!
    Otho. Do not mistake me, Gersa. That you may not,
Come, fair Auranthe, try if your soft hands
115   Can manage those hard rivets to set free
So brave a prince and soldier.
    Auranthe (sets him free).   Welcome task!
    Gersa. I am wound up in deep astonishment!
Thank you, fair lady—Otho!—Emperor!
You rob me of myself; my dignity
120   Is now your infant;—I am a weak child.
    Otho. Give me your hand, and let this kindly grasp
Live in our memories.
    Gersa.   In mine it will.
I blush to think of my unchasten'd tongue;
But I was haunted by the monstrous ghost
125   Of all our slain battalions. Sire, reflect,
And pardon you will grant, that, at this hour,
The bruised remnants of our stricken camp
Are huddling undistinguish'd, my dear friends
With common thousands, into shallow graves.
130   *Otho.* Enough, most noble Gersa. You are free
To cheer the brave remainder of your host
By your own healing presence, and that too,
Not as their leader merely, but their king;
For, as I hear, the wily enemy,
135   Who eas'd the crownet from your infant brows,
Bloody Taraxa, is among the dead.
    Gersa. Then I retire, so generous Otho please,
Bearing with me a weight of benefits
Too heavy to be borne.
    Otho.   It is not so;
140   Still understand me, King of Hungary,

Nor judge my open purposes awry.
Though I did hold you high in my esteem
For your self's sake, I do not personate
The stage-play emperor to entrap applause,

145   To set the silly sort o' the world agape,
And make the politic smile; no, I have heard
How in the Council you condemn'd this war,
Urging the perfidy of broken faith,—
For that I am your friend.
    Gersa.   If ever, sire,

150   You are my enemy, I dare here swear
'Twill not be Gersa's fault. Otho, farewell!
    Otho. Will you return, Prince, to our banquetting?
    Gersa. As to my father's board I will return.
    Otho. Conrad, with all due ceremony, give

155   The Prince a regal escort to his camp;
Albert, go thou and bear him company.
Gersa, farewell!
    Gersa.   All happiness attend you!
    Otho. Return with what good speed you may; for soon
We must consult upon our terms of peace.
                  [Exeunt GERSA *and* ALBERT, *with others.*

160   And thus a marble column do I build
To prop my empire's dome. Conrad, in thee
I have another steadfast one, to uphold
The portals of my state; and, for my own
Preeminence and safety, I will strive

165   To keep thy strength upon its pedestal.
For, without thee, this day I might have been
A show-monster about the streets of Prague,
In chains, as just now stood that noble prince:
And then to me no mercy had been shown,

170   For when the conquer'd lion is once dungeoned,
Who lets him forth again? or dares to give
An old lion sugar-cates of mild reprieve?
Not to thine ear alone I make confession,
But to all here, as, by experience,

175   I know how the great basement of all power
Is frankness, and a true tongue to the world;
And how intriguing secresy is proof
Of fear and weakness, and a hollow state.
Conrad, I owe thee much.
    Conrad.   To kiss that hand,

180   My Emperor, is ample recompense
     For a mere act of duty.
        Otho.   Thou art wrong;
     For what can any man on earth do more?
     We will make trial of your house's welcome,
     My bright Auranthe!
        Conrad.   How is Friedburg honoured!

           Enter ETHELBERT *and six Monks.*

185   *Ethelbert.* The benison of heaven on your head,
     Imperial Otho!
        Otho.   Who stays me? Speak! Quick!
     Ethelbert. Pause but one moment, mighty conqueror,
     Upon the threshold of this house of joy—
     Otho. Pray do not prose, good Ethelbert, but speak
190   What is your purpose.
     Ethelbert. The restoration of some captive maids,
     Devoted to heaven's pious ministries,
     Who, driven forth from their religious cells,
     And kept in thraldom by our enemy,
195   When late this province was a lawless spoil,
     Still weep amid the wild Hungarian camp,
     Though hemm'd around by thy victorious arms.
     Otho. Demand the holy sisterhood in our name
     From Gersa's tents. Farewell, old Ethelbert.
200   *Ethelbert.* The saints will bless you for this pious care.
     Otho. Daughter, your hand; Ludolph's would fit it best.
     Conrad. Ho! let the music sound!
       [*Music.* ETHELBERT *raises his hands, as in benediction of* OTHO.
       Exeunt severally. The scene closes on them.

        SCENE III. *The Country, with the Castle in the distance.*

          Enter LUDOLPH *and* SIGIFRED.

     Ludolph. You have my secret, let it not be breath'd.
     Sigifred. Still give me leave to wonder that the Prince
     Ludolph and the swift Arab are the same;
     Still to rejoice that 'twas a German arm
5   Death doing in a turban'd masquerade.
     Ludolph. The Emperor must not know it, Sigifred.
     Sigifred. I pr'ythee why? What happier hour of time

Could thy pleas'd star point down upon from heaven
With silver index, bidding thee make peace?
10   *Ludolph.* Still it must not be known, good Sigifred;
The star may point oblique.
        Sigifred.   If Otho knew
His son to be that unknown Mussleman
After whose spurring heels he sent me forth,
With one of his well-pleas'd Olympian oaths,
15   The charters of man's greatness, at this hour
He would be watching round the castle-walls,
And, like an anxious warder, strain his sight
For the first glimpse of such a son return'd;
Ludolph, that blast of the Hungarians,
20   That Saracenic meteor of the fight,
That silent fury, whose fell scymitar
Kept danger all aloof from Otho's head,
And left him space for wonder.
        Ludolph.   Say no more.
Not as a swordsman would I pardon claim,
25   But as a son. The bronz'd centurion,
Long toil'd in foreign wars, and whose high deeds
Are shaded in a forest of tall spears,
Known only to his troop, hath greater plea
Of favour with my sire than I can have.
30   *Sigifred.* My lord, forgive me that I cannot see
How this proud temper with clear reason squares.
What made you then, with such an anxious love,
Hover around that life, whose bitter days
You vext with bad revolt? Was't opium,
35   Or the mad-fumed wine—? Nay, do not frown,
I rather would grieve with you than upbraid.
        Ludolph. I do believe you. No, 'twas not to make
A father his son's debtor, or to heal
His deep heart-sickness for a rebel child.
40   'Twas done in memory of my boyish days,
Poor cancel for his kindness to my youth,
For all his calming of my childish griefs,
And all his smiles upon my merriment.
No, not a thousand foughten fields could sponge
45   Those days paternal from my memory,
Though now upon my head he heaps disgrace.
        Sigifred. My Prince, you think too harshly—
        Ludolph.   Can I so?

Hath he not gall'd my spirit to the quick?
And with a sullen rigour obstinate
50   Pour'd out a phial of wrath upon my faults?
Hunted me as a Tartar does the boar,
Driven me to the very edge o' the world,
And almost put a price upon my head?
    Sigifred. Remember how he spared the rebel-lords.
55   *Ludolph.* Yes, yes, I know he hath a noble nature
That cannot trample on the fallen. But his
Is not the only proud heart in his realm.
He hath wrong'd me, and I have done him wrong;
He hath lov'd me, and I have shown him kindness;
We should be almost equal.
60   *Sigifred.*   Yet, for all this,
I would you had appear'd among those lords,
And ta'en his favour.
    Ludolph.   Ha! till now I thought
My friend had held poor Ludolph's honour dear.
What! would you have me sue before his throne,
65   And kiss the courtier's missal, its silk steps?
Or hug the golden housings of his steed,
Amid a camp, whose steeled swarms I dar'd
But yesterday? And, at the trumpet sound,
Bow like some unknown mercenary's flag
70   And lick the soiled grass? No, no, my friend,
I would not, I, be pardon'd in the heap,
And bless indemnity with all that scum,—
Those men I mean, who on my shoulders propp'd
Their weak rebellion, winning me with lies,
75   And pitying forsooth my many wrongs;
Poor self-deceived wretches, who must think
Each one himself a king in embryo,
Because some dozen vassals cry'd—my lord!
Cowards, who never knew their little hearts,
80   Till flurried danger held the mirror up,
And then they own'd themselves without a blush,
Curling, like spaniels, round my father's feet.
Such things deserted me and are forgiven,
While I, least guilty, am an outcast still,
85   And will be, for I love such fair disgrace.
    Sigifred. I know the clear truth; so would Otho see,
For he is just and noble. Fain would I
Be pleader for you—

Ludolph.   He'll hear none of it;
You know his temper, hot, proud, obstinate;

90   Endanger not yourself so uselessly.
I will encounter his thwart spleen myself,
To-day, at the Duke Conrad's, where he keeps
His crowded state after the victory.
There will I be, a most unwelcome guest,

95   And parley with him, as a son should do,
Who doubly loathes a father's tyranny;
Tell him how feeble is that tyranny,
How the relationship of father and son
Is no more valid than a silken leash

100 Where lions tug adverse, if love grow not
From interchanged love through many years.
Aye, and those turreted Franconian walls,
Like to a jealous casket, hold my pearl—
My fair Auranthe! Yes, I will be there.

105 *Sigifred.* Be not so rash; wait till his wrath shall pass,
Until his royal spirit softly ebbs
Self-influenced; then, in his morning dreams
He will forgive thee, and awake in grief
To have not thy good morrow.
     Ludolph.   Yes, to-day

110 I must be there, while her young pulses beat
Among the new-plum'd minions of the war.
Have you seen her of late? No? Auranthe,
Franconia's fair sister, 'tis I mean.
She should be paler for my troublous days—

115 And there it is my father's iron lips
Have sworn divorcement 'twixt me and my right.
     Sigifred (aside). Auranthe! I had hoped this whim had pass'd.
     Ludolph. And, Sigifred, with all his love of justice,
When will he take that grandchild in his arms,

120 That, by my love I swear, shall soon be his?
This reconcilement is impossible,
For see—But who are these?
     Sigifred.   They are messengers
From our great Emperor; to you, I doubt not,
For couriers are abroad to seek you out.

Enter THEODORE *and* GONFRID.

125 *Theodore.* Seeing so many vigilant eyes explore
The province to invite your Highness back

To your high dignities, we are too happy.
  Gonfrid. We have no eloquence to colour justly
The Emperor's anxious wishes—
  Ludolph.   Go—I follow you.
              [*Exeunt* THEODORE *and* GONFRID.
130 I play the prude: it is but venturing—
Why should he be so earnest? Come, my friend,
Let us to Friedburg castle.

ACT II

SCENE I. *An Antichamber in the Castle.*

Enter LUDOLPH *and* SIGIFRED.

  Ludolph. No more advices, no more cautioning;
I leave it all to fate—to any thing!
I cannot square my conduct to time, place,
Or circumstance; to me 'tis all a mist!
  Sigifred. I say no more.
5   *Ludolph.*   It seems I am to wait
Here in the antiroom;—that may be a trifle.
You see now how I dance attendance here,
Without that tyrant temper, you so blame,
Snapping the rein. You have medicin'd me
10 With good advices; and I here remain,
In this most honourable antiroom,
Your patient scholar.
  Sigifred.   Do not wrong me, Prince.
By heavens, I'd rather kiss Duke Conrad's slipper,
When in the morning he doth yawn with pride,
15 Than see you humbled but a half degree!
Truth is, the Emperor would fain dismiss
The nobles ere he sees you.

Enter GONFRID, *from the Council-room.*

  Ludolph.   Well, sir! What!
  Gonfrid. Great honour to the Prince! The Emperor,
Hearing that his brave son had reappeared,
20 Instant dismiss'd the Council from his sight,
As Jove fans off the clouds. Even now they pass.   [*Exit.*

*Enter the Nobles from the Council-room. They cross the stage, bow-
ing with respect to* LUDOLPH, *he frowning on them.* CONRAD
follows. Exeunt Nobles.

Ludolph. Not the discoloured poisons of a fen,
Which he who breathes feels warning of his death,
Could taste so nauseous to the bodily sense,

25   As these prodigious sycophants disgust
The soul's fine palate.
Conrad.   Princely Ludolph, hail!
Welcome, thou younger scepter to the realm!
Strength to thy virgin crownet's golden buds,
That they, against the winter of thy sire,

30   May burst, and swell, and flourish round thy brows,
Maturing to a weighty diadem!
Yet be that hour far off; and may he live,
Who waits for thee, as the chapp'd earth for rain.
Set my life's star! I have liv'd long enough,

35   Since under my glad roof, propitiously,
Father and son each other repossess.
Ludolph. Fine wording, Duke! but words could never yet
Forestall the fates; have you not learnt that yet?
Let me look well: your features are the same,

40   Your gait the same, your hair of the same shade,
As one I knew some passed weeks ago,
Who sung far different notes into mine ears.
I have mine own particular comments on't;
You have your own perhaps.
Conrad.   My gracious Prince,

45   All men may err. In truth I was deceived
In your great father's nature, as you were.
Had I known that of him I have since known,
And what you soon will learn, I would have turn'd
My sword to my own throat, rather than held

50   Its threatening edge against a good king's quiet;
Or with one word fever'd you, gentle Prince,
Who seem'd to me, as rugged times then went,
Indeed too much oppress'd. May I be bold
To tell the Emperor you will haste to him?

55   *Ludolph.* Your dukedom's privilege will grant so much.
                                                    [*Exit* CONRAD.
He's very close to Otho, a tight leach!
Your hand—I go! Ha! here the thunder comes

Sullen against the wind! If in two angry brows
My safety lies, then, Sigifred, I'm safe.

Enter OTHO *and* CONRAD.

60   *Otho.* Will you make Titan play the lackey-page
To chattering pigmies? I would have you know
That such neglect of our high Majesty
Annuls all feel of kindred. What is son,—
Or friend,—or brother,—or all ties of blood,—
65   When the whole kingdom, centred in ourself,
Is rudely slighted? Who am I to wait?
By Peter's chair! I have upon my tongue
A word to fright the proudest spirit here!—
Death!—and slow tortures to the hardy fool
70   Who dares take such large charter from our smiles!
Conrad, we would be private! Sigifred!
Off! And none pass this way on pain of death!
                    [*Exeunt* CONRAD *and* SIGIFRED.
    Ludolph. This was but half expected, my good sire,
Yet I am griev'd at it, to the full height,
75   As though my hopes of favour had been whole.
    Otho. How you indulge yourself: what can you hope for?
    Ludolph. Nothing, my liege; I have to hope for nothing.
I come to greet you as a loving son,
And then depart, if I may be so free,
80   Seeing that blood of yours in my warm veins
Has not yet mitigated into milk.
    Otho. What would you, sir?
    Ludolph.   A lenient banishment;
So please you let me unmolested pass
This Conrad's gates, to the wide air again.
85   I want no more. A rebel wants no more.
    Otho. And shall I let a rebel loose again
To muster kites and eagles 'gainst my head?
No, obstinate boy, you shall be kept cag'd up,
Serv'd with harsh food, with scum for Sunday-drink.
    Ludolph. Indeed!
90   *Otho.*   And chains too heavy for your life;
I'll choose a jailor, whose swart monstrous face
Shall be a hell to look upon, and she—
    Ludolph. Ha!
    Otho. Shall be your fair Auranthe.

Ludolph.   Amaze! Amaze!
Otho. To-day you marry her.
95   *Ludolph.*   This is a sharp jest!
Otho. No. None at all. When have I said a lie?
Ludolph. If I sleep not, I am a waking wretch.
Otho. Not a word more. Let me embrace my child.
Ludolph. I dare not. 'Twould pollute so good a father!
100   O heavy crime! that your son's blinded eyes
Could not see all his parent's love aright,
As now I see it. Be not kind to me—
Punish me not with favour.
Otho.   Are you sure,
Ludolph, you have no saving plea in store?
Ludolph. My father, none!
105   *Otho.*   Then you astonish me.
Ludolph. No, I have no plea. Disobedience,
Rebellion, obstinacy, blasphemy,—
Are all my counsellors. If they can make
My crooked deeds show good and plausible,
110   Then grant me loving pardon,—but not else,—
Good gods! not else, in any way, my liege!
Otho. You are a most perplexing noble boy.
Ludolph. You not less a perplexing noble father.
Otho. Well! you shall have free passport through the gates.
Farewell!
115   *Ludolph.* Farewell! and by these tears believe,
And still remember, I repent in pain
All my misdeeds!
Otho.   Ludolph, I will! I will!
But, Ludolph, ere you go, I would enquire
If you, in all your wandering, ever met
120   A certain Arab haunting in these parts.
Ludolph. No, my good lord, I cannot say I did.
Otho. Make not your father blind before his time;
Nor let these arms paternal hunger more
For an embrace, to dull the appetite
125   Of my great love for thee, my supreme child!
Come close, and let me breathe into thine ear
I knew you through disguise. You are the Arab!
You can't deny it.   [*Embracing him.*
Ludolph.   Happiest of days!
Otho. We'll make it so.

   Ludolph.   'Stead of one fatted calf,
130 Ten hecatombs shall bellow out their last,
  Smote 'twixt the horns by the death-stunning mace
  Of Mars, and all the soldiery shall feast
  Nobly as Nimrod's masons, when the towers
  Of Nineveh new kiss'd the parted clouds!
135 *Otho.* Large as a god speak out, where all is thine.
   Ludolph. Aye, father;—but the fire in my sad breast
  Is quench'd with inward tears! I must rejoice
  For you, whose wings so shadow over me
  In tender victory,—but for myself
140 I still must mourn. The fair Auranthe mine!
  Too great a boon! I pr'ythee, let me ask
  What more than I know of could so have chang'd
  Your purpose touching her.
   Otho.   At a word, this:
  In no deed did you give me more offence
145 Than your rejection of Erminia.
  To my appalling, I saw too good proof
  Of your keen-eyed suspicion,—she is naught!
   Ludolph. You are convinc'd?
   Otho.   Aye, spite of her sweet looks.
  O, that my brother's daughter should so fall!
150 Her fame has pass'd into the grosser lips
  Of soldiers in their cups.
   Ludolph.   'Tis very sad.
   Otho. No more of her. Auranthe—Ludolph, come!
  This marriage be the bond of endless peace! [*Exeunt.*

     Scene II. *The entrance of* Gersa's *Tent*
      in the Hungarian Camp.

      Enter Erminia.

  Erminia. Where! Where! Where shall I find a messenger?
  A trusty soul? A good man in the camp?
  Shall I go myself? Monstrous wickedness!
  O cursed Conrad! devilish Auranthe!
5 Here is proof palpable as the bright sun!
  O for a voice to reach the Emperor's ears!
            [*Shouts in the Camp.*

Enter an Hungarian Captain.

 Captain. Fair prisoner, you hear these joyous shouts?
The King—aye, now our King,—but still your slave,
Young Gersa, from a short captivity
10 Has just return'd. He bids me say, bright dame,
That even the homage of his ranged chiefs
Cures not his keen impatience to behold
Such beauty once again.—What ails you, lady?
 Erminia. Say, is not that a German yonder? There!
15 *Captain.* Methinks by his stout bearing he should be—
Yes—it is Albert; a brave German knight,
And much in the Emperor's favor.
 Erminia.   I would fain
Enquire of friends and kinsfolk; how they fared
In these rough times. Brave soldier, as you pass
20 To royal Gersa with my humble thanks,
Will you send yonder knight to me?
 Captain.   I will.   [*Exit.*
 Erminia. Yes, he was ever known to be a man
Frank, open, generous; Albert I may trust.
O proof! proof! proof! Albert's an honest man;
25 Not Ethelbert the monk, if he were here,
Would I hold more trustworthy. Now!

Enter ALBERT.

 Albert.   Good gods!
Lady Erminia! are you prisoner
In this beleaguer'd camp? Or are you here
Of your own will? You pleas'd to send for me.
30 By Venus, 'tis a pity I knew not
Your plight before, and, by her son, I swear
To do you every service you can ask.
What would the fairest—?
 Erminia.   Albert, will you swear?
 Albert. I have. Well?
 Erminia.   Albert, you have fame to lose.
35 If men, in court and camp, lie not outright,
You should be, from a thousand, chosen forth
To do an honest deed. Shall I confide—?
 Albert. Aye, any thing to me, fair creature. Do,
Dictate my task. Sweet woman,—

    Erminia.   Truce with that.

40   You understand me not; and, in your speech,
     I see how far the slander is abroad.
     Without proof could you think me innocent?
        Albert. Lady, I should rejoice to know you so.
        Erminia. If you have any pity for a maid,

45   Suffering a daily death from evil tongues;
     Any compassion for that Emperor's niece,
     Who, for your bright sword and clear honesty,
     Lifted you from the crowd of common men
     Into the lap of honour;—save me, knight!

50   *Albert.* How? Make it clear; if it be possible,
     I by the banner of Saint Maurice swear
     To right you.
        Erminia.   Possible!—Easy! O my heart!
     This letter's not so soil'd but you may read it;—
     Possible! There—that letter! Read—read it!

                      [Gives him a letter.

55   *Albert (reads it).* "To the Duke Conrad. Forget the threat you
made at parting, and I will forget to send the Emperor letters
and papers of yours I have become possessed of. His life is no
trifle to me; his death you shall find none to yourself." (*Aside.*)
'Tis me—my life that's pleaded for! (*Reads.*) "He, for his own

60   sake, will be dumb as the grave. Erminia has my shame fix'd
upon her, sure as a wen. We are safe.

                        "Auranthe."

     A she devil! A dragon! I her imp!
     Fire of hell! Auranthe—lewd demon!

65   Where got you this? Where? When?
        Erminia. I found it in the tent, among some spoils
     Which, being noble, fell to Gersa's lot.
     Come in, and see.   *[They go in and return.*
        Albert.   Villainy! Villainy!
     Conrad's sword, his corslet, and his helm,

70   And his letter. Caitiff, he shall feel—
        Erminia. I see you are thunderstruck. Haste, haste away!
        Albert. O I am tortur'd by this villainy.
        Erminia. You needs must be. Carry it swift to Otho;
     Tell him, moreover, I am prisoner

75   Here in this camp, where all the sisterhood,
     Forc'd from their quiet cells, are parcell'd out
     For slaves among these Huns. Away! Away!
        Albert. I am gone.

Erminia.   Swift be your steed! Within this hour
The Emperor will see it.
    Albert.   Ere I sleep:
That I can swear.   [*Hurries out.*
80   *Gersa* (*without*). Brave captains, thanks! Enough
Of loyal homage now!

Enter GERSA.

Erminia.   Hail, royal Hun!
Gersa. What means this, fair one? Why in such alarm?
Who was it hurried by me so distract?
It seem'd you were in deep discourse together;
85   Your doctrine has not been so harsh to him
As to my poor deserts. Come, come, be plain.
I am no jealous fool to kill you both,
Or, for such trifles, rob th' adorned world
Of such a beauteous vestal.
    Erminia.   I grieve, my lord,
90   To hear you condescend to ribbald-phrase.
    Gersa. This is too much! Hearken, my lady pure,—
    Erminia. Silence! and hear the magic of a name—
Erminia! I am she,—the Emperor's niece!
Prais'd be the heavens, I now dare own myself!
95   *Gersa.* Erminia! Indeed! I've heard of her—
Prythee, fair lady, what chance brought you here?
    Erminia. Ask your own soldiers.
    Gersa.   And you dare own your name.
For loveliness you may—and for the rest
My vein is not censorious—
    Erminia.   Alas, poor me!
'Tis false indeed.
100   *Gersa.*   Indeed you are too fair:
The swan, soft leaning on her fledgy breast,
When to the stream she launches, looks not back
With such a tender grace; nor are her wings
So white as your soul is, if that but be
105   Twin picture to your face. Erminia!
To-day, for the first day, I am a king,
Yet would I give my unworn crown away
To know you spotless.
    Erminia.   Trust me one day more,
Generously, without more certain guarantee,

110　Than this poor face you deign to praise so much;
　　　After that, say and do whate'er you please.
　　　If I have any knowledge of you, sir,
　　　I think, nay I am sure, you will grieve much
　　　To hear my story. O be gentle to me,
115　For I am sick and faint with many wrongs,
　　　Tired out, and weary-worn with contumelies.
　　　　　Gersa. Poor lady!

Enter ETHELBERT.

　　　Erminia.　　　　Gentle Prince, 'tis false indeed.
　　　Good morrow, holy father! I have had
　　　Your prayers, though I look'd for you in vain.
120　　　*Ethelbert.* Blessings upon you, daughter! Sure you look
　　　Too cheerful for these foul pernicious days.
　　　Young man, you heard this virgin say 'twas false,—
　　　'Tis false, I say. What! can you not employ
　　　Your temper elsewhere, 'mong these burly tents,
125　But you must taunt this dove, for she hath lost
　　　The eagle Otho to beat off assault.
　　　Fie! Fie! But I will be her guard myself;
　　　In the Emperor's name, I here demand of you
　　　Herself, and all her sisterhood. She false!
130　　　*Gersa.* Peace! peace, old man! I cannot think she is.
　　　　　Ethelbert. Whom I have known from her first infancy,
　　　Baptis'd her in the bosom of the church,
　　　Watch'd her, as anxious husbandmen the grain,
　　　From the first shoot till the unripe mid-May,
135　Then to the tender ear of her June days,
　　　Which, lifting sweet abroad its timid green,
　　　Is blighted by the touch of calumny;
　　　You cannot credit such a monstrous tale.
　　　　　Gersa. I cannot. Take her. Fair Erminia,
140　I follow you to Friedburg,—is't not so?
　　　　　Erminia. Aye, so we purpose.
　　　　　Ethelbert.　　　　Daughter, do you so?
　　　How's this? I marvel! Yet you look not mad.
　　　　　Erminia. I have good news to tell you, Ethelbert.
　　　　　Gersa. Ho! Ho, there! Guards!
145　Your blessing, father! Sweet Erminia,
　　　Believe me, I am well nigh sure—
　　　　　Erminia.　　　　　　Farewell!

Short time will show.   [*Enter Chiefs.*
                          Yes, Father Ethelbert,
I have news precious as we pass along.
    Ethelbert. Dear daughter, you shall guide me.
    Erminia.   To no ill.
150   *Gersa.* Command an escort to the Friedburg lines.
                                      [*Exeunt Chiefs.*
Pray let me lead. Fair lady, forget not
Gersa, how he believ'd you innocent.
I follow you to Friedburg with all speed.   [*Exeunt.*

ACT III

SCENE I. *The Country.*

Enter ALBERT.

    Albert. O that the earth were empty, as when Cain
Had no perplexity to hide his head!
Or that the sword of some brave enemy
Had put a sudden stop to my hot breath,
5   And hurl'd me down the illimitable gulph
Of times past, unremember'd! Better so
Than thus fast limed in a cursed snare,
The limbo of a wanton. This the end
Of an aspiring life! My boyhood past
10   In feud with wolves and bears, when no eye saw
The solitary warfare, fought for love
Of honour 'mid the growling wilderness.
My sturdier youth, maturing to the sword,
Won by the syren-trumpets, and the ring
15   Of shields upon the pavement, when bright mail'd
Henry the Fowler pass'd the streets of Prague.
Was't to this end I louted and became
The menial of Mars, and held a spear
Sway'd by command, as corn is by the wind?
20   Is it for this, I now am lifted up
By Europe's throned Emperor, to see
My honour be my executioner,—
My love of fame, my prided honesty
Put to the torture for confessional?
25   Then the damn'd crime of blurting to the world

A woman's secret!—though a fiend she be,
Too tender of my ignominious life;
But then to wrong the generous Emperor
In such a searching point, were to give up
30   My soul for foot-ball at hell's holiday!
I must confess,—and cut my throat,—to-day?
To-morrow? Ho! some wine!

Enter SIGIFRED.

Sigifred.   A fine humour—
Albert. Who goes there? Count Sigifred? Ha! ha!
Sigifred. What, man, do you mistake the hollow sky
35   For a throng'd tavern,—and these stubbed trees
For old serge hangings,—me, your humble friend,
For a poor waiter? Why, man, how you stare!
What gipsies have you been carousing with?
No, no more wine; methinks you've had enough.
40   *Albert.* You well may laugh and banter. What a fool
An injury may make of a staid man!
You shall know all anon.
      Sigifred.   Some tavern-brawl?
Albert. 'Twas with some people out of common reach;
Revenge is difficult.
      Sigifred.   I am your friend;
45   We meet again to-day, and can confer
Upon it. For the present I'm in haste.
      Albert. Whither?
      Sigifred.   To fetch King Gersa to the feast.
The Emperor on this marriage is so hot,
Pray heaven it end not in apoplexy!
50   The very porters, as I pass'd the doors,
Heard his loud laugh, and answer'd in full choir.
I marvel, Albert, you delay so long
From these bright revelries; go, show yourself,
You may be made a duke.
      Albert.   Aye, very like.
55   Pray what day has his Highness fix'd upon?
      Sigifred. For what?
      Albert.   The marriage;—what else can I mean?
Sigifred. To-day! O I forgot you could not know;
The news is scarce a minute old with me.
      Albert. Married to-day!—to-day! You did not say so?

60   *Sigifred.* Now, while I speak to you, their comely heads
        Are bow'd before the mitre.
          Albert.   Oh! monstrous!
          Sigifred. What is this?
          Albert.   Nothing, Sigifred. Farewell!
        We'll meet upon our subject. Farewell, Count!   [*Exit.*
          Sigifred. Is this clear-headed Albert? He brain-turn'd!
65   'Tis as portentous as a meteor.   [*Exit.*

            SCENE II. *An Apartment in the Castle.*

        Enter, as from the Marriage, OTHO, LUDOLPH, AURANTHE,
        CONRAD, *Nobles, Knights, Ladies, etc., etc., etc. Music.*

          Otho. Now, Ludolph! Now, Auranthe, daughter fair!
        What can I find to grace your nuptial day
        More than my love, and these wide realms in fee?
          Ludolph. I have too much.
          Auranthe.   And I, my liege, by far.
5   *Ludolph.* Auranthe! I have! O, my bride,—my love,—
        Not all the gaze upon us can restrain
        My eyes, too long poor exiles from thy face,
        From adoration, and my foolish tongue
        From uttering soft responses to the love
10   I see in thy mute beauty beaming forth!
        Fair creature, bless me with a single word!
        All mine!
          Auranthe. Spare, spare me, my lord; I swoon else.
          Ludolph. Soft beauty! by to-morrow I should die,
        Wert thou not mine.   [*They talk apart.*
          First Lady.   How deep she has bewitch'd him!
15   *First Knight.* Ask you for her receipt for love philtres.
          Second Lady. They hold the Emperor in admiration.
          Otho. If ever king was happy, that am I!
        What are the cities 'yond the Alps to me,
        The provinces about the Danube's mouth,
20   The promise of fair sail beyond the Rhone,
        Or routing out of Hyperborean hordes,
        To these fair children, stars of a new age?
        Unless perchance I might rejoice to win
        This little ball of earth, and chuck it them
        To play with!
25   *Auranthe.* Nay, my lord, I do not know.

Ludolph. Let me not famish.
    Otho (to Conrad).   Good Franconia,
You heard what oath I sware, as the sun rose,
That, unless heaven would send me back my son,
My Arab, no soft music should enrich
30 The cool wine, kiss'd off with a soldier's smack:
Now all my empire, barter'd for one feast,
Seems poverty.
    Conrad.   Upon the neighbour-plain
The heralds have prepared a royal lists;
Your knights, found war-proof in the bloody field,
Speed to the game.
35   *Otho.*   Well, Ludolph, what say you?
    Ludolph. My lord!
    Otho.   A tourney?
    Conrad.   Or, if't please you best—
    Ludolph. I want no more!
    First Lady.   He soars!
    Second Lady.   Past all reason.
    Ludolph. Though heaven's choir
Should in a vast circumference descend,
40 And sing for my delight, I'd stop my ears!
Though bright Apollo's car stood burning here,
And he put out an arm to bid me mount,
His touch an immortality, not I!—
This earth,—this palace,—this room,—Auranthe!
45   *Otho.* This is a little painful; just too much.
Conrad, if he flames longer in this wise,
I shall believe in wizard-woven loves
And old romances; but I'll break the spell.
Ludolph!
    Conrad. He will be calm anon.
    Ludolph.   You call'd!
50 Yes, yes, yes, I offend. You must forgive me;
Not being quite recover'd from the stun
Of your large bounties. A tourney, is it not?
                       [*A sennet heard faintly.*
    Conrad. The trumpets reach us.
    Ethelbert (without).   On your peril, sirs,
Detain us!
    First Voice (without). Let not the abbot pass.
    Second Voice (without).   No,
On your lives!
55   *First Voice (without).* Holy father, you must not.

Ethelbert (without). Otho!
Otho.   Who calls on Otho?
Ethelbert (without).   Ethelbert!
Otho. Let him come in.
                              [*Enter* ETHELBERT, *leading in* ERMINIA.
                    Thou cursed abbot, why
Hast brought pollution to our holy rites?
Hast thou no fear of hangmen, or the faggot?
60   *Ludolph.* What portent—what strange prodigy is this?
Conrad. Away!
Ethelbert.   You, Duke?
Erminia.   Albert has surely fail'd me!
Look at the Emperor's brow upon me bent!
Ethelbert. A sad delay.
Conrad.   Away, thou guilty thing!
Ethelbert. You again, Duke? Justice, most noble Otho!
65   You—go to your sister there and plot again,
A quick plot, swift as thought to save your heads;
For lo! the toils are spread around your den,
The world is all agape to see dragg'd forth
Two ugly monsters.
Ludolph.   What means he, my lord?
Conrad. I cannot guess.
70   *Ethelbert.*   Best ask your lady sister,
Whether the riddle puzzles her beyond
The power of utterance.
Conrad.   Foul barbarian, cease;
The Princess faints!
Ludolph.   Stab him! O sweetest wife!
                              [*Attendants bear off* AURANTHE.
Erminia. Alas!
Ethelbert.   Your wife!
Ludolph.   Aye, Satan, does that yerk ye?
Ethelbert. Wife! so soon!
75   *Ludolph.*   Aye, wife! Oh, impudence!
Thou bitter mischief! Venemous bad priest!
How dar'st thou lift those beetle brows at me?
Me—the Prince Ludolph, in this presence here,
Upon my marriage-day, and scandalise
80   My joys with such opprobrious surprise?
Wife! Why dost linger on that syllable,
As if it were some demon's name pronounc'd
To summon harmful lightning, and make yawn

The sleepy thunder? Hast no sense of fear?
85   No ounce of man in thy mortality?
Tremble! for, at my nod, the sharpen'd axe
Will make thy bold tongue quiver to the roots,
Those grey lids wink, and thou not know it, monk!
     Ethelbert. O, poor deceived Prince, I pity thee!
Great Otho, I claim justice—
90   *Ludolph.*   Thou shalt have't!
Thine arms from forth a pulpit of hot fire
Shall sprawl distracted! O that that dull cowl
Were some most sensitive portion of thy life,
That I might give it to my hounds to tear!
95   Thy girdle some fine zealous-pained nerve
To girth my saddle! And those devil's beads
Each one a life, that I might, every day,
Crush one with Vulcan's hammer!
     Otho.   Peace, my son;
You far outstrip my spleen in this affair.
100 Let us be calm, and hear the abbot's plea
For this intrusion.
     Ludolph.   I am silent, sire.
     Otho. Conrad, see all depart not wanted here.
                    [*Exeunt Knights, Ladies, etc.*
Ludolph, be calm. Ethelbert, peace awhile.
This mystery demands an audience
105 Of a just judge, and that will Otho be.
     Ludolph. Why has he time to breathe another word?
     Otho. Ludolph, old Ethelbert, be sure, comes not
To beard us for no cause; he's not the man
To cry himself up an ambassador
Without credentials.
110   *Ludolph.*   I'll chain up myself.
     Otho. Old abbot, stand here forth. Lady Erminia,
Sit. And now, abbot, what have you to say?
Our ear is open. First we here denounce
Hard penalties against thee, if't be found
115 The cause for which you have disturb'd us here,
Making our bright hours muddy, be a thing
Of little moment.
     Ethelbert.   See this innocent!
Otho! thou father of the people call'd,
Is her life nothing? Her fair honour nothing?
120 Her tears from matins until even song

Nothing? Her burst heart nothing? Emperor!
Is this, your gentle niece—the simplest flower
Of the world's herbal, this fair lily blanch'd
Still with the dews of piety, this meek lady
125   Here sitting like an angel newly-shent,
Who vails its snowy wings and grows all pale—
Is she nothing?
    Otho.   What more to the purpose, abbot?
    Ludolph. Whither, whither is he winding?
    Conrad.   No clue yet!
    Ethelbert. You have heard, my liege, and so, no doubt, all here,
130   Foul, poisonous, malignant whisperings;
Nay open speech, rude mockery grown common,
Against the spotless nature and clear fame
Of the Princess Erminia, your niece.
I have intruded here thus suddenly,
135   Because I hold those base weeds with tight hand
Which now disfigure her fair growing stem,
Waiting but for your sign to pull them up
By the dark roots, and leave her palpable,
To all men's sight, a lady innocent.
140   The ignominy of that whisper'd tale
About a midnight-gallant, seen to climb
A window to her chamber neighbour'd near,
I will from her turn off, and put the load
On the right shoulders; on that wretch's head
145   Who, by close stratagems, did save herself,
Chiefly by shifting to this lady's room
A rope-ladder for false witness.
    Ludolph.   Most atrocious!
    Otho. Ethelbert, proceed.
    Ethelbert.   With sad lips I shall;
For, in the healing of one wound, I fear
150   To make a greater. His young Highness here
To-day was married.
    Ludolph.   Good.
    Ethelbert.   Would it were good!
Yet why do I delay to spread abroad
The names of those two vipers, from whose jaws
A deadly breath went forth to taint and blast
This guileless lady?
155   *Otho.*   Abbot, speak their names.

Ethelbert. A minute first. It cannot be—but may
I ask, great judge, if you to-day have put
A letter by unread?
  Otho.   Does't end in this?
  Conrad. Out with their names!
  Ethelbert.   Bold sinner, say you so?
  Ludolph. Out, tedious monk!
160 *Otho.*   Confess, or by the wheel—
  Ethelbert. My evidence cannot be far away;
And, though it never come, be on my head
The crime of passing an attaint upon
The slanderers of this virgin.
  Ludolph.   Speak aloud!
  Ethelbert. Auranthe! and her brother there—
165 *Conrad.*   Amaze!
  Ludolph. Throw them from the windows!
  Otho. Do what you will.
  Ludolph.   What shall I do with them?
Something of quick dispatch, for should she hear,
My soft Auranthe, her sweet mercy would
170 Prevail against my fury. Damned priest!
What swift death wilt thou die? As to the lady
I touch her not.
  Ethelbert. Illustrious Otho, stay!
An ample store of misery thou hast,
Choak not the granary of thy noble mind
175 With more bad bitter grain, too difficult
A cud for the repentance of a man
Grey-growing. To thee only I appeal,
Not to thy noble son, whose yeasting youth
Will clear itself, and crystal turn again.
180 A young man's heart, by heaven's blessing, is
A wide world, where a thousand new-born hopes
Empurple fresh the melancholy blood:
But an old man's is narrow, tenantless
Of hopes, and stuff'd with many memories,
185 Which, being pleasant, ease the heavy pulse,
Painful, clogg'd up and stagnate. Weigh this matter
Even as a miser balances his coin;
And, in the name of mercy, give command
That your knight Albert be brought here before you.
190 He will expound this riddle; he will show
A noon-day proof of bad Auranthe's guilt.

Otho. Let Albert straight be summon'd.

          [*Exit one of the Nobles.*

Ludolph.   Impossible!
I cannot doubt—I will not—no—to doubt
Is to be ashes!—wither'd up to death!

195 *Otho.* My gentle Ludolph, harbour not a fear;
You do yourself much wrong.

Ludolph.   O, wretched dolt!
Now, when my foot is almost on thy neck,
Wilt thou infuriate me? Proof! Thou fool!
Why wilt thou tease impossibility

200 With such a thick skull'd persevering suit?
Fanatic obstinacy! Prodigy!
Monster of folly! Ghost of a turn'd brain!
You puzzle me,—you haunt me,—when I dream
Of you my brain will split! Bald sorcerer!

205 Juggler! May I come near you! On my soul
I know not whether to pity, curse, or laugh.

       [*Enter* ALBERT, *and the Nobleman.*
Here, Albert, this old phantom wants a proof!
Give him his proof! A camel's load of proofs!

Otho. Albert, I speak to you as to a man

210 Whose words once utter'd pass like current gold;
And therefore fit to calmly put a close
To this brief tempest. Do you stand possess'd
Of any proof against the honourableness
Of Lady Auranthe, our new-spoused daughter?

215 *Albert.* You chill me with astonishment! How's this?
My liege, what proof should I have 'gainst a fame
Impossible of slur?   [OTHO *rises.*

Erminia.   O wickedness!

Ethelbert. Deluded monarch, 'tis a cruel lie.

Otho. Peace, rebel-priest!

Conrad.   Insult beyond credence!

Erminia. Almost a dream!

Ludolph.   We have awaken'd from!
A foolish dream that from my brow hath wrung
A wrathful dew. O folly! why did I
So act the lion with this silly gnat?
Let them depart. Lady Erminia,

225 I ever griev'd for you, as who did not?
But now you have, with such a brazen front,
So most maliciously, so madly striven

To dazzle the soft moon, when tenderest clouds
Should be unloop'd around to curtain her;
230   I leave you to the desert of the world
Almost with pleasure. Let them be set free
For me! I take no personal revenge
More than against a night-mare, which a man
Forgets in the new dawn.   [*Exit* LUDOLPH.
235   *Otho.* Still in extremes! No, they must not be loose.
    Ethelbert. Albert, I must suspect thee of a crime
So fiendish—
    Otho.   Fear'st thou not my fury, monk?
Conrad, be they in your safe custody,
Till we determine some fit punishment.
240   It is so mad a deed, I must reflect
And question them in private; for perhaps,
By patient scrutiny, we may discover
Whether they merit death, or should be plac'd
In care of the physicians.
             [*Exeunt* OTHO *and Nobles;* ALBERT *following.*
    Conrad. My guards, ho!
245   *Erminia.*   Albert, wilt thou follow there?
Wilt thou creep dastardly behind his back,
And shrink away from a weak woman's eye?
Turn, thou court-Janus, thou forget'st thyself;
Here is the Duke, waiting with open arms   [*Enter Guards.*
250   To thank thee; here congratulate each other;
Wring hands; embrace; and swear how lucky 'twas
That I, by happy chance, hit the right man
Of all the world to trust in.
    Albert.   Trust! to me!
    Conrad (*aside*). He is the sole one in this mystery.
255   *Erminia.* Well, I give up, and save my prayers for heaven!
You, who could do this deed, would ne'er relent,
Though, at my words, the hollow prison-vaults
Would groan for pity.
    Conrad.   Manacle them both!
    Ethelbert. I know it—it must be—I see it all!
Albert, thou art the minion!
260   *Erminia.*   Ah! too plain—
    Conrad. Silence! Gag up their mouths! I cannot bear
More of this brawling. That the Emperor
Had plac'd you in some other custody!
Bring them away.   [*Exeunt all but* ALBERT.

265   *Albert.* Though my name perish from the book of honour,
Almost before the recent ink is dry,
And be no more remember'd after death,
Than any drummer's in the muster-roll;
Yet shall I season high my sudden fall
270   With triumph o'er that evil-witted Duke!
He shall feel what it is to have the hand
Of a man drowning on his hateful throat.

Enter GERSA *and* SIGIFRED.

Gersa. What discord is at ferment in this house?
Sigifred. We are without conjecture; not a soul
275   We met could answer any certainty.
Gersa. Young Ludolph, like a fiery arrow, shot
By us.
Sigifred. The Emperor, with cross'd arms, in thought.
Gersa. In one room music, in another sadness,
Perplexity every where!
Albert.   A trifle mere!
280   Follow;—your presences will much avail
To tune our jarred spirits. I'll explain.   [*Exeunt.*

ACT IV

SCENE I. AURANTHE'S *Apartment.*

AURANTHE *and* CONRAD *discovered.*

Conrad. Well, well, I know what ugly jeopardy
We are cag'd in; you need not pester that
Into my ears. Pr'ythee, let me be spared
A foolish tongue, that I may bethink me
5   Of remedies with some deliberation.
You cannot doubt but 'tis in Albert's power
To crush or save us?
Auranthe.   No, I cannot doubt.
He has, assure yourself, by some strange means,
My secret; which I ever hid from him,
Knowing his mawkish honesty.
10   *Conrad.*   Curs'd slave!
Auranthe. Aye, I could almost curse him now myself.

Wretched impediment! evil genius!
A glue upon my wings, that cannot spread,
When they should span the provinces! A snake,
15   A scorpion, sprawling on the first gold step,
Conducting to the throne high canopied.
    Conrad. You would not hear my counsel, when his life
Might have been trodden out, all sure and hush'd;
Now the dull animal forsooth must be
20   Intreated, managed! When can you contrive
The interview he demands?
    Auranthe.   As speedily
It must be done as my bribed woman can
Unseen conduct him to me: but I fear
'Twill be impossible, while the broad day
25   Comes through the panes with persecuting glare.
Methinks, if't now were night, I could intrigue
With darkness, bring the stars to second me,
And settle all this trouble.
    Conrad.   Nonsense! Child!
See him immediately; why not now?
30   *Auranthe.* Do you forget that even the senseless door-posts
Are on the watch and gape through all the house;
How many whisperers there are about,
Hungry for evidence to ruin me;
Men I have spurn'd, and women I have taunted?
35   Besides, the foolish Prince sends, minute whiles,
His pages,—so they tell me,—to enquire
After my health, intreating, if I please,
To see me.
    Conrad. Well, suppose this Albert here;
What is your power with him?
    Auranthe.   He should be
40   My echo, my taught parrot! but I fear
He will be cur enough to bark at me;
Have his own say; read me some silly creed
'Bout shame and pity.
    Conrad.   What will you do then?
    Auranthe. What I shall do, I know not; what I would
45   Cannot be done; for see, this chamber-floor
Will not yield to the pickaxe and the spade,—
Here is no quiet depth of hollow ground.
    Conrad. Sister, you have grown sensible and wise,
Seconding, ere I speak it, what is now,

I hope, resolv'd between us.
50   *Auranthe.*   Say, what is't?
   Conrad. You need not be his sexton too: a man
May carry that with him shall make him die
Elsewhere,—give that to him; pretend the while
You will to-morrow succumb to his wishes,
55   Be what they may, and send him from the castle
On some fool's errand: let his latest groan
Frighten the wolves!
   Auranthe.   Alas! he must not die!
   Conrad. Would you were both hears'd up in stifling lead!
Detested—
   Auranthe. Conrad, hold! I would not bear
60   The little thunder of your fretful tongue,
Though I alone were taken in these toils,
And you could free me; but remember, sir,
You live alone in my security:
So keep your wits at work, for your own sake,
Not mine, and be more mannerly.
65   *Conrad.*   Thou wasp!
If my domains were emptied of these folk,
And I had thee to starve—
   Auranthe.   O, marvellous!
But, Conrad, now be gone; the host is look'd for;
Cringe to the Emperor, entertain the lords,
70   And, do ye mind, above all things, proclaim
My sickness, with a brother's sadden'd eye,
Condoling with Prince Ludolph. In fit time
Return to me.
   Conrad.   I leave you to your thoughts.   [*Exit.*
   Auranthe (*sola*). Down, down, proud temper! down, Auran-
     the's pride!
75   Why do I anger him when I should kneel?
Conrad! Albert! help! help! What can I do?
O wretched woman! lost, wreck'd, swallow'd up,
Accursed, blasted! O, thou golden crown,
Orbing along the serene firmament
80   Of a wide empire, like a glowing moon;
And thou, bright sceptre, lustrous in my eyes,—
There!—as the fabled fair Hesperian tree,
Bearing a fruit more precious! graceful thing,
Delicate, godlike, magic! must I leave
85   Thee to melt in the visionary air,

Ere, by one grasp, this common hand is made
Imperial? I do not know the time
When I have wept for sorrow; but methinks
I could now sit upon the ground, and shed
90   Tears, tears of misery. O, the heavy day!
How shall I bear my life till Albert comes?
Ludolph! Erminia! Proofs! O heavy day!
Bring me some mourning weeds, that I may 'tire
Myself, as fits one wailing her own death,—
95   Cut off these curls, and brand this lily hand,
And throw these jewels from my loathing sight,—
Fetch me a missal, and a string of beads,—
A cup of bitter'd water, and a crust,—
I will confess, O holy abbot!—How!
100   What is this? Auranthe, thou fool, dolt,
Whimpering ideot! up! up! and quell!
I am safe! Coward! why am I in fear?
Albert! he cannot stickle, chew the cud
In such a fine extreme,—impossible!
105   Who knocks?
                    [*Goes to the door, listens, and opens it. Enter* ALBERT.
Albert, I have been waiting for you here
With such an aching heart, such swooning throbs
On my poor brain, such cruel—cruel sorrow,
That I should claim your pity! Art not well?
        Albert. Yes, lady, well.
110   *Auranthe.*   You look not so, alas!
But pale, as if you brought some heavy news.
        Albert. You know full well what makes me look so pale.
        Auranthe. No! Do I? Surely I am still to learn
Some horror; all I know, this present, is
115   I am near hustled to a dangerous gulph,
Which you can save me from,—and therefore safe,
So trusting in thy love; that should not make
Thee pale, my Albert.
        Albert.   It doth make me freeze.
        Auranthe. Why should it, love?
        Albert.   You should not ask me that,
120   But make your own heart monitor, and save
Me the great pain of telling. You must know.
        Auranthe. Something has vext you, Albert. There are times
When simplest things put on a sombre cast;
A melancholy mood will haunt a man,

125   Until most easy matters take the shape
Of unachievable tasks; small rivulets
Then seem impassable.

    Albert.   Do not cheat yourself
With hope that gloss of words, or suppliant action,
Or tears, or ravings, or self-threatened death,
Can alter my resolve.

130   *Auranthe.*   You make me tremble;
Not so much at your threats, as at your voice,
Untun'd, and harsh, and barren of all love.

    Albert. You suffocate me! Stop this devil's parley,
And listen to me; know me once for all.

135   *Auranthe.* I thought I did. Alas! I am deceiv'd.

    Albert. No, you are not deceiv'd. You took me for
A man detesting all inhuman crime;
And therefore kept from me your demon's plot
Against Erminia. Silent? Be so still;

140   For ever! Speak no more; but hear my words,
Thy fate. Your safety I have bought to-day
By blazoning a lie, which in the dawn
I'll expiate with truth.

    Auranthe.   O cruel traitor!

    Albert. For I would not set eyes upon thy shame;

145   I would not see thee dragg'd to death by the hair,
Penanc'd, and taunted on a scaffolding!
To-night, upon the skirts of the blind wood
That blackens northward of these horrid towers,
I wait for you with horses. Choose your fate.
Farewell!

150   *Auranthe.* Albert, you jest; I'm sure you must.
You, an ambitious soldier! I, a queen,
One who could say,—here, rule these provinces!
Take tribute from those cities for thyself!
Empty these armouries, these treasuries,

155   Muster thy warlike thousands at a nod!
Go! conquer Italy!

    Albert.   Auranthe, you have made
The whole world chaff to me. Your doom is fixed.

    Auranthe. Out, villain! dastard!

    Albert.   Look there to the door!
Who is it?

    Auranthe. Conrad,—traitor!

    Albert.   Let him in.   [*Enter* CONRAD.

160   Do not affect amazement, hypocrite,

At seeing me in this chamber.
    Conrad.   Auranthe?
    Albert. Talk not with eyes, but speak your curses out
Against me, who would sooner crush and grind
A brace of toads, than league with them t' oppress

165   An innocent lady, gull an emperor,
More generous to me than autumn-sun
To ripening harvests.
    Auranthe.   No more insult, sir.
    Albert. Aye, clutch your scabbard; but, for prudence' sake,
Draw not the sword; 'twould make an uproar, Duke,

170   You would not hear the end of. At nightfall
Your lady sister, if I guess aright,
Will leave this busy castle. You had best
Take farewell too of worldly vanities.
    Conrad. Vassal!
    Albert.   To-morrow, when the Emperor sends

175   For loving Conrad, see you fawn on him.
Good even!
    Auranthe. You'll be seen!
    Albert.   See the coast clear then.
    Auranthe (as he goes). Remorseless Albert! Cruel, cruel wretch!
                              [*She lets him out.*

    Conrad. So, we must lick the dust?
    Auranthe.   I follow him.
    Conrad. How? Where? The plan of your escape?
    Auranthe.   He waits

180   For me, with horses by the forest-side
Northward.
    Conrad.   Good, good; he dies. You go, say you?
    Auranthe. Perforce.
    Conrad.   Be speedy, darkness! Till that comes,
Fiends keep you company!   [*Exit.*
    Auranthe.   And you! And you!
And all men! Vanish—Oh! Oh! Oh!
                    [*Retires to an inner apartment.*

SCENE II. *An Apartment in the Castle.*

Enter LUDOLPH *and Page.*

    Page. Still very sick, my lord; but now I went,
And there her women, in a mournful throng,
Stood in the passage whispering; if any

Moved, 'twas with careful steps, and hush'd as death:
They bade me stop.

5   *Ludolph.*   Good fellow, once again
Make soft inquiry; pr'ythee, be not stay'd
By any hindrance, but with gentlest force
Break through her weeping servants, till thou com'st
E'en to her chamber-door, and there, fair boy,—
10 If with thy mother's milk thou hast suck'd in
Any diviner eloquence,—woo her ears
With plaints for me, more tender than the voice
Of dying Echo, echoed.
    Page.   Kindest master!
To know thee sad thus, will unloose my tongue
15 In mournful syllables. Let but my words reach
Her ears, and she shall take them coupled with
Moans from my heart, and sighs not counterfeit.
May I speed better!   [*Exit Page.*
    Ludolph (*solus*).   Auranthe! My life!
Long have I loved thee, yet till now not loved:
20 Remembering, as I do, hard-hearted times
When I had heard e'en of thy death perhaps,
And, thoughtless! suffer'd thee to pass alone
Into Elysium!—now I follow thee,
A substance or a shadow, wheresoe'er
25 Thou leadest me,—whether thy white feet press,
With pleasant weight, the amorous-aching earth,
Or through the air thou pioneerest me,
A shade! Yet sadly I predestinate!
O, unbenignest Love, why wilt thou let
30 Darkness steal out upon the sleepy world
So wearily, as if night's chariot-wheels
Were clogg'd in some thick cloud? O, changeful Love,
Let not her steeds with drowsy-footed pace
Pass the high stars, before sweet embassage
35 Comes from the pillow'd beauty of that fair
Completion of all delicate nature's wit!
Pout her faint lips anew with rubious health;
And, with thine infant fingers, lift the fringe
Of her sick eye-lids; that those eyes may glow
40 With wooing light upon me, ere the morn
Peers with disrelish, grey, barren, and cold!
                   [*Enter* GERSA *and Courtiers.*
Otho calls me his lion,—should I blush

To be so tamed? so—
 Gersa.   Do me the courtesy,
Gentlemen, to pass on.
 First Knight.   We are your servants.
           [Exeunt Courtiers.

45 *Ludolph.* It seems then, sir, you have found out the man
You would confer with;—me?
 Gersa.   If I break not
Too much upon your thoughtful mood, I will
Claim a brief while your patience.
 Ludolph.   For what cause
Soe'er, I shall be honour'd.
 Gersa.   I not less.
50 *Ludolph.* What may it be? No trifle can take place
Of such deliberate prologue, serious 'haviour.
But, be it what it may, I cannot fail
To listen with no common interest;
For though so new your presence is to me,
55 I have a soldier's friendship for your fame.
Please you explain.
 Gersa.   As thus:—for, pardon me,
I cannot, in plain terms, grossly assault
A noble nature; and would faintly sketch
What your quick apprehension will fill up;
So finely I esteem you.
60 *Ludolph.*   I attend.
 Gersa. Your generous father, most illustrious Otho,
Sits in the banquet-room among his chiefs;
His wine is bitter, for you are not there;
His eyes are fix'd still on the open doors,
65 And ev'ry passer in he frowns upon,
Seeing no Ludolph comes.
 Ludolph.   I do neglect.
 Gersa. And for your absence may I guess the cause?
 Ludolph. Stay there! No—guess? More princely you must be
Than to make guesses at me. 'Tis enough.
I'm sorry I can hear no more.
70 *Gersa.*   And I
As griev'd to force it on you so abrupt;
Yet, one day, you must know a grief, whose sting
Will sharpen more the longer 'tis conceal'd.
 Ludolph. Say it at once, sir! dead—dead—is she dead?
75 *Gersa.* Mine is a cruel task: she is not dead,

And would, for your sake, she were innocent.
Ludolph. Hungarian! Thou amazest me beyond
All scope of thought, convulsest my heart's blood
To deadly churning! Gersa, you are young,
80   As I am; let me observe you, face to face:
Not grey-brow'd like the poisonous Ethelbert,
No rheumed eyes, no furrowing of age,
No wrinkles, where all vices nestle in
Like crannied vermin,—no! but fresh, and young,
85   And hopeful featur'd. Ha! by heaven you weep!
Tears, human tears! Do you repent you then
Of a curs'd torturer's office? Why shouldst join,—
Tell me,—the league of devils? Confess—confess—
The lie!
     Gersa. Lie!—but begone all ceremonious points
90   Of honour battailous! I could not turn
My wrath against thee for the orbed world.
     Ludolph. Your wrath, weak boy? Tremble at mine, unless
Retraction follow close upon the heels
Of that late stounding insult! Why has my sword
95   Not done already a sheer judgment on thee?
Despair, or eat thy words! Why, thou wast nigh
Whimpering away my reason! Hark 'e, sir,—
It is no secret, that Erminia,
Erminia, sir, was hidden in your tent,—
100 O bless'd asylum! Comfortable home!
Begone! I pity thee; thou art a gull,
Erminia's fresh puppet!
     Gersa.   Furious fire!
Thou mak'st me boil as hot as thou canst flame!
And in thy teeth I give thee back the lie!
105 Thou liest! Thou, Auranthe's fool! A wittol!
     Ludolph. Look! look at this bright sword;
There is no part of it, to the very hilt,
But shall indulge itself about thine heart!
Draw! but remember thou must cower thy plumes,
110 As yesterday the Arab made thee stoop.
     Gersa. Patience! Not here; I would not spill thy blood
Here, underneath this roof where Otho breathes,—
Thy father,—almost mine.
     Ludolph.   O faltering coward!   [*Enter Page.*
Stay, stay; here is one I have half a word with.
Well? What ails thee, child?
     Page.   My lord!

115   *Ludolph.*   What wouldst say?
        Page. They are fled!
        Ludolph.   They! Who?
        Page.   When anxiously
        I hasten'd back, your grieving messenger,
        I found the stairs all dark, the lamps extinct,
        And not a foot or whisper to be heard.
120   I thought her dead, and on the lowest step
        Sat listening; when presently came by
        Two muffled up,—one sighing heavily,
        The other cursing low, whose voice I knew
        For the Duke Conrad's. Close I follow'd them
125   Through the dark ways they chose to the open air;
        And, as I follow'd, heard my lady speak.
            Ludolph. Thy life answer the truth!
            Page.   The chamber's empty!
            Ludolph. As I will be of mercy! So, at last,
        This nail is in my temples!
            Gersa.   Be calm in this.
            Ludolph. I am.
130   *Gersa.*   And Albert too has disappear'd;
        Ere I met you, I sought him every where;
        You would not hearken.
            Ludolph.   Which way went they, boy?
            Gersa. I'll hunt with you.
            Ludolph.   No, no, no. My senses are
        Still whole. I have surviv'd. My arm is strong,—
135   My appetite sharp—for revenge! I'll no sharer
        In my feast; my injury is all my own,
        And so is my revenge, my lawful chattels!
        Terrier, ferret them out! Burn—burn the witch!
        Trace me their footsteps! Away!   [*Exeunt.*

ACT V

SCENE I. *A part of the Forest.*

Enter CONRAD *and* AURANTHE.

Auranthe. Go no further; not a step more. Thou art
A master-plague in the midst of miseries.
Go,—I fear thee! I tremble every limb,
Who never shook before. There's moody death

5   In thy resolved looks! Yes, I could kneel
      To pray thee far away! Conrad, go! go!—
      There! yonder underneath the boughs I see
      Our horses!
            Conrad.   Aye, and the man.
            Auranthe.   Yes, he is there!
      Go, go,—no blood! no blood!—go, gentle Conrad!
            Conrad. Farewell!
10   *Auranthe.*   Farewell! For this heaven pardon you!
                                        [*Exit* AURANTHE.
            Conrad. If he survive one hour, then may I die
      In unimagined tortures, or breathe through
      A long life in the foulest sink o' the world!
      He dies! 'Tis well she do not advertise
15   The caitiff of the cold steel at his back.   [*Exit* CONRAD.

                   Enter LUDOLPH *and Page.*

      Ludolph. Miss'd the way, boy? Say not that on your peril!
      Page. Indeed, indeed I cannot trace them further.
      Ludolph. Must I stop here? Here solitary die?
      Stifled beneath the thick oppressive shade
20   Of these dull boughs,—this oven of dark thickets,—
      Silent,—without revenge,—pshaw!—bitter end,—
      A bitter death,—a suffocating death,—
      A gnawing—silent—deadly, quiet death!
      Escap'd?—fled?—vanish'd? melted into air?
25   She's gone! I cannot clutch her! no revenge!
      A muffled death, ensnared in horrid silence!
      Suck'd to my grave amid a dreary calm!
      O, where is that illustrious noise of war,
      To smother up this sound of labouring breath,
      This rustle of the trees!   [AURANTHE *shrieks at a distance.*
30   *Page.*   My lord, a noise!
      This way—hark!
            Ludolph.   Yes, yes! A hope! A music!
      A glorious clamour! Now I live again!   [*Exeunt.*

              SCENE II. *Another part of the Forest.*

                   Enter ALBERT (*wounded*).

      Albert. Oh! for enough life to support me on
      To Otho's feet!

Enter LUDOLPH.

Ludolph.   Thrice villanous, stay there!
Tell me where that detested woman is,
Or this is through thee!
    Albert.   My good Prince, with me
5   The sword has done its worst; not without worst
Done to another,—Conrad has it home!
I see you know it all!
    Ludolph.   Where is his sister?

Enter AURANTHE.

Auranthe. Albert!
    Ludolph.   Ha! There! there!—He is the paramour!—
There—hug him—dying! O, thou innocence,
10   Shrive him and comfort him at his last gasp,
Kiss down his eyelids! Was he not thy love?
Wilt thou forsake him at his latest hour?
Keep fearful and aloof from his last gaze,
His most uneasy moments, when cold death
15   Stands with the door ajar to let him in?
    Albert. O that that door with hollow slam would close
Upon me sudden! for I cannot meet,
In all the unknown chambers of the dead,
Such horrors!
    Ludolph.   Auranthe! what can he mean?
20   What horrors? Is it not a joyous time?
Am I not married to a paragon
"Of personal beauty and untainted soul"?
A blushing fair-eyed purity? A sylph,
Whose snowy timid hand has never sinn'd
25   Beyond a flower pluck'd, white as itself?
Albert, you do insult my bride—your mistress—
To talk of horrors on our wedding-night!
    Albert. Alas! poor Prince, I would you knew my heart!
'Tis not so guilty—
    Ludolph.   Hear, he pleads not guilty!
30   You are not? or, if so, what matters it?
You have escap'd me, free as the dusk air,
Hid in the forest, safe from my revenge,
I cannot catch you! You should laugh at me,
Poor cheated Ludolph! Make the forest hiss
35   With jeers at me! You tremble—faint at once,

You will come to again. O cockatrice,
I have you! Whither wander those fair eyes
To entice the devil to your help, that he
May change you to a spider, so to crawl
40   Into some cranny to escape my wrath?
    Albert. Sometimes the counsel of a dying man
Doth operate quietly when his breath is gone:
Disjoin those hands—part—part—do not destroy
Each other—forget her!—Our miseries
Are equal shared, and mercy is—
45   *Ludolph.*   A boon
When one can compass it. Auranthe, try
Your oratory; your breath is not so hitch'd.
Aye, stare for help!   [ALBERT *dies.*
               There goes a spotted soul
Howling in vain along the hollow night!
50   Hear him! He calls you—sweet Auranthe, come!
    Auranthe. Kill me!
    Ludolph.   No! What? Upon our marriage-night?
The earth would shudder at so foul a deed!
A fair bride! A sweet bride! An innocent bride!
No! we must revel it, as 'tis in use
55   In times of delicate brilliant ceremony:
Come, let me lead you to our halls again!
Nay, linger not; make no resistance, sweet;—
Will you? Ah, wretch, thou canst not, for I have
The strength of twenty lions 'gainst a lamb!
60   Now—one adieu for Albert!—Come away!   [*Exeunt.*

SCENE III. *An inner Court of the Castle.*

Enter SIGIFRED, GONFRID, *and* THEODORE, *meeting.*

    Theodore. Was ever such a night?
    Sigifred.   What horrors more?
Things unbeliev'd one hour, so strange they are,
The next hour stamps with credit.
    Theodore.   Your last news?
    Gonfrid. After the page's story of the death
Of Albert and Duke Conrad?
5   *Sigifred.*   And the return
Of Ludolph with the Princess.

Gonfrid.   No more, save
Prince Gersa's freeing Abbot Ethelbert,
And the sweet lady, fair Erminia,
From prison.
  Theodore.   Where are they now? Hast yet heard?
10 *Gonfrid.* With the sad Emperor they are closeted;
I saw the three pass slowly up the stairs,
The lady weeping, the old abbot cowl'd.
  Sigifred. What next?
  Theodore.   I ache to think on't.
  Gonfrid.   'Tis with fate.
  Theodore. One while these proud towers are hush'd as death.
15 *Gonfrid.* The next our poor Prince fills the arched rooms
With ghastly ravings.
  Sigifred.   I do fear his brain.
  Gonfrid. I will see more. Bear you so stout a heart?
            [Exeunt into the Castle.

SCENE IV. *A Cabinet, opening towards a Terrace.*

OTHO, ERMINIA, ETHELBERT, *and a Physician, discovered.*

Otho. O, my poor boy! My son! My son! My Ludolph!
Have ye no comfort for me, ye physicians
Of the weak body and soul?
  Ethelbert.   'Tis not in medicine,
Either of heaven or earth, can cure, unless
5 Fit time be chosen to administer.
  Otho. A kind forbearance, holy abbot. Come,
Erminia; here sit by me, gentle girl;
Give me thy hand; hast thou forgiven me?
  Erminia. Would I were with the saints to pray for you!
10 *Otho.* Why will ye keep me from my darling child?
  Physician. Forgive me, but he must not see thy face.
  Otho. Is then a father's countenance a Gorgon?
Hath it not comfort in it? Would it not
Console my poor boy, cheer him, heal his spirits?
15 Let me embrace him; let me speak to him;
I will! Who hinders me? Who's Emperor?
  Physician. You may not, sire; 'twould overwhelm him quite,
He is so full of grief and passionate wrath;
Too heavy a sigh would kill him, or do worse.

20   He must be sav'd by fine contrivances;
      And, most especially, we must keep clear
      Out of his sight a father whom he loves;
      His heart is full, it can contain no more,
      And do its ruddy office.
        Ethelbert.   Sage advice;
25   We must endeavour how to ease and slacken
      The tight-wound energies of his despair,
      Not make them tenser.
        Otho.   Enough! I hear, I hear.
      Yet you were about to advise more,—I listen.
        Ethelbert. This learned doctor will agree with me,
30   That not in the smallest point should he be thwarted,
      Or gainsaid by one word; his very motions,
      Nods, becks, and hints, should be obey'd with care,
      Even on the moment; so his troubled mind
      May cure itself.
        Physician.   There are no other means.
35   *Otho.* Open the door; let's hear if all is quiet.
      Physician. Beseech you, sire, forbear.
      Erminia.   Do, do.
      Otho.   I command!
      Open it straight;—hush!—quiet!—my lost boy!
      My miserable child!
        Ludolph (*indistinctly without*). Fill, fill my goblet,—here's a
          health!
40   *Erminia.* O, close the door!
      Otho. Let, let me hear his voice; this cannot last;
      And fain would I catch up his dying words,
      Though my own knell they be! This cannot last!
      O let me catch his voice—for lo! I hear
45   A whisper in this silence that he's dead!
      It is so!—Gersa?

                Enter GERSA.

      Physician.   Say, how fares the Prince?
      Gersa. More calm; his features are less wild and flush'd;
      Once he complain'd of weariness.
        Physician.   Indeed!
      'Tis good,—'tis good; let him but fall asleep,
      That saves him.
50   *Otho.*   Gersa, watch him like a child;

Ward him from harm,—and bring me better news!
Physician. Humour him to the height. I fear to go;
For should he catch a glimpse of my dull garb,
It might affright him, fill him with suspicion
55 That we believe him sick, which must not be.
Gersa. I will invent what soothing means I can.

[*Exit* GERSA.

Physician. This should cheer up your Highness; the weari-
ness
Is a good symptom, and most favourable;
It gives me pleasant hopes. Please you, walk forth
60 Upon the terrace; the refreshing air
Will blow one half of your sad doubts away.   [*Exeunt.*

SCENE V. *A Banquetting Hall, brilliantly illuminated, and set
forth with all costly magnificence, with supper-tables, laden with
services of gold and silver. A door in the back scene, guarded by two
Soldiers. Lords, Ladies, Knights, Gentlemen, etc., whispering sadly,
and ranging themselves; part entering and part discovered.*

First Knight. Grievously are we tantalised, one and all;
Sway'd here and there, commanded to and fro,
As though we were the shadows of a sleep,
And link'd to a dreaming fancy. What do we here?
5 *Gonfrid.* I am no seer; you know we must obey
The Prince from A to Z, though it should be
To set the place in flames. I pray, hast heard
Where the most wicked Princess is?
First Knight.   There, sir,
In the next room; have you remark'd those two
Stout soldiers posted at the door?
10 *Gonfrid.*   For what?   [*They whisper.*
First Lady. How ghast a train!
Second Lady. Sure this should be some splendid burial.
First Lady. What fearful whispering!—See, see,—Gersa
there!

Enter GERSA.

Gersa. Put on your brightest looks; smile if you can;
15 Behave as all were happy; keep your eyes
From the least watch upon him; if he speaks

To any one, answer, collectedly,
Without surprise, his questions, howe'er strange.
Do this to the utmost,—though, alas! with me

20   The remedy grows hopeless! Here he comes,—
Observe what I have said,—show no surprise.

Enter LUDOLPH, *followed by* SIGIFRED *and Page.*

Ludolph. A splendid company! rare beauties here!
I should have Orphean lips, and Plato's fancy,
Amphion's utterance, toned with his lyre,

25   Or the deep key of Jove's sonorous mouth,
To give fit salutation. Methought I heard,
As I came in, some whispers,—what of that?
'Tis natural men should whisper; at the kiss
Of Psyche given by Love, there was a buzz

30   Among the gods!—and silence is as natural.
These draperies are fine, and, being a mortal,
I should desire no better; yet, in truth,
There must be some superior costliness,
Some wider-domed high magnificence!

35   I would have, as a mortal I may not,
Hangings of heaven's clouds, purple and gold,
Slung from the spheres; gauzes of silver mist,
Loop'd up with cords of twisted wreathed light,
And tassell'd round with weeping meteors!

40   These pendent lamps and chandeliers are bright
As earthly fires from dull dross can be cleans'd;
Yet could my eyes drink up intenser beams
Undazzled,—this is darkness,—when I close
These lids, I see far fiercer brilliances,—

45   Skies full of splendid moons, and shooting stars,
And spouting exhalations, diamond fires,
And panting fountains quivering with deep glows!
Yes—this is dark—is it not dark?
    Sigifred.   My lord,
'Tis late; the lights of festival are ever
Quench'd in the morn.

50   *Ludolph.*   'Tis not to-morrow then?
    Sigifred. 'Tis early dawn.
    Gersa.   Indeed full time we slept;
Say you so, Prince?
    Ludolph.   I say I quarrell'd with you;

We did not tilt each other,—that's a blessing,—
Good gods! no innocent blood upon my head!
   Sigifred. Retire, Gersa!
55   *Ludolph.*   There should be three more here:
For two of them, they stay away perhaps,
Being gloomy-minded, haters of fair revels,—
They know their own thoughts best. As for the third,
We'll have her presently; aye, you shall see her,
60 And wonder at her, friends, she is so fair;
Deep blue eyes, semi-shaded in white lids,
Finish'd with lashes fine for more soft shade,
Completed by her twin-arch'd ebon-brows;
White temples, of exactest elegance,
65 Of even mould, felicitous and smooth;
Cheeks fashion'd tenderly on either side,
So perfect, so divine, that our poor eyes
Are dazzled with the sweet proportioning,
And wonder that 'tis so,—the magic chance!
70 Her nostrils, small, fragrant, fairy-delicate;
Her lips—I swear no human bones e'er wore
So taking a disguise;—you shall behold her!
She is the world's chief jewel, and, by heaven,
She's mine by right of marriage!—she is mine!
75 Patience, good people, in fit time I send
A summoner,—she will obey my call,
Being a wife most mild and dutiful.
First I would hear what music is prepared
To herald and receive her; let me hear!
80   *Sigifred.* Bid the musicians soothe him tenderly.
                          [*A soft strain of music.*
   Ludolph. Ye have none better? No, I am content;
'Tis a rich sobbing melody, with reliefs
Full and majestic; it is well enough,
And will be sweeter, when ye see her pace
85 Sweeping into this presence, glisten'd o'er
With emptied caskets, and her train upheld
By ladies, habited in robes of lawn
Sprinkled with golden crescents, others bright
In silks with spangles shower'd, and bow'd to
90 By duchesses and pearled margravines!
Sad, that the fairest creature of the earth—
I pray you mind me not—'tis sad, I say,
That the extremest beauty of the world

Should so entrench herself away from me,
95   Behind a barrier of engender'd guilt!
 Second Lady. Ah! what a moan!
 First Knight.   Most piteous indeed!
 Ludolph. She shall be brought before this company,
And then—then—
 First Lady. He muses.
 Gersa.   O, Fortune, where will this end!
100   *Sigifred.* I guess his purpose! Indeed he must not have
That pestilence brought in,—that cannot be,
There we must stop him.
 Gersa.   I am lost! Hush, hush!
He is about to rave again.
 Ludolph. A barrier of guilt! I was the fool,
105   She was the cheater! Who's the cheater now,
And who the fool? The entrapp'd, the caged fool,
The bird-lim'd raven? She shall croak to death!
Secure! Methinks I have her in my fist,
To crush her with my heel! Wait; wait! I marvel
110   My father keeps away. Good friend—ah! Sigifred?—
Do bring him to me,—and Erminia
I fain would see before I sleep,—and Ethelbert,
That he may bless me, as I know he will,
Though I have curs'd him.
 Sigifred.   Rather suffer me
To lead you to them.
115   *Ludolph.*   No, excuse me,—no!
The day is not quite done. Go, bring them hither.
            [*Exit* SIGIFRED.

Certes, a father's smile should, like sunlight,
Slant on my sheeved harvest of ripe bliss.
Besides, I thirst to pledge my lovely bride
120   In a deep goblet: let me see—what wine?
The strong Iberian juice? or mellow Greek?
Or pale Calabrian? or the Tuscan grape?
Or of old Ætna's pulpy wine-presses,
Black stain'd with the fat vintage, as it were
125   The purple slaughter-house, where Bacchus' self
Prick'd his own swollen veins! Where is my page?
 Page. Here—here!
 Ludolph. Be ready to obey me; anon thou shalt
Bear a soft message for me; for the hour

130   Draws near when I must make a winding up
        Of bridal-mysteries—a fine-spun vengeance!
        Carve it on my tomb, that, when I rest beneath,
        Men shall confess,—this prince was gull'd and cheated,
        But from the ashes of disgrace he rose
135   More than a fiery dragon, and did burn
        His ignominy up in purging fires!
        Did I not send, sir, but a moment past,
        For my father?
        Gersa.   You did.
        Ludolph.   Perhaps 'twould be
        Much better he came not.
        Gersa.   He enters now!

        Enter OTHO, ERMINIA, ETHELBERT, SIGIFRED, *and Physician.*

140   *Ludolph.* Oh! thou good man, against whose sacred head
        I was a mad conspirator, chiefly too
        For the sake of my fair newly wedded wife,
        Now to be punish'd,—do not look so sad!
        Those charitable eyes will thaw my heart,
145   Those tears will wash away a just resolve,
        A verdict ten-times sworn! Awake—awake—
        Put on a judge's brow, and use a tongue
        Made iron-stern by habit! Thou shalt see
        A deed to be applauded, 'scribed in gold!
150   Join a loud voice to mine, and so denounce
        What I alone will execute!
        Otho.   Dear son,
        What is it? By your father's love, I sue
        That it be nothing merciless!
        Ludolph.   To that demon?
        Not so! No! She is in temple-stall
155   Being garnish'd for the sacrifice, and I,
        The priest of justice, will immolate her
        Upon the altar of wrath! She stings me through!—
        Even as the worm doth feed upon the nut,
        So she, a scorpion, preys upon my brain!
160   I feel her gnawing here!—Let her but vanish,
        Then, father, I will lead your legions forth,
        Compact in steeled squares, and speared files,
        And bid our trumpets speak a fell rebuke

To nations drows'd in peace!
   Otho.   To-morrow, son,
Be your word law; forget to-day—
165   *Ludolph.*   I will
When I have finish'd it! Now,—now, I'm pight,
Tight-footed for the deed!
   Erminia.   Alas! Alas!
   Ludolph. What angel's voice is that? Erminia!
Ah! gentlest creature, whose sweet innocence
170 Was almost murder'd; I am penitent,
Wilt thou forgive me? And thou, holy man,
Good Ethelbert, shall I die in peace with you?
   Erminia. Die, my lord!
   Ludolph.   I feel it possible.
   Otho.   Physician?
   Physician. I fear me he is past my skill.
   Otho.   Not so!
175   *Ludolph.* I see it—I see it—I have been wandering!
Half mad—not right here—I forget my purpose.
Bestir—bestir—Auranthe! Ha! ha! ha!
Youngster! Page! go bid them drag her to me!
Obey! This shall finish it!   *[Draws a dagger.*
   Otho.   Oh, my son! my son!
   Sigifred. This must not be—stop there!
180 *Ludolph.*   Am I obey'd?
A little talk with her—no harm—haste! haste!   *[Exit Page.*
Set her before me—never fear I can strike.
   Several Voices. My lord! My lord!
   Gersa.   Good Prince!
   Ludolph. Why do ye trouble me? out—out—away!
185 There she is! take that! and that! no, no,
That's not well done.—Where is she?
     [The doors open. Enter Page. Several women are seen grouped
     about AURANTHE *in the inner-room.*
   Page. Alas! My lord, my lord! they cannot move her!
Her arms are stiff,—her fingers clench'd and cold!
   Ludolph. She's dead!   *[Staggers and falls into their arms.*
   Ethelbert.   Take away the dagger.
   Gersa.   Softly! so!
   Otho. Thank God for that!
190 *Sigifred.*   It could not harm him now.
   Gersa. No!—brief be his anguish!

Ludolph. She's gone! I am content—nobles, good night!
Where is your hand, father?—what sultry air!
We are all weary—faint—set ope the doors—
195   I will to bed!—To-morrow—   [*Dies.*

THE CURTAIN FALLS.

Lamia

PART I

Upon a time, before the faery broods
Drove Nymph and Satyr from the prosperous woods,
Before King Oberon's bright diadem,
Sceptre, and mantle, clasp'd with dewy gem,

5   Frighted away the Dryads and the Fauns
From rushes green, and brakes, and cowslip'd lawns,
The ever-smitten Hermes empty left
His golden throne, bent warm on amorous theft:
From high Olympus had he stolen light,

10   On this side of Jove's clouds, to escape the sight
Of his great summoner, and made retreat
Into a forest on the shores of Crete.
For somewhere in that sacred island dwelt
A nymph, to whom all hoofed Satyrs knelt;

15   At whose white feet the languid Tritons poured
Pearls, while on land they wither'd and adored.
Fast by the springs where she to bathe was wont,
And in those meads where sometime she might haunt,
Were strewn rich gifts, unknown to any Muse,

20   Though Fancy's casket were unlock'd to choose.
Ah, what a world of love was at her feet!
So Hermes thought, and a celestial heat
Burnt from his winged heels to either ear,
That from a whiteness, as the lily clear,

25   Blush'd into roses 'mid his golden hair,
Fallen in jealous curls about his shoulders bare.

From vale to vale, from wood to wood, he flew,
Breathing upon the flowers his passion new,
And wound with many a river to its head,

30   To find where this sweet nymph prepar'd her secret bed:
In vain; the sweet nymph might nowhere be found,
And so he rested, on the lonely ground,
Pensive, and full of painful jealousies
Of the Wood-Gods, and even the very trees.

35   There as he stood, he heard a mournful voice,
Such as once heard, in gentle heart, destroys
All pain but pity: thus the lone voice spake:

"When from this wreathed tomb shall I awake!
When move in a sweet body fit for life,
40   And love, and pleasure, and the ruddy strife
Of hearts and lips! Ah, miserable me!"
The God, dove-footed, glided silently
Round bush and tree, soft-brushing, in his speed,
The taller grasses and full-flowering weed,
45   Until he found a palpitating snake,
Bright, and cirque-couchant in a dusky brake.

    She was a gordian shape of dazzling hue,
Vermilion-spotted, golden, green, and blue;
Striped like a zebra, freckled like a pard,
50   Eyed like a peacock, and all crimson barr'd;
And full of silver moons, that, as she breathed,
Dissolv'd, or brighter shone, or interwreathed
Their lustres with the gloomier tapestries—
So rainbow-sided, touch'd with miseries,
55   She seem'd, at once, some penanced lady elf,
Some demon's mistress, or the demon's self.
Upon her crest she wore a wannish fire
Sprinkled with stars, like Ariadne's tiar:
Her head was serpent, but ah, bitter-sweet!
60   She had a woman's mouth with all its pearls complete:
And for her eyes: what could such eyes do there
But weep, and weep, that they were born so fair?
As Proserpine still weeps for her Sicilian air.
Her throat was serpent, but the words she spake
65   Came, as through bubbling honey, for Love's sake,
And thus; while Hermes on his pinions lay,
Like a stoop'd falcon ere he takes his prey.

    "Fair Hermes, crown'd with feathers, fluttering light,
I had a splendid dream of thee last night:
70   I saw thee sitting, on a throne of gold,
Among the Gods, upon Olympus old,
The only sad one; for thou didst not hear
The soft, lute-finger'd Muses chaunting clear,
Nor even Apollo when he sang alone,
75   Deaf to his throbbing throat's long, long melodious moan.
I dreamt I saw thee, robed in purple flakes,
Break amorous through the clouds, as morning breaks,
And, swiftly as a bright Phœbean dart,

Strike for the Cretan isle; and here thou art!
80   Too gentle Hermes, hast thou found the maid?"
Whereat the star of Lethe not delay'd
His rosy eloquence, and thus inquired:
"Thou smooth-lipp'd serpent, surely high inspired!
Thou beauteous wreath, with melancholy eyes,
85   Possess whatever bliss thou canst devise,
Telling me only where my nymph is fled,—
Where she doth breathe!" "Bright planet, thou hast said,"
Return'd the snake, "but seal with oaths, fair God!"
"I swear," said Hermes, "by my serpent rod,
90   And by thine eyes, and by thy starry crown!"
Light flew his earnest words, among the blossoms blown.
Then thus again the brilliance feminine:
"Too frail of heart! for this lost nymph of thine,
Free as the air, invisibly, she strays
95   About these thornless wilds; her pleasant days
She tastes unseen; unseen her nimble feet
Leave traces in the grass and flowers sweet;
From weary tendrils, and bow'd branches green,
She plucks the fruit unseen, she bathes unseen:
100   And by my power is her beauty veil'd
To keep it unaffronted, unassail'd
By the love-glances of unlovely eyes,
Of Satyrs, Fauns, and blear'd Silenus' sighs.
Pale grew her immortality, for woe
105   Of all these lovers, and she grieved so
I took compassion on her, bade her steep
Her hair in weïrd syrops, that would keep
Her loveliness invisible, yet free
To wander as she loves, in liberty.
110   Thou shalt behold her, Hermes, thou alone,
If thou wilt, as thou swearest, grant my boon!"
Then, once again, the charmed God began
An oath, and through the serpent's ears it ran
Warm, tremulous, devout, psalterian.
115   Ravish'd, she lifted her Circean head,
Blush'd a live damask, and swift-lisping said,
"I was a woman, let me have once more
A woman's shape, and charming as before.
I love a youth of Corinth—O the bliss!
120   Give me my woman's form, and place me where he is.
Stoop, Hermes, let me breathe upon thy brow,

And thou shalt see thy sweet nymph even now."
The God on half-shut feathers sank serene,
She breath'd upon his eyes, and swift was seen
125   Of both the guarded nymph near-smiling on the green.
It was no dream; or say a dream it was,
Real are the dreams of Gods, and smoothly pass
Their pleasures in a long immortal dream.
One warm, flush'd moment, hovering, it might seem
130   Dash'd by the wood-nymph's beauty, so he burn'd;
Then, lighting on the printless verdure, turn'd
To the swoon'd serpent, and with languid arm,
Delicate, put to proof the lythe Caducean charm.
So done, upon the nymph his eyes he bent
135   Full of adoring tears and blandishment,
And towards her stept: she, like a moon in wane,
Faded before him, cower'd, nor could restrain
Her fearful sobs, self-folding like a flower
That faints into itself at evening hour:
140   But the God fostering her chilled hand,
She felt the warmth, her eyelids open'd bland,
And, like new flowers at morning song of bees,
Bloom'd, and gave up her honey to the lees.
Into the green-recessed woods they flew;
145   Nor grew they pale, as mortal lovers do.

    Left to herself, the serpent now began
To change; her elfin blood in madness ran,
Her mouth foam'd, and the grass, therewith besprent,
Wither'd at dew so sweet and virulent;
150   Her eyes in torture fix'd, and anguish drear,
Hot, glaz'd, and wide, with lid-lashes all sear,
Flash'd phosphor and sharp sparks, without one cooling tear.
The colours all inflam'd throughout her train,
She writh'd about, convuls'd with scarlet pain:
155   A deep volcanian yellow took the place
Of all her milder-mooned body's grace;
And, as the lava ravishes the mead,
Spoilt all her silver mail, and golden brede;
Made gloom of all her frecklings, streaks and bars,
160   Eclips'd her crescents, and lick'd up her stars:
So that, in moments few, she was undrest
Of all her sapphires, greens, and amethyst,
And rubious-argent: of all these bereft,

Nothing but pain and ugliness were left.
165 Still shone her crown; that vanish'd, also she
Melted and disappear'd as suddenly;
And in the air, her new voice luting soft,
Cried, "Lycius! gentle Lycius!"—Borne aloft
With the bright mists about the mountains hoar
170 These words dissolv'd: Crete's forests heard no more.

Whither fled Lamia, now a lady bright,
A full-born beauty new and exquisite?
She fled into that valley they pass o'er
Who go to Corinth from Cenchreas' shore;
175 And rested at the foot of those wild hills,
The rugged founts of the Peræan rills,
And of that other ridge whose barren back
Stretches, with all its mist and cloudy rack,
South-westward to Cleone. There she stood
180 About a young bird's flutter from a wood,
Fair, on a sloping green of mossy tread,
By a clear pool, wherein she passioned
To see herself escap'd from so sore ills,
While her robes flaunted with the daffodils.

185 Ah, happy Lycius!—for she was a maid
More beautiful than ever twisted braid,
Or sigh'd, or blush'd, or on spring-flowered lea
Spread a green kirtle to the minstrelsy:
A virgin purest lipp'd, yet in the lore
190 Of love deep learned to the red heart's core:
Not one hour old, yet of sciential brain
To unperplex bliss from its neighbour pain;
Define their pettish limits, and estrange
Their points of contact, and swift counterchange;
195 Intrigue with the specious chaos, and dispart
Its most ambiguous atoms with sure art;
As though in Cupid's college she had spent
Sweet days a lovely graduate, still unshent,
And kept his rosy terms in idle languishment.

200 Why this fair creature chose so fairily
By the wayside to linger, we shall see;
But first 'tis fit to tell how she could muse
And dream, when in the serpent prison-house,

Of all she list, strange or magnificent:
205 How, ever, where she will'd, her spirit went;
Whether to faint Elysium, or where
Down through tress-lifting waves the Nereids fair
Wind into Thetis' bower by many a pearly stair;
Or where God Bacchus drains his cups divine,
210 Stretch'd out, at ease, beneath a glutinous pine;
Or where in Pluto's gardens palatine
Mulciber's columns gleam in far piazzian line.
And sometimes into cities she would send
Her dream, with feast and rioting to blend;
215 And once, while among mortals dreaming thus,
She saw the young Corinthian Lycius
Charioting foremost in the envious race,
Like a young Jove with calm uneager face,
And fell into a swooning love of him.
220 Now on the moth-time of that evening dim
He would return that way, as well she knew,
To Corinth from the shore; for freshly blew
The eastern soft wind, and his galley now
Grated the quaystones with her brazen prow
225 In port Cenchreas, from Egina isle
Fresh anchor'd; whither he had been awhile
To sacrifice to Jove, whose temple there
Waits with high marble doors for blood and incense rare.
Jove heard his vows, and better'd his desire;
230 For by some freakful chance he made retire
From his companions, and set forth to walk,
Perhaps grown wearied of their Corinth talk:
Over the solitary hills he fared,
Thoughtless at first, but ere eve's star appeared
235 His phantasy was lost, where reason fades,
In the calm'd twilight of Platonic shades.
Lamia beheld him coming, near, more near—
Close to her passing, in indifference drear,
His silent sandals swept the mossy green;
240 So neighbour'd to him, and yet so unseen
She stood: he pass'd, shut up in mysteries,
His mind wrapp'd like his mantle, while her eyes
Follow'd his steps, and her neck regal white
Turn'd—syllabling thus, "Ah, Lycius bright,
245 And will you leave me on the hills alone?
Lycius, look back! and be some pity shown."

He did; not with cold wonder fearingly,
But Orpheus-like at an Eurydice;
For so delicious were the words she sung,
250   It seem'd he had lov'd them a whole summer long:
And soon his eyes had drunk her beauty up,
Leaving no drop in the bewildering cup,
And still the cup was full,—while he, afraid
Lest she should vanish ere his lip had paid
255   Due adoration, thus began to adore;
Her soft look growing coy, she saw his chain so sure:
"Leave thee alone! Look back! Ah, Goddess, see
Whether my eyes can ever turn from thee!
For pity do not this sad heart belie—
260   Even as thou vanishest so I shall die.
Stay! though a Naiad of the rivers, stay!
To thy far wishes will thy streams obey:
Stay! though the greenest woods be thy domain,
Alone they can drink up the morning rain:
265   Though a descended Pleiad, will not one
Of thine harmonious sisters keep in tune
Thy spheres, and as thy silver proxy shine?
So sweetly to these ravish'd ears of mine
Came thy sweet greeting, that if thou shouldst fade
270   Thy memory will waste me to a shade:—
For pity do not melt!"—"If I should stay,"
Said Lamia, "here, upon this floor of clay,
And pain my steps upon these flowers too rough,
What canst thou say or do of charm enough
275   To dull the nice remembrance of my home?
Thou canst not ask me with thee here to roam
Over these hills and vales, where no joy is,—
Empty of immortality and bliss!
Thou art a scholar, Lycius, and must know
280   That finer spirits cannot breathe below
In human climes, and live: Alas! poor youth,
What taste of purer air hast thou to soothe
My essence? What serener palaces,
Where I may all my many senses please,
285   And by mysterious sleights a hundred thirsts appease?
It cannot be—Adieu!" So said, she rose
Tiptoe with white arms spread. He, sick to lose
The amorous promise of her lone complain,
Swoon'd, murmuring of love, and pale with pain.

290 The cruel lady, without any show
Of sorrow for her tender favourite's woe,
But rather, if her eyes could brighter be,
With brighter eyes and slow amenity,
Put her new lips to his, and gave afresh
295 The life she had so tangled in her mesh:
And as he from one trance was wakening
Into another, she began to sing,
Happy in beauty, life, and love, and every thing,
A song of love, too sweet for earthly lyres,
300 While, like held breath, the stars drew in their panting fires.
And then she whisper'd in such trembling tone,
As those who, safe together met alone
For the first time through many anguish'd days,
Use other speech than looks; bidding him raise
305 His drooping head, and clear his soul of doubt,
For that she was a woman, and without
Any more subtle fluid in her veins
Than throbbing blood, and that the self-same pains
Inhabited her frail-strung heart as his.
310 And next she wonder'd how his eyes could miss
Her face so long in Corinth, where, she said,
She dwelt but half retir'd, and there had led
Days happy as the gold coin could invent
Without the aid of love; yet in content
315 Till she saw him, as once she pass'd him by,
Where 'gainst a column he leant thoughtfully
At Venus' temple porch, 'mid baskets heap'd
Of amorous herbs and flowers, newly reap'd
Late on that eve, as 'twas the night before
320 The Adonian feast; whereof she saw no more,
But wept alone those days, for why should she adore?
Lycius from death awoke into amaze,
To see her still, and singing so sweet lays;
Then from amaze into delight he fell
325 To hear her whisper woman's lore so well;
And every word she spake entic'd him on
To unperplex'd delight and pleasure known.
Let the mad poets say whate'er they please
Of the sweets of Fairies, Peris, Goddesses,
330 There is not such a treat among them all,
Haunters of cavern, lake, and waterfall,
As a real woman, lineal indeed

From Pyrrha's pebbles or old Adam's seed.
Thus gentle Lamia judg'd, and judg'd aright,
335   That Lycius could not love in half a fright,
So threw the goddess off, and won his heart
More pleasantly by playing woman's part,
With no more awe than what her beauty gave,
That, while it smote, still guaranteed to save.
340   Lycius to all made eloquent reply,
Marrying to every word a twinborn sigh;
And last, pointing to Corinth, ask'd her sweet,
If 'twas too far that night for her soft feet.
The way was short, for Lamia's eagerness
345   Made, by a spell, the triple league decrease
To a few paces; not at all surmised
By blinded Lycius, so in her comprized.
They pass'd the city gates, he knew not how,
So noiseless, and he never thought to know.

350   As men talk in a dream, so Corinth all,
Throughout her palaces imperial,
And all her populous streets and temples lewd,
Mutter'd, like tempest in the distance brew'd,
To the wide-spreaded night above her towers.
355   Men, women, rich and poor, in the cool hours,
Shuffled their sandals o'er the pavement white,
Companion'd or alone; while many a light
Flared, here and there, from wealthy festivals,
And threw their moving shadows on the walls,
360   Or found them cluster'd in the corniced shade
Of some arch'd temple door, or dusky colonnade.

Muffling his face, of greeting friends in fear,
Her fingers he press'd hard, as one came near
With curl'd gray beard, sharp eyes, and smooth bald crown,
365   Slow-stepp'd, and robed in philosophic gown:
Lycius shrank closer, as they met and past,
Into his mantle, adding wings to haste,
While hurried Lamia trembled: "Ah," said he,
"Why do you shudder, love, so ruefully?
370   Why does your tender palm dissolve in dew?"—
"I'm wearied," said fair Lamia: "tell me who
Is that old man? I cannot bring to mind
His features:—Lycius! wherefore did you blind

Yourself from his quick eyes?" Lycius replied,
375   "'Tis Apollonius sage, my trusty guide
And good instructor; but to-night he seems
The ghost of folly haunting my sweet dreams."

   While yet he spake they had arrived before
A pillar'd porch, with lofty portal door,
380   Where hung a silver lamp, whose phosphor glow
Reflected in the slabbed steps below,
Mild as a star in water; for so new,
And so unsullied was the marble hue,
So through the crystal polish, liquid fine,
385   Ran the dark veins, that none but feet divine
Could e'er have touch'd there. Sounds Æolian
Breath'd from the hinges, as the ample span
Of the wide doors disclos'd a place unknown
Some time to any, but those two alone,
390   And a few Persian mutes, who that same year
Were seen about the markets: none knew where
They could inhabit; the most curious
Were foil'd, who watch'd to trace them to their house:
And but the flitter-winged verse must tell,
395   For truth's sake, what woe afterwards befel,
'Twould humour many a heart to leave them thus,
Shut from the busy world of more incredulous.

PART II

Love in a hut, with water and a crust,
Is—Love, forgive us!—cinders, ashes, dust;
Love in a palace is perhaps at last
More grievous torment than a hermit's fast:—
5   That is a doubtful tale from faery land,
Hard for the non-elect to understand.
Had Lycius liv'd to hand his story down,
He might have given the moral a fresh frown,
Or clench'd it quite: but too short was their bliss
10   To breed distrust and hate, that make the soft voice hiss.
Besides, there, nightly, with terrific glare,
Love, jealous grown of so complete a pair,
Hover'd and buzz'd his wings, with fearful roar,

Above the lintel of their chamber door,
15   And down the passage cast a glow upon the floor.

For all this came a ruin: side by side
They were enthroned, in the even tide,
Upon a couch, near to a curtaining
Whose airy texture, from a golden string,
20   Floated into the room, and let appear
Unveil'd the summer heaven, blue and clear,
Betwixt two marble shafts:—there they reposed,
Where use had made it sweet, with eyelids closed,
Saving a tythe which love still open kept,
25   That they might see each other while they almost slept;
When from the slope side of a suburb hill,
Deafening the swallow's twitter, came a thrill
Of trumpets—Lycius started—the sounds fled,
But left a thought, a buzzing in his head.
30   For the first time, since first he harbour'd in
That purple-lined palace of sweet sin,
His spirit pass'd beyond its golden bourn
Into the noisy world almost forsworn.
The lady, ever watchful, penetrant,
35   Saw this with pain, so arguing a want
Of something more, more than her empery
Of joys; and she began to moan and sigh
Because he mused beyond her, knowing well
That but a moment's thought is passion's passing bell.
40   "Why do you sigh, fair creature?" whisper'd he:
"Why do you think?" return'd she tenderly:
"You have deserted me;—where am I now?
Not in your heart while care weighs on your brow:
No, no, you have dismiss'd me; and I go
45   From your breast houseless: ay, it must be so."
He answer'd, bending to her open eyes,
Where he was mirror'd small in paradise,
"My silver planet, both of eve and morn!
Why will you plead yourself so sad forlorn,
50   While I am striving how to fill my heart
With deeper crimson, and a double smart?
How to entangle, trammel up and snare
Your soul in mine, and labyrinth you there
Like the hid scent in an unbudded rose?
55   Ay, a sweet kiss—you see your mighty woes.

My thoughts! shall I unveil them? Listen then!
What mortal hath a prize, that other men
May be confounded and abash'd withal,
But lets it sometimes pace abroad majestical,
60 And triumph, as in thee I should rejoice
Amid the hoarse alarm of Corinth's voice.
Let my foes choke, and my friends shout afar,
While through the thronged streets your bridal car
Wheels round its dazzling spokes."—The lady's cheek
65 Trembled; she nothing said, but, pale and meek,
Arose and knelt before him, wept a rain
Of sorrows at his words; at last with pain
Beseeching him, the while his hand she wrung,
To change his purpose. He thereat was stung,
70 Perverse, with stronger fancy to reclaim
Her wild and timid nature to his aim:
Besides, for all his love, in self despite,
Against his better self, he took delight
Luxurious in her sorrows, soft and new.
75 His passion, cruel grown, took on a hue
Fierce and sanguineous as 'twas possible
In one whose brow had no dark veins to swell.
Fine was the mitigated fury, like
Apollo's presence when in act to strike
80 The serpent—Ha, the serpent! certes, she
Was none. She burnt, she lov'd the tyranny,
And, all subdued, consented to the hour
When to the bridal he should lead his paramour.
Whispering in midnight silence, said the youth,
85 "Sure some sweet name thou hast, though, by my truth,
I have not ask'd it, ever thinking thee
Not mortal, but of heavenly progeny,
As still I do. Hast any mortal name,
Fit appellation for this dazzling frame?
90 Or friends or kinsfolk on the citied earth,
To share our marriage feast and nuptial mirth?"
"I have no friends," said Lamia, "no, not one;
My presence in wide Corinth hardly known:
My parents' bones are in their dusty urns
95 Sepulchred, where no kindled incense burns,
Seeing all their luckless race are dead, save me,
And I neglect the holy rite for thee.
Even as you list invite your many guests;

But if, as now it seems, your vision rests
100   With any pleasure on me, do not bid
Old Apollonius—from him keep me hid."
Lycius, perplex'd at words so blind and blank,
Made close inquiry; from whose touch she shrank,
Feigning a sleep; and he to the dull shade
105   Of deep sleep in a moment was betray'd.

    It was the custom then to bring away
The bride from home at blushing shut of day,
Veil'd, in a chariot, heralded along
By strewn flowers, torches, and a marriage song,
110   With other pageants: but this fair unknown
Had not a friend. So being left alone,
(Lycius was gone to summon all his kin)
And knowing surely she could never win
His foolish heart from its mad pompousness,
115   She set herself, high-thoughted, how to dress
The misery in fit magnificence.
She did so, but 'tis doubtful how and whence
Came, and who were her subtle servitors.
About the halls, and to and from the doors,
120   There was a noise of wings, till in short space
The glowing banquet-room shone with wide-arched grace.
A haunting music, sole perhaps and lone
Supportress of the faery-roof, made moan
Throughout, as fearful the whole charm might fade.
125   Fresh carved cedar, mimicking a glade
Of palm and plantain, met from either side,
High in the midst, in honour of the bride:
Two palms and then two plantains, and so on,
From either side their stems branch'd one to one
130   All down the aisled place; and beneath all
There ran a stream of lamps straight on from wall to wall.
So canopied, lay an untasted feast
Teeming with odours. Lamia, regal drest,
Silently paced about, and as she went,
135   In pale contented sort of discontent,
Mission'd her viewless servants to enrich
The fretted splendour of each nook and niche.
Between the tree-stems, marbled plain at first,
Came jasper pannels; then, anon, there burst
140   Forth creeping imagery of slighter trees,

And with the larger wove in small intricacies.
Approving all, she faded at self-will,
And shut the chamber up, close, hush'd and still,
Complete and ready for the revels rude,
145   When dreadful guests would come to spoil her solitude.

The day appear'd, and all the gossip rout.
O senseless Lycius! Madman! wherefore flout
The silent-blessing fate, warm cloister'd hours,
And show to common eyes these secret bowers?
150   The herd approach'd; each guest, with busy brain,
Arriving at the portal, gaz'd amain,
And enter'd marveling: for they knew the street,
Remember'd it from childhood all complete
Without a gap, yet ne'er before had seen
155   That royal porch, that high-built fair demesne;
So in they hurried all, maz'd, curious and keen:
Save one, who look'd thereon with eye severe,
And with calm-planted steps walk'd in austere;
'Twas Apollonius: something too he laugh'd,
160   As though some knotty problem, that had daft
His patient thought, had now begun to thaw,
And solve and melt:—'twas just as he foresaw.

He met within the murmurous vestibule
His young disciple. "'Tis no common rule,
165   Lycius," said he, "for uninvited guest
To force himself upon you, and infest
With an unbidden presence the bright throng
Of younger friends; yet must I do this wrong,
And you forgive me." Lycius blush'd, and led
170   The old man through the inner doors broad-spread;
With reconciling words and courteous mien
Turning into sweet milk the sophist's spleen.

Of wealthy lustre was the banquet-room,
Fill'd with pervading brilliance and perfume:
175   Before each lucid pannel fuming stood
A censer fed with myrrh and spiced wood,
Each by a sacred tripod held aloft,
Whose slender feet wide-swerv'd upon the soft
Wool-woofed carpets: fifty wreaths of smoke
180   From fifty censers their light voyage took

To the high roof, still mimick'd as they rose
Along the mirror'd walls by twin-clouds odorous.
Twelve sphered tables, by silk seats insphered,
High as the level of a man's breast rear'd
185   On libbard's paws, upheld the heavy gold
Of cups and goblets, and the store thrice told
Of Ceres' horn, and, in huge vessels, wine
Come from the gloomy tun with merry shine.
Thus loaded with a feast the tables stood,
190   Each shrining in the midst the image of a God.

When in an antichamber every guest
Had felt the cold full sponge to pleasure press'd,
By minist'ring slaves, upon his hands and feet,
And fragrant oils with ceremony meet
195   Pour'd on his hair, they all mov'd to the feast
In white robes, and themselves in order placed
Around the silken couches, wondering
Whence all this mighty cost and blaze of wealth could spring.

Soft went the music the soft air along,
200   While fluent Greek a vowel'd undersong
Kept up among the guests, discoursing low
At first, for scarcely was the wine at flow;
But when the happy vintage touch'd their brains,
Louder they talk, and louder come the strains
205   Of powerful instruments:—the gorgeous dyes,
The space, the splendour of the draperies,
The roof of awful richness, nectarous cheer,
Beautiful slaves, and Lamia's self, appear,
Now, when the wine has done its rosy deed,
210   And every soul from human trammels freed,
No more so strange; for merry wine, sweet wine,
Will make Elysian shades not too fair, too divine.

Soon was God Bacchus at meridian height;
Flush'd were their cheeks, and bright eyes double bright:
215   Garlands of every green, and every scent
From vales deflower'd, or forest-trees branch-rent,
In baskets of bright osier'd gold were brought
High as the handles heap'd, to suit the thought
Of every guest; that each, as he did please,
220   Might fancy-fit his brows, silk-pillow'd at his ease.

What wreath for Lamia? What for Lycius?
What for the sage, old Apollonius?
Upon her aching forehead be there hung
The leaves of willow and of adder's tongue;
225 And for the youth, quick, let us strip for him
The thyrsus, that his watching eyes may swim
Into forgetfulness; and, for the sage,
Let spear-grass and the spiteful thistle wage
War on his temples. Do not all charms fly
230 At the mere touch of cold philosophy?
There was an awful rainbow once in heaven:
We know her woof, her texture; she is given
In the dull catalogue of common things.
Philosophy will clip an Angel's wings,
235 Conquer all mysteries by rule and line,
Empty the haunted air, and gnomed mine—
Unweave a rainbow, as it erewhile made
The tender-person'd Lamia melt into a shade.

By her glad Lycius sitting, in chief place,
240 Scarce saw in all the room another face,
Till, checking his love trance, a cup he took
Full brimm'd, and opposite sent forth a look
'Cross the broad table, to beseech a glance
From his old teacher's wrinkled countenance,
245 And pledge him. The bald-head philosopher
Had fix'd his eye, without a twinkle or stir
Full on the alarmed beauty of the bride,
Brow-beating her fair form, and troubling her sweet pride.
Lycius then press'd her hand, with devout touch,
250 As pale it lay upon the rosy couch:
'Twas icy, and the cold ran through his veins;
Then sudden it grew hot, and all the pains
Of an unnatural heat shot to his heart.
"Lamia, what means this? Wherefore dost thou start?
255 Know'st thou that man?" Poor Lamia answer'd not.
He gaz'd into her eyes, and not a jot
Own'd they the lovelorn piteous appeal:
More, more he gaz'd: his human senses reel:
Some hungry spell that loveliness absorbs;
260 There was no recognition in those orbs.
"Lamia!" he cried—and no soft-toned reply.
The many heard, and the loud revelry

Grew hush; the stately music no more breathes;
The myrtle sicken'd in a thousand wreaths.
265   By faint degrees, voice, lute, and pleasure ceased;
A deadly silence step by step increased,
Until it seem'd a horrid presence there,
And not a man but felt the terror in his hair.
"Lamia!" he shriek'd; and nothing but the shriek
270   With its sad echo did the silence break.
"Begone, foul dream!" he cried, gazing again
In the bride's face, where now no azure vein
Wander'd on fair-spaced temples; no soft bloom
Misted the cheek; no passion to illume
275   The deep-recessed vision:—all was blight;
Lamia, no longer fair, there sat a deadly white.
"Shut, shut those juggling eyes, thou ruthless man!
Turn them aside, wretch! or the righteous ban
Of all the Gods, whose dreadful images
280   Here represent their shadowy presences,
May pierce them on the sudden with the thorn
Of painful blindness; leaving thee forlorn,
In trembling dotage to the feeblest fright
Of conscience, for their long offended might,
285   For all thine impious proud-heart sophistries,
Unlawful magic, and enticing lies.
Corinthians! look upon that gray-beard wretch!
Mark how, possess'd, his lashless eyelids stretch
Around his demon eyes! Corinthians, see!
290   My sweet bride withers at their potency."
"Fool!" said the sophist, in an under-tone
Gruff with contempt; which a death-nighing moan
From Lycius answer'd, as heart-struck and lost,
He sank supine beside the aching ghost.
295   "Fool! Fool!" repeated he, while his eyes still
Relented not, nor mov'd; "from every ill
Of life have I preserv'd thee to this day,
And shall I see thee made a serpent's prey?"
Then Lamia breath'd death breath; the sophist's eye,
300   Like a sharp spear, went through her utterly,
Keen, cruel, perceant, stinging: she, as well
As her weak hand could any meaning tell,
Motion'd him to be silent; vainly so,
He look'd and look'd again a level—No!
305   "A Serpent!" echoed he; no sooner said,

Than with a frightful scream she vanished:
And Lycius' arms were empty of delight,
As were his limbs of life, from that same night.
On the high couch he lay!—his friends came round—
310   Supported him—no pulse, or breath they found,
And, in its marriage robe, the heavy body wound.*

* "Philostratus, in his fourth book *de Vita Apollonii,* hath a memorable instance
in this kind, which I may not omit, of one Menippus Lycius, a young man twenty-
five years of age, that going betwixt Cenchreas and Corinth, met such a phantasm
in the habit of a fair gentlewoman, which taking him by the hand, carried him
home to her house, in the suburbs of Corinth, and told him she was a Phœnician
by birth, and if he would tarry with her, he should hear her sing and play, and
drink such wine as never any drank, and no man should molest him; but she,
being fair and lovely, would live and die with him, that was fair and lovely to behold. The young man, a philosopher, otherwise staid and discreet, able to moderate his passions, though not this of love, tarried with her a while to his great content, and at last married her, to whose wedding, amongst other guests, came
Apollonius; who, by some probable conjectures, found her out to be a serpent, a
lamia; and that all her furniture was, like Tantalus' gold, described by Homer, no
substance but mere illusions. When she saw herself descried, she wept, and desired Apollonius to be silent, but he would not be moved, and thereupon she,
plate, house, and all that was in it, vanished in an instant: many thousands took
notice of this fact, for it was done in the midst of Greece."
Burton's "Anatomy of Melancholy." Part 3. Sect. 2. Memb. 1. Subs. 1.

Pensive they sit, and roll their languid eyes

Pensive they sit, and roll their languid eyes,
Nibble their toasts, and cool their tea with sighs,
Or else forget the purpose of the night,
Forget their tea—forget their appetite.
5   See, with cross'd arms they sit—ah hapless crew,
The fire is going out, and no one rings
For coals, and therefore no coals Betty brings.
A fly is in the milk pot—must he die
Circled by a humane society?
10   No, no, there Mr. Werter takes his spoon,
Inverts it—dips the handle, and lo, soon
The little struggler, sav'd from perils dark,
Across the teaboard draws a long wet mark.

Romeo! Arise! take snuffers by the handle;
15   There's a large cauliflower in each candle,
A winding-sheet—Ah me! I must away
To No. 7, just beyond the Circus gay.
"Alas, my friend! your coat sits very well:
Where may your taylor live?" "I may not tell—
20   O pardon me—I'm absent now and then.
Where *might* my taylor live?—I say again
I cannot tell. Let me no more be teas'd—
He lives in Wapping, *might* live where he pleas'd."

To Autumn

1

Season of mists and mellow fruitfulness,
   Close bosom-friend of the maturing sun;
Conspiring with him how to load and bless
   With fruit the vines that round the thatch-eves run;
5   To bend with apples the moss'd cottage-trees,
   And fill all fruit with ripeness to the core;
     To swell the gourd, and plump the hazel shells
   With a sweet kernel; to set budding more,
And still more, later flowers for the bees,
10   Until they think warm days will never cease,
     For summer has o'er-brimm'd their clammy cells.

2

Who hath not seen thee oft amid thy store?
   Sometimes whoever seeks abroad may find
Thee sitting careless on a granary floor,
15   Thy hair soft-lifted by the winnowing wind;
Or on a half-reap'd furrow sound asleep,
   Drows'd with the fume of poppies, while thy hook
   Spares the next swath and all its twined flowers:
And sometimes like a gleaner thou dost keep
20   Steady thy laden head across a brook;
   Or by a cyder-press, with patient look,
     Thou watchest the last oozings hours by hours.

3

Where are the songs of spring? Ay, where are they?
   Think not of them, thou hast thy music too,—

25   While barred clouds bloom the soft-dying day,
       And touch the stubble-plains with rosy hue;
     Then in a wailful choir the small gnats mourn
       Among the river sallows, borne aloft
        Or sinking as the light wind lives or dies;
30   And full-grown lambs loud bleat from hilly bourn;
       Hedge-crickets sing; and now with treble soft
     The red-breast whistles from a garden-croft;
     And gathering swallows twitter in the skies.

The Fall of Hyperion:
A Dream

CANTO I

Fanatics have their dreams, wherewith they weave
A paradise for a sect; the savage too
From forth the loftiest fashion of his sleep
Guesses at heaven: pity these have not
5   Trac'd upon vellum or wild Indian leaf
The shadows of melodious utterance.
But bare of laurel they live, dream, and die;
For Poesy alone can tell her dreams,
With the fine spell of words alone can save
10   Imagination from the sable charm
And dumb enchantment. Who alive can say
"Thou art no poet; may'st not tell thy dreams"?
Since every man whose soul is not a clod
Hath visions, and would speak, if he had lov'd
15   And been well nurtured in his mother tongue.
Whether the dream now purposed to rehearse
Be poet's or fanatic's will be known
When this warm scribe my hand is in the grave.

      Methought I stood where trees of every clime,
20   Palm, myrtle, oak, and sycamore, and beech,
With plantane, and spice blossoms, made a screen;
In neighbourhood of fountains, by the noise
Soft showering in mine ears, and, by the touch
Of scent, not far from roses. Turning round,
25   I saw an arbour with a drooping roof
Of trellis vines, and bells, and larger blooms,

Like floral-censers swinging light in air;
Before its wreathed doorway, on a mound
Of moss, was spread a feast of summer fruits,
30   Which, nearer seen, seem'd refuse of a meal
By angel tasted, or our mother Eve;
For empty shells were scattered on the grass,
And grape stalks but half bare, and remnants more,
Sweet smelling, whose pure kinds I could not know.
35   Still was more plenty than the fabled horn
Thrice emptied could pour forth, at banqueting
For Proserpine return'd to her own fields,
Where the white heifers low. And appetite
More yearning than on earth I ever felt
40   Growing within, I ate deliciously;
And, after not long, thirsted, for thereby
Stood a cool vessel of transparent juice,
Sipp'd by the wander'd bee, the which I took,
And, pledging all the mortals of the world,
45   And all the dead whose names are in our lips,
Drank. That full draught is parent of my theme.
No Asian poppy, nor elixir fine
Of the soon fading jealous caliphat;
No poison gender'd in close monkish cell
50   To thin the scarlet conclave of old men,
Could so have rapt unwilling life away.
Among the fragrant husks and berries crush'd,
Upon the grass I struggled hard against
The domineering potion; but in vain:
55   The cloudy swoon came on, and down I sunk
Like a Silenus on an antique vase.
How long I slumber'd 'tis a chance to guess.
When sense of life return'd, I started up
As if with wings; but the fair trees were gone,
60   The mossy mound and arbour were no more;
I look'd around upon the carved sides
Of an old sanctuary with roof august,
Builded so high, it seem'd that filmed clouds
Might spread beneath, as o'er the stars of heaven;
65   So old the place was, I remembered none
The like upon the earth; what I had seen
Of grey cathedrals, buttress'd walls, rent towers,
The superannuations of sunk realms,
Or nature's rocks toil'd hard in waves and winds,

70 Seem'd but the faulture of decrepit things
To that eternal domed monument.
Upon the marble at my feet there lay
Store of strange vessels, and large draperies,
Which needs had been of dyed asbestus wove,
75 Or in that place the moth could not corrupt,
So white the linen; so, in some, distinct
Ran imageries from a sombre loom.
All in a mingled heap confus'd there lay
Robes, golden tongs, censer, and chafing dish,
80 Girdles, and chains, and holy jewelries.

  Turning from these with awe, once more I rais'd
My eyes to fathom the space every way;
The embossed roof, the silent massy range
Of columns north and south, ending in mist
85 Of nothing, then to eastward, where black gates
Were shut against the sunrise evermore.
Then to the west I look'd, and saw far off
An image, huge of feature as a cloud,
At level of whose feet an altar slept,
90 To be approach'd on either side by steps,
And marble balustrade, and patient travail
To count with toil the innumerable degrees.
Towards the altar sober-pac'd I went,
Repressing haste, as too unholy there;
95 And, coming nearer, saw beside the shrine
One minist'ring; and there arose a flame.
When in mid-May the sickening east wind
Shifts sudden to the south, the small warm rain
Melts out the frozen incense from all flowers,
100 And fills the air with so much pleasant health
That even the dying man forgets his shroud;
Even so that lofty sacrificial fire,
Sending forth Maian incense, spread around
Forgetfulness of every thing but bliss,
105 And clouded all the altar with soft smoke,
From whose white fragrant curtains thus I heard
Language pronounc'd. "If thou canst not ascend
These steps, die on that marble where thou art.
Thy flesh, near cousin to the common dust,
110 Will parch for lack of nutriment—thy bones
Will wither in few years, and vanish so

That not the quickest eye could find a grain
Of what thou now art on that pavement cold.
The sands of thy short life are spent this hour,
115   And no hand in the universe can turn
Thy hour glass, if these gummed leaves be burnt
Ere thou canst mount up these immortal steps."
I heard, I look'd: two senses both at once
So fine, so subtle, felt the tyranny
120   Of that fierce threat, and the hard task proposed.
Prodigious seem'd the toil; the leaves were yet
Burning,—when suddenly a palsied chill
Struck from the paved level up my limbs,
And was ascending quick to put cold grasp
125   Upon those streams that pulse beside the throat:
I shriek'd; and the sharp anguish of my shriek
Stung my own ears—I strove hard to escape
The numbness; strove to gain the lowest step.
Slow, heavy, deadly was my pace: the cold
130   Grew stifling, suffocating, at the heart;
And when I clasp'd my hands I felt them not.
One minute before death, my iced foot touch'd
The lowest stair; and as it touch'd, life seem'd
To pour in at the toes: I mounted up,
135   As once fair angels on a ladder flew
From the green turf to heaven.—"Holy Power,"
Cried I, approaching near the horned shrine,
"What am I that should so be sav'd from death?
What am I that another death come not
140   To choak my utterance sacrilegious here?"
Then said the veiled shadow—"Thou hast felt
What 'tis to die and live again before
Thy fated hour. That thou hadst power to do so
Is thy own safety; thou hast dated on
145   Thy doom."—"High Prophetess," said I, "purge off
Benign, if so it please thee, my mind's film."
"None can usurp this height," return'd that shade,
"But those to whom the miseries of the world
Are misery, and will not let them rest.
150   All else who find a haven in the world,
Where they may thoughtless sleep away their days,
If by a chance into this fane they come,
Rot on the pavement where thou rotted'st half."—
"Are there not thousands in the world," said I,

155   Encourag'd by the sooth voice of the shade,
       "Who love their fellows even to the death;
       Who feel the giant agony of the world;
       And more, like slaves to poor humanity,
       Labour for mortal good? I sure should see
160   Other men here: but I am here alone."
       "They whom thou spak'st of are no vision'ries,"
       Rejoin'd that voice—"They are no dreamers weak,
       They seek no wonder but the human face;
       No music but a happy-noted voice—
165   They come not here, they have no thought to come—
       And thou art here, for thou art less than they.
       What benefit canst thou do, or all thy tribe,
       To the great world? Thou art a dreaming thing;
       A fever of thyself—think of the earth;
170   What bliss even in hope is there for thee?
       What haven? Every creature hath its home;
       Every sole man hath days of joy and pain,
       Whether his labours be sublime or low—
       The pain alone; the joy alone; distinct:
175   Only the dreamer venoms all his days,
       Bearing more woe than all his sins deserve.
       Therefore, that happiness be somewhat shar'd,
       Such things as thou art are admitted oft
       Into like gardens thou didst pass erewhile,
180   And suffer'd in these temples; for that cause
       Thou standest safe beneath this statue's knees."
       "That I am favored for unworthiness,
       By such propitious parley medicin'd
       In sickness not ignoble, I rejoice,
185   Aye, and could weep for love of such award."
       So answer'd I, continuing, "If it please,
       Majestic shadow, tell me: sure not all
       Those melodies sung into the world's ear
       Are useless: sure a poet is a sage;
190   A humanist, physician to all men.
       That I am none I feel, as vultures feel
       They are no birds when eagles are abroad.
       What am I then? Thou spakest of my tribe:
       What tribe?"—The tall shade veil'd in drooping white
195   Then spake, so much more earnest, that the breath
       Mov'd the thin linen folds that drooping hung
       About a golden censer from the hand

Pendent.—"Art thou not of the dreamer tribe?
The poet and the dreamer are distinct,
200   Diverse, sheer opposite, antipodes.
The one pours out a balm upon the world,
The other vexes it." Then shouted I
Spite of myself, and with a Pythia's spleen,
"Apollo! faded, far flown Apollo!
205   Where is thy misty pestilence to creep
Into the dwellings, through the door crannies,
Of all mock lyrists, large self worshipers,
And careless hectorers in proud bad verse.
Though I breathe death with them it will be life
210   To see them sprawl before me into graves.
Majestic shadow, tell me where I am:
Whose altar this; for whom this incense curls:
What image this, whose face I cannot see,
For the broad marble knees; and who thou art,
215   Of accent feminine, so courteous."
Then the tall shade in drooping linens veil'd
Spake out, so much more earnest, that her breath
Stirr'd the thin folds of gauze that drooping hung
About a golden censer from her hand
220   Pendent; and by her voice I knew she shed
Long treasured tears. "This temple sad and lone
Is all spar'd from the thunder of a war
Foughten long since by giant hierarchy
Against rebellion: this old image here,
225   Whose carved features wrinkled as he fell,
Is Saturn's; I, Moneta, left supreme
Sole priestess of his desolation."—
I had no words to answer; for my tongue,
Useless, could find about its roofed home
230   No syllable of a fit majesty
To make rejoinder to Moneta's mourn.
There was a silence while the altar's blaze
Was fainting for sweet food: I look'd thereon
And on the paved floor, where nigh were pil'd
235   Faggots of cinnamon, and many heaps
Of other crisped spice-wood—then again
I look'd upon the altar and its horns
Whiten'd with ashes, and its lang'rous flame,
And then upon the offerings again;
240   And so by turns—till sad Moneta cried,

"The sacrifice is done, but not the less
Will I be kind to thee for thy good will.
My power, which to me is still a curse,
Shall be to thee a wonder; for the scenes
245 Still swooning vivid through my globed brain
With an electral changing misery
Thou shalt with those dull mortal eyes behold,
Free from all pain, if wonder pain thee not."
As near as an immortal's sphered words
250 Could to a mother's soften, were these last:
But yet I had a terror of her robes,
And chiefly of the veils, that from her brow
Hung pale, and curtain'd her in mysteries
That made my heart too small to hold its blood.
255 This saw that Goddess, and with sacred hand
Parted the veils. Then saw I a wan face,
Not pin'd by human sorrows, but bright blanch'd
By an immortal sickness which kills not;
It works a constant change, which happy death
260 Can put no end to; deathwards progressing
To no death was that visage; it had pass'd
The lily and the snow; and beyond these
I must not think now, though I saw that face—
But for her eyes I should have fled away.
265 They held me back, with a benignant light,
Soft mitigated by divinest lids
Half closed, and visionless entire they seem'd
Of all external things—they saw me not,
But in blank splendor beam'd like the mild moon,
270 Who comforts those she sees not, who knows not
What eyes are upward cast. As I had found
A grain of gold upon a mountain's side,
And twing'd with avarice strain'd out my eyes
To search its sullen entrails rich with ore,
275 So at the view of sad Moneta's brow,
I ached to see what things the hollow brain
Behind enwombed: what high tragedy
In the dark secret chambers of her skull
Was acting, that could give so dread a stress
280 To her cold lips, and fill with such a light
Her planetary eyes; and touch her voice
With such a sorrow. "Shade of Memory!"
Cried I, with act adorant at her feet,

"By all the gloom hung round thy fallen house,
285   By this last temple, by the golden age,
By great Apollo, thy dear foster child,
And by thy self, forlorn divinity,
The pale Omega of a wither'd race,
Let me behold, according as thou said'st,
290   What in thy brain so ferments to and fro."—
No sooner had this conjuration pass'd
My devout lips, than side by side we stood,
(Like a stunt bramble by a solemn pine)
Deep in the shady sadness of a vale,
295   Far sunken from the healthy breath of morn,
Far from the fiery noon, and eve's one star.
Onward I look'd beneath the gloomy boughs,
And saw, what first I thought an image huge,
Like to the image pedestal'd so high
300   In Saturn's temple. Then Moneta's voice
Came brief upon mine ear,—"So Saturn sat
When he had lost his realms."—Whereon there grew
A power within me of enormous ken,
To see as a God sees, and take the depth
305   Of things as nimbly as the outward eye
Can size and shape pervade. The lofty theme
At those few words hung vast before my mind,
With half unravel'd web. I set myself
Upon an eagle's watch, that I might see,
310   And seeing ne'er forget. No stir of life
Was in this shrouded vale, not so much air
As in the zoning of a summer's day
Robs not one light seed from the feather'd grass,
But where the dead leaf fell there did it rest:
315   A stream went voiceless by, still deaden'd more
By reason of the fallen divinity
Spreading more shade: the Naiad mid her reeds
Press'd her cold finger closer to her lips.
Along the margin sand large footmarks went
320   No farther than to where old Saturn's feet
Had rested, and there slept, how long a sleep!
Degraded, cold, upon the sodden ground
His old right hand lay nerveless, listless, dead,
Unsceptred; and his realmless eyes were clos'd,
325   While his bow'd head seem'd listening to the Earth,
His antient mother, for some comfort yet.

It seem'd no force could wake him from his place;
But there came one who with a kindred hand
Touch'd his wide shoulders, after bending low
330   With reverence, though to one who knew it not.
Then came the griev'd voice of Mnemosyne,
And griev'd I hearken'd. "That divinity
Whom thou saw'st step from yon forlornest wood,
And with slow pace approach our fallen King,
335   Is Thea, softest-natur'd of our brood."
I mark'd the goddess in fair statuary
Surpassing wan Moneta by the head,
And in her sorrow nearer woman's tears.
There was a listening fear in her regard,
340   As if calamity had but begun;
As if the vanward clouds of evil days
Had spent their malice, and the sullen rear
Was with its stored thunder labouring up.
One hand she press'd upon that aching spot
345   Where beats the human heart; as if just there,
Though an immortal, she felt cruel pain;
The other upon Saturn's bended neck
She laid, and to the level of his hollow ear
Leaning, with parted lips, some words she spake
350   In solemn tenor and deep organ tune;
Some mourning words, which in our feeble tongue
Would come in this-like accenting; how frail
To that large utterance of the early Gods!—
"Saturn! look up—and for what, poor lost King?
355   I have no comfort for thee, no—not one:
I cannot cry, *Wherefore thus sleepest thou?*
For heaven is parted from thee, and the earth
Knows thee not, so afflicted, for a God;
And ocean too, with all its solemn noise,
360   Has from thy sceptre pass'd, and all the air
Is emptied of thine hoary majesty.
Thy thunder, captious at the new command,
Rumbles reluctant o'er our fallen house;
And thy sharp lightning in unpracticed hands
365   Scorches and burns our once serene domain.
With such remorseless speed still come new woes
That unbelief has not a space to breathe.
Saturn, sleep on:—Me thoughtless, why should I
Thus violate thy slumbrous solitude?

370   Why should I ope thy melancholy eyes?
       Saturn, sleep on, while at thy feet I weep."

       As when, upon a tranced summer night,
       Forests, branch-charmed by the earnest stars,
       Dream, and so dream all night, without a noise,
375   Save from one gradual solitary gust,
       Swelling upon the silence; dying off;
       As if the ebbing air had but one wave;
       So came these words, and went; the while in tears
       She press'd her fair large forehead to the earth,
380   Just where her fallen hair might spread in curls,
       A soft and silken mat for Saturn's feet.
       Long, long, those two were postured motionless,
       Like sculpture builded up upon the grave
       Of their own power. A long awful time
385   I look'd upon them; still they were the same;
       The frozen God still bending to the earth,
       And the sad Goddess weeping at his feet;
       Moneta silent. Without stay or prop
       But my own weak mortality, I bore
390   The load of this eternal quietude,
       The unchanging gloom, and the three fixed shapes
       Ponderous upon my senses a whole moon.
       For by my burning brain I measured sure
       Her silver seasons shedded on the night,
395   And every day by day methought I grew
       More gaunt and ghostly. Oftentimes I pray'd
       Intense, that death would take me from the vale
       And all its burthens. Gasping with despair
       Of change, hour after hour I curs'd myself:
400   Until old Saturn rais'd his faded eyes,
       And look'd around, and saw his kingdom gone,
       And all the gloom and sorrow of the place,
       And that fair kneeling Goddess at his feet.
       As the moist scent of flowers, and grass, and leaves
405   Fills forest dells with a pervading air
       Known to the woodland nostril, so the words
       Of Saturn fill'd the mossy glooms around,
       Even to the hollows of time-eaten oaks,
       And to the windings in the foxes' hole,
410   With sad low tones, while thus he spake, and sent
       Strange musings to the solitary Pan.

"Moan, brethren, moan; for we are swallow'd up
And buried from all godlike exercise
Of influence benign on planets pale,
415 And peaceful sway above man's harvesting,
And all those acts which deity supreme
Doth ease its heart of love in. Moan and wail.
Moan, brethren, moan; for lo! the rebel spheres
Spin round, the stars their antient courses keep,
420 Clouds still with shadowy moisture haunt the earth,
Still suck their fill of light from sun and moon,
Still buds the tree, and still the sea-shores murmur.
There is no death in all the universe,
No smell of death—there shall be death—Moan, moan,
425 Moan, Cybele, moan, for thy pernicious babes
Have chang'd a God into a shaking palsy.
Moan, brethren, moan; for I have no strength left,
Weak as the reed—weak—feeble as my voice—
O, O, the pain, the pain of feebleness.
430 Moan, moan; for still I thaw—or give me help:
Throw down those imps and give me victory.
Let me hear other groans, and trumpets blown
Of triumph calm, and hymns of festival
From the gold peaks of heaven's high piled clouds;
435 Voices of soft proclaim, and silver stir
Of strings in hollow shells; and let there be
Beautiful things made new for the surprize
Of the sky children."—So he feebly ceas'd,
With such a poor and sickly sounding pause,
440 Methought I heard some old man of the earth
Bewailing earthly loss; nor could my eyes
And ears act with that pleasant unison of sense
Which marries sweet sound with the grace of form,
And dolorous accent from a tragic harp
445 With large limb'd visions. More I scrutinized:
Still fix'd he sat beneath the sable trees,
Whose arms spread straggling in wild serpent forms,
With leaves all hush'd: his awful presence there
(Now all was silent) gave a deadly lie
450 To what I erewhile heard: only his lips
Trembled amid the white curls of his beard.
They told the truth, though, round, the snowy locks
Hung nobly, as upon the face of heaven
A midday fleece of clouds. Thea arose

455   And stretch'd her white arm through the hollow dark,
       Pointing some whither: whereat he too rose
       Like a vast giant seen by men at sea
       To grow pale from the waves at dull midnight.
       They melted from my sight into the woods:
460   Ere I could turn, Moneta cried—"These twain
       Are speeding to the families of grief,
       Where roof'd in by black rocks they waste in pain
       And darkness for no hope."—And she spake on,
       As ye may read who can unwearied pass
465   Onward from the antichamber of this dream,
       Where even at the open doors awhile
       I must delay, and glean my memory
       Of her high phrase: perhaps no further dare.

                    CANTO II

       "Mortal, that thou may'st understand aright,
       I humanize my sayings to thine ear,
       Making comparisons of earthly things;
       Or thou might'st better listen to the wind,
5   Whose language is to thee a barren noise,
       Though it blows legend-laden through the trees.
       In melancholy realms big tears are shed,
       More sorrow like to this, and such-like woe,
       Too huge for mortal tongue, or pen of scribe.
10   The Titans fierce, self-hid, or prison-bound,
       Groan for the old allegiance once more,
       Listening in their doom for Saturn's voice.
       But one of our whole eagle-brood still keeps
       His sov'reignty, and rule, and majesty;
15   Blazing Hyperion on his orbed fire
       Still sits, still snuffs the incense teeming up
       From man to the Sun's God: yet unsecure;
       For as upon the earth dire prodigies
       Fright and perplex, so also shudders he:
20   Nor at dog's howl, or gloom-bird's even screech,
       Or the familiar visitings of one
       Upon the first toll of his passing bell:
       But horrors portion'd to a giant nerve
       Make great Hyperion ache. His palace bright,
25   Bastion'd with pyramids of glowing gold,

And touch'd with shade of bronzed obelisks,
Glares a blood red through all the thousand courts,
Arches, and domes, and fiery galeries:
And all its curtains of Aurorian clouds
30   Flush angerly: when he would taste the wreaths
Of incense breath'd aloft from sacred hills,
Instead of sweets, his ample palate takes
Savour of poisonous brass and metals sick.
Wherefore when harbour'd in the sleepy west,
35   After the full completion of fair day,
For rest divine upon exalted couch
And slumber in the arms of melody,
He paces through the pleasant hours of ease,
With strides colossal, on from hall to hall;
40   While, far within each aisle and deep recess,
His winged minions in close clusters stand
Amaz'd, and full of fear; like anxious men
Who on a wide plain gather in sad troops,
When earthquakes jar their battlements and towers.
45   Even now, while Saturn, rous'd from icy trance,
Goes, step for step, with Thea from yon woods,
Hyperion, leaving twilight in the rear,
Is sloping to the threshold of the west.
Thither we tend."—Now in clear light I stood,
50   Reliev'd from the dusk vale. Mnemosyne
Was sitting on a square edg'd polish'd stone,
That in its lucid depth reflected pure
Her priestess-garments. My quick eyes ran on
From stately nave to nave, from vault to vault,
55   Through bowers of fragrant and enwreathed light,
And diamond paved lustrous long arcades.
Anon rush'd by the bright Hyperion;
His flaming robes stream'd out beyond his heels,
And gave a roar, as if of earthly fire,
60   That scar'd away the meek ethereal hours
And made their dove-wings tremble: on he flared

   *   *   *   *   *   *   *   *   *   *   *   *

The day is gone, and all its sweets are gone

The day is gone, and all its sweets are gone!
　　Sweet voice, sweet lips, soft hand, and softer breast,
Warm breath, light whisper, tender semi-tone,
　　Bright eyes, accomplish'd shape, and lang'rous waist!
5　Faded the flower and all its budded charms,
　　Faded the sight of beauty from my eyes,
Faded the shape of beauty from my arms,
　　Faded the voice, warmth, whiteness, paradise,
Vanish'd unseasonably at shut of eve,
10　　When the dusk holiday—or holinight—
Of fragrant curtain'd Love begins to weave
　　The woof of darkness, thick, for hid delight;
But, as I've read Love's missal through to-day,
He'll let me sleep, seeing I fast and pray.

I cry your mercy—pity—love!—aye, love

I cry your mercy—pity—love!—aye, love,
　　Merciful love that tantalises not,
One-thoughted, never wand'ring, guileless love,
　　Unmask'd, and being seen—without a blot!
5　O, let me have thee whole,—all,—all—be mine!
　　That shape, that fairness, that sweet minor zest
Of love, your kiss, those hands, those eyes divine,
　　That warm, white, lucent, million-pleasured breast,—
Yourself—your soul—in pity give me all,
10　　Withhold no atom's atom or I die,
Or living on perhaps, your wretched thrall,
　　Forget, in the mist of idle misery,
Life's purposes,—the palate of my mind
Losing its gust, and my ambition blind.

What can I do to drive away

What can I do to drive away
Remembrance from my eyes? for they have seen,
Aye, an hour ago, my brilliant queen!
Touch has a memory. O say, Love, say,
5　What can I do to kill it and be free

In my old liberty?
When every fair one that I saw was fair,
Enough to catch me in but half a snare,
Not keep me there:
10 When, howe'er poor or particolour'd things,
My muse had wings,
And ever ready was to take her course
Whither I bent her force,
Unintellectual, yet divine to me;—
15 Divine, I say!—What sea-bird o'er the sea
Is a philosopher the while he goes
Winging along where the great water throes?

   How shall I do
To get anew
20 Those moulted feathers, and so mount once more
Above, above
The reach of fluttering Love,
And make him cower lowly while I soar?
Shall I gulp wine? No, that is vulgarism,
25 A heresy and schism,
Foisted into the canon law of love;—
No,—wine is only sweet to happy men;
More dismal cares
Seize on me unawares,—
30 Where shall I learn to get my peace again?
To banish thoughts of that most hateful land,
Dungeoner of my friends, that wicked strand
Where they were wreck'd and live a wretched life;
That monstrous region, whose dull rivers pour
35 Ever from their sordid urns unto the shore,
Unown'd of any weedy-haired gods;
Whose winds, all zephyrless, hold scourging rods,
Iced in the great lakes, to afflict mankind;
Whose rank-grown forests, frosted, black, and blind,
40 Would fright a Dryad; whose harsh herbaged meads
Make lean and lank the starv'd ox while he feeds;
There flowers have no scent, birds no sweet song,
And great unerring Nature once seems wrong.

   O, for some sunny spell
45 To dissipate the shadows of this hell!
Say they are gone,—with the new dawning light

Steps forth my lady bright!
O, let me once more rest
My soul upon that dazzling breast!
50   Let once again these aching arms be placed,
The tender gaolers of thy waist!
And let me feel that warm breath here and there
To spread a rapture in my very hair,—
O, the sweetness of the pain!
55   Give me those lips again!
Enough! Enough! it is enough for me
To dream of thee!

To Fanny

Physician Nature! let my spirit blood!
O ease my heart of verse and let me rest;
Throw me upon thy tripod, till the flood
Of stifling numbers ebbs from my full breast.
5   A theme! a theme! Great Nature! give a theme;
Let me begin my dream.
I come—I see thee, as thou standest there,
Beckon me out into the wintry air.

Ah! dearest love, sweet home of all my fears
10   And hopes and joys and panting miseries,—
To-night, if I may guess, thy beauty wears
A smile of such delight,
As brilliant and as bright,
As when with ravished, aching, vassal eyes,
15   Lost in a soft amaze,
I gaze, I gaze!

Who now, with greedy looks, eats up my feast?
What stare outfaces now my silver moon!
Ah! keep that hand unravished at the least;
20   Let, let the amorous burn—
But, prithee, do not turn
The current of your heart from me so soon:
O save, in charity,
The quickest pulse for me.

25 Save it for me, sweet love! though music breathe
      Voluptuous visions into the warm air,
    Though swimming through the dance's dangerous wreath,
        Be like an April day,
        Smiling and cold and gay,
30   A temperate lily, temperate as fair;
        Then, heaven! there will be
        A warmer June for me.

    Why this, you'll say—my Fanny!—is not true;
      Put your soft hand upon your snowy side,
35 Where the heart beats: confess—'tis nothing new—
        Must not a woman be
        A feather on the sea,
      Swayed to and fro by every wind and tide?
        Of as uncertain speed
40   As blow-ball from the mead?

    I know it—and to know it is despair
      To one who loves you as I love, sweet Fanny,
    Whose heart goes fluttering for you every where,
        Nor when away you roam,
45   Dare keep its wretched home:
      Love, love alone, has pains severe and many;
        Then, loveliest! keep me free
        From torturing jealousy.

    Ah! if you prize my subdued soul above
50   The poor, the fading, brief pride of an hour:
    Let none profane my Holy See of Love,
        Or with a rude hand break
        The sacramental cake:
      Let none else touch the just new-budded flower;
55   If not—may my eyes close,
        Love, on their last repose!

King Stephen:
A Fragment of a Tragedy

Dramatis Personæ

KING STEPHEN
EARL OF GLOCESTER
EARL OF CHESTER
EARL BALDWIN DE REDVERS
DE KAIMS

THE EMPRESS MAUD, *or* MATILDA

ACT I

SCENE I. *Field of Battle.*

Alarum. Enter KING STEPHEN, *Knights, and Soldiers.*

Stephen. If shame can on a soldier's vein-swoll'n front
Spread deeper crimson than the battle's toil,
Blush in your casing helmets!—for see, see!
Yonder my chivalry, my pride of war,
5   Wrench'd with an iron hand from firm array,
Are routed loose about the plashy meads,
Of honour forfeit. O, that my known voice
Could reach your dastard ears and fright you more!
Fly, cowards, fly! Glocester is at your backs!
10   Throw your slack bridles o'er the flurried manes,
Ply well the rowel with faint trembling heels,
Scampering to death at last!
   First Knight.   The enemy
Bears his flaunt standard close upon their rear.
   Second Knight. Sure of a bloody prey, seeing the fens
Will swamp them girth deep.
15   *Stephen.*   Over head and ears,
No matter! 'Tis a gallant enemy;
How like a comet he goes streaming on.
But we must plague him in the flank,—hey, friends?
We are well breathed,—follow!
              [*Enter* EARL BALDWIN, *and Soldiers, as defeated.*
                 De Redvers!

20   What is the monstrous bugbear that can fright
       Baldwin?
           Baldwin. No scarecrow, but the fortunate star
       Of boisterous Chester, whose fell truncheon now
       Points level to the goal of victory.
       This way he comes, and if you would maintain
25   Your person unaffronted by vile odds,
       Take horse, my lord.
           Stephen.   And which way spur for life?
       Now I thank heaven I am in the toils,
       That soldiers may bear witness how my arm
       Can burst the meshes. Not the eagle more
30   Loves to beat up against a tyrannous blast,
       Than I to meet the torrent of my foes.
       This is a brag,—be't so,—but if I fall,
       Carve it upon my 'scutcheon'd sepulchre.
       On, fellow soldiers! Earl of Redvers, back!
35   Not twenty Earls of Chester shall brow-beat
       The diadem!   [*Exeunt. Alarums.*

SCENE II. *Another part of the Field.*

Trumpets sounding a victory. Enter GLOCESTER,
Knights, and forces.

       Glocester. Now may we lift our bruised visors up,
       And take the flattering freshness of the air,
       While the wide din of battle dies away
       Into times past, yet to be echoed sure
5   In the silent pages of our chroniclers.
           First Knight. Will Stephen's death be mark'd there, my good
               lord,
       Or that we gave him lodging in yon towers?
           Glocester. Fain would I know the great usurper's fate.

Enter two Captains, severally.

       First Captain. My lord!
       Second Captain.   Most noble Earl!
       First Captain.   The King—
       Second Captain.   The Empress greets—
       Glocester. What of the King?

10 *First Captain.*   He sole and lone maintains
A hopeless bustle 'mid our swarming arms;
And with a nimble savageness attacks,
Escapes, makes fiercer onset, then anew
Eludes death, giving death to most that dare
15 Trespass within the circuit of his sword:—
He must by this have fallen. Baldwin is taken;
And for the Duke of Bretagne, like a stag
He flies, for the Welch beagles to hunt down.
God save the Empress.
 Glocester.   Now our dreaded Queen—
What message from her Highness?
20 *Second Captain.*   Royal Maud
From the throng'd towers of Lincoln hath look'd down,
Like Pallas from the walls of Ilion,
And seen her enemies havock'd at her feet.
She greets most noble Glocester from her heart,
25 Intreating him, his captains, and brave knights
To grace a banquet. The high city gates
Are envious which shall see your triumph pass.
The streets are full of music—

Enter Second Knight.

 Glocester.   Whence come you?
 Second Knight. From Stephen, my good Prince—Stephen—
  Stephen—
30 *Glocester.* Why do you make such echoing of his name?
 Second Knight. Because I think, my lord, he is no man,
But a fierce demon 'nointed safe from wounds
And misbaptised with a Christian name.
 Glocester. A mighty soldier. Does he still hold out?
35 *Second Knight.* He shames our victory. His valour still
Keeps elbow room amid our eager swords,
And holds our bladed falchions all aloof.
His gleaming battle axe being slaughter sick,
Smote on the morion of a Flemish knight,
40 Broke short in his hand; upon the which he flung
The heft away with such a vengeful force
It paunch'd the Earl of Chester's horse, who then
Spleen-hearted came in full career at him.
 Glocester. Did no one take him at a vantage then?
45 *Second Knight.* Three then with tiger leap upon him flew,

Whom, with his sword swift-drawn and nimbly held,
He stung away again, and stood to breathe,
Smiling. Anon upon him rush'd once more
A throng of foes; and in this renew'd strife
50   My sword met his and snapp'd off at the hilts.
    Glocester. Come, lead me to this Mars—and let us move
In silence, not insulting his sad doom
With clamourous trumpets. To the Empress bear
My salutation as befits the time.
                  [*Exeunt* GLOCESTER *and forces.*

SCENE III. *The field of Battle.*

Enter STEPHEN *unarm'd.*

    Stephen. Another sword! and what if I could seize
One from Bellona's gleaming armoury,
Or choose the fairest of her sheaved spears!
Where are my enemies? Here, close at hand,
5   Here comes the testy brood. O for a sword!
I'm faint—a biting sword! A noble sword!
A hedge-stake—or a ponderous stone to hurl
With brawny vengeance, like the labourer Cain.
Come on! Farewell my kingdom, and all hail
10   Thou superb, plum'd, and helmeted renown,
All hail—I would not truck this brilliant day
To rule in Pylos with a Nestor's beard.
Come on!
           Enter DE KAIMS *and Knights, etc.*

    De Kaims. Is't madness or a hunger after death
15   That makes thee thus unarm'd throw taunts at us?
Yield, Stephen, or my sword's point dip in
The gloomy current of a traitor's heart.
    Stephen. Do it, De Kaims, I will not budge an inch.
    De Kaims. Yes, of thy madness thou shalt take the meed—
    Stephen. Darest thou?
20   *De Kaims.*   How dare, against a man disarm'd?
    Stephen. What weapon has the lion but himself?
Come not near me, De Kaims, for by the price
Of all the glory I have won this day,
Being a king, I will not yield alive

25   To any but the second man of the realm,
      Robert of Glocester.
          De Kaims.   Thou shalt vail to me.
          Stephen. Shall I, when I have sworn against it, sir?
      Thou think'st it brave to take a breathing king,
      That, on a court day bow'd to haughty Maud,
30   The awed presence chamber may be bold
      To whisper, there's the man who took alive
      Stephen—me—prisoner. Certes, De Kaims,
      The ambition is a noble one.
          De Kaims.   'Tis true,
      And, Stephen, I must compass it—
          Stephen.   No, no—
35   Do not tempt me to throttle you on the gorge,
      Or with my gauntlet crush your hollow breast,
      Just when your knighthood is grown ripe and full
      For lordship.
          A Soldier. Is an honest yeoman's spear
      Of no use at a need? Take that—
          Stephen.   Ah dastard!
40   *De Kaims.* What, you are vulnerable! my prisoner!
          Stephen. No, not yet—I disclaim it, and demand
      Death as a sovereign right unto a king
      Who 'sdains to yield to any but his peer,
      If not in title yet in noble deeds,
45   The Earl of Glocester. Stab to the hilts, De Kaims,
      For I will never by mean hands be led
      From this so famous field—D'ye hear! be quick!
          [*Trumpets. Enter the* EARL *of* CHESTER *and Knights.*

SCENE IV. *A Presence Chamber.*

QUEEN MAUD *in a chair of state. The* EARLS *of* GLOCESTER
      and CHESTER, *Lords, Attendants.*

      Maud. Glocester, no more: I will behold that Boulogne:
      Set him before me. Not for the poor sake
      Of regal pomp and a vainglorious hour,
      As thou with wary speech, yet near enough,
      Hast hinted.
5   *Glocester.* Faithful counsel have I given,
      If wary, for your Highness' benefit—

Maud. The heavens forbid that I should not think so.
For by thy valour have I won this realm,
Which by thy wisdom will I ever keep.
10 To sage advisers let me ever bend
A meek attentive ear, so that they treat
Of the wide kingdom's rule and government,
Not trenching on our actions personal.
Advised, not school'd, I would be, and henceforth
15 Spoken to in clear, plain, and open terms,
Not sideways sermon'd at.
    Glocester.   Then in plain terms,
Once more for the fall'n King—
    Maud.   Your pardon, brother,
I would no more of that; for, as I said,
'Tis not for worldly pomp I wish to see
20 The rebel, but as a dooming judge to give
A sentence something worthy of his guilt.
    Glocester. If't must be so I'll bring him to your presence.
                              [*Exit* GLOCESTER.
    Maud. A meaner summoner might do as well—
My Lord of Chester, is't true what I hear
25 Of Stephen of Boulogne, our prisoner,
That he, as a fit penance for his crimes,
Eats wholesome, sweet, and palatable food
Off Glocester's golden dishes—drinks pure wine,
Lodges soft?
    Chester.   More than that, most gracious Queen,
30 Has anger'd me. The noble Earl, methinks,
Full soldier as he is, and without peer
In Council, dreams too much among his books.
It may read well, but sure 'tis out of date
To play the Alexander with Darius.
35   *Maud.* Truth! I think so—by heavens, it shall not last.
    Chester. It would amaze your Highness now to mark
How Glocester overstrains his courtesy
To that crime-loving rebel; that Boulogne—
    Maud. That ingrate!
    Chester.   For whose vast ingratitude
40 To our late sovereign lord, your noble sire,
The generous Earl condoles in his mishaps,
And with a sort of lackeying friendliness
Talks off the mighty frowning from his brow,
Woos him to hold a duet in a smile,

45   Or if it please him play an hour at chess—
    Maud. A perjur'd slave!
     Chester.   And for his perjury
    Glocester has fit rewards—nay, I believe
    He sets his bustling household's wits at work
    For flatteries to ease this Stephen's hours,
50   And make a heaven of his purgatory,
    Adorning bondage with the pleasant gloss
    Of feasts and music, and all idle shows
    Of indoor pageantry; while syren whispers,
    Predestin'd for his ear, scape as half check'd
55   From lips the courtliest and the rubiest
    Of all the realm, admiring of his deeds.
    Maud. A frost upon his summer!
     Chester.   A queen's nod
    Can make his June December—here he comes.

This living hand, now warm and capable

This living hand, now warm and capable
Of earnest grasping, would, if it were cold
And in the icy silence of the tomb,
So haunt thy days and chill thy dreaming nights
5   That thou would wish thine own heart dry of blood,
So in my veins red life might stream again,
And thou be conscience-calm'd. See, here it is—
I hold it towards you.

The Jealousies:
A Faery Tale, by Lucy Vaughan Lloyd
of China Walk, Lambeth

1

In midmost Ind, beside Hydaspes cool,
There stood, or hover'd, tremulous in the air,
A faery city, 'neath the potent rule
Of Emperor Elfinan; famed ev'rywhere
5   For love of mortal women, maidens fair,
Whose lips were solid, whose soft hands were made
Of a fit mould and beauty, ripe and rare,

To pamper his slight wooing, warm yet staid:
He lov'd girls smooth as shades, but hated a mere shade.

2

10   This was a crime forbidden by the law;
And all the priesthood of his city wept,
For ruin and dismay they well foresaw,
If impious prince no bound or limit kept,
And faery Zendervester overstept;
15   They wept, he sinn'd, and still he would sin on,
They dreamt of sin, and he sinn'd while they slept;
In vain the pulpit thunder'd at the throne,
Caricature was vain, and vain the tart lampoon.

3

Which seeing, his high court of parliament
20   Laid a remonstrance at his Highness' feet,
Praying his royal senses to content
Themselves with what in faery land was sweet,
Befitting best that shade with shade should meet:
Whereat, to calm their fears, he promised soon
25   From mortal tempters all to make retreat,—
Aye, even on the first of the new moon,
An immaterial wife to espouse as heaven's boon.

4

Meantime he sent a fluttering embassy
To Pigmio, of Imaus sovereign,
30   To half beg, and half demand, respectfully,
The hand of his fair daughter Bellanaine;
An audience had, and speeching done, they gain
Their point, and bring the weeping bride away;
Whom, with but one attendant, safely lain
35   Upon their wings, they bore in bright array,
While little harps were touch'd by many a lyric fay.

5

As in old pictures tender cherubim
A child's soul through the sapphired canvas bear,
So, through a real heaven, on they swim
40   With the sweet Princess on her plumaged lair,
Speed giving to the winds her lustrous hair;

And so she journey'd, sleeping or awake,
Save when, for healthful exercise and air,
She chose to "promener à l'aile," or take
45   A pigeon's somerset, for sport or change's sake.

6

"Dear Princess, do not whisper me so loud,"
Quoth Corallina, nurse and confidant,
"Do not you see there, lurking in a cloud,
Close at your back, that sly old Crafticant?
50   He hears a whisper plainer than a rant:
Dry up your tears, and do not look so blue;
He's Elfinan's great state-spy militant,
His running, lying, flying foot-man too,—
Dear mistress, let him have no handle against you!

7

55   "Show him a mouse's tail, and he will guess,
With metaphysic swiftness, at the mouse;
Show him a garden, and with speed no less,
He'll surmise sagely of a dwelling-house,
And plot, in the same minute, how to chouse
60   The owner out of it; show him a—" "Peace!
Peace! nor contrive thy mistress' ire to rouse,"
Return'd the Princess, "my tongue shall not cease
Till from this hated match I get a free release.

8

"Ah, beauteous mortal!" "Hush!" quoth Coralline,
65   "Really you must not talk of him, indeed."
"You hush!" replied the mistress, with a shine
Of anger in her eyes, enough to breed
In stouter hearts than nurse's fear and dread:
'Twas not the glance itself made nursey flinch,
70   But of its threat she took the utmost heed;
Not liking in her heart an hour-long pinch,
Or a sharp needle run into her back an inch.

9

So she was silenced, and fair Bellanaine,
Writhing her little body with ennui,
75   Continued to lament and to complain,
That Fate, cross-purposing, should let her be

Ravish'd away far from her dear countree;
That all her feelings should be set at nought,
In trumping up this match so hastily,
80   With lowland blood; and lowland blood she thought
Poison, as every staunch true-born Imaian ought.

10

Sorely she grieved, and wetted three or four
White Provence rose-leaves with her faery tears,
But not for this cause;—alas! she had more
85   Bad reasons for her sorrow, as appears
In the famed memoirs of a thousand years,
Written by Crafticant, and published
By Parpaglion and Co., (those sly compeers
Who raked up ev'ry fact against the dead,)
90   In Scarab Street, Panthea, at the Jubal's Head.

11

Where, after a long hypercritic howl
Against the vicious manners of the age,
He goes on to expose, with heart and soul,
What vice in this or that year was the rage,
95   Backbiting all the world in ev'ry page;
With special strictures on the horrid crime,
(Section'd and subsection'd with learning sage,)
Of faeries stooping on their wings sublime
To kiss a mortal's lips, when such were in their prime.

12

100   Turn to the copious index, you will find
Somewhere in the column headed letter B
The name of Bellanaine, if you're not blind;
Then pray refer to the text, and you will see
An article made up of calumny
105   Against this highland princess, rating her
For giving way, so over fashionably,
To this new-fangled vice, which seems a burr
Stuck in his moral throat, no coughing e'er could stir.

13

There he says plainly that she loved a man!
110   That she around him flutter'd, flirted, toy'd,
Before her marriage with great Elfinan;

That after marriage too, she never joy'd
In husband's company, but still employ'd
Her wits to 'scape away to Angle-land;
115   Where liv'd the youth, who worried and annoy'd
Her tender heart, and its warm ardours fann'd
To such a dreadful blaze, her side would scorch her hand.

14

But let us leave this idle tittle tattle
To waiting-maids, and bed-room coteries,
120   Nor till fit time against her fame wage battle.
Poor Elfinan is very ill at ease—
Let us resume his subject if you please:
For it may comfort and console him much,
To rhyme and syllable his miseries;
125   Poor Elfinan! whose cruel fate was such,
He sat and cursed a bride he knew he could not touch.

15

Soon as (according to his promises)
The bridal embassy had taken wing,
And vanish'd, bird-like, o'er the suburb trees,
130   The Emperor, empierced with the sharp sting
Of love, retired, vex'd and murmuring
Like any drone shut from the fair bee-queen,
Into his cabinet, and there did fling
His limbs upon a sofa, full of spleen,
135   And damn'd his House of Commons, in complete chagrin.

16

"I'll trounce some of the members," cried the Prince,
"I'll put a mark against some rebel names,
I'll make the opposition-benches wince,
I'll show them very soon, to all their shames,
140   What 'tis to smother up a prince's flames;
That ministers should join in it, I own,
Surprises me!—they too at these high games!
Am I an Emperor? Do I wear a crown?
Imperial Elfinan, go hang thyself or drown!

17

145   "I'll trounce 'em!—there's the square-cut chancellor,
His son shall never touch that bishopric;

And for the nephew of old Palfior,
I'll show him that his speeches made me sick,
And give the colonelcy to Phalaric;
150 The tiptoe marquis, moral and gallant,
Shall lodge in shabby taverns upon tick;
And for the Speaker's second cousin's aunt,
She sha'n't be maid of honour,—by heaven that she sha'n't!

18

"I'll shirk the Duke of A.; I'll cut his brother;
155 I'll give no garter to his eldest son;
I won't speak to his sister or his mother!
The Viscount B. shall live at cut-and-run;
But how in the world can I contrive to stun
That fellow's voice, which plagues me worse than any,
160 That stubborn fool, that impudent state-dun,
Who sets down ev'ry sovereign as a zany,—
That vulgar commoner, Esquire Biancopany?

19

"Monstrous affair! Pshaw! pah! what ugly minx
Will they fetch from Imaus for my bride?
165 Alas! my wearied heart within me sinks,
To think that I must be so near allied
To a cold dullard fay,—ah, woe betide!
Ah, fairest of all human loveliness!
Sweet Bertha! what crime can it be to glide
170 About the fragrant plaitings of thy dress,
Or kiss thine eyes, or count thy locks, tress after tress?"

20

So said, one minute's while his eyes remain'd
Half lidded, piteous, languid, innocent;
But, in a wink, their splendour they regain'd,
175 Sparkling revenge with amorous fury blent.
Love thwarted in bad temper oft has vent:
He rose, he stampt his foot, he rang the bell,
And order'd some death-warrants to be sent
For signature:—somewhere the tempest fell,
180 As many a poor felon does not live to tell.

21

"At the same time, Eban,"—(this was his page,
A fay of colour, slave from top to toe,

Sent as a present, while yet under age,
From the Viceroy of Zanguebar,—wise, slow
185   His speech, his only words were "yes" and "no,"
But swift of look, and foot, and wing was he,)—
"At the same time, Eban, this instant go
To Hum the soothsayer, whose name I see
Among the fresh arrivals in our empery.

22

190   "Bring Hum to me! But stay—here take my ring,
The pledge of favour, that he not suspect
Any foul play, or awkward murdering,
Though I have bowstrung many of his sect;
Throw in a hint, that if he should neglect
195   One hour, the next shall see him in my grasp,
And the next after that shall see him neck'd,
Or swallow'd by my hunger-starved asp,—
And mention ('tis as well) the torture of the wasp."

23

These orders given, the Prince, in half a pet,
200   Let o'er the silk his propping elbow slide,
Caught up his little legs, and, in a fret,
Fell on the sofa on his royal side.
The slave retreated backwards, humble-eyed,
And with a slave-like silence closed the door,
205   And to old Hum through street and alley hied;
He "knew the city," as we say, of yore,
For shortest cuts and turns, was nobody knew more.

24

It was the time when wholesale houses close
Their shutters with a moody sense of wealth,
210   But retail dealers, diligent, let loose
The gas (objected to on score of health),
Convey'd in little solder'd pipes by stealth,
And make it flare in many a brilliant form,
That all the power of darkness it repell'th,
215   Which to the oil-trade doth great scaith and harm,
And supersedeth quite the use of the glow-worm.

25

Eban, untempted by the pastry-cooks,
(Of pastry he got store within the palace,)

With hasty steps, wrapp'd cloak, and solemn looks,
220   Incognito upon his errand sallies,
His smelling-bottle ready for the allies;
He pass'd the hurdy-gurdies with disdain,
Vowing he'd have them sent on board the gallies;
Just as he made his vow, it 'gan to rain,
225   Therefore he call'd a coach, and bade it drive amain.

26

"I'll pull the string," said he, and further said,
"Polluted jarvey! Ah, thou filthy hack!
Whose springs of life are all dried up and dead,
Whose linsey-wolsey lining hangs all slack,
230   Whose rug is straw, whose wholeness is a crack;
And evermore thy steps go clatter-clitter;
Whose glass once up can never be got back,
Who prov'st, with jolting arguments and bitter,
That 'tis of modern use to travel in a litter.

27

235   "Thou inconvenience! thou hungry crop
For all corn! thou snail-creeper to and fro,
Who while thou goest ever seem'st to stop,
And fiddle-faddle standest while you go;
I' the morning, freighted with a weight of woe,
240   Unto some lazar-house thou journeyest,
And in the evening tak'st a double row
Of dowdies, for some dance or party drest,
Besides the goods meanwhile thou movest east and west.

28

"By thy ungallant bearing and sad mien,
245   An inch appears the utmost thou couldst budge;
Yet at the slightest nod, or hint, or sign,
Round to the curb-stone patient dost thou trudge,
School'd in a beckon, learned in a nudge,
A dull-eyed Argus watching for a fare;
250   Quiet and plodding, thou dost bear no grudge
To whisking tilburies, or phaetons rare,
Curricles, or mail-coaches, swift beyond compare."

29

Philosophising thus, he pull'd the check,
And bade the coachman wheel to such a street,

255   Who, turning much his body, more his neck,
       Louted full low, and hoarsely did him greet:
       "Certes, monsieur were best take to his feet,
       Seeing his servant can no further drive
       For press of coaches, that to-night here meet,
260   Many as bees about a straw-capp'd hive,
       When first for April honey into faint flowers they dive."

                          30
       Eban then paid his fare, and tiptoe went
       To Hum's hotel; and, as he on did pass
       With head inclined, each dusky lineament
265   Show'd in the pearl-paved street, as in a glass;
       His purple vest, that ever peeping was
       Rich from the fluttering crimson of his cloak,
       His silvery trowsers, and his silken sash
       Tied in a burnish'd knot, their semblance took
270   Upon the mirror'd walls, wherever he might look.

                          31
       He smiled at self, and, smiling, show'd his teeth,
       And seeing his white teeth, he smiled the more;
       Lifted his eye-brows, spurn'd the path beneath,
       Show'd teeth again, and smiled as heretofore,
275   Until he knock'd at the magician's door;
       Where, till the porter answer'd, might be seen,
       In the clear panel, more he could adore,—
       His turban wreath'd of gold, and white, and green,
       Mustachios, ear-ring, nose-ring, and his sabre keen.

                          32
280   "Does not your master give a rout to-night?"
       Quoth the dark page; "Oh, no!" return'd the Swiss,
       "Next door but one to us, upon the right,
       The *Magazin des Modes* now open is
       Against the Emperor's wedding;—and, sir, this
285   My master finds a monstrous horrid bore;
       As he retired, an hour ago I wis,
       With his best beard and brimstone, to explore
       And cast a quiet figure in his second floor.

                          33
       "Gad! he's obliged to stick to business!
290   For chalk, I hear, stands at a pretty price;

And as for aqua vitæ—there's a mess!
The *dentes sapientiæ* of mice
Our barber tells me too are on the rise,—
Tinder's a lighter article,—nitre pure
295   Goes off like lightning,—grains of paradise
At an enormous figure!—stars not sure!—
Zodiac will not move without a sly douceur!

34

"Venus won't stir a peg without a fee,
And master is too partial, *entre nous,*
300   To—" "Hush—hush!" cried Eban, "sure that is he
Coming down stairs,—by St. Bartholomew!
As backwards as he can,—is't something new?
Or is't his custom, in the name of fun?"
"He always comes down backward, with one shoe"—
305   Return'd the porter—"off, and one shoe on,
Like, saving shoe for sock or stocking, my man John!"

35

It was indeed the great magician,
Feeling, with careful toe, for every stair,
And retrograding careful as he can,
310   Backwards and downwards from his own two pair:
"Salpietro!" exclaim'd Hum, "is the dog there?
He's always in my way upon the mat!"
"He's in the kitchen, or the Lord knows where,"—
Replied the Swiss,—"the nasty, whelping brat!"
315   "Don't beat him!" return'd Hum, and on the floor came pat.

36

Then facing right about, he saw the page,
And said: "Don't tell me what you want, Eban;
The Emperor is now in a huge rage,—
'Tis nine to one he'll give you the rattan!
320   Let us away!" Away together ran
The plain-dress'd sage and spangled blackamoor,
Nor rested till they stood to cool, and fan,
And breathe themselves at th' Emperor's chamber door,
When Eban thought he heard a soft imperial snore.

37

325   "I thought you guess'd, foretold, or prophesied,
That 's Majesty was in a raving fit."

"He dreams," said Hum, "or I have ever lied,
That he is tearing you, sir, bit by bit."
"He's not asleep, and you have little wit,"
330   Replied the page; "that little buzzing noise,
Whate'er your palmistry may make of it,
Comes from a play-thing of the Emperor's choice,
From a Man-Tiger-Organ, prettiest of his toys."

38

Eban then usher'd in the learned seer:
335   Elfinan's back was turn'd, but, ne'ertheless,
Both, prostrate on the carpet, ear by ear,
Crept silently, and waited in distress,
Knowing the Emperor's moody bitterness;
Eban especially, who on the floor 'gan
340   Tremble and quake to death,—he feared less
A dose of senna-tea, or nightmare Gorgon,
Than the Emperor when he play'd on his Man-Tiger-Organ.

39

They kiss'd nine times the carpet's velvet face
Of glossy silk, soft, smooth, and meadow-green,
345   Where the close eye in deep rich fur might trace
A silver tissue, scantly to be seen,
As daisies lurk'd in June-grass, buds in treen;
Sudden the music ceased, sudden the hand
Of majesty, by dint of passion keen,
350   Doubled into a common fist, went grand,
And knock'd down three cut glasses, and his best ink-stand.

40

Then turning round, he saw those trembling two:
"Eban," said he, "as slaves should taste the fruits
Of diligence, I shall remember you
355   To-morrow, or the next day, as time suits,
In a finger conversation with my mutes,—
Begone!—for you, Chaldean! here remain;
Fear not, quake not, and as good wine recruits
A conjurer's spirits, what cup will you drain?
360   Sherry in silver, hock in gold, or glass'd champagne?"

41

"Commander of the faithful!" answer'd Hum,
"In preference to these, I'll merely taste

A thimble-full of old Jamaica rum."
"A simple boon!" said Elfinan, "thou may'st
365   Have nantz, with which my morning-coffee's laced."*
"I'll have a glass of nantz, then,"—said the seer,—
"Made racy—(sure my boldness is misplaced!)—
With the third part—(yet that is drinking dear!)—
Of the least drop of *crème de citron* crystal clear."

42

370   "I pledge you, Hum! and pledge my dearest love,
My Bertha!" "Bertha! Bertha!" cried the sage,
"I know a many Berthas!" "Mine's above
All Berthas!" sighed the Emperor. "I engage,"
Said Hum, "in duty, and in vassalage,
375   To mention all the Berthas in the earth;—
There's Bertha Watson,—and Miss Bertha Page,—
This famed for languid eyes, and that for mirth,—
There's Bertha Blount of York,—and Bertha Knox of Perth."

43

"You seem to know"—"I do know," answer'd Hum,
380   "Your Majesty's in love with some fine girl
Named Bertha; but her surname will not come,
Without a little conjuring." "'Tis Pearl,
'Tis Bertha Pearl! What makes my brains so whirl?
And she is softer, fairer than her name!"
385   "Where does she live?" ask'd Hum. "Her fair locks curl
So brightly, they put all our fays to shame!—
Live!—O! at Canterbury, with her old grand-dame."

44

"Good! good!" cried Hum, "I've known her from a child!
She is a changeling of my management;
390   She was born at midnight in an Indian wild;
Her mother's screams with the striped tiger's blent,
While the torch-bearing slaves a halloo sent
Into the jungles; and her palanquin,
Rested amid the desert's dreariment,
395   Shook with her agony, till fair were seen
The little Bertha's eyes ope on the stars serene."

---

* "Mr. Nisby is of opinion that laced coffee is bad for the head." *Spectator.*

45

"I can't say," said the monarch, "that may be
Just as it happen'd, true or else a bam!
Drink up your brandy, and sit down by me,
400   Feel, feel my pulse, how much in love I am;
And if your science is not all a sham,
Tell me some means to get the lady here."
"Upon my honour!" said the son of Cham,*
"She is my dainty changeling, near and dear,
405   Although her story sounds at first a little queer."

46

"Convey her to me, Hum, or by my crown,
My sceptre, and my cross-surmounted globe,
I'll knock you—" "Does your Majesty mean—*down?*
No, no, you never could my feelings probe
410   To such a depth!" The Emperor took his robe,
And wept upon its purple palatine,
While Hum continued, shamming half a sob,—
"In Canterbury doth your lady shine?
But let me cool your brandy with a little wine."

47

415   Whereat a narrow Flemish glass he took,
That since belong'd to Admiral De Witt,
Admired it with a connoisseuring look,
And with the ripest claret crowned it,
And, ere one lively bead could burst and flit,
420   He turned it quickly, nimbly upside down,
His mouth being held conveniently fit
To catch the treasure: "Best in all the town!"
He said, smack'd his moist lips, and gave a pleasant frown.

48

"Ah! good my Prince, weep not!" And then again
425   He fill'd a bumper. "Great sire, do not weep!
Your pulse is shocking, but I'll ease your pain."
"Fetch me that ottoman, and prithee keep
Your voice low," said the Emperor, "and steep

* Cham is said to have been the inventor of magic. Lucy learnt this from
Bayle's Dictionary, and had copied a long Latin note from that work.

　　　　Some lady's fingers nice in Candy wine;
430　　And prithee, Hum, behind the screen do peep
　　　　For the rose-water vase, magician mine!
　　And sponge my forehead,—so my love doth make me pine."

49

　　　　"Ah, cursed Bellanaine!" "Don't think of her,"
　　　　Rejoin'd the mago, "but on Bertha muse;
435　　For, by my choicest best barometer,
　　　　You shall not throttled be in marriage noose;
　　　　I've said it, sire; you only have to choose
　　　　Bertha or Bellanaine." So saying, he drew
　　　　From the left pocket of his threadbare hose,
440　　A sampler hoarded slyly, good as new,
　　Holding it by his thumb and finger full in view.

50

　　　　"Sire, this is Bertha Pearl's neat handy-work,
　　　　Her *name,* see here, *Midsummer, ninety-one.*"
　　　　Elfinan snatch'd it with a sudden jerk,
445　　And wept as if he never would have done,
　　　　Honouring with royal tears the poor homespun;
　　　　Whereon were broider'd tigers with black eyes,
　　　　And long-tail'd pheasants, and a rising sun,
　　　　Plenty of posies, great stags, butterflies
450　　Bigger than stags,—a moon,—with other mysteries.

51

　　　　The monarch handled o'er and o'er again
　　　　These day-school hieroglyphics with a sigh;
　　　　Somewhat in sadness, but pleas'd in the main,
　　　　Till this oracular couplet met his eye
455　　Astounded,—*Cupid, I / do thee defy!*
　　　　It was too much. He shrunk back in his chair,
　　　　Grew pale as death, and fainted—very nigh!
　　　　"Pho! nonsense!" exclaim'd Hum, "now don't despair:
　　She does not mean it really. Cheer up, hearty—there!

52

460　　"And listen to my words. You say you won't,
　　　　On any terms, marry Miss Bellanaine;
　　　　It goes against your conscience—good! Well, don't.

You say you love a mortal. I would fain
Persuade your honour's Highness to refrain
465   From peccadilloes. But, sire, as I say,
What good would that do? And, to be more plain,
You would do me a mischief some odd day,
Cut off my ears and hands, or head too, by my fay!

53

"Besides, manners forbid that I should pass any
470   Vile strictures on the conduct of a prince
Who should indulge his genius, if he has any,
Not, like a subject, foolish matters mince.
Now I think on't, perhaps I could convince
Your Majesty there is no crime at all
475   In loving pretty little Bertha, since
She's very delicate,—not over tall,—
A fairy's hand, and in the waist, why—very small."

54

"Ring the repeater, gentle Hum!" " 'Tis five,"
Said gentle Hum; "the nights draw in apace;
480   The little birds I hear are all alive;
I see the dawning touch'd upon your face;
Shall I put out the candles, please your Grace?"
"Do put them out, and, without more ado,
Tell me how I may that sweet girl embrace,—
485   How you can bring her to me." "That's for you,
Great Emperor! to adventure, like a lover true."

55

"I fetch her!"—"Yes, an't like your Majesty;
And as she would be frighten'd wide awake
To travel such a distance through the sky,
490   Use of some soft manœuvre you must make,
For your convenience, and her dear nerves' sake;
Nice way would be to bring her in a swoon;
Anon, I'll tell what course were best to take;
You must away this morning." "Hum! so soon?"
495   "Sire, you must be in Kent by twelve o'clock at noon."

56

At this great Cæsar started on his feet,
Lifted his wings, and stood attentive-wise.
"Those wings to Canterbury you must beat,

If you hold Bertha as a worthy prize.
500   Look in the Almanack—*Moore* never lies—
April the twenty-fourth,—this coming day,
Now breathing its new bloom upon the skies,
Will end in St. Mark's eve;—you must away,
For on that eve alone can you the maid convey."

57

505   Then the magician solemnly 'gan frown,
So that his frost-white eyebrows, beetling low,
Shaded his deep green eyes, and wrinkles brown
Plaited upon his furnace-scorched brow:
Forth from his hood that hung his neck below,
510   He lifted a bright casket of pure gold,
Touch'd a spring-lock, and there in wool, or snow
Charm'd into ever freezing, lay an old
And legend-leaved book, mysterious to behold.

58

"Take this same book,—it will not bite you, sire;
515   There, put it underneath your royal arm;
Though it's a pretty weight, it will not tire,
But rather on your journey keep you warm:
This is the magic, this the potent charm,
That shall drive Bertha to a fainting fit!
520   When the time comes, don't feel the least alarm;
Uplift her from the ground, and swiftly flit
Back to your palace, where I wait for guerdon fit."

59

"What shall I do with this same book?" "Why merely
Lay it on Bertha's table, close beside
525   Her work-box, and 'twill help your purpose dearly;
I say no more." "Or good or ill betide,
Through the wide air to Kent this morn I glide!"
Exclaim'd the Emperor; "When I return,
Ask what you will,—I'll give you my new bride!
530   And take some more wine, Hum;—O, heavens! I burn
To be upon the wing! Now, now, that minx I spurn!"

60

"Leave her to me," rejoin'd the magian:
"But how shall I account, illustrious fay!

For thine imperial absence? Pho! I can
535   Say you are very sick, and bar the way
To your so loving courtiers for one day;
If either of their two Archbishops' graces
Should talk of extreme unction, I shall say
You do not like cold pig with Latin phrases,
540   Which never should be used but in alarming cases."

61

"Open the window, Hum; I'm ready now!"
"Zooks!" exclaim'd Hum, as up the sash he drew,
"Behold, your Majesty, upon the brow
Of yonder hill, what crowds of people!" "Whew!
545   The monster's always after something new,"
Return'd his Highness; "they are piping hot
To see my pigsney Bellanaine. Hum! do
Tighten my belt a little,—so, so,—not
Too tight,—the book!—my wand!—so, nothing is forgot."

62

550   "Wounds! how they shout!" said Hum, "and there,—see,
        see,
Th' Ambassador's return'd from Pigmio!
The morning's very fine,—uncommonly!
See, past the skirts of yon white cloud they go,
Tinging it with soft crimsons! Now below
555   The sable-pointed heads of firs and pines
They dip, move on, and with them moves a glow
Along the forest side! Now amber lines
Reach the hill top, and now throughout the valley shines."

63

"Why, Hum, you're getting quite poetical!
560   Those *nows* you managed in a special style."
"If ever you have leisure, sire, you shall
See scraps of mine will make it worth your while,
Tit-bits for Phœbus!—yes, you well may smile.
Hark! hark! the bells!" "A little further get,
565   Good Hum, and let me view this mighty coil."
Then the great Emperor full graceful set
His elbow for a prop, and snuff'd his mignionette.

64

The morn was full of holiday; loud bells
With rival clamours rang from every spire;
570   Cunningly-station'd music dies and swells
In echoing places; when the winds respire,
Light flags stream out like gauzy tongues of fire;
A metropolitan murmur, lifeful, warm,
Came from the northern suburbs; rich attire
575   Freckled with red and gold the moving swarm;
While here and there clear trumpets blew a keen alarm.

65

And now the fairy escort was seen clear,
Like the old pageant of Aurora's train,
Above a pearl-built minster, hovering near;
580   First wily Crafticant, the chamberlain,
Balanced upon his grey-grown pinions twain,
His slender wand officially reveal'd;
Then black gnomes scattering sixpences like rain;
Then pages three and three; and next, slave-held,
585   The Imaian 'scutcheon bright,—one mouse in argent field.

66

Gentlemen pensioners next; and after them,
A troop of winged janizaries flew;
Then slaves, as presents bearing many a gem;
Then twelve physicians fluttering two and two;
590   And next a chaplain in a cassock new;
Then lords in waiting; then (what head not reels
For pleasure?)—the fair Princess in full view,
Borne upon wings,—and very pleased she feels
To have such splendour dance attendance at her heels.

67

595   For there was more magnificence behind:
She waved her handkerchief. "Ah, very grand!"
Cried Elfinan, and closed the window-blind;
"And, Hum, we must not shilly-shally stand,—
Adieu! adieu! I'm off for Angle-land!
600   I say, old hocus, have you such a thing
About you,—feel your pockets, I command,—

I want, this instant, an invisible ring,—
Thank you, old mummy!—now securely I take wing."

68

Then Elfinan swift vaulted from the floor,
605   And lighted graceful on the window-sill;
Under one arm the magic book he bore,
The other he could wave about at will;
Pale was his face, he still look'd very ill:
He bow'd at Bellanaine, and said—"Poor Bell!
610   Farewell! farewell! and if for ever! still
For ever fare thee well!"—and then he fell
A laughing!—snapp'd his fingers!—shame it is to tell!

69

"By'r Lady! he is gone!" cries Hum, "and I,—
(I own it,)—have made too free with his wine;
615   Old Crafticant will smoke me, by-the-bye!
This room is full of jewels as a mine,—
Dear valuable creatures, how ye shine!
Sometime to-day I must contrive a minute,
If Mercury propitiously incline,
620   To examine his scrutoire, and see what's in it,
For of superfluous diamonds I as well may thin it.

70

"The Emperor's horrid bad; yes, that's my cue!"
Some histories say that this was Hum's last speech;
That, being fuddled, he went reeling through
625   The corridor, and scarce upright could reach
The stair-head; that being glutted as a leach,
And used, as we ourselves have just now said,
To manage stairs reversely, like a peach
Too ripe, he fell, being puzzled in his head
630   With liquor and the staircase: verdict—*found stone dead.*

71

This as a falsehood Crafticanto treats;
And as his style is of strange elegance,
Gentle and tender, full of soft conceits,
(Much like our Boswell's), we will take a glance
635   At his sweet prose, and, if we can, make dance

His woven periods into careless rhyme;
O, little faery Pegasus! rear—prance—
Trot round the quarto—ordinary time!
March, little Pegasus, with pawing hoof sublime!

72

640   Well, let us see,—*tenth book and chapter nine,*—
Thus Crafticant pursues his diary:—
" 'Twas twelve o'clock at night, the weather fine,
Latitude thirty-six; our scouts descry
A flight of starlings making rapidly
645   Tow'rds Thibet. Mem.:—birds fly in the night;
From twelve to half-past—wings not fit to fly
For a thick fog—the Princess sulky quite—
Call'd for an extra shawl, and gave her nurse a bite.

73

"Five minutes before one—brought down a moth
650   With my new double-barrel—stew'd the thighs,
And made a very tolerable broth—
Princess turn'd dainty, to our great surprise,
Alter'd her mind, and thought it very nice:
Seeing her pleasant, tried her with a pun—
655   She frown'd; a monstrous owl across us flies
About this time,—a sad old figure of fun;
Bad omen—this new match can't be a happy one.

74

"From two to half-past, dusky way we made,
Above the plains of Gobi,—desert, bleak;
660   Beheld afar off, in the hooded shade
Of darkness, a great mountain (strange to speak),
Spitting, from forth its sulphur-baken peak,
A fan-shaped burst of blood-red, arrowy fire,
Turban'd with smoke, which still away did reek,
665   Solid and black from that eternal pyre,
Upon the laden winds that scantly could respire.

75

"Just upon three o'clock, a falling star
Created an alarm among our troop,
Kill'd a man-cook, a page, and broke a jar,

670   A tureen, and three dishes, at one swoop,
       Then passing by the Princess, singed her hoop:
       Could not conceive what Coralline was at—
       She clapp'd her hands three times, and cried out 'Whoop!'—
       Some strange Imaian custom. A large bat
675   Came sudden 'fore my face, and brush'd against my hat.

                              76
       "Five minutes thirteen seconds after three,
       Far in the west a mighty fire broke out—
       Conjectured, on the instant, it might be
       The city of Balk—'twas Balk beyond all doubt:
680   A griffin, wheeling here and there about,
       Kept reconnoitring us—doubled our guard—
       Lighted our torches, and kept up a shout,
       Till he sheer'd off—the Princess very scared—
And many on their marrow-bones for death prepared.

                              77
685   "At half-past three arose the cheerful moon—
       Bivouac'd for four minutes on a cloud—
       Where from the earth we heard a lively tune
       Of tambourines and pipes, serene and loud,
       While on a flowery lawn a brilliant crowd
690   Cinque-parted danced, some half asleep reposed
       Beneath the green-fan'd cedars, some did shroud
       In silken tents, and 'mid light fragrance dozed,
Or on the open turf their soothed eyelids closed.

                              78
       "Dropp'd my gold watch, and kill'd a kettle-drum—
695   It went for apoplexy—foolish folks!—
       Left it to pay the piper—a good sum—
       (I've got a conscience, maugre people's jokes:)
       To scrape a little favour, 'gan to coax
       Her Highness' pug-dog—got a sharp rebuff—
700   She wish'd a game at whist—made three revokes—
       Turn'd from myself, her partner, in a huff;
His Majesty will know her temper time enough.

79

"She cried for chess—I play'd a game with her—
Castled her king with such a vixen look,
705 It bodes ill to his Majesty—(refer
To the second chapter of my fortieth book,
And see what hoity-toity airs she took:)
At half-past four the morn essay'd to beam—
Saluted, as we pass'd, an early rook—
710 The Princess fell asleep, and, in her dream,
Talk'd of one Master Hubert, deep in her esteem.

80

"About this time,—making delightful way,—
Shed a quill-feather from my larboard wing—
Wish'd, trusted, hoped 'twas no sign of decay—
715 Thank heaven, I'm hearty yet!—'twas no such thing:—
At five the golden light began to spring,
With fiery shudder through the bloomed east;
At six we heard Panthea's churches ring—
The city all her unhived swarms had cast,
720 To watch our grand approach, and hail us as we pass'd.

81

"As flowers turn their faces to the sun,
So on our flight with hungry eyes they gaze,
And, as we shaped our course, this, that way run,
With mad-cap pleasure, or hand-clasp'd amaze:
725 Sweet in the air a mild-toned music plays,
And progresses through its own labyrinth;
Buds gather'd from the green spring's middle-days,
They scatter'd,—daisy, primrose, hyacinth,—
Or round white columns wreath'd from capital to plinth.

82

730 "Onward we floated o'er the panting streets,
That seem'd throughout with upheld faces paved;
Look where we will, our bird's-eye vision meets
Legions of holiday; bright standards waved,
And fluttering ensigns emulously craved
735 Our minute's glance; a busy thunderous roar,
From square to square, among the buildings raved,

As when the sea, at flow, gluts up once more
The craggy hollowness of a wild-reefed shore.

83

"And 'Bellanaine for ever!' shouted they,
740   While that fair Princess, from her winged chair,
Bow'd low with high demeanour, and, to pay
Their new-blown loyalty with guerdon fair,
Still emptied, at meet distance, here and there,
A plenty horn of jewels. And here I
745   (Who wish to give the devil her due) declare
Against that ugly piece of calumny,
Which calls them Highland pebble-stones not worth a fly.

84

"Still 'Bellanaine!' they shouted, while we glide
'Slant to a light Ionic portico,
750   The city's delicacy, and the pride
Of our Imperial Basilic; a row
Of lords and ladies, on each hand, make show
Submissive of knee-bent obeisance,
All down the steps; and, as we enter'd, lo!
755   The strangest sight—the most unlook'd-for chance—
All things turn'd topsy-turvy in a devil's dance.

85

"'Stead of his anxious Majesty and court
At the open doors, with wide saluting eyes,
Congées and scrape-graces of every sort,
760   And all the smooth routine of gallantries,
Was seen, to our immoderate surprise,
A motley crowd thick gather'd in the hall,
Lords, scullions, deputy-scullions, with wild cries
Stunning the vestibule from wall to wall,
765   Where the Chief Justice on his knees and hands doth crawl.

86

"Counts of the palace, and the state purveyor
Of moth's down, to make soft the royal beds,
The Common Council and my fool Lord Mayor
Marching a-row, each other slipshod treads;
770   Powder'd bag-wigs and ruffy-tuffy heads

Of cinder wenches meet and soil each other;
Toe crush'd with heel ill-natured fighting breeds,
Frill-rumpling elbows brew up many a bother,
And fists in the short ribs keep up the yell and pother.

87

775
"A poet, mounted on the court-clown's back,
Rode to the Princess swift with spurring heels,
And close into her face, with rhyming clack,
Began a prothalamion;—she reels,
She falls, she faints! while laughter peals
780
Over her woman's weakness. 'Where,' cried I,
'Where is his Majesty?' No person feels
Inclined to answer; wherefore instantly
I plunged into the crowd to find him or to die.

88

"Jostling my way I gain'd the stairs, and ran
785
To the first landing, where, incredible!
I met, far gone in liquor, that old man,
That vile impostor Hum,——"
                              So far so well,—
For we have proved the mago never fell
Down stairs on Crafticanto's evidence;
790
And therefore duly shall proceed to tell,
Plain in our own original mood and tense,
The sequel of this day, though labour 'tis immense!

89

Now Hum, new fledg'd with high authority,
Came forth to quell the hubbub in the hall.

*   *   *   *   *   *   *   *   *   *   *

In after time a sage of mickle lore

In after time a sage of mickle lore,
Yclep'd Typographus, the giant took
And did refit his limbs as heretofore,
And made him read in many a learned book,
5   And into many a lively legend look;
Thereby in goodly themes so training him,
That all his brutishness he quite forsook,
When, meeting Artegall and Talus grim,
The one he struck stone blind, the other's eyes wox dim.

Abbreviations

In references to books here and in the Selected Bibliography and Commentary, the place of publication is given only when it is not London.

1817	Keats, *Poems,* 1817
1818	Keats, *Endymion: A Poetic Romance,* 1818
1820	Keats, *Lamia, Isabella, The Eve of St. Agnes, and Other Poems,* 1820
1848	*Life, Letters, and Literary Remains, of John Keats,* ed. Richard Monckton Milnes, 2 vols., 1848
1876	*The Poetical Works of John Keats,* ed. Lord Houghton [R. M. Milnes], 1876
EC	*Essays in Criticism*
ELH	*ELH* (formerly *ELH: A Journal of English Literary History*)
ELN	*English Language Notes*
JEGP	*Journal of English and Germanic Philology*
KC	*The Keats Circle: Letters and Papers, 1816–1878,* ed. Hyder Edward Rollins, 2 vols., Cambridge, Mass., 1948
K-SJ	*Keats-Shelley Journal*
K-SMB	*Keats-Shelley Memorial Bulletin*
Letters	*The Letters of John Keats,* ed. Hyder Edward Rollins, 2 vols., Cambridge, Mass., 1958
N&Q	*Notes and Queries*
OED	*The Oxford English Dictionary,* 12 vols. with supplement, 1933
PDWJ	*The Plymouth and Devonport Weekly Journal*
PMLA	*PMLA: Publications of the Modern Language Association of America*
PQ	*Philological Quarterly*
SEL	*Studies in English Literature*
SIR	*Studies in Romanticism*
TLS	*The Times Literary Supplement*
W¹, W², W³	Three collections of transcripts by Richard Woodhouse (the first two at Harvard, the third in the Morgan Library, New York)

Selected Bibliography

Bibliographical Guides

MacGillivray, J. R., *Keats: A Bibliography and Reference Guide with an Essay on Keats' Reputation* (Toronto, 1949).

Rice, Sister Pio Maria, "John Keats: A Classified Bibliography of Critical Writings . . . 1947–1961," *Bulletin of Bibliography*, 24 (1965), 167–168, 187–192.

Thorpe, Clarence D., and David Perkins, "Keats," in *The English Romantic Poets: A Review of Research and Criticism*, 3rd rev. ed., ed. Frank Jordan (New York, 1972), pp. 379–448.

The three most useful annual bibliographies of research are (1) that begun in *PMLA* (1922–1969) and continued in the *MLA International Bibliography* (1970–   ); (2) that begun in *ELH* (1937–1949), continued in *PQ* (1950–1964) and *ELN* (1965–1979), and now being issued by Garland Publishing, Inc.; and (3) that in *K-SJ* (1952–   ). The first thirty-five bibliographies of the *ELH-PQ-ELN* sequence are reprinted with an index volume in *The Romantic Movement Bibliography, 1936–1970: A Master Cumulation*, ed. A. C. Elkins, Jr., and L. J. Forstner, 7 vols. (Ann Arbor, 1973); those of the first twenty-five volumes of *K-SJ* are reprinted with indexes in two volumes entitled *Keats, Shelley, Byron, Hunt, and Their Circles: A Bibliography*, ed. David Bonnell Green and Edwin Graves Wilson (Lincoln, Neb., 1964) and Robert A. Hartley (Lincoln, Neb., 1978).

Editions and Concordance

The Poems of John Keats, ed. Jack Stillinger (Cambridge, Mass., 1978)—based on the editor's study of MSS and early printings in *The Texts of Keats's Poems* (Cambridge, Mass., 1974); supersedes H. W. Garrod's *The Poetical Works of John Keats* (Oxford, 1939; 2nd ed., 1958) as the standard textual edition.

The Poems of John Keats, ed. Miriam Allott (1970; 3rd impression, with corrections, 1975)—the most fully annotated of the critical editions, with special emphasis on historical context, sources, and analogues. Three other usefully annotated complete editions of the poetry are *The Poems*, ed. E. de Selincourt (1905; 5th ed., 1926); *Complete Poems and Selected Letters*, ed. Clarence DeWitt Thorpe (New York, 1935); and *The Complete Poems*, ed. John Barnard (Harmondsworth, 1973; 2nd ed., 1976). The best of the selected editions is Douglas Bush's *Selected Poems and Letters* (Boston, 1959).

The Poetical Works and Other Writings of John Keats ("Hampstead Edition"), ed. H. Buxton Forman, revised by Maurice Buxton Forman, 8 vols. (New York, 1938–1939)—the latest of H. B. Forman's numerous editions (which began with 4 vols. in 1883); still useful for Keats's magazine reviews, marginalia, and some other miscellanea.

The Letters of John Keats, ed. Hyder Edward Rollins, 2 vols. (Cambridge, Mass., 1958). This is the standard edition, but Robert Gittings' *Letters of John Keats: A New Selection* (1970) has independent value.

The Keats Circle: Letters and Papers, 1816–1878, ed. Hyder Edward Rollins, 2 vols. (Cambridge, Mass., 1948).

Becker, Michael G., et al., *A Concordance to the Poems of John Keats* (New York, 1981)—supersedes the concordance by Dane Lewis Baldwin et al. (Washington, 1917).

Biographies

Bate, Walter Jackson, *John Keats* (Cambridge, Mass., 1963).

Colvin, Sidney, *John Keats: His Life and Poetry, His Friends, Critics, and After-Fame* (1917; 3rd ed., 1920).

Gittings, Robert, *John Keats* (Boston, 1968).

Hewlett, Dorothy, *Adonais: A Life of John Keats* (1937; 3rd rev. ed., *A Life of John Keats,* 1970).

Lowell, Amy, *John Keats,* 2 vols. (Boston, 1925).

Ward, Aileen, *John Keats: The Making of a Poet* (New York, 1963).

Critical Studies

Bate, Walter Jackson, ed., *Keats: A Collection of Critical Essays* (Englewood Cliffs, N.J., 1964).

Bate, Walter Jackson, *The Stylistic Development of Keats* (New York, 1945).

Blackstone, Bernard, *The Consecrated Urn: An Interpretation of Keats in Terms of Growth and Form* (1959).

Bloom, Harold, *The Visionary Company: A Reading of English Romantic Poetry* (Garden City, N.Y., 1961).

Bush, Douglas, *John Keats: His Life and Writings* (New York, 1966).

Caldwell, James Ralston, *John Keats' Fancy: The Effect on Keats of the Psychology of His Day* (Ithaca, 1945).

D'Avanzo, Mario L., *Keats's Metaphors for the Poetic Imagination* (Durham, N.C., 1967).

Dickstein, Morris, *Keats and His Poetry: A Study in Development* (Chicago, 1971).

Ende, Stuart A., *Keats and the Sublime* (New Haven, 1976).

Evert, Walter H., *Aesthetic and Myth in the Poetry of Keats* (Princeton, 1965).

Finney, Claude Lee, *The Evolution of Keats's Poetry,* 2 vols. (Cambridge, Mass., 1936).

Fogle, Richard Harter, *The Imagery of Keats and Shelley: A Comparative Study* (Chapel Hill, 1949).

Ford, Newell F., *The Prefigurative Imagination of John Keats: A Study of the Beauty-Truth Identification and Its Implications* (Stanford, 1951).

Gittings, Robert, *John Keats: The Living Year* (1954).

Gittings, Robert, *The Mask of Keats: A Study of Problems* (1956).

Hirst, Wolf Z., *John Keats* (Boston, 1981).

Jack, Ian, *Keats and the Mirror of Art* (Oxford, 1967).

Jones, John, *John Keats's Dream of Truth* (1969).

Little, Judy, *Keats as a Narrative Poet: A Test of Invention* (Lincoln, Neb., 1975).

Matthews, G. M., ed., *Keats: The Critical Heritage* (1971).

Muir, Kenneth, ed., *John Keats: A Reassessment* (Liverpool, 1958).

Murry, John Middleton, *Keats* (1955)—the 4th ed., "revised and enlarged," of a work first published in 1930 as *Studies in Keats.*

Patterson, Charles I., Jr., *The Daemonic in the Poetry of John Keats* (Urbana, 1970).

Perkins, David, *The Quest for Permanence: The Symbolism of Wordsworth, Shelley, and Keats* (Cambridge, Mass., 1959).

Pettet, E. C., *On the Poetry of Keats* (Cambridge, Eng., 1957).

Ricks, Christopher, *Keats and Embarrassment* (Oxford, 1974).

Ridley, M. R., *Keats' Craftsmanship: A Study in Poetic Development* (Oxford, 1933).

Ryan, Robert M., *Keats: The Religious Sense* (Princeton, 1976).

Sharp, Ronald A., *Keats, Skepticism, and the Religion of Beauty* (Athens, Ga., 1979).

Slote, Bernice, *Keats and the Dramatic Principle* (Lincoln, Neb., 1958).

Sperry, Stuart M., *Keats the Poet* (Princeton, 1973).

Stillinger, Jack, *The Hoodwinking of Madeline and Other Essays on Keats's Poems* (Urbana, 1971).

Wasserman, Earl R., *The Finer Tone: Keats' Major Poems* (Baltimore, 1953).

Commentary

Imitation of Spenser

Written probably in 1814 (when Keats was eighteen); first published in *1817*. Charles Brown, a close friend and early biographer, calls the poem Keats's "earliest attempt": "It was the 'Faery Queen' that awakened his genius. In Spenser's fairy land he was enchanted, breathed in a new world, and became another being; till, enamoured of the stanza, he attempted to imitate it, and succeeded" (*KC*, II, 55–56). *1817*'s asterisks at the beginning and end of the text may be typographical ornaments, but more probably were intended as indications of fragmentariness.

On Peace

Written perhaps in April 1814 (Napoleon surrendered on 11 April and departed for Elba shortly afterward) or somewhat later; first published in *N&Q*, 4 February 1905.

8 mountain nymph: "The mountain nymph, sweet Liberty" in Milton's *L'Allegro* 36.

Lines Written on 29 May, the Anniversary of Charles's Restoration, on Hearing the Bells Ringing

Written probably in 1814 or 1815; first published in Amy Lowell's biography, 1925.

5 Sydney's, Russell's, Vane's: Algernon Sydney (1622–1683), Lord William Russell (1639–1683), Sir Henry Vane (1613–1662), opponents of Charles II who were executed for treason.

Stay, ruby breasted warbler, stay

Written probably in 1814; first published in *1876*. According to a note by Richard Woodhouse originally opposite one of his *W*³ transcripts, "This song was written at the request of some young ladies who were tired of singing the words printed with the air. & desired fresh words to the same tune." A later note in the *W*² book of transcripts adds the information that the song "was written off in a few Minutes" and that the young ladies were Caroline and Ann Mathew, cousins of the recipient of Keats's *To George Felton Mathew*.

Reginald Spofforth's *Julia to the Wood Robin* ("A Favorite Canzonet, with an Accompaniment for the Piano Forte") was published in London, c. 1799, with the following lyrics:

> Stay, sweet Enchanter of the grove;
> Leave not so soon thy native tree;
> O warble still those notes of love,
> While my fond heart responds to thee.
>
> Rest thy soft bosom on the spray
> Till chilly Autumn frowns severe;
> Then charm me with thy parting lay,
> And I will answer with a tear.
>
> But soon as Spring, enwreath'd with flow'rs,
> Comes dancing o'er the new drest Plain,
> Return and cheer thy natal bow'rs,
> My Robin, with those notes again.

Spofforth's tune requires the words to be rather awkwardly drawn out—for example, "the" in the first line is held for three eighth notes—and the piano accompaniment has triplets in the left hand and a great many trills (for bird calls) in the right. The device ("Stay . . ." or, more commonly, "Stay . . . stay") was a popular one; Burns's *Address to the Woodlark* ("O stay, sweet warbling woodlark, stay") is a typical example.

Fill for me a brimming bowl

Written in August 1814; first published in *N&Q*, 4 February 1905. According to notes in two transcripts, Keats told Woodhouse in February 1819 that he was alluding in 10 ff. to the same woman, casually seen at Vauxhall, who later inspired *When I have fears* 9–10 and *Time's sea hath been*. The epigraph from Terence's *Eunuchus* is a translation of the fifth line of II.iii in modern editions, line 296 of the play.

24 "the joy of grief": An eighteenth-century commonplace, in Burke's *Enquiry*, Macpherson's Ossian poems, Campbell's *The Pleasures of Hope* (I.182), etc. (see Larry L. Stewart, *ELN*, 15 [1977], 29–32).

As from the darkening gloom a silver dove

Written in December 1814; first published in *1876*. According to a note originally opposite the W^2 transcript, Keats told Woodhouse in February 1819 that "he had written it on the death of his grandmother, about five days afterward, but that he had never told any one before (not even his brother) the occasion upon which it was written. He said he was tenderly attached to her."

To Lord Byron

Written in December 1814; first published in *1848*.

Oh Chatterton! how very sad thy fate

Written in 1815; first published in *1848*. Thomas Chatterton (1752–1770), brilliant fabricator of the purportedly fifteenth-century Rowley poems, who, starving in a garret, committed suicide at the age of seventeen, was a hero to all the Romantics. Keats dedicated *Endymion* to him.

Written on the Day That Mr. Leigh Hunt Left Prison

Written on 2 February 1815 (the day on which Hunt was released from Horsemonger Lane Prison after serving a two-year sentence for libel against the Prince Regent); first published in *1817*. C. C. Clarke (in Charles and Mary Cowden Clarke, *Recollections of Writers*, 1878, p. 127) tells that on the occasion of his walking to London to see Hunt, then just out of prison, Keats accompanied him part of the way, and "At the last field-gate, when taking leave, he gave me the sonnet entitled, 'Written on the day that Mr. Leigh Hunt left Prison.' This I feel to be the first proof I had received of his having committed himself in verse; and how clearly do I recall the conscious look and hesitation with which he offered it!"

To Hope

Written in February 1815; first published in *1817*.
3 "mind's eye": *Hamlet* I.i.112, ii.185.

Ode to Apollo

Written in February 1815; first published in *1848*.
14 Maro: Virgil (Publius Vergilius Maro), who describes funeral pyres in *Aeneid* IV.494–705, VI.212–235, and XI.1–212.   **33 chastity:** The subject of *The Faerie Queene* III.

To Some Ladies

Written in the summer of 1815; first published in *1817*. The addressees are the Mathew sisters, Caroline and Ann, who were on holiday at Hastings with their cousin G. F. Mathew.
20 Tighe: The Irish poetess Mary Tighe (1772–1810), author of *Psyche* (1805).

On Receiving a Curious Shell, and a Copy of Verses, from the Same Ladies

Written in the summer of 1815; first published in *1817*. According to a note by Woodhouse in the W^3 papers, the knight in the poem ("Sir Knight" in 17, "Eric" in 41) is G. F. Mathew, cousin of the ladies addressed in the preceding poem. "Copy of Verses" in the title and "this scroll" in 21 refer to a MS copy of Thomas Moore's *The Wreath and the Chain* (a short poem first published in Moore's *Epistles, Odes, and Other Poems*, 1806) that one of the ladies had made for Keats.

8 Armida . . . Rinaldo: Principal characters in Tasso's *Gerusalemme liberata.* **12 Britomartis:** Heroine of *The Faerie Queene* III.   **25 This canopy:** The "Curious Shell" of the title (see *To Some Ladies* 15–24).

O come, dearest Emma! the rose is full blown

Written probably in 1815; first published in Forman's edition of 1883. "Emma," most likely a poetic pseudonym (like one of Wordsworth's) for Keats's future sister-in-law Georgiana Wylie or for one of the Mathew sisters, remains unidentified. A slightly different version in George Keats's handwriting substitutes "Georgiana" for "Emma" (plus adjective) in 1 and 11.

Woman! when I behold thee flippant, vain

Written in 1815 or 1816; first published in *1817.*
12–13 Calidore . . . Red Cross Knight: Heroes of *The Faerie Queene* VI and I.   **31–32 God . . . protection:** According to Woodhouse's shorthand note in his interleaved *1817,* "When Keats had written these lines he burst into tears overpowered by the tenderness of his own imagination." But the basis for this is questionable; Woodhouse almost certainly had not met Keats at this time.

O Solitude! if I must with thee dwell

Written in 1815 or 1816; first published in the *Examiner,* 5 May 1816 (Keats's first appearance in print). For biographical and critical comment see Stuart M. Sperry, *Huntington Library Quarterly,* 29 (1966), 191–197.

To George Felton Mathew

Written in November 1815; first published in *1817.* Mathew (on whom see the comprehensive note in *Letters,* I, 100) met Keats through his cousins Caroline and Ann, the "ladies" of *To Some Ladies* and *On Receiving a Curious Shell,* and became a close friend of the poet in 1815. He published verses addressed to Keats (*To a Poetical Friend,* echoing several of Keats's early poems) in the *European Magazine,* October 1816, and later reviewed *1817* in the same periodical, May 1817.
5 brother Poets: Beaumont and Fletcher.   **18 soft . . . airs":** *L'Allegro* 136.   **75 "a . . . place":** *The Faerie Queene* I.iii.4.   **76–93:** Mathew himself took this account of his "travels strange" quite seriously; see *KC,* II, 186–188.

Had I a man's fair form, then might my sighs

Written in 1815 or 1816 (possibly, like the next poem, a valentine to Mary Frogley, a member of the Mathew circle and cousin of Woodhouse); first published (under the heading "To * * * * * *") in *1817.* Older critics usually read the sonnet as an expression of Keats's feelings about his short stature (he was only a fraction of an inch over five feet tall), and Woodhouse's own interpretation, noted in his interleaved *1817,* would seem to lend support to the idea. But J. Burke

Severs, *K-SJ*, 6 (1957), 109–113, has convincingly argued that the speaker is a fairy addressing a loved one who is human. If so, we have here the earliest instance of the mortal-nonmortal love match (or mismatch) that figures prominently in a number of later poems—*Endymion*, *La Belle Dame*, and *Lamia*, to name the best known.

Hadst thou liv'd in days of old

Written on or shortly before 14 February 1816 (as a valentine for George Keats to send to Mary Frogley); first published (under the heading "To * * * *") in *1817*.

I am as brisk

Written probably in 1816 (the lines appear on the second page of the extant holograph of the preceding poem); first published in Garrod's edition of 1939.

Give me women, wine, and snuff

Written toward the end of 1815 or during the first half of 1816 (scribbled in pencil on the cover of a lecture notebook belonging to a fellow student at Guy's Hospital); first published in Forman's one-volume edition of 1884.
   2 "hold, enough!": *Macbeth* V.viii.34.

Specimen of an Induction to a Poem

Written in 1816, probably in the spring sometime after the publication (in February) of Hunt's *The Story of Rimini*, an obvious influence especially on Keats's style; first published in *1817*.
   6 Archimago: The evil magician of *The Faerie Queene* I and II.   **61 Libertas:** Leigh Hunt (the name is used again in the epistles *To My Brother George* 24 and *To Charles Cowden Clarke* 44).

Calidore

Written in 1816, probably in the spring just after the preceding poem; first published in *1817*. Calidore is presumably named after the hero of *The Faerie Queene* VI.

To one who has been long in city pent

Written in June 1816; first published in *1817*. The opening line is a pointed allusion to *Paradise Lost* IX.445.

Oh! how I love, on a fair summer's eve

Written in 1816, perhaps in the summer; first published in *1848*.
   10 Sydney: See the note to *Lines Written on 29 May* 5.

To a Friend Who Sent Me Some Roses

Written on 29 June 1816; first published in *1817*. The "Friend" was the poet Charles Jeremiah Wells, who knew the Keats brothers when he was in school at Edmonton (see Molly Tatchell, *K-SMB*, 22 [1971], 7–17, and Priscilla Johnston, *K-SJ*, 26 [1977], 72–87). The poet Thomas Wade briefly explains the occasion of the poem in a letter to R. M. Milnes of 27 January 1845: "Keats and [Wells] quarrelled about some trifle or other; the quarrel being ended by Wells' present of roses" (*KC*, II, 115).

Happy is England! I could be content

Written perhaps in 1816; first published in *1817*.

To My Brother George (sonnet)

Written at Margate in August 1816; first published in *1817*.

To My Brother George (epistle)

Written at Margate in August 1816; first published in *1817*. This is one of the three most substantial pieces in Keats's first volume (*I stood tip-toe* and *Sleep and Poetry*, at the beginning and the end of the volume, are the other two; this one comes almost exactly in the middle). The subject, as in the other two (and throughout *1817* more generally), is whether Keats can and should be a poet; the poem deals with inspiration and the poetic process (1–66), fame—"posterity's award"—and the good influence of poetry (67–109), and then the question of Keats's personal aims (109 ff.). Note in particular the description of the poetic trance (19–54, a process that literally or metaphorically is central in many later poems), the emphasis on seeing (21, 26, 35, 36, 43, 44, 53, 57, 63, 65), and the fact that what is seen—"enchanted portals," "golden halls," "wonders strange"—is clearly outside and above the natural world (at the farthest, it is a realm that "no mortal eye can reach," 44).
   19 bay: Laurel, symbol of poetic fame.   **24 Libertas:** Leigh Hunt.   **83–90:** Syntactically incomplete in both Keats's fair copy MS and *1817* ("Gay villagers" has no main verb).   **121 for you:** Woodhouse noted in his interleaved *1817* that *Hadst thou liv'd in days of old, To G. A. W.*, and "perhaps" *O Solitude* "were written *for* his brother" and that the present poem, the preceding sonnet, and *To My Brothers* "were written *to* his Brother." Even so, "for you" in the context at hand surely means "to be read by you."

To Charles Cowden Clarke

Written at Margate in September 1816; first published in *1817*. Clarke, son of the master of the Enfield school that Keats and his brothers attended, was the friend who most influenced the poet's early reading.
   6 the . . . courts: It is not clear whether the object of "courts" is intended to

be "Zephyr" (who then, in the inverted syntax, would be courted by a masculine swan represented as female Naiad) or a feminine-masculine composite, "Naiad-Zephyr." **27 Helicon:** A mountain sacred to the Muses; here either an error on Keats's part or a metonym for Hippocrene, Helicon's famous fountain whose waters were supposed to inspire poets. "Helicon" as wine also occurs in the original draft text of *Lamia,* in a passage subsequently discarded following II.162. **29 Baiæ:** An ancient resort on the Bay of Naples. Tasso was educated in a Jesuit school in Naples. Armida's garden (31) is described in *Gerusalemme liberata* XVI.i–xvi.   **33 Mulla's stream:** A river near Spenser's home in Ireland. "Maidens . . . cream" (34) is an allusion to Spenser's *Epithalamion* 175, and Belphoebe, Una, and Archimago are characters in *The Faerie Queene* I–IV.   **44 Libertas:** Leigh Hunt, "wrong'd" by political persecution.

How many bards gild the lapses of time

Written probably in 1816; first published in *1817.* The sonnet shows that, even relatively early in his career, Keats's "anxiety of influence" was well under control. On the sources of the poem, Spenser and Milton in particular, see Robert F. Gleckner, *K-SJ,* 27 (1978), 14–22.

On First Looking into Chapman's Homer

Written in October 1816, on a morning after Keats had stayed up all night reading George Chapman's translation of Homer with C. C. Clarke; first published in the *Examiner,* 1 December 1816. Clarke explains the circumstances (*Recollections of Writers,* pp. 128–130):

> A beautiful copy of the folio edition of Chapman's translation of Homer had been lent me . . . and to work we went, turning to some of the "famousest" passages, as we had scrappily known them in Pope's version. . . . Chapman supplied us with many an after-treat; but it was in the teeming wonderment of this his [Keats's] first introduction, that, when I came down to breakfast the next morning, I found upon my table a letter with no other enclosure than his famous sonnet, "On First Looking into Chapman's Homer." We had parted . . . at day-spring, yet he contrived that I should receive the poem from a distance of, may be, two miles by ten o'clock.

This is universally regarded as the finest of the short poems in Keats's first volume, and one of his best sonnets. On its imagery, structure, theme, and language see especially J. M. Murry, *Keats* (1955), pp. 145–165 (an influential essay first published in 1928); Carl Woodring, *K-SJ,* 14 (1965), 15–22; Paul McNally, *JEGP,* 79 (1980), 530–540; and Lawrence Lipking, *The Life of the Poet: Beginning and Ending Poetic Careers* (Chicago, 1981), pp. 3–11.

11 Cortez: It was of course Balboa, not Cortez, who discovered the Pacific (from the Isthmus of Darien, in Panama). But none of Keats's contemporaries noticed the error.

Keen, fitful gusts are whisp'ring here and there

Written in October or November 1816 (shortly after meeting Hunt, whose cottage is referred to in 10); first published in *1817*.

On Leaving Some Friends at an Early Hour

Written in October or November 1816; first published in *1817*. The "Friends" were Hunt, John Hamilton Reynolds, and probably C. C. Clarke.

To My Brothers

Written on Tom Keats's seventeenth birthday, 18 November 1816; first published in *1817*.

Addressed to Haydon

Written in 1816; first published in *1817*. The historical painter Benjamin Robert Haydon is the friend who later introduced Keats to the Elgin Marbles.

6 "singleness of aim": Wordsworth, *Character of the Happy Warrior* 40.

Addressed to the Same

Written on 20 November 1816, after an evening with Haydon that Keats says "wrought me up" (*Letters*, I, 117); first published in *1817*. On the following day Keats made a copy for Haydon to forward to Wordsworth, but the painter instead sent his own transcript of the poem on the last day of the year (for Wordsworth's response, 20 January 1817, see *The Letters of William and Dorothy Wordsworth: The Middle Years*, Part II, ed. Ernest de Selincourt, 2nd ed., rev. Mary Moorman and Alan G. Hill, Oxford, 1970, pp. 360–361). The "Great spirits" are Wordsworth (2–4), Hunt (5–6), and Haydon (7–8).

3 Helvellyn: Mountain a few miles from Wordsworth's home in the Lake District.   **13:** Originally a full pentameter line, "Of mighty Workings in a distant Mart?" The omission of the last four words was suggested by Haydon (see *Letters*, I, 118).

To G. A. W.

Written in December 1816; first published in *1817*. Woodhouse noted in shorthand in his interleaved *1817*, "this sonnet was written by the author at the request of his brother George, to be sent by the latter to Miss Georgiana Ann [*Woodhouse's mistake for* Augusta] Wylie the lady to whom G. K. was afterward married."

To Kosciusko

Written in December 1816; first published in the *Examiner*, 16 February 1817. The famous Polish patriot, a hero to English liberals, was seventy years old at this time.

Sleep and Poetry

Written sometime during October–December 1816; first published in *1817*. "It was in the library at Hunt's cottage, where an extemporary bed had been made up for him on the sofa, that [Keats] composed the frame-work and many lines of the poem . . . the last sixty or seventy being an inventory of the art garniture of the room" (Clarke, *Recollections of Writers,* pp. 133–134). This is the final (and climactic) poem in Keats's first volume, and it both justifies much of the earlier verse in the volume ("the realm . . . Of Flora, and old Pan," 101 ff.) and outlines a program for development to more significant achievement in the future (the "nobler life" of 123 ff.). The epigraph is from *The Flower and the Leaf* (17–21), a 600-line allegorical poem that in Keats's time was attributed to Chaucer.

89 Montmorenci: A river in southern Quebec with a waterfall 275 feet high.   **171–180:** Referring primarily to Elizabethan poetry.   **181–206:** Referring to Augustan poetry (whose principles were most fully articulated in Boileau's *L'Art poétique,* 1674).   **198 certain . . . wit:** See Genesis 30:31–43.   **202 bright Lyrist:** Apollo.   **218–219 some . . . die:** Woodhouse noted in his interleaved *1817,* "alluding to H Kirke White—Chatterton—& other poets of great promise, neglected by the age, who died young."   **224–226 some . . . bill:** Probably referring to the Lake Poets, especially Wordsworth, as Woodhouse noted in his *1817.* Robert Gittings, *John Keats* (Boston, 1968), p. 105, thinks the allusion is to Lake Leman (Lake Geneva) and Byron's *Childe Harold* III.   **226–229 from . . . earth:** Referring to Hunt's poetry.   **230–245 yet . . . life:** Probably referring to Byron, as Woodhouse twice noted in his *1817,* though Hunt, reviewing *1817* in the *Examiner,* 13 July 1817, p. 443, read the passage as an objection to "the morbidity that taints the productions of the Lake Poets."   **245–247, 267–268:** This idea of poetry as solace runs throughout *1817.* Cf. (in the order in which the poems were arranged in the volume) *I stood tip-toe* 138–139, *On Receiving a Curious Shell* 19–20 and 43–44, *Imitation of Spenser* 19–22, *To George Felton Mathew* 63–65, and *To My Brother George* (epistle) 73–109.

I stood tip-toe upon a little hill

Completed in December 1816 (possibly begun several months earlier); first published in *1817.* This is (if we set aside the dedicatory sonnet *To Leigh Hunt, Esq.*) the opening poem in Keats's first volume. It is part description, part vision, part apostrophe, and has to do principally with the relationship between nature and poetry. After detailing his actual surroundings in the first paragraph (1–28), Keats launches into a vision—of nature advanced from the present reality of early spring ("sweet buds," "scantly leaved . . . stems" in 3, 5) to an imaginatively conceived midsummer (37)—and this leads him eventually to an element of nature, the moon, that he apostrophizes as "Maker of sweet poets" (116). In the apostrophe, which continues to the end of the poem, he arrives at his main subject, the equation of nature with poetic inspiration (see especially 125–126), inspiration that, just as in the epistle *To My Brother George* and *Sleep and Poetry,* paradoxically takes the poet out of nature into a higher realm (139, 185–192,

242). While he was writing it Keats referred to the poem as "Endymion," and a transcript by Tom Keats, the latest of the authoritative texts before *1817*, is headed with that title. The epigraph is from Leigh Hunt's *The Story of Rimini* (1816), III.430. For discussion of the poem from a phenomenological point of view see Marjorie Norris, *K-SJ*, 25 (1976), 43–54.

15–22: This activity of the "greediest eye"—first "peering about," then "picturing," and finally "guessing"—occurs frequently in Keats's poems (the most notable instance being the middle stanzas of *Ode to a Nightingale*, where the speaker sees certain things and then "cannot see . . . But . . . guess[es]"). **141 ff.:** Keats's depiction of the origin of myths (the four examples are Cupid and Psyche in 141–150, Pan and Syrinx in 151–162, Narcissus and Echo in 163–180, and Endymion and Cynthia in 181–204) is based on Wordsworth's account in *The Excursion* IV.718–762, 847–887. **241 Was . . . born:** Several meanings are possible—Was there a poet conceived in the "greater blisses" (239) of Endymion's and Cynthia's wedding night? Was there a poet born in the original imagining of the tale (181 ff.)? Was there a poet born *in Keats* in the retelling here? The connection between 242 and 190–192 (like the earlier similarity of 1 and 194) would seem to clinch the personal application of the question.

Written in Disgust of Vulgar Superstition

Written on 22 December 1816; first published in *1876*. Tom Keats's note on the original draft, "Written in 15 Minutes," suggests that the sonnet was, like *On the Grasshopper and Cricket, To the Nile,* and possibly *On Receiving a Laurel Crown,* the product of a sonnet-writing competition.

7 Lydian airs: Keats puts the same words in quotes in *To George Felton Mathew* 18 (from *L'Allegro* 136).

On the Grasshopper and Cricket

Written on 30 December 1816; first published in *1817*. Woodhouse explains the circumstances in a note in his interleaved *1817:* "The author & Leigh Hunt challenged each other to write a sonnet in a Quarter of an hour.—'The Grasshopper & Cricket' was the subject.—Both performed the task within the time allotted." A longer account in Clarke, *Recollections of Writers,* pp. 135–136, adds that "Keats won as to time." Keats's and Hunt's sonnets were later published together in both the *Examiner,* 21 September 1817, and the *Monthly Repository,* October 1817.

After dark vapours have oppressed our plains

Written on 31 January 1817; first published in the *Examiner,* 23 February 1817.

To a Young Lady Who Sent Me a Laurel Crown

Written perhaps in 1816 or 1817; first published in *1848*. The young lady has not been identified.

On Receiving a Laurel Crown from Leigh Hunt

Written at the end of 1816 or early in 1817; first published in *The Times* (London), 18 May 1914. Woodhouse describes the occasion of this poem in a note opposite the W^2 transcript of *God of the golden bow:*

> As Keats & Leigh Hunt were taking their Wine together after dinner, at the house of the latter, the whim seized them (probably at Hunt's instigation) to crown themselves with laurel after the fashion of the elder Bards.—While they were thus attired, two of Hunt's friends happened to call upon him—Just before their entrance H. removed the wreath from his own brows, and suggested to K. that he might as well do the same. K however in his mad enthusiastic way, vowed that he would not take off his crown for any human being: and he accordingly wore it, without any explanation, as long as the visit lasted.—
>
> He mentioned the circumstance afterwards to some of his friends, along with his sense of the folly (and I believe presumption) of his conduct—And he said he was determined to record it, by an apologetic Ode to Apollo on the occasion—He shortly after wrote this fragment [*God of the golden bow*].

Keats apparently alludes to this incident in a now lost letter to George Keats that he quotes to Benjamin Bailey on 8 October 1817, "I put on no Laurels till I shall have finished Endymion, and I hope Apollo is [not] angered at my having made a Mockery at him at Hunt's" (*Letters*, I, 170). References to the passing of time in 1 and 9 suggest that he is here engaged in another sonnet-writing contest (see the note to *Written in Disgust of Vulgar Superstition*).

To the Ladies Who Saw Me Crown'd

Written at the end of 1816 or early in 1817 (same occasion as that of the preceding poem); first published in *The Times* (London), 18 May 1914.

God of the golden bow

Written at the end of 1816 or early in 1817; first published in the *Western Messenger* (Louisville, Ky.), June 1836. For the occasion see the note to *On Receiving a Laurel Crown from Leigh Hunt*.

This pleasant tale is like a little copse

Written in February 1817; first published in the *Examiner*, 16 March 1817. Clarke told Milnes in a letter of 20 December 1846 that Keats composed the poem "in my Chaucer, while I lay asleep on his Sofa" (*KC*, II, 170) and elsewhere describes the writing of it as "an extempore effusion . . . without the alteration of a single word" (*Recollections of Writers*, p. 139), but the extant holograph in Clarke's Chaucer looks much more like a fair copy than a draft. The "pleasant tale" is *The*

Flower and the Leaf, which at the time was included among Chaucer's writings. J. H. Reynolds wrote an answering sonnet (dated 27 February 1817) that is preserved among Woodhouse's W^2 transcripts and has been published in (among other places) Reynolds' *Poetry and Prose,* ed. George L. Marsh (1928), p. 174.

To Leigh Hunt, Esq.

Written in February 1817; first published (as the "Dedication" of the volume) in *1817.* In some biographical notes on Keats that he wrote out for Milnes in March 1846, Clarke cites this poem as "proof of [Keats's] facility in composition": "he was surrounded by several of his friends when the last proof-sheet of his little book [*1817*] was brought in; and he was requested to send the dedication, if he intended one. He went to a side-table, and in a few minutes, while all had been talking, he returned and read the Dedicatory Sonnett. . . . The subject of this Sonnett may have lain in the bud of his mind, and had blossomed at his then bidding" (*KC,* II, 150). Clarke's more detailed account in *Recollections of Writers,* pp. 137–138, adds that Keats wrote the poem without a single alteration—"a circumstance that was noted at the time."

On Seeing the Elgin Marbles

Written on 1 or 2 March 1817; first published on the same day in both the *Champion* and the *Examiner,* 9 March 1817. Keats saw the Elgin Marbles (the famous sculptures and friezes from the Parthenon, brought to England by Lord Elgin) for the first time, in the British Museum, in the company of B. R. Haydon, and wrote this and the next poem shortly afterward. We have Haydon's enthusiastic response in a note to Keats of 3 March (*Letters,* I, 122). For a survey of previous interpretations and a new one emphasizing the theme of art's mortality see E. B. Murray, *K-SJ,* 20 (1971), 22–36.

To Haydon with a Sonnet Written on Seeing the Elgin Marbles

Written on 1 or 2 March 1817; first published (with the preceding poem) in both the *Champion* and the *Examiner,* 9 March 1817.

On a Leander Which Miss Reynolds, My Kind Friend, Gave Me

Written probably in March 1817; first published in *The Gem* (1829). The Leander was one of James Tassie's popular "gems," glass-paste reproductions (frequently used on letter seals) of ancient cameo medallions. Woodhouse noted in W^2, "I believe it was once Keats's intention to write a series of Sonnets & short poems on Some of Tassie's gems." For a picture of the gem that best accords with the details of the present poem (Leander about to drown in the Hellespont) see Ian Jack, *Keats and the Mirror of Art* (Oxford, 1967), Plate IXb, facing p. 104. "Miss Reynolds" was one of J. H. Reynolds' four sisters—Jane, Mariane, Eliza, or Charlotte.

On The Story of Rimini

Written in March 1817 (before the 25th); first published in *1848*. Leigh Hunt's *The Story of Rimini*, a poem that exerted considerable influence on Keats's early style (especially in *Specimen of an Induction* and *Calidore*), appeared in February 1816.

On the Sea

Written at Carisbrooke, Isle of Wight (where Keats had gone to begin writing *Endymion*), probably on 17 April 1817; first published in the *Champion*, 17 August 1817. Keats tells Reynolds in a letter containing the poem, "From want of regular rest, I have been rather *narvus*—and the passage in Lear—'Do you not hear the Sea?' [IV.vi.4]—has haunted me intensely" (*Letters*, I, 132).

Unfelt, unheard, unseen

Written in 1817 (before the middle of August); first published in *1848*.
    12 "love . . . bounds": Keats's source (if the words are an exact quotation) has not been identified. The idea was a commonplace (e.g., in *Romeo and Juliet* II.ii.67, 133–135), and Burton Stevenson's *The Home Book of Quotations*, 10th ed. (New York, 1967), pp. 1191–92, includes several items beginning "Love knows no . . . ," of which the closest to Keats's wording is Phineas Fletcher's *Piscatory Eclogues* III.119, "Love knows no mean or measure."

Hither, hither, love

Written perhaps in 1817 or 1818; first published in the *Ladies' Companion* (New York), August 1837.

You say you love; but with a voice

Written perhaps in 1817 or 1818; first published in *TLS*, 16 April 1914. Though Keats could not have known the work, there is an uncanny resemblance here to one of Byron's poems *To Caroline* ("You say you love, and yet your eye / No symptom of that love conveys"), included in the privately printed *Fugitive Pieces* (1806) but then not reprinted until 1898.

Before he went to live with owls and bats

Written perhaps in 1817; first published in *Literary Anecdotes of the Nineteenth Century*, ed. W. Robertson Nicoll and Thomas J. Wise, vol. II (1896). The poem is based on Daniel 2–4. For interpretation as political allegory (parodic comment on the Tory government's persecution of its critics) see Aileen Ward, *PQ*, 34 (1955), 177–188.
    5 "good . . . cats": *Romeo and Juliet* III.i.77.   **14 "Ye . . . gold":** Daniel 2:38 ("Thou art this head of gold").

The Gothic looks solemn

Written at Oxford probably in September 1817; first published in Forman's edition of 1883. Woodhouse's transcripts preserve the following from a now lost letter from Keats to Reynolds containing the poem:

> Wordworth sometimes, though in a fine way, gives us sentences in the Style of School exercises—for Instance
>
> > The lake doth glitter
> > Small birds twitter &c.
>
> Now I think this is an excellent method of giving a very clear description of an interesting place such as Oxford is. (*Letters,* I, 151–152)

The lines that Keats quotes above (presumably from memory) are Wordsworth's *Written in March While Resting on the Bridge at the Foot of Brother's Water* 4 and 3.

9 trencher: Trencher-cap, mortarboard (the black tassel indicating that its wearer was a commoner rather than a nobleman).

O grant that like to Peter I

No evidence for dating; first published in J. M. Murry's edition of 1930.

Think not of it, sweet one, so

Written about 11 November 1817; first published in *1848*.

Endymion

Begun toward the end of April 1817 and first completed in draft form on 28 November 1817. Keats pretty well kept to the timetable that he announces at the outset of the poem (I.39–57). He started writing at Carisbrooke sometime after 18 April and continued with Book I at Margate, Canterbury, Hastings, and Hampstead. Book II was written at Hampstead during the summer months, Book III at Oxford in September, and Book IV at Hampstead and Burford Bridge, Surrey, in October and November. He recopied the poem, revising as he wrote it out, in January–March 1818; the proofs of Book I began arriving in the middle of February, while he was still revising the later parts. First published (as a separate volume, *1818*) toward the end of April.

The poem, as Keats told his brother George in the spring of 1817 (in a now lost letter quoted to Bailey on 8 October 1817), was conceived as

> a test, a trial of my Powers of Imagination and chiefly of my invention which is a rare thing indeed—by which I must make 4000 Lines of one bare circumstance and fill them with Poetry; and when I consider that this is a great task, and that when done it will take me but a dozen paces

towards the Temple of Fame—it makes me say—God forbid that I should be without such a task! I have heard Hunt say and [I] may be asked—why endeavour after a long Poem? To which I should answer— Do not the Lovers of Poetry like to have a little Region to wander in where they may pick and choose, and in which the images are so numerous that many are forgotten and found new in a second Reading: which may be food for a Week's stroll in the Summer. . . . Besides a long Poem is a test of Invention which I take to be the Polar Star of Poetry, as Fancy is the Sails, and Imagination the Rudder. Did our great Poets ever write short Pieces? I mean in the shape of Tales—This same invention seems i[n]deed of late Years to have been forgotten as a Poetical excellence. (*Letters,* I, 169–170)

The "one bare circumstance" was of course the legend of Endymion, which Keats had read in Lemprière's *Classical Dictionary* and other works of Greek mythology when he was a schoolboy (see Clarke, *Recollections of Writers,* p. 124) and had already written about in the last sixty-two lines of *I stood tip-toe* (a poem originally titled "Endymion"). He briefly recounts the legend and characterizes the hero in a letter to his sister Fanny of 10 September 1817:

Many Years ago there was a young handsome Shepherd who fed his flocks on a Mountain's Side called Latmus—he was a very contemplative sort of a Person and lived solitry among the trees and Plains little thinking—that such a beautiful Creature as the Moon was growing mad in Love with him—However so it was; and when he was asleep on the Grass, she used to come down from heaven and admire him excessively [for] a long time; and at last could not refrain from carying him away in her arms to the top of that high Mountain Latmus while he was dreaming. (*Letters,* I, 154)

In his elaboration of this simple story—to 4050 lines, just fifty more than the 4000 he originally planned—Keats introduced several themes that recur significantly in his later poems: "fellowship with essence," the imaginative joining or identification with things or persons outside oneself that leads, at its highest reach, to union with some ideal (see I.777 ff.); "gradations of Happiness," a valuation scale of "essences" (see the letter to John Taylor of 30 January 1818 as quoted below in the note to I.777–781); the conflict of self and solitude with love and humanitarian activities; the opposing claims of human and immortal realms of existence; and the question of the authenticity of dreams (which here, as in a number of Keats's later poems, may be taken to symbolize the visionary imagination). Keats's extended preoccupation with this last in Books I and IV is surely a response to Shelley's different treatment of the same subject in *Alastor,* published in March 1816.

The poem has received serious attention in virtually all the full-length biographical and critical treatments of Keats's career. Among specialized studies, see Jacob D. Wigod, *PMLA,* 68 (1953), 779–790; Glen O. Allen, *K-SJ,* 6 (1957), 37–57; Carroll Arnett, *Texas Studies in English,* 36 (1957), 100–109; Clarisse Godfrey in *John Keats: A Reassessment,* ed. Kenneth Muir (Liverpool, 1958), pp. 20–38; Albert Gérard, *University of Toronto Quarterly,* 28 (1959), 160–175 (the essay is reprinted in revised form in Gérard's *English Romantic Poetry,* Berkeley and Los Angeles, 1968, pp. 194–214); Stuart M. Sperry, *SIR,* 2 (1962), 38–53 (see also Sperry's *Keats the Poet,* Princeton, 1973, pp. 90–116); Walter H. Evert, *Aesthetic and Myth in the Poetry of Keats* (Princeton, 1965), pp. 88–176; Bruce E. Miller, *K-SJ,* 14 (1965), 33–54; Mario L. D'Avanzo, *K-SJ,* 16 (1967), 61–72; Helen E. Haworth, *Humanities Association Bulletin,* 18 (1967), 80–91; Northrop Frye, *A Study of English Romanticism* (New York, 1968), pp. 125–165; Morris Dickstein, *Keats and His Poetry* (Chicago, 1971), pp. 53–129; Leon Waldoff, *EC,* 21 (1971), 152–158; Jack Stillinger, *The Hoodwinking of Madeline* (Urbana, 1971), pp. 14–30; Miriam Allott in *Literature of the Romantic Period,* ed. R. T. Davies and B. G. Beatty (Liverpool, 1976), pp. 151–170; and William Garrett, *K-SJ,* 27 (1978), 23–34. For surveys of the interpretations of important earlier critics—among them Robert Bridges, Ernest de Selincourt, Sidney Colvin, Amy Lowell, Clarence D. Thorpe, J. M. Murry, Leonard Brown, Douglas Bush, C. L. Finney, and Newell F. Ford—see in particular the essays by Wigod, Sperry, and Miller.

Though friends admired and defended the poem, the principal contemporary reviews—in the *British Critic* (June 1818), *Blackwood's* (August 1818), and the *Quarterly Review* (April 1818, appearing in September)—were unfavorable, the last so severe that Shelley in *Adonais* attributed Keats's early death to it. Keats's own dissatisfaction with the poem first surfaces in a letter to Haydon of 28 September 1817, just after the completion of Book III—"My Ideas with respect to it . . . are very low—and I would write the subject thoroughly again. but I am tired of it" (*Letters,* I, 168)—and continues on into the published Preface of April 1818; in other letters he called the poem "slip-shod" and said that in writing it his "mind was like a pack of scattered cards" (I, 374, II, 323). But he knew that it was valuable apprentice work, and he took the hostile reviews in stride. As he told J. A. Hessey on 8 October 1818,

> Praise or blame has but a momentary effect on the man whose love of beauty in the abstract makes him a severe critic on his own Works. My own domestic criticism has given me pain without comparison beyond what Blackwood or the Quarterly could possibly inflict. . . . I have written independently *without Judgment*—I may write independently *&* *with judgment* hereafter. . . . In Endymion, I leaped headlong into the Sea, and thereby have become better acquainted with the Soundings, the quicksands, & the rocks, than if I had stayed upon the green shore, and piped a silly pipe, and took tea & comfortable advice.—I was never afraid of failure; for I would sooner fail than not be among the greatest.
> (I, 373–374)

It is noteworthy, in the face of this external criticism, that on the title page of his next (and last) volume, *1820,* Keats is identified as "Author of Endymion."

The epigraph, which Keats first thought of in November 1817 ("a capital Motto for my Poem," *Letters,* I, 189), is from Shakespeare's Sonnet XVII.12. In the last sentence of the Preface ("I wish to try once more") he is looking ahead to *Hyperion* (see the note below to IV.774).

Book I.   **25 essences:** The word (which, as Sperry has suggested in *Keats the Poet,* pp. 45–49, probably was associated in Keats's thinking with the chemical process of distillation) occurs again in I.99, 779, II.740, 905, III.172, 700, 983.   **63 Latmos:** A mountain in Caria, in Asia Minor.   **78 ay:** *1818* consistently uses "ay" for the adverb ("ever") and "aye" for the interjection ("yes," "ah"). *1817* and *1820* also regularly distinguish between the two but reverse the spellings. (In his MSS Keats wrote "aye" for all meanings.)   **134 old Chaucer:** Keats told his publishers Taylor and Hessey on 16 May 1817, "This Evening I go to Canterbury. . . . I hope the Remembrance of Chaucer will set me forward like a Billiard-Ball" (*Letters,* I, 146–147).   **138 younglings:** Young plants.   **232–306:** Keats recited this "Hymn to Pan" to Wordsworth at their first meeting, in the middle of December 1817, and the older poet responded by calling it a "pretty piece of Paganism." The most authoritative of several accounts of this event is by Haydon, in a letter of 29 November 1845 (*KC,* II, 143–144), but Haydon's interpretation of Keats's reaction to the remark—"Keats felt it *deeply* . . . he never forgave him"—has been called into question by recent biographers (see W. J. Bate, *John Keats,* Cambridge, Mass., 1963, pp. 265–268, and Gittings, *John Keats,* pp. 167–168).   **256 chuckling:** Clucking.   **320 genitors:** Progenitors.   **334 raft:** Archaic form of "reft," torn off.   **405–406 marble . . . Arabian:** Many characters are turned to stone in Arabian tales. Perhaps the reference is to the half-marble man in "The History of the Young King of the Black Isles" (in *The Arabian Nights Entertainments*).   **466 ff.:** Keats told his brothers in a letter of 23–24 January 1818, "Leigh Hunt . . . says the conversation is unnatural & too high-flown for the Brother & Sister. Says it should be simple forgetting . . . that they are both overshadowed by a Supernatural Power, & of force could not speak like Franchesca in the Rimini. He must first prove that Caliban's poetry is unnatural,—This with me completely overturns his objections" (*Letters,* I, 213–214).   **495 Dryope:** A nymph who was ravished by Apollo and later, with her infant son, was transformed into a lotus tree. This is not the same mythological figure as Dryope the mother of Pan in I.290.   **555 ditamy:** Dittany.   **756–760 nothing . . . dream:** Peona's words are echoed in Endymion's renunciation of dreams at IV.636–638.   **777–781:** In sending these revised lines to Taylor on 30 January 1818 Keats commented, "You must indulge me by putting this in for setting aside the badness of the other [the original version of the passage], such a preface is necessary to the Subject. The whole thing [Endymion's long speech beginning in 769] must I think have appeared to you, who are a consequitive Man, as a thing almost of mere words—but I assure you that when I wrote it, it was a regular stepping of the Imagination towards a Truth. My having written that Argument will perhaps be of the greatest Service to me of any thing I ever did—It set before me at once the gradations of Happiness even like a kind of Pleasure Thermometer—and is my first Step towards the chief Attempt in the Drama—the playing of different Natures with Joy and Sorrow" (*Letters,* I, 218–219). His earlier remarks to Bailey on 22 November 1817, declaring certainty about "the authenticity of Imagination," are relevant to both the "Argument" here and the concerns and action of Books I and IV more generally: "I am certain of nothing but of the holiness of the Heart's affections and the truth of Imagination—What the imagination seizes as Beauty must be truth —whether it existed before or not—for I have the same Idea of all our Passions as of Love they are all in their sublime, creative of essential Beauty—In a Word, you may know my favorite Speculation by my first book [of *Endymion*] and the little song I sent in my last [the first five stanzas of the song beginning at IV.146] —which is a representation from the fancy of the probable mode of operating in these Matters—The Imagination may be compared to Adam's dream [in *Paradise Lost* VIII.283–311 or 452–490]—he awoke and found it truth. . . . O for a Life of Sensations rather than of Thoughts! It is 'a Vision in the form of Youth' a Shadow of reality to come—and this consideration has further conv[i]nced me for it has come as auxiliary to another favorite Speculation of mine, that we shall enjoy ourselves here after by having what we called happiness on Earth repeated in a finer tone and so repeated. . . . Adam's dream will do here and seems to be a conviction that Imagination and its empyreal reflection is the same as human Life and its spiritual repetition" (*Letters*, I, 184–185).   **792 giant battle:** The war between the Titans and the Olympian gods (see the note below to IV.774).   **815 like . . . brood:** With the mother's own blood.   **862 Latona:** Mother of Diana and Apollo.   **866 outraught:** Stretched out, extended (archaic past participle of "outreach").

Book II.   6 pine: Cause to pine.   **13 close:** Union, embrace.   **22–23 owl . . . mast:** *"Plutarch* reports, that when *Themistocles* was consulting with the other Officers, upon the uppermost Deck of the Ship, and most of them opposed him, being unwilling to hazard a Battle, an Owl coming upon the Right side of the Ship, and lighting upon the Mast, so animated them, that they unanimously concurred with him, and prepared themselves for the Fight" (John Potter, *Archaeologia Graeca: or The Antiquities of Greece,* 1697–98; 5th ed., 1728, I, 326). **31–32 Hero . . . Imogen . . . Pastorella:** Heroines of Marlowe's *Hero and Leander,* Shakespeare's *Cymbeline,* and *The Faerie Queene* VI.ix–xii.   **60 pight:** Settled, alighted (archaic past participle of "pitch").   **253–254 The . . . England:** I.e., the poets.   **277 the . . . elf:** Ignis fatuus.   **282 raught:** Archaic past tense of "reach."   **298 chief:** Head, upper end.   **360 Arion:** Poet and musician of Lesbos who, when thrown overboard by sailors, was rescued by dolphins who had gathered around the ship to hear his music.   **374 clear:** Clearness, clear space or sky.   **396 coverlids:** Coverlets.   **443:** Ariadne is associated with Bacchus (see *Sleep and Poetry* 334–336) and therefore with wine.   **537 quell:** Power or means to quell; here specifically Cupid's bow (see II.584).   **579–584:** In some notes that he sent Milnes in March 1846 C. C. Clarke remarks, "I have often thought of that Sunday afternoon, when [Keats] read to Mʳ Severn and myself the description of the 'Bower of Adonis'; and the conscious pleasure with which he looked up when he came to the passage that tells the ascent of the car of Venus" (*KC,* II, 151).   **674 Hesperean:** Possibly westward (after Hesperus, which appears in the west), but more probably Keats intended the same meaning as "Hesperidean," in this context denoting a tread like that of someone in the garden of the Hesperides.   **689 those . . . seven:** The Pleiades.   **761 Ida:** The mountain near Troy where Paris awarded Venus the prize for beauty; here probably a metonym for Venus herself.   **854 turn:** Return.   **875 Alecto:** One of the Furies.   **885 snort:** "Eject or discharge through the nostrils with a snort" (*OED,* citing this passage); possibly a reference to the spouting of whales.   **938 her prayer:** For protection from Alpheus, in answer to which Diana changed the nymph Arethusa into a river.   **961 Oread-Queen:** Diana.

Book III.   1–21: Woodhouse noted in his interleaved *1818* that "K said, with much simplicity, 'It will be easily seen what I think of the present Ministers, by the beginning of the 3ᵈ Book.'"   **7–8 Fire . . . hopes:** See Judges 15:4–5.   **31 bourne:** "*Incorrectly* for: Realm, domain" (*OED,* citing this passage).   **70 spooming:** Foaming.   **71 Tellus:** The Earth, mother of Saturn and the other Titans. Keats is describing the weight of the (moon-caused) tides.   **192 An old man:** Glaucus, first named in III.400.   **218–225:** In a letter to Milnes of 7 May 1849 Bailey describes Keats's recitation of this passage "immediately after its composition": "I remember his upward look when he read of the 'magic ploughs'" (*KC,* II, 271).   **234, 255 Thou . . . man:** 2 Samuel 12:7.   **243 that giant:** Typhon.   **251 Sisters three:** The Fates.   **364 Æthon:** One of Apollo's horses.   **406:** Hercules, dying from the effects of a poisoned tunic, "wound up his story" on a funeral pyre on Oeta, a mountain rising between Thessaly and Macedonia.   **415 Æǽ's isle:** An island off the coast of Italy where Circe ("Phœbus' daughter" in 414) was born and also where she lived after she was expelled from Colchis.   **856 raught:** Reached.   **899–902:** According to some authorities, Glaucus was the son of Neptune and the sea nymph Nais.   **918 Cytherea:** Keats's error for "Cythera," the Greek island sacred to Venus. "Cytherea" (used correctly in II.492, III.975) is a name for Venus.   **1000 Doris:** Wife of Nereus and mother of the Nereides.

Book IV.   1–29: Keats copied these lines in a letter to Bailey of 28–30 October 1817 with the comment, "you will see from the Manner I had not an opportunity of mentioning any Poets, for fear of spoiling the effect of the passage by particularising them" (*Letters,* I, 172).   **15 Ausonia:** One of the ancient names of Italy.   **146–181:** See Keats's comment on these stanzas (as illustrating the creativity of passion) in the letter to Bailey, 22 November 1817, quoted above in the note to I.777–781.   **157 spry:** Obsolete form of "spray."   **424 Hours:** The Horae.   **441–442 He . . . sun:** Icarus.   **459 dædale:** Daedalian, cunning (here with the suggestion of artfully deceiving).   **485 throe:** Suffer throes.   **536 Semele:** Mother of Bacchus.   **576 latter-mint:** "? A late kind of mint" (*OED,* citing this passage).   **606 Danae's Son:** Perseus.   **685 dew-claw'd:** Woodhouse noted in his interleaved *1818,* "The dew-claw, is the small short claw in the back part of the animal's leg, above the foot."   **686 syrinx flag:** The reedlike plant that Syrinx was transformed into.   **713 Delphos:** Oracle.   **774 Thy . . . brother:** Apollo, the hero of *Hyperion,* who becomes "brother" (brother-in-law) upon the marriage of his sister Diana to Endymion. For other anticipations of *Hyperion* in the present poem see the last sentence of Keats's Preface and I.792, II.993–994, III.129–131, 993–994, IV.943, 956–957.   **929 father:** Apollo (as the sun).   **943 Titan's foe:** Jupiter.   **950 seemlihed:** Seemliness.   **989–993:** For the first two of these obstacles earlier in the poem, see II.777–781 (her "foolish fear"), and II.123–128, 293, 574–575,

III.297–299, 708, 759, 1023, IV.976, and *Letters*, I, 207, 213 ("decrees of fate"). The "unlook'd for change" that "spiritualizes" Endymion is most often taken to refer to his freeing of Glaucus and the dead lovers in Book III.

In drear nighted December

Written in December 1817; first published in the *Literary Gazette*, 19 September 1829.

7 glue: Prevent (by gluing).

Apollo to the Graces

Written perhaps early in 1818; first published in *TLS*, 16 April 1914. According to Woodhouse's heading in the W^2 transcript, the lines were composed to the tune of an air in a pantomime about Don Giovanni (*Harlequin's Vision, or, The Feast of the Statue*) that Keats had seen at Drury Lane in December 1817 and then reviewed in the *Champion* on 4 January 1818.

To Mrs. Reynolds's Cat

Written on 16 January 1818; first published in Thomas Hood's *The Comic Annual* (1830). Mrs. Reynolds was the mother of J. H. Reynolds and his four sisters.

1 grand climacteric: The sixty-third year of human life. Possibly Mrs. Reynolds' cat (through some weak joke based on 63 divided by 9 lives—see Bernard Richards, *N&Q*, June 1978, p. 225) is represented as having just completed its seventh year.

Lines on Seeing a Lock of Milton's Hair

Written on 21 January 1818; first published in *PDWJ*, 15 November 1838. In a letter to Bailey of 23 January, containing a copy of the poem, Keats explains, "I was at Hunt's the other day, and he surprised me with a real authenticated Lock of *Milton's Hair*. . . . This I did at Hunt's at his request—perhaps I should have done something better alone and at home" (*Letters*, I, 210, 212). Hunt's collection of locks of hair is now at the University of Texas at Austin.

35 vassal: Apparently Keats (perhaps misunderstanding "vassals of his anger" in *Paradise Lost* II.90) meant something like "manifestation" or "reminder"; there is no *OED* definition of "vassal" that fits the context here.

On Sitting Down to Read King Lear Once Again

Written on 22 January 1818; first published in *PDWJ*, 8 November 1838. Keats mentions the poem in a letter to Bailey of 23 January: "I sat down to read King Lear yesterday, and felt the greatness of the thing up to the writing of a Sonnet preparatory thereto" (*Letters*, I, 212). Later on the same day he copied the sonnet for his brothers with a more elaborate comment: "I think a little change has taken place in my intellect lately—I cannot bear to be uninterested or unemployed, I, who for so long a time, have been addicted to passiveness—Nothing is finer for the purposes of great productions, than a very gradual ripening of the intellectual powers—As an instance of this—observe—I sat down yesterday to read King Lear once again the thing appeared to demand the prologue of a Sonnet, I wrote it & began to read" (I, 214).

When I have fears that I may cease to be

Written toward the end of January 1818; first published in *1848*. For interpretive analysis see M. A. Goldberg, *Modern Language Quarterly*, 18 (1957), 125–131.

9 fair . . . hour: According to Woodhouse's W^2 notes, this is the same unidentified woman earlier described in *Fill for me a brimming bowl* and later addressed in *Time's sea hath been.*

Lines on the Mermaid Tavern

Written probably during the last week of January 1818 (see Leonidas M. Jones, *ELN,* 15 [1978], 186–188); first published in *1820*. The Mermaid Tavern, in Cheapside, is supposed to have been a frequent resort of Shakespeare, Jonson, Beaumont, Fletcher, and other dramatists. See Keats's comment on "the old Poets" in the letter to Reynolds quoted below in the note to *Robin Hood.*

12 bowse: Drink, tipple ("Sup" earlier in the line also means to drink).

O blush not so! O blush not so

Written probably on 31 January 1818 (drafted or copied in a letter to Reynolds of that date); first published in Forman's edition of 1883. This may be one of the poems that Brown later described to Milnes as being "of an exceptionable kind . . . written and copied for the purpose of preventing the young blue-stocking ladies from asking for the loan of [Keats's] MS Poems" (*KC,* II, 103).

Hence burgundy, claret, and port

Written in a letter to Reynolds on 31 January 1818; first published in *1848*. Keats tells Reynolds, "I purposed to write to you a serious poetical Letter. . . . Yet I cannot write in prose, It is a sun-shiny day and I cannot so here goes"—and then writes the present poem and *God of the meridian* (*Letters,* I, 220).

11 Caius: Reynolds' pseudonymous signature in three articles that he published in the *Yellow Dwarf* in February 1818.

God of the meridian

Written on 31 January 1818; first published in *1848*.

1 God . . . meridian: Apollo (at the end of the preceding poem, which this immediately follows in the letter to Reynolds).

Robin Hood

Written at the beginning of February 1818; first published in *1820*. Keats was responding to two sonnets on Robin Hood that Reynolds had recently sent him (they were subsequently published in the *Yellow Dwarf* on 21 February 1818 and reprinted in Reynolds' *The Garden of Florence*, 1821). In a letter of 3 February, after some remarks on the egotism of modern poets, Keats tells Reynolds, "I don't mean to deny Wordsworth's grandeur & Hunt's merit, but I mean to say we need not be teazed with grandeur & merit—when we can have them uncontaminated & unobtrusive. Let us have the old Poets, & robin Hood Your letter and its sonnets gave me more pleasure than will the 4th Book of Childe Harold & the whole of any body's life & opinions. In return . . . I have gathered a few Catkins [the present poem and *Lines on the Mermaid Tavern*]. . . . I hope you will like them they are at least written in the Spirit of Outlawry" (*Letters*, I, 224–225).

30 pasture: Probably intended to mean "pastured" or "pastoral" (*OED* does not recognize the word as an adjective).   **34 song of Gamelyn:** The medieval *Tale of Gamelyn*.   **36 "grenè shawe":** Chaucer's *The Friar's Tale* 86 ("grene-wode shawe" in modern texts, III [D].1386, but "grene shawe" in the editions of Keats's time).

Welcome joy, and welcome sorrow

Written in 1818; first published in *1848*. The epigraph (perhaps a quotation from memory) is based on *Paradise Lost* II.898 ff.:

> For Hot, Cold, Moist, and Dry, four champions fierce,
> Strive here for mast'ry, and to battle bring
> Their embryon atoms; they around the flag
> Of each his faction, in their several clans,
> Light-armed or heavy, sharp, smooth, swift or slow,
> Swarm populous. . . .

Time's sea hath been five years at its slow ebb

Written on 4 February 1818; first published in *Hood's Magazine*, September 1844. In a note added to his clerk's transcript Woodhouse says that the addressee was a "Lady whom [Keats] saw for some few moments at Vauxhall"; other notes in W^2 further identify her as the same woman described in *Fill for me a brimming bowl* and alluded to in *When I have fears* 9–10.

To the Nile

Written on 4 February 1818, in a sonnet-writing competition with Shelley and Hunt; first published in *PDWJ*, 19 July 1838. According to Woodhouse's note in W^2, the poems were to be done in fifteen minutes; "K. & [Shelley] had theirs ready within the time—Leigh Hunt remained up till 2 oClock in the Morning before his was finished." Shelley's sonnet (beginning "Month after month the gathered rains descend") was first published in the *St. James's Magazine,* March 1876; Hunt's ("It flows through old hushed Egypt and its sands") first appeared in his *Foliage* volume (1818).

Spenser, a jealous honorer of thine

Written on 5 February 1818; first published in *1848.*
7 quell: Bow (see *God of the golden bow* 1 and the note to *Endymion* II.537).

Blue! —'Tis the life of heaven — the domain

Written on 8 February 1818; first published in *1848.* The poem is a response to the concluding lines of Reynolds' sonnet *Sweet poets of the gentle antique line* (later published in *The Garden of Florence,* 1821): "dark eyes are dearer far / Than orbs that mock the hyacynthine-bell."

O thou whose face hath felt the winter's wind

Written on 19 February 1818; first published in *1848.* In a letter to Reynolds containing this unrhymed sonnet Keats extols at length a state of "delicious diligent Indolence," and then says, "I was led into these thoughts . . . by the beauty of the morning operating on a sense of Idleness—I have not read any Books—the Morning said I was right—I had no Idea but of the Morning and the Thrush said I was right—seeming to say—" The poem immediately follows, after which Keats adds, "Now I am sensible all this is a mere sophistication, however it may neighbour to any truths, to excuse my own indolence" (*Letters,* I, 231–233).

Extracts from an Opera

Written in 1818; first published in *1848.* The opera, if there ever was one, has not been identified.

Four seasons fill the measure of the year

Written at Teignmouth in the second week of March 1818; first published in Leigh Hunt's *Literary Pocket-Book* for 1819 (1818). In a letter containing the sonnet, 13 March, Keats tells Bailey,

> I am sometimes so very sceptical as to think Poetry itself a mere Jack a lanthern to amuse whoever may chance to be struck with its brilliance— As Tradesmen say every thing is worth what it will fetch, so probably every mental pursuit takes its reality and worth from the ardour of the pursuer—being in itself a nothing—Ethereal thing[s] may at least be thus real, divided under three heads . . . Things real—such as existences of Sun Moon & Stars and passages of Shakspeare—Things semireal such as Love, the Clouds &c which require a greeting of the Spirit to make them wholly exist—and Nothings which are made Great

and dignified by an ardent pursuit. . . . I have written a Sonnet here of a somewhat collateral nature. (*Letters,* I, 242–243)

For there's Bishop's Teign

Written at Teignmouth in a letter to Haydon on 21 March 1818; first published in Tom Taylor's *Life of Benjamin Robert Haydon* (1853). The opening line and 2, 3, 7, and 13 are based on the names of various places near Teignmouth—Bishopsteignton, Kingsteignton, Combeinteignhead, Arch Brook, and Wildwoods Point and Copse. "Larch Brook" (8), if there was such a stream, is no longer identifiable.

19 Newton Marsh: In Keats's time the marshes at the head of the Teign estuary extended inland to what is now the center of the town of Newton Abbot. The "level" described in 21–24 was probably either the central area of Newton Abbot now used as a recreation ground and car park (not far from the present Market Street) or the ground now occupied by the racecourse (northwest of the railway sidings). R. S. Sincock, Secretary of the Teignbridge District Council, who supplied these details in a letter to the present editor in 1975, adds that "spear grass harsh" (20) still grows in the region.   **25 barton:** Farmland.   **35 plight:** Attire.   **36 spike:** An ear of grain.   **39 dack'd hair'd:** Keats frequently wrote "a" for "o" in his MSS, and may have intended "dock'd hair'd" (short-haired).

Where be ye going, you Devon maid

Written at Teignmouth in a letter to Haydon on 21 March 1818; first published in Tom Taylor's *Life of . . . Haydon* (1853).

Over the hill and over the dale

Written at Teignmouth on 23 or 24 March 1818 (the annual fair at Dawlish, three miles north of Teignmouth, was this year held on the 23rd); first published in Amy Lowell's biography, 1925 (lines 1–4 earlier in *1848*).
5 Rantipole: Wild, disorderly, rakish.   **16 venus:** Slang term for prostitute.

Dear Reynolds, as last night I lay in bed

Written at Teignmouth on 25 March 1818; first published in *1848*. Reynolds was ill in London, and Keats sent him these lines, as he says in the prose accompanying them, "In hopes of cheering you through a Minute or two": "you will excuse the unconnected subject, and careless verse—You know, I am sure, Claude's Enchanted Castle and I wish you may be pleased with my remembrance of it" (*Letters,* I, 263). The first sixty-six lines describe a series of ridiculous and fantastic dreams that Keats says he had the previous night; a middle paragraph (67–85) comments on the relationship between such dreamings and one's daytime awareness and concerns; a third section (86–105) tells of a vision the poet has had of nature's cruelty, "an eternal fierce destruction"; and the concluding lines (105–

113) dismiss the whole as "Moods of one's mind." All critics relate 20–22 to similar images more than a year later in *Ode on a Grecian Urn;* the feelingful lines on imagination (76–85), which mark a midpoint in Keats's development from the realm of Flora and old Pan in the poems of 1816–1817 to the "nobler life" of the poems of 1819, have specific connections with both that ode and *Ode to a Nightingale.* For interpretive discussion see Albert Gérard, *K-SJ,* 11 (1962), 17–29 (the essay is reprinted in revised form in Gérard's *English Romantic Poetry,* pp. 215–236); Walter H. Evert, *Aesthetic and Myth in the Poetry of Keats,* pp. 194–211; Mary Visick, *K-SJ,* 15 (1966), 87–98; Stuart M. Sperry, *ELH,* 36 (1969), 562–574 (also Sperry's *Keats the Poet,* pp. 117–131); and David Luke, *SEL,* 19 (1979), 661–672.

10 Miss Edgeworth: The novelist Maria Edgeworth (1767–1849).   **11 Junius Brutus:** Probably the actor Junius Brutus Booth (1796–1852).   **11 so so:** Slang term for tipsy.   **20–22:** The details come not from Titian (19) but from Claude's *Landscape with the Father of Psyche Sacrificing at the Milesian Temple of Apollo* (reproduced from an engraving in Ian Jack, *Keats and the Mirror of Art,* Plate XXXV, following p. 220), which Keats could have seen exhibited at the British Institution in the spring of 1816 (according to Sidney Colvin, *John Keats,* 1917, p. 264, it was hung next to Titian's *Europa*).   **26 the . . . Castle:** Keats probably knew Claude's *The Enchanted Castle* (described in 26–66) from the 1782 engraving by François Vivares and William Woollett (reproduced in Jack, Plate XII, facing p. 128).   **29 Urganda:** An enchantress in the fifteenth-century *Amadis of Gaul* (available in Southey's translated abridgment, 1803).   **34 Merlin's hall:** In Ariosto's *Orlando furioso* XXXIII.3 ff.   **42 santon:** Holy man.   **44 Cuthbert . . . Aldebrim:** Probably a name that Keats made up, though S. R. Swaminathan, *N&Q,* September 1974, pp. 333–334, points out some possible connections with an historical Cuthbert (of Lindisfarne) as described in Scott's *Marmion.*   **88 lampit:** Scottish spelling of "limpet."   **110 Tom the same:** His brother Tom (at this time with Keats at Teignmouth) was ill with tuberculosis.   **111 new romance:** Presumably a reference to *Isabella.*   **112 centaine dose:** A hundred(-line) dose.   **113 "here . . . prose":** *Twelfth Night* II.v.142.

To J. R.

Written perhaps in April 1818; first published in *1848.* J. R. was James Rice, a friend whom Keats had met a year earlier through Reynolds.

Isabella

Written in London and Teignmouth in February–April 1818; first published in *1820.* Keats and Reynolds had together planned a volume of versified stories from Boccaccio's *Decameron,* a project probably suggested by a remark of Hazlitt in a lecture on 3 February 1818: "[Dryden's] Tales have been, upon the whole, the most popular of his works; and I should think that a translation of some of the other serious tales in Boccaccio and Chaucer, as that of Isabella . . . could not fail to succeed in the present day" (*The Complete Works of William Hazlitt,* ed. P. P. Howe, 1930–1934, V, 82). After first seeing *Isabella* in October 1818, however, Reynolds withdrew from the collaboration, telling Keats that "I give over all intention and you ought to be alone. I can never write anything now—my mind is taken the other way" (*Letters,* I, 377); when he subsequently published two versified stories of his own in *The Garden of Florence* (1821), he explained in the Advertisement that "illness on [Keats's] part, and distracting engagements on mine, prevented us from accomplishing our plan at the time."

According to Woodhouse's note in W^2, Keats's specific source for the story was the fifth edition (1684) of a 1620 English translation perhaps by John Florio, *The Novels and Tales of the Renowned John Boccacio* (Fifth Novel, Fourth Day), pp. 182–185, a relatively innocent and somewhat romanticized version that sets the events in Messina rather than Florence, gives Isabella three brothers rather than two, and assigns no motive for the murder other than that Lorenzo was "a trusty Factor or Servant" and that the lovers' devotion to each other "was altogether against [the brothers'] liking." Nine extracts from the translation are given in the notes below (each of the last eight immediately follows the preceding extract; taken together, the passages constitute about nine-tenths of the complete text). It will be seen that a great many of the narrative details in Keats's poem and almost all of the dialogue, as well as his comments on unhappy lovers (89–104), his characterization of the brothers (105–144), his apology to Boccaccio (145–160), the stanzas linking love and selfishness (233–248), the stanzas of "wormy circumstance" (353–360, 385–392), and the apostrophes to Melancholy and the other personifications (433–448, 481–488), have no counterpart in this source.

In his review of *1820* (in the *New Times,* 19 July 1820), Charles Lamb called *Isabella* "The finest thing in the volume," and Matthew Arnold and the Pre-Raphaelites also praised it highly, but Keats himself was dissatisfied. After a recent meeting with the poet, Woodhouse told Taylor on 19 September 1819 that Keats "said he could not bear [*Isabella*] now. It appeared to him mawkish" (*Letters,* II, 162). Three days later, on the 22nd, Keats further explained his feelings in a letter to Woodhouse: "I will give you a few reasons why I shall persist in not publishing The Pot of Basil—It is too smokeable. . . . There is too much inexperience of [life], and simplicity of knowlege in it—which might do very well after one's death—but not while one is alive. There are very few would look to the reality. . . . Isabella is what I should call were I a reviewer 'A weak-sided Poem' with an amusing sober-sadness about it. . . . If I may so say, in my dramatic capacity I enter fully into the feeling: but in Propria Persona I should be apt to quiz it myself" (II, 174). Woodhouse never relinquished his own good opinion of the poem (*KC,* I, 79; *Letters,* II, 162), possibly in part because he had himself, in the course of making four transcripts of it, contributed to the final wording of some thirty or more of its lines.

In the present century, writers on Keats have generally not found a great deal to admire in it; standard procedure has been to condemn its sentimentality, mawkishness, and vulgarity (all the qualities we call Huntian), then to praise Keats's idealization of the lovers in the first half of the poem and the strength of some of the descriptive stanzas in the latter half, and finally to label the poem transitional and rush on to *The Eve of St. Agnes, Hyperion,* and the odes. The most recent criticism, however, focusing on realistic and even antiromantic elements, as well as the narrator's posture as "modern" reteller of an old story that he considers, in Boccaccio's original, too simple and naive for his own time, has made the poem more compatible with the serious shorter pieces of the winter and spring of 1818 and more logically a precursor of the later narratives and lyrics. See in particular Stillinger, *The Hoodwinking of Madeline*, pp. 31–45; Billy T. Boyar, *K-SJ*, 21–22 (1972–73), 160–169; and Louise Z. Smith, *SIR*, 13 (1974), 299–311.

1–88: Keats's source, after a short paragraph introducing the teller of the story, begins as follows: "In *Messina* there dwelt three young men, Brethren, and Merchants by their common Profession, who becoming very Rich by the death of their Father, lived in very good fame and repute. . . . [They] had a Sister named *Isabella*, young, beautiful, and well condition'd; who upon some occasion, as yet remained unmarryed. A proper youth, being a Gentleman born in *Pisa*, and named *Lorenzo*, as a trusty Factor or Servant, had the managing of the Brethrens business and affairs. This *Lorenzo* being of comely personage, affable, and excellent in his behaviour, grew so gracious in the Eyes of *Isabella*, that she afforded him many respective looks, yea kindnesses of no common quality. Which *Lorenzo* taking notice of, and observing by degrees from time to time, gave over all Beauties in the City, which might allure any Affection from him, and only fixed his Heart on her, so that their love grew to a mutual embracing, both equally respecting one another, and entertaining kindnesses, as occasion gave leave."   **95 Theseus' spouse:** Ariadne.   **107 swelt:** Swelter.   **124 lazar stairs:** Stairs in a lazar hospital.   **150 ghittern:** A type of guitar.   **161–172:** Keats's source goes on: "Long time continued this Amorous League of Love, yet not so cunninly concealed, but at length the secret meeting of *Lorenzo* and *Isabella*, to ease their poor Souls of Loves oppressions, was discovered by the Eldest of the Brethren, unknown to them who were thus betrayed. He being a man of great discretion, although this sight was highly displeasing to him: yet notwithstanding he kept it to himself till the next morning, labouring his brain what might best be done in so urgent a case. When day was come, he resorted to his Brethren, and told them what he had seen. . . . Many deliberations passed on in this case; but after all, thus they concluded together, to let it proceed on with patient supportance, that no scandal might ensue to them or their Sister, no evil Act being (as yet) committed. And seeming as if they knew not of their Love, had a wary Eye still upon her secret walks, awaiting for some convenient time, when without their own prejudice, or *Isabellaes* knowledge, they might safely break off this stolen Love, which was altogether against their liking."   **177–228:** Source: "So, shewing no worse Countenance to *Lorenzo*, than formerly they had done, but employing and conversing with him in kind manner; it fortuned, that riding (all three) to recreate themselves out of the City, they took *Lorenzo*, in their company, and when they came to a solitary place, such as suited best with their vile purpose: they ran suddenly upon *Lorenzo*, slew him, and afterward enterr'd his Body, where hardly it could be discover'd by any one. Then they returned back to *Messina*, and gave it forth (as a credible Report) that they had sent him abroad about their Affairs, as formerly they were wont to do: which every one verily believed, because they knew no reason why they should conceit any otherwise."   **233–261:** Source: "*Isabella*, living in expectation of his return, and perceiving his stay to her was so offensive long: made many demands to her Brethren, into what parts they had sent him, that his tarrying was so quite from all wonted course. Such was her importunate speeches to them, that they taking it very discontentedly, one of them returned her this frowning Answer. What is your meaning Sister, by so many questionings after *Lorenzo*? What urgent Affairs have you with him, that makes you so impatient upon his Absence? If hereafter you make any more Demands for him, we shall shape you such a Reply, as will be but little to your liking. At these harsh words *Isabella* fell into abundance of Tears, where-among she mingled many Sighs and Groans, such as were able to overthrow a far greater constitution: so that being full of fear and dismay, yet no way distrusting her Brethrens so wicked and hainous a cruel deed; she durst not question any more after him." **262 Hinnom's vale:** In 2 Kings 23:10 and 2 Chronicles 28:3. **273–322:** Source: "In the silence of dark Night, as she lay afflicted in her Bed, oftentimes would she call for *Lorenzo*, entreating his speedy return to her. And then again, as if he had been present with her, she checkt and reproved him for his long Absence. One Night among the rest, she being grown almost hopeless, of ever seeing him again, having a long while wept and grievously lamented; her senses and faculties utterly spent and tyred, that she could not utter any more Complaints, she fell into a Trance or Sleep, and dreamed that the Ghost of *Lorenzo* appeared unto her, in torn and unbefitting Garments, his looks pale, meager, and starving, and (as she thought) thus spake to her. My dear Love *Isabella*, thou dost nothing but torment thy self, with calling on me, accusing me for overlong tarrying from thee: I am come therefore to let thee know, that thou canst not enjoy my Company any more, because the very same day when last thou sawest me, thy Brethren most bloodily murther'd me. And acquainting her with the place where they had buryed his mangled body, he strictly charged her not to call him at any time afterward, and so vanished away." **328–408:** Source: "The Young Damosel awaking, and giving some credit to her Vision, sighed and wept exceedingly; and after she was risen in the Morning, not daring to say any thing to her Brethren, she resolutely determined to go see the place formerly appointed her, only to make tryal, if that which she seemed to see in her Sleep, should carry any likely-hood of Truth. Having obtained favour of her Brethren, to ride a days journey from the City, in company of her trusty Nurse, who long time had attended on her in the house, and knew the secret passages of her Love: they rode directly to the designed place, which being covered with some store of dryed leaves, and more deeply sunk than any other part of the Ground thereabout, they digged not far, but they found the body of the murthered *Lorenzo*, as yet very little corrupted or impaired, and then perceived the truth of her Vision. . . . Gladly would she have carryed the whole body with her, secretly to bestow honourable Enterment on it, but yet exceeded the compass of her Ability. Wherefore, in regard she could not have all, yet she would be possessed of a part, and having brought a keen Razor with her, by help of the Nurse, she divided the Head from the Body, wrapped it up in a Napkin, which the Nurse conveyed into her Lap, and then laid the Body in the Ground again. Thus being undiscovered by any, they departed thence, and arrived at home in convenient time, where being alone by themselves in the Chamber: she washed the Head over and over with her tears, and bestowed infinite kisses thereon." **393 Perséan sword:** The sword with which Perseus in a single blow severed the Medusa's head.   **397:** A reference to the heading of Boccaccio's story in the English translation: "The Fifth Novel. / Wherein is plainly proved, That Love cannot be rooted up, by any Humane Power or Providence; especially in such a Soul, where it hath been really apprehended."   **409–432:** Source: "Not long after, the Nurse having brought her a large Earthen Pot, such as we use to set Basile, Marjoram, Flowers, or other sweet Hearbs in; and shrowding the Head in a Silken Scarf, putting it into the Pot, covering it with Earth, and planting divers Roots of excellent Basile therein, which she never watered but either with her Tears, Rosewater, or water distilled from the Flowers of Oranges. This Pot she used continually to sit by, either in her Chamber, or any where else: for she carryed it always with her. . . . So long she held on in this mourning manner, that, what by the continual watering of the Basile, and putrefaction of the Head, so buried in the Pot of Earth; it grew very flourishing, and most odoriferous to such as scented it, that as no other Basile could possibly yield so sweet a savour."   **432 leafits:** Leaflets.   **452–480:** Source: "The Neighbours noting this behaviour in her, observing the long continuance thereof, how much her bright Beauty was defaced, and the Eyes sunk into her Head by incessant weeping, made many kind and friendly motions, to understand the reason of her so violent oppressions. . . . Her Brethren also waxed weary of this cariage in her; and having very often reprov'd her for it, without any other alteration in her: at length, they closely stole away the Pot of Basile from her, for which she made infinite woful lamentations. . . . Perceiving that she could not have the Pot again, she fell into an extreme Sickness, occasioned only by her ceaseless weeping; and never urged she to have any thing, but the restoring of the Basile-Pot. Her Brethren grew greatly amazed thereat . . . and thereupon were very desirous to ransack the Pot to the very bottom. Having emptied out all the Earth, they found the Scarf of Silk, wherein the Head of *Lorenzo* was wrapped; which was (as yet) not so much consumed, but by the Locks of Hair, they knew it to be *Lorenzo's* Head. . . . Fearing lest their offence might come to open publication, they buried it very secretly; and before any could take notice thereof, they departed from *Messina,* and went to dwell at *Naples.*"   **489–504:** Source: "*Isabella* crying and calling still for her Pot of Basile, being unable to give over Mourning, dyed within a few days after. . . . Within no long while after, when this Accident came to be publickly known, an excellent Ditty was composed thereof, beginning thus: *Cruel and unkind was the Christian, / That rob'd me of my Basiles bliss,* &c."

Mother of Hermes! and still youthful Maia

Written at Teignmouth on 1 May 1818; first published in *1848.* In sending a copy of the lines to Reynolds on 3 May, Keats comments: "With respect to the affections and Poetry you must know by a sympathy my thoughts that way; and I dare say these few lines will be but a ratification: I wrote them on May-day—and intend to finish the ode all in good time" (*Letters,* I, 278). The addressee of the fragment, Maia, was one of the Pleiades and mother of Mercury (Hermes) by Jupiter.   **3 Baiæ:** Presumably a reference to Tasso (see the note to *To Charles Cowden Clarke* 29), though Keats may have been primarily concerned to find a rhyme with "Maia" in 1.   **5 earlier Sicilian:** A reference to Theocritus and the other earliest known pastoral poets.

To Homer

Written in 1818; first published in *1848*. For explication see Thomas Cook, *K-SJ*, 11 (1962), 8–12.

Give me your patience, sister, while I frame

Written at Wythburn, Cumberland, in a letter to George and Georgiana Keats on 27 June 1818; first published in the New York *World*, 25 June 1877. Keats had recently begun a walking tour with Brown through the Lake District and Scotland. The initial letters of the lines spell the new name of Georgiana Wylie, who had married George Keats a month earlier. The couple at this time were en route to settle in America, and Keats's original letter containing these lines, addressed to them at Liverpool, never reached them. As he explains in a letter to them of September 1819, in which he recopied the lines: "On looking over some Letters I found the one I wrote intended for you from the foot of Helvellyn to Liverpool —but you had sail'd and therefore It was returned to me. It contained among other nonsense an Acrostic of my Sister's name—and a pretty long name it is. I wrote it in a great hurry which you will see. Indeed I would not copy it if I thought it would ever be seen by any but yourselves" (*Letters*, II, 195).

Sweet, sweet is the greeting of eyes

Written at Keswick in a letter to George and Georgiana Keats on 28 June 1818; first published in Amy Lowell's biography, 1925.

On Visiting the Tomb of Burns

Written at Dumfries on 1 July 1818; first published in *1848*. Keats comments in a letter to his brother Tom, "Burns' tomb is . . . not very much to my taste, though on a scale, large enough to show they wanted to honour him. . . . This Sonnet I have written in a strange mood, half asleep. I know not how it is, the Clouds, the sky, the Houses, all seem anti Grecian & anti Charlemagnish" (*Letters*, I, 309). For interpretive discussion see J. C. Maxwell, *K-SJ*, 4 (1955), 77–80, and George Yost, Jr., *JEGP*, 57 (1958), 220–229.

Old Meg she was a gipsey

Written at Auchencairn, Kirkcudbrightshire, in a letter to Fanny Keats on 3 July 1818; first published in *PDWJ*, 22 November 1838. Brown, who had told Keats about Meg Merrilies, the old gypsy in Scott's *Guy Mannering*, on their walk from Dalbeattie to Auchencairn before breakfast on the 3rd, records in his "Life" of Keats that the poet "was much interested in the character. There was [a] little spot, close to our path-way,—'There', he said, in an instant positively realising a creation of the novellist, 'in that very spot, without a shadow of doubt, has old Meg Merrilies often boiled her kettle!' It was among pieces of rock, and brambles, and broom, ornamented with a profusion of honeysuckle, wild roses, and foxglove, all in the very blush and fullness of blossom" (*KC*, II, 61).

25 Margaret Queen: Probably Margaret of Anjou, wife of Henry VI (in Shakespeare's *Henry VI*).   **28 chip hat:** A hat made of thin strips of wood or wood fiber.

There was a naughty boy

Written at Kirkcudbright in a letter to Fanny Keats on 3 July 1818; first published in Forman's edition of 1883. Keats describes this as "a song about myself" and comments after the last line, "My dear Fanny I am ashamed of writing you such stuff, nor would I if it were not for being tired after my days walking" (*Letters*, I, 312, 315).

76 Tittlebat: A variant form of "stickleback."

Ah! ken ye what I met the day

Written at Ballantrae, Ayrshire, on 9 or 10 July 1818; first published in Forman's edition of 1883. Keats tells his brother Tom in a letter of the 10th, "The reason for my writing these lines was that Brown wanted to impose a galloway song upon dilke [Brown's old schoolfellow, Charles Wentworth Dilke]—but it wont do— The subject I got from meeting a wedding just as we came down into this place [Ballantrae]" (*Letters*, I, 328).

2 owre: Over.   **3 craggis:** Apparently an invented form for the plural of "crag."   **5 goud:** Gold.   **5 yeve:** Give.   **35 daffed:** Daunted.

To Ailsa Rock

Written at Girvan, Ayrshire, on 10 July 1818; first published in Leigh Hunt's *Literary Pocket-Book* for 1819 (1818). Keats had first seen Ailsa Rock on the preceding day and describes his reaction in a letter to Tom Keats containing a copy of the poem: "we had a gradual ascent and got among the tops of the Mountains whence In a little time I descried in the Sea Ailsa Rock 940 feet hight—it was 15 Miles distant and seemed close upon us—The effect of ailsa with the peculiar perspective of the Sea in connection with the ground we stood on, and the misty rain then falling gave me a complete Idea of a deluge—Ailsa struck me very suddenly—really I was a little alarmed." After copying the poem, he says, "This is the only Sonnet of any worth I have of late written" (*Letters*, I, 329, 330).

8 coverlid: Coverlet.

This mortal body of a thousand days

Written in the cottage in which Burns was born, at Ayr, on 11 July 1818; first published in *1848*. Keats twice comments on the poem in letters to Reynolds and Tom Keats on the 13th: "We went to the Cottage and took some Whiskey—I wrote a sonnet for the mere sake of writing some lines under the roof—they are so bad I cannot transcribe them—The Man at the Cottage was a great Bore with his Anecdotes—I hate the rascal. . . . The flat dog made me write a flat sonnet"; "We drank some Toddy to Burns's Memory with an old Man who knew Burns—damn him—and damn his Anecdotes—he was a great bore. . . . I was determined to write a sonnet in the Cottage—I did—but it is so bad I cannot venture it here" (*Letters*, I, 324–325, 332; see also I, 343). In his "Life" of Keats Brown adds that the "conversion [of the cottage] into a whiskey-shop, together with its drunken landlord, went far towards the annihilation of his poetic power" (*KC*, II, 62).

All gentle folks who owe a grudge

Written at Cairndow, Argyllshire, on 17 July 1818; first published in Forman's edition of 1883. Keats explains in a letter to Tom Keats containing the poem (probably the original draft) that he has "just been bathing in Loch fine a saltwater Lake . . . quite pat and fresh but for the cursed Gad flies—damn 'em they have been at me ever since I left the Swan and two necks [in London]" (*Letters*, I, 334).

21 Lowther: Either William Lowther (1787–1872), later the second Earl of Lonsdale, or his brother Henry Cecil Lowther (1790–1867), both of whom were at this time Tory M.P.'s for Westmorland. Keats had been distressed three weeks earlier when, upon inquiring after Wordsworth at Bowness on Windermere, he was told that the older poet had been canvassing for the Lowthers' reelection (see *Letters*, I, 299).   **30, 32:** "Mr. D——" and "Mr. V——" have never been satisfactorily identified. The references may be to Joseph Dykes Ballentine Dykes (d. 1830) and Sir Frederick Fletcher Vane (1760–1832), property owners who were active in the Westmorland election of July 1818 (see *The Letters of William and Dorothy Wordsworth: The Middle Years*, Part II, p. 466 and nn.).   **40 Mister Lovels:** Lovel, the hero of Scott's *The Antiquary*.   **44 wert:** Archaic spelling of "wart."   **46–47 seven . . . pray'd:** See Psalm 119:164.

Of late two dainties were before me plac'd

Written on 17 or 18 July 1818 (Keats saw Augustus von Kotzebue's *The Stranger* at Inveraray, Argyllshire, on the evening of the 17th and wrote this sonnet about the performance either that night or the next day); first published in the *Athenaeum*, 7 June 1873. Keats describes the occasion in a letter to Tom Keats containing the poem:

> On ente[r]ing Inverary we saw a Play Bill—Brown was knock'd up from new shoes—so I went to the Barn alone where I saw the Stranger accompanied by a Bag pipe—There they went on about 'interesting creaters' and 'human nater'—till the Curtain fell and then Came the Bag pipe—When Mrs Haller [the heroine of the play] fainted down went the Curtain and out came the Bagpipe—at the heartrending, shoemending reconciliation the Piper blew amain—I never read or saw

this play before; not the Bag pipe, nor the wretched players themselves were little in comparison with it—thank heaven it has been scoffed at lately almost to a fashion. (*Letters*, I, 336–337)

14 Mumchance: Silent, tongue-tied.

There is a joy in footing slow across a silent plain

Written in July 1818; first published in the *Examiner*, 14 July 1822 (lines 1–6, 25–26, 41–48 earlier in the *New Monthly Magazine*, March 1822). In a letter to Bailey on the 22nd, in which he copied these lines, Keats characterizes them as "cousin-german to the Circumstance" that produced *This mortal body* on the 11th, and says that he composed them "a few days afterwards" (*Letters*, I, 344, 343). In the earliest extant holograph the piece is titled, "Lines written in the highlands after a visit to Burns's Country."

Not Aladdin magian

Written between 24 and 26 July 1818 (Keats visited Fingal's Cave on the island of Staffa on the 24th and either drafted or, more probably, copied the poem in a letter to Tom Keats on the 26th); first published in the *Western Messenger* (Louisville, Ky.), July 1836. Keats describes Staffa and Fingal's Cave in the letter to Tom as follows:

> One may compare the surface of the Island to a roof—this roof is supported by grand pillars of basalt standing together as thick as honey combs The finest thing is Fingal's Cave—it is entirely a hollowing out of Basalt Pillars. Suppose now the Giants who rebelled against Jove had taken a whole Mass of black Columns and bound them together like bunches of matches—and then with immense Axes had made a cavern in the body of these columns—of course the roof and floor must be composed of the broken ends of the Columns—such is fingal's Cave except that the Sea has done the work of excavations and is continually dashing there—so that we walk along the sides of the cave on the pillars which are left as if for convenient Stairs—the roof is arched somewhat gothic wise and the length of some of the entire side pillars is 50 feet—About the island you might seat an army of Men each on a pillar—The length of the Cave is 120 feet and from its extremity the view into the sea through the large Arch at the entrance—the colour of the colums is a sort of black with a lurking gloom of purple therin—For solemnity and grandeur it far surpasses the finest Cathedrall.

After drafting or copying the poem he adds, "I am sorry I am so indolent as to write such stuff as this—it cant be help'd" (*Letters*, I, 348–349, 351). Brown calls the poem "a fragment . . . which I never could induce him to finish" (*KC*, II, 63).

3 Wizard . . . Dee: Perhaps Merlin, but more probably Keats was drawing on

Lycidas 55, "Nor yet where Deva spreads her wizard stream" ("wizard" because the Dee's changes of flow were supposed to be good or bad omens for England and Wales).   **5–7 St. John . . . seven:** In Revelation 1:4, 9, 11, 20.   **26 funeral minstrelsy:** Specifically Milton's famous elegy. Keats may have chosen Lycidas as his speaker because of the speculation that his bones were "hurled . . . beyond the stormy Hebrides" (*Lycidas* 155–156).   **50–52:** Keats wrote to Tom Keats from Oban on 21 July 1818, "Staffa . . . is a fashionable place and therefore every one concerned with it either in this town or the Island are what you call up [i.e., well-to-do]. . . . this irritated me and Brown was not best pleased" (*Letters*, I, 339).

Read me a lesson, Muse, and speak it loud

Written on the top of Ben Nevis on 2 August 1818; first published in *PDWJ*, 6 September 1838. Brown says in his "Life" that "When on the summit of this mountain, we were enveloped in a cloud, and, waiting till it was slowly wafted away, [Keats] sat on the stones, a few feet from the edge of that fearful precipice, fifteen hundred feet perpendicular from the valley below, and wrote this sonnet" (*KC*, II, 63; see also Keats's description of the mountain in *Letters*, I, 352–354).

Upon my life, Sir Nevis, I am piqu'd

Written at Letterfinlay, Inverness-shire, in a letter to Tom Keats on 3 August 1818; first published in Forman's edition of 1883. Keats introduces the dialogue by explaining that "there was one Mrs Cameron of 50 years of age and the fattest woman in all inverness shire who got up this Mountain [Ben Nevis] some few years ago—true she had her servants but then she had her self—She ought to have hired Sysiphus. . . . 'T is said a little conversation took place between the mountain and the Lady—After taking a glass of Wiskey as she was tolerably seated at ease she thus begun" (*Letters*, I, 354).   **2 reek'd:** Perspired.   **4 bate:** Stop for rest (probably an archaic form of "bait" rather than the aphetic form of "abate").   **66 snub:** Perhaps (from its use in "snub nose") intended to mean something like "nuzzle."   **74:** Keats adds in the letter to Tom, after the final line, "But what surprises me above all is how this Lady got down again—I felt it horribly—'T was the most vile descent" (*Letters*, I, 357).

On Some Skulls in Beauley Abbey, near Inverness

Written jointly by Keats and Brown early in August 1818 (they arrived at Inverness on the 6th, and Keats sailed for London on the 8th), or possibly some weeks or even months later; first published in the *New Monthly Magazine*, January 1822. According to Woodhouse (who got the information from Keats and recorded it in a now lost transcript printed by Colvin, *John Keats*, pp. 553–556), Keats was responsible for line 1, the first four words of 2, and all of 7–12, 43–48, and 55–60. The first epigraph is from Wordsworth's sonnet *"Beloved Vale!" I said, "when I shall con,"* 7–9 (the text of 1807–1820, which Wordsworth revised to a different wording after Keats's death); the second is from *Richard III*, I.iv.33. Lines 6–16 refer to the Reformation in general, but the events are not specifically associated with Beauly Priory, which was founded in 1230 and was handed over to the sixth Lord Lovat toward the end of the sixteenth century.

61 "undivulged crime": *King Lear* III.ii.52.

Nature withheld Cassandra in the skies

Translated from Ronsard on or shortly before 21 September 1818; first published in *1848*. The lines are based on the second sonnet in *Le Premier Livre des amours*, which Keats read in the text that first appeared in the seventh collected edition of Ronsard's *Oeuvres* in 1587:

> Nature ornant Cassandre qui devoit
> De sa douceur forcer les plus rebelles,
> La composa de cent beautez nouvelles
> Que dés mille ans en espargne elle avoit.
>
>   De tous les biens qu'Amour au ciel couvoit
> Comme un tresor cherement sous ses ailes,
> Elle enrichit les graces immortelles
> De son bel œil, qui les Dieux esmouvoit.
>
>   Du Ciel à peine elle estoit descendue
> Quand je la vey, quand mon ame esperdue
> En devint folle, & d'un si poignant trait
>
>   Amour coula ses beautez en mes veines,
> Qu'autres plaisirs je ne sens que mes peines,
> Ny autre bien qu'adorer son pourtrait.

> (*Les Oeuvres de Pierre de Ronsard: Texte de 1587,* ed. Isidore Silver, Chicago and Paris, 1966–1970, I, 72)

In a letter to Reynolds in which he copied the lines Keats calls his work "a free translation" and explains, "I had not the original by me when I wrote it, and did not recollect the purport of the last lines" (*Letters*, I, 371).

Fragment of Castle-builder

Written in 1818; lines 24–71 first published in *1848,* and 1–23 first in *TLS*, 16 April 1914. "Castle-builder" may be a private reference to Brown ("C. B.").

4, 9 Convent Garden: The original name of the London district now called Covent Garden (once the convent garden of St. Peter's, Westminster), in Keats's time notable for its market and theater.   **22–23:** A reference to the French army's retreat from Moscow in 1812.   **54 "Mene . . . Upharsin":** The handwriting on the wall in Daniel 5:25.   **67 Salvator:** Salvator Rosa (1615–1673), Italian landscape painter.

And what is Love?—It is a doll dress'd up

Written in 1818; first published in *1848*.

15–16 that . . . melted: Cleopatra is said to have toasted Antony with a pearl dissolved in acid.

'Tis the "witching time of night"

Written in a letter to George and Georgiana Keats on 14 October 1818; first published in the *Ladies' Companion* (New York), August 1837. Keats introduces the lines by saying, "If I had a prayer to make for any great good, next to Tom's recovery, it should be that one of your Children should be the first American Poet. I have a great mind to make a prophecy and they say prophecies work out their own fullfillment" (*Letters*, I, 398). Georgiana was at this time pregnant with their first child, Georgiana Emily Keats, born early in 1819.

1 "witching . . . night": *Hamlet* III.ii.388.   **20–21 linnen . . . tree:** Keats's errors (linen comes from flax, and cotton does not grow on trees).

Where's the Poet? Show him! show him

Written in 1818; first published in *1848*. Most scholars who comment on the fragment connect it with Keats's "camelion Poet" letter to Woodhouse of 27 October 1818 (*Letters*, I, 386–388).

Fancy

Written toward the end of 1818; first published in *1820*. In copying them out for his brother and sister-in-law on 2 January 1819, Keats calls this poem and the next one "specimens of a sort of rondeau which I think I shall become partial to—because you have one idea amplified with greater ease and more delight and freedom than in the sonnet" (*Letters*, II, 26). In *1820* the lines immediately follow *Ode to Psyche*, which mentions "the gardener Fancy" (cultivating "some untrodden region" of the speaker's mind) in the last stanza.

81 Ceres' daughter: Proserpine.   **82 God of Torment:** Pluto.

Bards of passion and of mirth

Written toward the end of 1818; first published (under the heading "Ode") in *1820*. In sending the poem to his brother and sister-in-law (see the note to the preceding piece), Keats explains that "it is on the double immortality of Poets" (*Letters*, II, 25). The only extant holograph version is written in an edition of Jonson, Beaumont, and Fletcher, on a blank page facing the beginning of *The Fair Maid of the Inn;* the "Poets" that Keats had in mind may be specifically Beaumont and Fletcher.

Spirit here that reignest

Written perhaps in 1818; first published in *1848*.

I had a dove, and the sweet dove died

Written at the end of December 1818 or the beginning of January 1819; first published in *1848*. In copying it for George and Georgiana Keats on 2 January 1819, Keats calls the poem "a little thing I wrote off to some Music as it was playing" (*Letters*, II, 27).

Hush, hush, tread softly, hush, hush, my dear

Written in 1818; first published in *Hood's Magazine*, April 1845. J. H. Reynolds' youngest sister, Charlotte, told H. B. Forman that Keats "was passionately fond of music, and would sit for hours while she played the piano to him. It was to a Spanish air which she used to play that the song 'Hush, hush! tread softly!' was composed" (Forman's preface to his edition of 1883, I, xxix–xxx). An anonymous writer in the *Athenaeum*, 15 October 1859, p. 505, reviewing "The Autumn Opera Season in Paris," offhandedly remarks that Keats wrote the song to a tune by Daniel Steibelt (1765–1823) but without identifying the specific composition. Robert Gittings, *John Keats: The Living Year* (1954), pp. 57–60, and *The Mask of Keats* (1956), pp. 45–53, argues that it dramatizes an affair, or at least a meeting, between Keats and Mrs. Isabella Jones, a friend of Taylor and other members of the Keats circle (she apparently is the Hastings "Lady" mentioned in *Letters*, I, 402–403, II, 65). Perhaps the poem served several purposes at once (see Bate's comment, *John Keats*, p. 382 n.).

Ah! woe is me! poor Silver-wing

Written in 1818 or 1819; first published in *PDWJ*, 25 October 1838. The poem is headed "Faery Song" in Brown's transcript, and "Faery Dirge" in the *PDWJ* text (which Brown supplied).

The Eve of St. Agnes

Drafted mainly or entirely at Chichester and Bedhampton during the last two weeks of January and perhaps also the first few days of February 1819, and revised at Winchester in September; first published in *1820*. In a contemporary source, Henry Ellis' 1813 revision of John Brand's *Observations on Popular Antiquities*, I, 32, St. Agnes (whose feast is celebrated on 21 January and whose eve therefore is the 20th) is described as

> a Roman virgin and martyr, who suffered in the tenth persecution under the Emperor Dioclesian, A. D. 306. She was condemned to be debauched in the public stews before her execution, but her virginity was miraculously preserved by lightning and thunder from Heaven. About eight days after her execution, her parents going to lament and pray at her tomb, they saw a vision of angels, among whom was their daughter, and a lamb standing by her as white as snow, on which account it is that in every graphic representation of her, there is a lamb pictured by her side.

On the eve of her day many kinds of divination are practised by virgins to discover their future husbands.

According to Woodhouse's note in W^2, the poem was written at the suggestion of Isabella Jones, but we do not know whether she merely proposed the general subject—Keats told Bailey on 14 August 1819 that the poem was "on a popular superstition" (*Letters,* II, 139)—or provided Keats with specific details of the plot as well. The "popular superstition" was the ritual of "fasting St. Agnes' Fast," for which Ellis in the 1813 work cited above quotes references in Jonson's masque *Entertainment . . . at Althrope* 74–77, Aubrey's *Miscellanies,* and Burton's *Anatomy of Melancholy;* an expanded edition of 1848 adds several others, including the following from an undated chapbook entitled *Mother Bunch's Closet Newly Broke Open:*

> On that day thou must be sure that no man salute thee, nor kiss thee; I mean neither man, woman, nor child, must kiss thy lips on that day; and then, at night, before thou goest into thy bed, thou must be sure to put on a clean shift, and the best thou hast, then the better thou mayst speed. And when thou liest down, lay thy right hand under thy head, saying these words, *Now the god of Love send me my desire;* make sure to sleep as soon as thou canst, and thou shalt be sure to dream of him who shall be thy husband, and see him stand before thee, and thou wilt take great notice of him and his complexion, and, if he offers to salute thee, do not deny him.

Keats's revision of the poem—in particular his rewriting of 314–322 to make the sexual consummation more explicit—shocked Woodhouse and drew a very strong reaction from Taylor. Woodhouse told Taylor about the changes in a letter of 19–20 September 1819:

> [Keats] had the Eve of St A. copied fair: He has made trifling alterations, inserted an additional stanza early in the poem [see the note below to 54/55] to make the *legend* more intelligible, and correspondent with what afterwards takes place, particularly with respect to the supper & the playing on the Lute.—he retains the name of Porphyro—has altered the last 3 lines to leave on the reader a sense of pettish disgust, by bringing Old Angela in (only) dead stiff & ugly.—He says he likes that the poem should leave off with this Change of Sentiment—it was what he aimed at, & was glad to find from my objections to it that he had succeeded. . . . There was another alteration [see the note below to 314–322], which I abused for "a full hour by the *Temple* clock." You know if a thing has a decent side, I generally look no further—As the Poem was $orig^y$ written, *we* innocent ones (ladies & myself) might very well have supposed that Porphyro, when acquainted with Madeline's love for him, & when "he arose, Etherial flush^d &c &c (turn to it) set himself at once to persuade her to go off with him, & succeeded & went over the "Dartmoor black" (now changed for some other place) to be married, in right

honest chaste & sober wise. But, as it is now altered, as soon as M. has confessed her love, P. winds by degrees his arm round her, presses breast to breast, and acts all the acts of a bonâ fide husband, while she fancies she is only playing the part of a Wife in a dream. This alteration is of about 3 stanzas; and tho' there are no improper expressions but all is left to inference, and tho' profanely speaking, the Interest on the reader's imagination is greatly heightened, yet I do apprehend it will render the poem unfit for ladies, & indeed scarcely to be mentioned to them among the "things that are."—He says he does not want ladies to read his poetry: that he writes for men—& that if in the former poem there was an opening for doubt what took place, it was his fault for not writing clearly & comprehensibly—that he sh^d despise a man who would be such an eunuch in sentiment as to leave a maid, with that Character about her, in such a situation: & sho^d despise himself to write about it &c &c &c—and all this sort of Keats-like rhodomontade. (*Letters,* II, 162–163)

Taylor wrote back to Woodhouse on 25 September:

This Folly of Keats is the most stupid piece of Folly I can conceive. . . . I don't know how the Meaning of the new Stanzas is wrapped up, but I will not be accessary (I can answer also for H[essey] I think) towards publishing any thing which can only be read by Men. . . . As it is, the flying in the Face of all Decency & Discretion is doubly offensive from its being accompanied with so preposterous a Conceit on his part of being able to overcome the best founded Habits of our Nature.—Had he known truly what the Society and what the Suffrages of Women are worth, he would never have thought of depriving himself of them.—So far as he is unconsciously silly in this Proceeding I am sorry for him, but for the rest I cannot but confess to you that it excites in me the Strongest Sentiments of Disapprobation—Therefore . . . if he will not so far concede to my Wishes as to leave the passage as it originally stood, I must be content to admire his Poems with some other Imprint, & in so doing I can reap as much Delight from the Perusal of them as if they were our own property, without having the disquieting Consideration attached to them of our approving, by the "Imprimatur," those Parts which are unfit for publication. (*Letters,* II, 182–183)

From this correspondence and Woodhouse's cryptic sentence in his note in W^2, "K. left it to his Publishers to adopt which [readings] they pleased, & to revise the Whole," it is clear that the *1820* text, a composite of original and revised MS readings along with some new readings not in any MS, is the joint product of Keats's writing and Woodhouse's and Taylor's editing, and that some of the editorial changes from the revised text were made by the publishers against the poet's wishes.

Apart from the above, there are only a few brief comments on the poem in the extant letters. On 22 September 1819, remarking on a weakness in *Isabella*—"in my dramatic capacity I enter fully into the feeling: but in Propria Persona I should be apt to quiz it myself"—Keats told Woodhouse that "There is no objection of this kind to Lamia—A good deal to St Agnes Eve—only not so glaring" (*Letters,* II, 174). And on 17 November he mentions a wish "to diffuse the colouring of St Agnes eve throughout a Poem in which Character and Sentiment would be the figures to such drapery—Two or three such Poems, if God should spare me, written in the course of the next six years, would be a famous gradus ad Parnassum altissimum" (II, 234). In March 1820 he liked it well enough to want it printed as the opening piece in *1820* (II, 276), though ultimately that position was given to *Lamia.*

Modern interpretation of the poem may be said to begin with Earl R. Wasserman, *The Finer Tone: Keats' Major Poems* (Baltimore, 1953), pp. 97–137, and Stillinger, *Studies in Philology,* 58 (1961), 533–555 (the essay is reprinted in revised form in *The Hoodwinking of Madeline,* pp. 67–93), the one taking a metaphysical view of the goings on, relating them to passages in Keats's letters about the authenticity of imagination and human life as a "Mansion of Many Apartments" (*Letters,* I, 184–185, 280–281), the other taking a more down-to-earth view, with emphasis on Madeline as self-deluded dreamer, "Hoodwink'd with faery fancy" (70) in the superstitious ritual she is practicing. Much of the more recent criticism has attempted to mediate between these extremes. See in particular C. F. Burgess, *English Journal,* 54 (1965), 389–394; Marian H. Cusac, *K-SJ,* 17 (1968), 113–119; Stuart M. Sperry, *SIR,* 10 (1971), 27–43 (also Sperry's *Keats the Poet,* pp. 198–220); Allan Danzig, ed., *Twentieth Century Interpretations of "The Eve of St. Agnes"* (Englewood Cliffs, N.J., 1971); G. Douglas Atkins, *Tennessee Studies in Literature,* 18 (1973), 113–132; Michael Ragussis, *ELH,* 42 (1975), 378–394 (the essay is revised in Ragussis' *The Subterfuge of Art,* Baltimore, 1978, pp. 70–84); Gail M. Gibson, *K-SJ,* 26 (1977), 39–50; Leon Waldoff, *JEGP,* 76 (1977), 177–194; Constance Rooke, *English Studies in Canada,* 4 (1978), 25–40; and David Wiener, *K-SJ,* 29 (1980), 120–130.

54/55: The revised text has an additional stanza at this point:

> 'Twas said her future lord would there appear
> Offering, as sacrifice—all in the dream—
> Delicious food, even to her lips brought near,
> Viands, and wine, and fruit, and sugar'd cream,
> To touch her palate with the fine extreme
> Of relish: then soft music heard, and then
> More pleasures follow'd in a dizzy stream
> Palpable almost: then to wake again
> Warm in the virgin morn, no weeping Magdalen.

71 lambs unshorn: A reference to the traditional offering of lambs' wool at the altar on St. Agnes' Day, to be spun and woven by the nuns (see 115–117).   **133 brook:** Apparently intended to mean "prevent" or "hold back" (there is no definition in the *OED* that covers Keats's use of the word in this context).   **170–171:** None of the recorded stories of Merlin fits the specific details of the allusion here. Since Merlin and "his Demon" are categorized as "lovers" (170), Keats must have been thinking of some aspect of Merlin's betrayal and perpetual imprisonment by his mistress, the Lady of the Lake (sometimes called Nimue or Vivien).   **261:** Keats told Clarke that this line "came into my head when I remembered how I used to listen in bed to your music at school" (Clarke, *Recollections of Writers,* p. 143).   **292 "La . . . mercy":** The title of a poem by Alain Chartier (c. 1385–1433), the English translation of which, under the same title, was in Keats's time sometimes attributed to Chaucer. Here, however, as in his own *La Belle Dame* written three months later, Keats was simply making use of the title; Chartier's "ancient ditty" is more than twice the length of *The Eve of St. Agnes.*   **314–322:** The revised text substitutes the following:

> See, while she speaks his arms encroaching slow,
> Have zoned her, heart to heart,—loud, loud the dark winds blow!

> For on the midnight came a tempest fell;
> More sooth, for that his quick rejoinder flows
> Into her burning ear: and still the spell
> Unbroken guards her in serene repose.
> With her wild dream he mingled, as a rose
> Marrieth its odour to a violet.
> Still, still she dreams, louder the frost wind blows,

353 dragons: It is not clear whether Keats meant mythical monsters or soldiers ("dragon" was a variant spelling of "dragoon").

The Eve of St. Mark

Written between 13 and 17 February 1819; first published in *1848.* Keats copied out 1–114 in a letter to his brother and sister-in-law on 20 September 1819 with the following introduction: "Some time since I began a Poem call'd 'the Eve of St Mark quite in the spirit of Town quietude. I th[i]nk it will give you the sensation of walking about an old county Town in a coolish evening. I know not yet whether I shall ever finish it—I will give it far as I have gone. *Ut tibi placent!*" After the text he adds, "I hope you will like this for all its Carelessness" (*Letters,* II, 201, 204).

St. Mark's feast is celebrated on 25 April (and therefore his eve is the 24th). Various commentators beginning with D. G. Rossetti have suggested that Keats intended to develop the poem in accordance with the popular superstition of "watching St. Mark's Eve," which Henry Ellis explains in his 1813 revision of Brand's *Observations on Popular Antiquities,* I, 166:

> It is customary in Yorkshire . . . for the common people to sit and watch in the church porch on St. Mark's Eve, from eleven o'clock at night till one in the morning. The third year (for this must be done thrice), they are supposed to see the ghosts of all those who are to die the next year, pass by into the church. When any one sickens that is thought to have been seen in this manner, it is presently whispered about that he

will not recover, for that such, or such an one, who has watched St. Mark's Eve, says so.

This superstition is in such force, that, if the patients themselves hear of it, they almost despair of recovery. Many are said to have actually died by their imaginary fears on the occasion.

There is nothing of this in the poem as it stands, but Keats did recount the superstition in a separate fragment written on the reverse side of a preliminary draft of the present poem's 99–114:

> Gif ye wol stonden hardie wight—
> Amiddes of the blacke night—
> Righte in the churche porch, pardie
> Ye wol behold a companie
> Appouchen thee Full dolourouse
> For sooth to sain from everich house
> Be it in City or village
> Wol come the Phantom and image
> Of ilka gent and ilka carle
> Whom coldè Deathè hath in parle
> And wol some day that very year
> Touchen with foulè venìme spear
> And sadly do them all to die—
> Hem all shalt thou see verilie—
> And everichon shall by thee pass
> All who must die that year Alas

For diverse interpretations of the poem, and in particular of why Bertha is a "poor cheated soul" (69), see Walter E. Houghton, *ELH,* 13 (1946), 64–78, and Stillinger, *The Hoodwinking of Madeline,* pp. 94–98. Oddly, Keats appears to be recalling this Bertha in *The Jealousies* 370 ff.; see the note below to 519 of that poem.   **33 Aaron's breastplate:** In Exodus 28:4, 15–30; Leviticus 8:8.   **33–34 the . . . heaven:** Revelation 1:12–13, 20, 2:1.   **35 winged Lion:** The traditional emblem of St. Mark (derived from Revelation 4:7–8).   **36–38 Covenantal . . . Cherubim:** Exodus 25:10–22; Hebrews 9:4–5.   **38 golden mice:** 1 Samuel 6:4, 11, 18.   **81 av'davat:** An Indian songbird.   **99–114:** In his letter copy for George and Georgiana, Keats pauses between 98 and 99 to comment, "What follows is an imitation of the Authors in Chaucer's time—'t is more ancient than Chaucer himself and perhaps betwe[e]n him and Gower" (*Letters,* II, 204).   **99 Als:** Also.   **101 hir . . . hem:** Their, them.   **105 Gif:** If.   **107 croce:** Cross.   **112 Somdel:** Somewhat.   **117 holy shrine:** St. Mark's Basilica, in Venice.

Why did I laugh tonight? No voice will tell

Written in March 1819 (before the 19th); first published in *1848.* Keats included the poem in a letter to his brother and sister-in-law with the following comment:

I am ever affraid that your anxiety for me will lead you to fear for the violence of my temperament continually smothered down: for that reason I did not intend to have sent you the following sonnet—but look over the last two pages [of the letter] and ask yourselves whether I have not that in me which will well bear the buffets of the world. It will be the best comment on my sonnet; it will show you that it was written with no Agony but that of ignorance; with no thirst of any thing but knowledge when pushed to the point though the first steps to it were throug[h] my human passions—they went away, and I wrote with my Mind—and perhaps I must confess a little bit of my heart.

After copying the poem Keats adds, "I went to bed, and enjoyed an uninterrupted sleep—Sane I went to bed and sane I arose" (*Letters*, II, 81–82).

When they were come unto the Faery's court

Written in a letter to George and Georgiana Keats on 15 April 1819 (Keats calls it "a little extempore"—*Letters*, II, 85); lines 1–17 first published in *Macmillan's Magazine*, August 1888, and a complete text first in Forman's supplementary volume, *Poetry and Prose by John Keats*, 1890.

   14 Otaheitan: "Otaheite" (see also 79) is a former name of Tahiti.   **80 'Aye . . . king':** *King Lear* IV.vi.107.   **80 'Fortune's fool':** *Romeo and Juliet* III.i.136.   **96:** Keats breaks off after this line with the comment, "Brown is gone to bed—and I am tired of rhyming" (*Letters*, II, 88).

As Hermes once took to his feathers light

Written in April 1819 (on or shortly before the 16th); first published in the *Indicator*, 28 June 1820. Keats copied the poem in a letter to his brother and sister-in-law with the following introductory remarks:

> The fifth canto of Dante [the *Inferno*, which Keats read in H. F. Cary's translation] pleases me more and more—it is that one in which he meets with Paulo and Francesca—I had passed many days in rather a low state of mind and in the midst of them I dreamt of being in that region of Hell. The dream was one of the most delightful enjoyments I ever had in my life—I floated about the whirling atmosphere as it is described with a beautiful figure to whose lips mine were joined [as] it seem'd for an age—and in the midst of all this cold and darkness I was warm—even flowery tree tops sprung up and we rested on them sometimes with the lightness of a cloud till the wind blew us away again—I tried a Sonnet upon it—there are fourteen lines but nothing of what I felt in it—o that I could dream it every night. (*Letters*, II, 91)

Character of C. B.

Written on 16 April 1819; first published in *1848*. The lines are an ironic portrayal of Brown, who, as Keats explains in a letter containing them, "this morning is writing some spenserian stanzas against Mrs Miss Brawne and me; so I shall amuse myself with him a little: in the manner of Spenser." After the last line he adds, "This character would ensure him a situation in the establishment of patient Griselda" (*Letters,* II, 89, 90). **20 Tipping the wink:** Warning or signaling with a wink. **21 olden Tom . . . ruin blue:** Two kinds of gin. **22 nantz:** A kind of brandy (after Nantes, in France, the place of manufacture). **26–27:** See Isaiah 3:16.

Bright star, would I were stedfast as thou art

Written in 1819; first published in *PDWJ,* 27 September 1838. Keats made a copy of this sonnet (in a volume of Shakespeare's *Poetical Works,* opposite the beginning of *A Lover's Complaint*) when he was aboard ship on his way to Italy at the end of September or the beginning of October 1820, and for a long time it was known by the mistaken heading that Milnes gave it in *1848,* "Keats's Last Sonnet." For interpretive discussion see Martin Kallich, *Forum* (Ball State University), 5 (Winter 1964), 11–16, and David Ormerod, *K-SJ,* 16 (1967), 73–77.

Hyperion

Begun in the closing months of 1818 (perhaps by 27 October and certainly by 17 December) and abandoned in or before April 1819 (Woodhouse copied the poem as we now have it on 20 April, and about the same time noted in his interleaved *1818,* opposite *Endymion* IV.774, "*April 1819.* K. lent me the Fragment here alluded to for perusal. . . . He said he was dissatisfied with what he had done of it; and should not complete it"); first published in *1820.*

Keats had the poem in mind for a year or more before he began writing it. He alludes to the Titans several times in *Endymion* and specifically in IV.774 (drafted in November 1817) and at the end of the printed Preface (April 1818) openly announces his intention to do the later poem. He presumably refers to *Hyperion* in speaking of "a new Romance which I have in my eye for next summer" in a letter to Haydon of 28 September 1817 (*Letters,* I, 168), and first mentions it by name, again to Haydon, on 23 January 1818: "in Endymion I think you may have many bits of the deep and sentimental cast—the nature of *Hyperion* will lead me to treat it in a more naked and grecian Manner—and the march of passion and endeavour will be undeviating—and one great contrast between them will be— that the Hero of the written tale [Endymion] being mortal is led on, like Buonaparte, by circumstance; whereas the Apollo in Hyperion being a fore-seeing God will shape his actions like one" (I, 207). His remarks to C. W. Dilke on 20 September 1818, "I am obliged to write, and plunge into abstract images," and to Reynolds a few days later, "I have relapsed into those abstractions which are my only life" (I, 369, 370), are sometimes taken to mean that he had then begun writing the poem; there is also the mention of "cogitating on the Characters of saturn and Ops" in a letter to Woodhouse of 27 October (I, 387). But the earliest unambiguous evidence of actual composition appears in a letter to George and Georgiana Keats on 18 December ("I went on a little with it last night"—II, 12), and subsequent references in the letters, from 22 December to the following 8 March, are mainly comments on *not* writing it (see II, 14–15, 18, 21, 42, 62). There is a four-week hiatus in Keats's productivity between the middle of March 1819 (*Why did I laugh*) and the middle of April (*When they were come unto the Faery's court*), and it is possible that he wrote some sizable portion of *Hyperion* during that period. But the terminal dating, like that of the beginning, remains a matter of speculation. We know only that he gave up the poem by 20 April (though he of course took it up again in writing *The Fall of Hyperion* a few months later).

The legend of the overthrow of the Titans by the Olympian gods was available in the same works of Greek mythology that supplied the basic materials for *Endymion,* and, just as in the earlier long mythological poem, most of the specific details and the characterizations and speeches are original with Keats. But the thematic intent is much less clear in *Hyperion,* and there are several interpretive problems that continue to cause difficulties—the question of where Keats's sympathy lies in the struggle between the Titans and the Olympians; some apparent inconsistency concerning who has power over whom, and why; the significance of the many comparisons made between divine and human affairs; and especially the relationship of the deification of Apollo in Book III to the war between the gods that is the main subject of Books I and II. Some of these matters are fundamental to the structure of the work, and it may have been his own uncertainty concerning one or more of them that led Keats to abandon the effort in the first place.

He did not want the fragment published; according to the Advertisement following the title page in *1820,* "it was printed at [the publishers'] particular request, and contrary to the wish of the author." It was, however, the most highly regarded of his works at publication and throughout the nineteenth century, and it has continued to attract readers and critics. Virtually every major Keats scholar has written on the work. Bate, *John Keats,* pp. 388–417, provides especially valuable general treatment; Evert, *Aesthetic and Myth in the Poetry of Keats,* pp. 225–243, offers a convincing explanation of why Keats abandoned the fragment; Brian Wilkie, *Romantic Poets and Epic Tradition* (Madison and Milwaukee, 1965), pp. 145–187, has the most comprehensive discussion in print taking the fragment as a unified whole. Among more recent studies, see Helen E. Haworth, *SEL,* 10 (1970), 637–649; Geoffrey H. Hartman, *EC,* 24 (1974), 1–20 (the essay is reprinted in Hartman's *The Fate of Reading,* Chicago, 1975, pp. 57–73, 319–320); Nancy M. Goslee, *PQ,* 53 (1974), 205–219, and *K-SJ,* 30 (1981), 118–151; Pierre Vitoux, *SIR,* 14 (1975), 165–183; Michael Ragussis, *The Subterfuge of Art,* pp. 35–69; Paul Sherwin, *PMLA,* 93 (1978), 383–395; and Anya Taylor, *SEL,* 19 (1979), 673–687. See also the note to *The Fall of Hyperion,* below.

Book I.   1–7: In a letter to Milnes of 7 May 1849 Bailey uses this passage to illustrate Keats's "principle of melody in Verse . . . particularly in the management of open & close vowels. . . . Keats's theory was, that the vowels should be so managed as not to clash one with another so as to mar the melody,—& yet that they should be interchanged, like differing notes of music to prevent monotony" (*KC,* II, 277).   **1 vale:** In his copy of *Paradise Lost* that he later gave to Mrs. Dilke Keats underscored I.321 ("To slumber here, as in the vales of Heaven") and commented in the margin, "There is a cool pleasure in the very sound of vale. The english word is of the happiest chance. Milton has put vales in heaven and hell with the very utter affection and yearning of a great Poet. It is a sort of delphic Abstraction—a beautiful—thing made more beautiful by being reflected and put in a Mist" (*The Romantics on Milton*, ed. J. A. Wittreich, Jr., Cleveland, 1970, p. 554).   **23 one:** Thea, wife of Hyperion.   **61 reluctant:** In his copy of *Paradise Lost* Keats underscored IV.58–59 ("reluctant flames, the sign / Of wrath awaked") and commented, " 'Reluctant' with its original and modern meaning combined and woven together, with all its shades of signification has a powerful effect" (*The Romantics on Milton*, p. 559). The "original" (literal) meaning of the word is "struggling."   **147 The . . . three:** Saturn's sons, Jupiter, Neptune, and Pluto.   **216 Hours:** The Horae.   **246 Tellus:** The Earth, mother of the Titans (see I.20–21).   **274 colure:** The colures are "two great circles which intersect each other at right angles at the poles, and divide the equinoctial and the ecliptic into four equal parts" (*OED*). Keats got the word from *Paradise Lost* IX.66.   **307 Cœlus:** Another name for Uranus (the Sky), father of the Titans.   **323 first-born:** Saturn.   **326 wox:** Archaic past tense of "wax."

Book II.   4 Cybele: Wife of Saturn and mother of the Olympian gods (see II.389); she is called by another of her names, Ops, in II.78, 113.   **29 straying . . . world:** Explained in III.50–79.   **39 shroud:** Archaic past participle (= "shrouded").   **45 plashy:** "Marked as if splashed with colour" (*OED*, citing this passage).   **70 that . . . war:** The war of the Giants against the Olympian gods (see the note below to III.136).   **161 engine:** "Find engines or instruments for" (*OED*, citing this passage).   **232 God . . . Seas:** Neptune.   **244 poz'd:** Probably intended to mean "puzzled," "baffled," but the word is also interpretable as "affected," "feigned."   **252 O Father:** Clymene is a daughter of the preceding speaker, Oceanus.   **281–289:** Joseph Severn told Milnes in a letter of 6 October 1845 that a "beautifull air of Glucks . . . furnishd the groundwork of the coming of Apollo in Hyperion" (*KC*, II, 133).   **376:** According to Lemprière's *Classical Dictionary*, Memnon's statue (the "image" of 374) "had the wonderful property of uttering a melodious sound every day, at sun-rising, like that which is heard at the breaking of the string of a harp when it is wound up. This was effected by the rays of the sun when they fell upon it. At the setting of the sun, and in the night, the sound was lugubrious."

Book III.   29 Giant . . . Sun: Hyperion.   **31–32 mother . . . sister:** Latona and Diana.   **46 Goddess:** Mnemosyne.   **81–82 while . . . syllables:** According to some rough notes written by Woodhouse in 1820, Keats "said, that he has often not been aware of the beauty of some thought or expr^n until after he has composed & written it down— It has then struck him with astonishm^t—& seemed rather the prod^n of another person than his own— He has wondered how he came to hit upon it. This was the case with the descr^n of Apollo in the 3 b. of Hyp^n white melodious throat. . . . Such Keats s^d was his Sensation of astonishm^t & pleasure when he had prod^d the lines 'His white melod^s &c— It seemed to come by chance or magic—to be as it were something given to him" (*KC*, I, 129). Critics frequently take the passage in question to be Apollo's speech in 82–120, but Woodhouse's words make it fairly clear that he was referring to the specific bit of description in 81–82 preceding the speech.   **136:** Woodhouse noted in his interleaved *1818*, in connection with some extracts that he copied

from Book II, "The poem, if completed, would have treated of the dethronement of Hyperion, the former God of the Sun, by Apollo—and incidentally of
Oceanus by Neptune, of Saturn by Jupiter &c and of the war of the Giants for
Saturn's reestablishment—with other events, of which we have but very dark
hints in the Mythological poets of Greece & Rome. In fact, the incidents would
have been pure creations of the Poet's brain."

La Belle Dame sans Merci

Written in a letter to George and Georgiana Keats on 21 or 28 April 1819; first
published in the *Indicator,* 10 May 1820. Keats took his title, but practically
nothing else, from a medieval work by Alain Chartier (see the note above to *The
Eve of St. Agnes* 292). For the poem itself scholars have proposed a considerable
array of sources in Spenser, Shakespeare, Burton, and other Renaissance writers,
H. F. Cary's translation of Dante, several specific ballads (e.g., *Thomas the Rhymer*)
as well as the ballad tradition in general, and a number of contemporary writers.
The Faerie Queene is the work most often cited—Duessa's seduction of the Red
Cross Knight in I.ii (especially stanzas 28–30, 45), Arthur's dream of the Faerie
Queene in I.ix.13–15, the encounter of Phaedria and Cymochles in II.vi.2–18,
the story of the false Florimel in III–IV (Keats mentions this last character in his
spring journal letter just two pages before the draft of *La Belle Dame*)—and much
has been made of some passages in Burton's *Anatomy of Melancholy* (Part I, Sect.
III, mem. i, subs. 2, 3) describing persons suffering certain symptoms of melancholy:

> As *Bellerophon* in *Homer* . . .
>
> > That wandered in the woods sad all alone,
> > Forsaking men's society, making great moan;
>
> they delight in floods & waters, desert places, to walk alone in orchards,
> gardens, private walks, back-lanes, averse from company. . . . *they are
> much given to weeping, and delight in waters, ponds, pools, rivers, fishing, fowl-
> ing, &c.* . . . they are pale of colour, slothful, apt to sleep, heavy; *much
> troubled with head-ache* . . . .

For this one poem, as an illustration of the kinds of connection that can be made
between Keats's phrasings and earlier works, the notes below give a sampling of
what used to be called "echoes and borrowings" (for the most part they are here
echoed and borrowed from the scholarship of Ernest de Selincourt, C. L. Finney,
Robert Gittings, Douglas Bush, and Miriam Allott). As Kenneth Muir and F. W.
Bateson point out, in an important statement that applies to Keats's sources more
generally (*EC,* 4 [1954], 432–440), some of these citations are of questionable or
doubtful usefulness, and in any case they represent merely some of the possible
literary sources; the nonliterary sources—which most probably include something of Keats's feelings about Fanny Brawne, the recent experience of Tom
Keats's death, some serious thinking about poetry and the nature of human life
(the famous "vale of Soul-making" speculations occur only a few pages later in

the same journal letter), and a great many other things that we know nothing about—are of course much more difficult to pin down.

One possible literary source that is not widely cited is Joseph Addison's illustration, in the third of the *Spectator* papers on "The Pleasures of the Imagination" (No. 413, 24 June 1712), of what happens when the qualities of color, light, and shade are removed from our perception of nature:

> We are every where entertained with pleasing Shows and Apparitions, we discover imaginary Glories in the Heavens, and in the Earth, and see some of this Visionary Beauty poured out upon the whole Creation; but what a rough unsightly Sketch of Nature should we be entertained with, did all her Colouring disappear, and the several Distinctions of Light and Shade vanish? In short, our Souls are at present delightfully lost and bewildered in a pleasing Delusion, and we walk about like the Enchanted Hero of a Romance, who sees beautiful Castles, Woods and Meadows; and at the same time hears the warbling of Birds, and the purling of Streams; but upon the finishing of some secret Spell, the fantastick Scene breaks up, and the disconsolate Knight finds himself on a barren Heath, or in a solitary Desert.

Keats certainly read this passage, and since Addison is describing a hypothetical failure of imagination, one might be tempted to class Keats's knight with other dreamers in the poems whose imaginary experiences are not wholly successful—to think of him, say, as a Madeline abandoned (rather than finally rescued?) by Porphyro or as a Lycius who has survived, but just barely, the vanishing of Lamia. But the elemental character of the poem at hand makes possible and justifiable a variety of interpretations. The most substantial discussions are by Wasserman, *The Finer Tone*, pp. 65–83; Charles I. Patterson, Jr., *The Daemonic in the Poetry of John Keats* (Urbana, 1970), pp. 125–150 (with a convenient summary of earlier scholarship in the first four pages); and Sperry, *Keats the Poet*, pp. 231–241.

1–4: Cf. Thomas Love Peacock, *Rhododaphne* I.134–135, 143, "What ails thee, stranger? Leaves are sear, / And flowers are dead, and fields are drear . . . And streams are bright, and sweet birds sing."   **1 knight at arms:** Perhaps adapted from the opening of Milton's Sonnet VIII, "Captain or colonel, or knight in arms."   **2:** Cf. Chaucer, *The Knight's Tale* 1364–66, "His hewe falow and pale as asshen colde, / And solitarie he was and evere allone, / And waillynge al the nyght, makynge his mone" (a passage quoted in and marked by Keats in his copy of Burton's *Anatomy*).   **4:** Cf. William Browne, *Britannia's Pastorals* II.i.244, "Let no bird sing."   **9–10:** Cf. Cary's translation of Dante, *Inferno* III.122–123, "with clammy dews / Fear chills my brow," and William Sotheby's translation of C. M. Wieland's *Oberon* I.16, "Fear stands upon his brow in dew-drops chill."   **10 anguish moist:** Cf. Hunt, *The Story of Rimini* IV.65, "moist anguish."   **11:** Cf. Bion's lament for Adonis 18 (in Francis Fawkes's translation), "And on his lips the roses fade away," and Mary Tighe, *Psyche* I.254, "The fading roses of her cheek."   **15–16:** Cf. Coleridge, *The Rime of the Ancient Mariner* 190–191, "*Her* lips were red, *her* looks were free, / Her locks were yellow as gold," and Wordsworth, *Her eyes are wild* 1, "Her eyes are wild, her head is bare."   **17:**

Cf. *The Knight's Tale* 1054, "To make a subtil gerland for hire hede," and *The Faerie Queene* (hereafter *F.Q.*) I.ii.30, "to frame / A girlond for her dainty forehead fit, / He pluckt a bough," and III.vii.17, "Girlonds of flowres sometimes for her faire hed / He fine would dight."   **20 made . . . moan:** Cf. "making great moan" in the couplet translated from the *Iliad* in the Burton passage quoted in the main note above, "makynge his mone" in the Chaucer lines cited for 2, and *F.Q.* II.vi.3, "Making sweet solace to her selfe alone."   **21:** Cf. *F.Q.* I.ii.45, "He set her on her steede."   **26 honey . . . dew:** Cf. "hony dew" in both *F.Q.* III.xi.31 and Coleridge's *Kubla Khan* 53.   **30 sigh'd . . . sore:** Cf. *F.Q.* IV.viii.64, "sigh full sore" (and also "sighing sore" in the same work eight times in Books I, III, IV, and VI).   **32 kisses four:** Keats explains in his letter containing the poem, "Why four kisses—you will say—why four because I wish to restrain the headlong impetuosity of my Muse—she would have fain said 'score' without hurting the rhyme—but we must temper the Imagination as the Critics say with Judgment. I was obliged to choose an even number that both eyes might have fair play: and to speak truly I think two a piece quite sufficient—Suppose I had said seven; there would have been three and a half a piece—a very awkward affair—and well got out of on my side" (*Letters*, II, 97).   **33:** Cf. *F.Q.* II.vi.18, "By this she had him lulled fast a sleepe."   **37–42:** Cf. *F.Q.* III.xi.29, "mighty kings and kesars, into thraldome brought," and Shakespeare, *Pericles* I.i.34–40, "Yon sometimes famous princes . . . Tell thee, with speechless tongues and semblance pale, / That . . . Here they stand martyrs, slain in Cupid's wars; / And with dead cheeks advise thee to desist / For going on death's net, whom none resist."   **40:** Cf. Cary's Dante, *Inferno* V.125, "How him love thrall'd."   **43–44:** Cf. *F.Q.* I.ix.15, "When I awoke, and found her place deuoyd, / And nought but pressed gras, where she had lyen, / I sorrowed all so much, as earst I ioyd."

Song of Four Fairies

Written in a letter to George and Georgiana Keats toward the end of April 1819; first published in *1848*.

Sonnet to Sleep

Written probably toward the end of April 1819; first published in *PDWJ*, 11 October 1838.

Ode to Psyche

Written probably toward the end of April 1819; first published in *1820*. In copying the ode for his brother and sister-in-law on or shortly after 30 April Keats comments:

> The following Poem—the last I have written is the first and the only one with which I have taken even moderate pains—I have for the most part dash'd of[f] my lines in a hurry—This I have done leisurely—I think it reads the more richly for it and will I hope encourage me to write other thing[s] in even a more peacable and healthy spirit. You must recollect

that Psyche was not embodied as a goddess before the time of Apulieus the Platonist who lived afteir the Agustan age, and consequently the Goddess was never worshipped or sacrificed to with any of the ancient fervour—and perhaps never thought of in the old religion—I am more orthodox [than] to let a hethen Goddess be so neglected. (*Letters*, II, 105–106)

This is the first of Keats's five "great odes" in the present volume (the others are *Nightingale, Grecian Urn, Melancholy,* and *Autumn*), and probably it was the earliest to be written, though the datings are uneven among the five and the chronological relationships to an extent unsettled. The most precisely datable ode, *To Autumn,* was written on 19 September 1819; the next most precisely datable, *Ode to Psyche,* was "the last I have written" when Keats mentioned it in the letter quoted above (but the exact date of this part of his journal letter is uncertain — it is somewhere between 30 April and 3 May); *Nightingale* is dated "May 1819" in several sources deriving from a lost MS by Brown and presumably came after *Psyche,* since Keats describes *Psyche* as "the first and the only one with which I have taken even moderate pains." But *Grecian Urn* and *Melancholy* are dated only "1819" in reliable sources, and, while scholars usually assign them to the spring or even more specifically to May (in part on the basis of misrepresentation of the MS evidence), each could have been written at any time during the year, even before *Psyche* or after *Autumn.* The five poems were included in *1820* but not as a distinct group; *Nightingale, Grecian Urn,* and *Psyche* follow the three narrative poems with which the volume begins (see the Appendix), and *Autumn* and *Melancholy* are together (in that order) at a later point, just before the final piece, *Hyperion.*

These odes all have distinctive personas speaking dramatically in a variety of moods—puzzlement, anxiety, distress, excitement, peremptoriness, celebration—and they express or imply a great many (not always harmonious) attitudes about life, love, nature, death, visionary escape, timelessness, and other large concerns; the poems are generally well structured (things happen, oppositions are established and played upon, ideas and feelings develop naturally); stylistically they represent Keats's achievement at its very best. They have of course attracted an immense amount of critical attention and have been the subjects of many hundreds of interpretations. In addition to the standard full-length works on Keats, virtually all of which consider the odes in detail, see the separate pieces collected in Stillinger, ed., *Twentieth Century Interpretations of Keats's Odes* (Englewood Cliffs, N.J., 1968—the introductory essay is reprinted in *The Hoodwinking of Madeline,* pp. 99–119); David Perkins' discussion of likenesses in imagery and wording between the odes and passages in Keats's letters, *K-SJ,* 2 (1953), 51–60; Robert Gittings' presentation of facsimiles of Keats's extant drafts in *The Odes of Keats and Their Earliest Known Manuscripts* (1970); and the following studies specially focusing on the unity of the group and problems of interpretation: John Holloway, *Cambridge Journal,* 5 (1952), 416–425 (the essay is reprinted in Holloway's *The Charted Mirror,* 1960, pp. 40–52); Robert F. Gleckner, *SEL,* 5 (1965), 577–585; Gillian Beer, *Modern Language Review,* 64 (1969), 742–748; Helen Vendler, *SIR,* 12 (1973), 591–606; and Paul H. Fry, *The Poet's Calling in the English Ode* (New Haven, 1980), chs. 9 and 10.

Psyche is not so clearly organized as the other odes and has frequently seemed the most difficult to integrate with the rest in a unified scheme. But a number of Keatsian motifs are present—dreaming versus seeing "with awaken'd eyes" (5–6, 35, 43, 49), thought versus thoughtlessness (7, 52, 65), physicality versus insubstantiality (7–20, 52–65), coolness and stasis versus warmth and activity (13–20, 64–67), simple days of "happy pieties" versus "these days" of the more complicated present (36–41), imaginative creativity versus mere fancy and feigning (50–63)—and these reflect some of the concerns coming together in Keats's mind that surface repeatedly in the work of his best period. Among articles the most helpful are by Kenneth Allott, *EC*, 6 (1956), 278–301 (the essay is reprinted in *John Keats: A Reassessment*, ed. Muir, pp. 74–94); Leonidas M. Jones, *K-SMB*, 9 (1958), 22–26; Max F. Schulz, *Criticism*, 2 (1960), 55–65; Robert D. Wagner, *K-SJ*, 13 (1964), 29–41; James H. Bunn, *ELH*, 37 (1970), 581–594; and Leon Waldoff, *PMLA*, 92 (1977), 410–419.

On Fame ("*Fame, like a wayward girl*")

Written on 30 April 1819; first published in the *Ladies' Companion* (New York), August 1837.

9 Nilus born: Gypsies were thought to have come from Egypt.   **10 Potiphar:** In Genesis 39.

On Fame ("*How fever'd is the man*")

Written in a letter to George and Georgiana Keats on 30 April 1819; first published in *1848*.

12 undisturbed lake: Woodhouse noted in W^2 that Keats's revision of 7–8 (which originally read, "As if a clear Lake meddling with itself / Should Cloud its pureness with a muddy gloom") "left an allusion in the 12th line to those thus erased."

If by dull rhymes our English must be chain'd

Written toward the end of April or at the beginning of May 1819; first published in the *Plymouth, Devonport, and Stonehouse News*, 15 October 1836. Keats introduces a letter copy of the poem as follows: "I have been endeavouring to discover a better sonnet stanza than we have. The legitimate [the Italian or Petrarchan] does not suit the language over-well from the pouncing rhymes—the other kind [the English or Shakespearean] appears too elegaic—and the couplet at the end of it has seldom a pleasing effect—I do not pretend to have succeeded—it will explain itself" (*Letters*, II, 108). For interpretive analysis of the poem see Mario L. D'Avanzo, *Research Studies* (Washington State University), 38 (1970), 29–35.

Two or three posies

Written in a letter to Fanny Keats probably on 1 May 1819; first published in Forman's edition of 1883. Keats tells Fanny that "M^r & Mrs Dilke are coming to dine with us to day—they will enjoy the country after Westminster," and then exclaims:

> O there is nothing like fine weather, and health, and Books, and a fine country, and a contented Mind, and Diligent-habit of reading and thinking, and an amulet against the ennui—and, please heaven, a little claret-wine cool out of a cellar a mile deep—with a few or a good many ratafia cakes—a rocky basin to bathe in, a strawberry bed to say your prayers to Flora in, a pad nag to go you ten miles or so; two or three sensible people to chat with; two or th[r]ee spiteful folkes to spar with; two or three odd fishes to laugh at and two or three numskuls to argue with—instead of using dumb bells on a rainy day.

At this point he breaks into verse, writing the present poem (*Letters,* II, 56).

20 Mrs. ——: "Mrs. Abbeys," a reference to the wife of Richard Abbey, who was guardian of the Keats children and a trustee of their grandmother's estate. Fanny was living with the Abbeys at this time. Keats adds "mum!" in the margin beside this line in his letter.

Ode to a Nightingale

Written in May 1819; first published in *Annals of the Fine Arts,* July 1819. Brown recalls the circumstances of composition in his "Life" of Keats, written seventeen years after the event, as follows:

> In the spring of 1819 a nightingale had built her nest near my house. Keats felt a tranquil and continual joy in her song; and one morning he took his chair from the breakfast-table to the grass-plot under a plum-tree, where he sat for two or three hours. When he came into the house, I perceived he had some scraps of paper in his hand, and these he was quietly thrusting behind the books. On inquiry, I found those scraps, four or five in number, contained his poetic feeling on the song of our nightingale. The writing was not well legible; and it was difficult to arrange the stanzas on so many scraps. With his assistance I succeeded, and this was his *Ode to a Nightingale,* a poem which has been the delight of every one. (*KC,* II, 65)

Brown is probably exaggerating his role in the history of the poem, and his description of the draft MS is almost surely mistaken (the extant draft, in the Fitzwilliam Museum, Cambridge, consists of two half-sheets, neither of them a "scrap"), but some of the other details may have been remembered accurately. Oddly, Keats himself says virtually nothing in his letters or any recorded comment about this and the next two odes, and he did not copy them, as he did so many other poems, for his brother and sister-in-law.

As to interpretation, the speaker's problem has always seemed fairly clear—dissatisfaction with the real world of mortality and mutability, movingly described in 23–30, and desire to escape that world by imaginatively joining an invisible bird in "the forest dim"—but the attempts at solution, and even more so the attitudes that the poem takes toward them, continue to be a matter of dispute. In some readings the poem is seen to depict, after the initial statement of the problem, an almost systematic cutting off, one after another, of all the escapes the speaker can think of: alcohol is the first to be rejected (32); then the nightingale's forest is found to have "no light" and the speaker "cannot see" the beauties of the transient natural world he has left behind (38–50); the romantic attractiveness of death is undermined by the speaker's awareness that he would "become a sod" (51–60); and a further imaginative journey, this time into the past, leads ultimately to "faery lands forlorn" (61–70). In the final stanza the speaker is back in the real world where he started, and the nightingale is divested of its symbolism as it flies off and the speaker locates it not in another ideal forest but in the familiar landscape of "the near meadows . . . the still stream . . . the hillside . . . the next valley-glades." But the ending, just as in a number of other major poems in this volume, is full of ambiguity; the speaker himself doesn't even know whether he is awake or dreaming.

On the great odes as a group see the note above to *Ode to Psyche.* On *Nightingale* in particular most of the best critical work has been done in the full-length general studies (especially those by Earl Wasserman, David Perkins, Walter Evert, and Morris Dickstein), but see, among separate pieces, Allen Tate, *American Scholar,* 15 (1945–46), 55–63, 189–197 (the essay is reprinted in Tate's *On the Limits of Poetry,* New York, 1948, pp. 165–184); R. H. Fogle, *PMLA,* 68 (1953), 211–222 (essay reprinted in Fogle's *The Permanent Pleasure,* Athens, Ga., 1974, pp. 100–115); Andrew J. Kappel, *ELH,* 45 (1978), 270–279, 282–284; and Allan Chavkin, *Research Studies* (Washington State University), 47 (1979), 108–115.

Ode on a Grecian Urn

Written in 1819; first published in *Annals of the Fine Arts,* January 1820. In this ode, whose structure parallels that of *Nightingale* (but without the additional complexity resulting in stanza 6 from the wish to die), the hypothetical ideal is the realm of art. The seesaw opposition of earthly and urnly values gets under way immediately with the implications of unnaturalness in "unravish'd bride" and "foster-child," and it continues with increasing intensity through the first three stanzas. In the fourth stanza the speaker takes a fresh look at the urn, worries more onesidedly about the perpetual immobility of the sacrificial procession and the permanent emptiness of the unseen town whence the people have come, and with "desolate" in 40 (cf. "forlorn" in *Nightingale*) arrives at a final acceptance of the real world of time and mortality. The closing lines present a special problem in interpretation, but it seems clear that, while the urn is not entirely rejected at the end, its value lies in its character as a work of art and not in its being a desirable alternative to life in the real world.

For guidance through the first 125 years of criticism on this poem see Harvey T. Lyon, *Keats' Well-Read Urn* (New York, 1958). The most useful of the earlier essays are those by Kenneth Burke, *Accent,* 4 (1943), 30–42 (reprinted in Burke's *A Grammar of Motives,* New York, 1945, pp. 447–463); Cleanth Brooks, *Sewanee Review,* 52 (1944), 89–101 (reprinted in Brooks's *The Well Wrought Urn,* New

York, 1947, pp. 139–152); Charles I. Patterson, *ELH,* 21 (1954), 208–220; and Jacob D. Wigod, *PMLA,* 72 (1957), 113–121. Among more recent studies see Bruce E. Miller, *K-SJ,* 20 (1971), 62–70; Jean-Claude Sallé, *SIR,* 11 (1972), 79–93; James Shokoff, *K-SJ,* 24 (1975), 102–107; and Pratap Biswas, *University of Toronto Quarterly,* 47 (1977–78), 95–111. For interesting discussion, with illustrations, of the kinds of urn and other art works that might have influenced Keats while he was writing the poem, see Jack, *Keats and the Mirror of Art,* pp. 214–224, and James Dickie, *Bulletin of the John Rylands Library,* 52 (1969), 96–114.

49–50: In Brown's transcript the penultimate line reads "Beauty is Truth,— Truth Beauty,—that is all" and the *Annals* text has "Beauty is Truth, Truth Beauty.—That is all" (neither contains the quotation marks around "Beauty . . . beauty" that are unique to the third of the authoritative texts, that of *1820,* followed in this volume). With or without the quotes there is considerable uncertainty about who speaks the last thirteen words of the poem, and to whom. The four most frequently mentioned possibilities are (1) poet to reader, (2) poet to urn, (3) poet to figures on the urn, and (4) urn to reader—but serious objections have been raised in each case (see Appendix III in *The Hoodwinking of Madeline,* pp. 167–173). "Beauty" and "truth" were commonplace as aesthetic values in the literary and especially the art criticism of the eighteenth and early nineteenth centuries, and the union or equation of the two was often emphasized (e.g., in Mark Akenside's *The Pleasures of Imagination* I.374–375, "Truth and Good are one, / And Beauty dwells in them, and they in her"); the terms appear together frequently in Haydon's comments on the Elgin Marbles (see James A. Notopoulos, *Modern Language Review,* 61 [1966], 180–182), and three times in Keats's own letters (*Letters,* I, 184, 192, II, 19). Critics sometimes relate "beauty" to poetry and "truth" to philosophy, but it is probably best not to attempt this sort of translation.

Ode on Melancholy

Written in 1819; first published in *1820.* At one time (but not, as is usually reported, in the earliest version) the poem had an additional stanza at the beginning, to introduce the other three, but this was canceled before it got into print:

> Though you should build a bark of dead men's bones,
>   And rear a phantom gibbet for a mast,
> Stitch creeds together for a sail, with groans
>   To fill it out, bloodstained and aghast;
> Although your rudder be a Dragon's tail,
>   Long sever'd, yet still hard with agony,
>   Your cordage large uprootings from the skull
> Of bald Medusa; certes you would fail
>   To find the Melancholy, whether she
>   Dreameth in any isle of Lethe dull.

Melancholy is the most logically constructed of the major odes: the first stanza tells what not to do "when the melancholy fit shall fall," the second stanza advises what to do instead, and the third presents a rationale for these injunctions (and the clearest statement in all Keats's poetry concerning the interconnectedness of pleasure and pain in human life). This does not, however, mean that there are no complications. "Wakeful anguish" is presented as a state to be valued (10); the "weeping cloud" of melancholy is associated with both nourishment and death (12–14); the deep enjoyment of the mistress' "peerless eyes" seems to depend on her "rich anger" (18–20); the heroic figure capable of bursting "Joy's grape" ends up a cloudy trophy (27–30). For recent critical discussion see Barbara H. Smith, *SEL*, 6 (1966), 679–691, and Horace G. Posey, Jr., *Concerning Poetry*, 8 (Fall 1975), 61–69.

Ode on Indolence

Written in the spring of 1819, probably after 19 March, when Keats described "a sort of temper indolent" in his journal letter to his brother and sister-in-law (see just below), and certainly before 9 June, when he told Miss Jeffrey (or Jeffery) that "the thing I have most enjoyed this year has been writing an ode to Indolence" (*Letters*, II, 116); first published in *1848*. The passage in the earlier letter is as follows:

> This morning I am in a sort of temper indolent and supremely careless: I long after a stanza or two of Thompson's Castle of indolence—My passions are all alseep from my having slumbered till nearly eleven and weakened the animal fibre all over me to a delightful sensation about three degrees on this side of faintness—if I had teeth of pearl and the breath of lillies I should call it langour—but as I am I must call it Laziness—In this state of effeminacy the fibres of the brain are relaxed in common with the rest of the body, and to such a happy degree that pleasure has no show of enticement and pain no unbearable frown. Neither Poetry, nor Ambition, nor Love have any alertness of countenance as they pass by me: they seem rather like three figures on a greek vase— a Man and two women—whom no one but myself could distinguish in their disguisement. This is the only happiness; and is a rare instance of advantage in the body overpowering the Mind. (II, 78–79)

There are several details of image and wording here that also appear in the poem, but the chronological relationship of poem and letter is unsettled.

Indolence is occasionally classed with *Psyche* and the others as a sixth "great ode," but it lacks the dramatic tension and sharpness of imagery characteristic of the more famous examples. The speaker refuses to engage in serious conflict with Love, Ambition, and Poesy, and the poem genuinely reflects the indolence that is its subject. For critical comment see Margaret Y. Robertson, *Style*, 4 (1970), 133–143; Howard H. Hinkel, *Tennessee Studies in Literature*, 20 (1975), 26–36; and William F. Zak, *K-SJ*, 25 (1976), 55–64 (the first two of these, however, interpret a text that has the stanzas in the wrong order). The epigraph is from Matthew 6:28.

10 Phidian: After Phidias (fifth century B.C.), the sculptor thought to have been responsible for the designs of the Elgin Marbles.

Shed no tear—O shed no tear

Written probably in 1819; first published (under the heading "The Faery Bird's Song") in *PDWJ*, 18 October 1838. Keats composed the song for inclusion in Brown's unfinished romance "The Fairies' Triumph" (MS at Keats House, Hampstead), at a point where the princes Elury and Azameth, disregarding an old man's warning, have thoughtlessly plucked a flower, seen it shrivel to dust, and heard the voice of their supposedly dead brother moaning, "Ah! who has been so cruel?" The princes "stood there like statues of grief. At length immediately above their heads they heard a most enchanting melody breathed forth; and looking up they saw, perched upon a slender bough, a bird of lovely form, and brilliant plumage, and it gazed down on them with its mild dove-like eyes, and warbled its song to cheer them." The song is then followed by the heading of a new chapter (the fifth), which opens, "Our youths were awakened from their trance of grief by this song, and having regained their horses . . . they proceeded slowly, exchanging but few words along the road." For a fuller account of the context in Brown's MS see *K-SJ*, 10 (1961), 6–8.

Otho the Great

Written by Keats and Brown at Shanklin (on the Isle of Wight) and Winchester in July–August 1819, with further revisions in December 1819 and January 1820; first published in *1848*. In general Brown was responsible for the plot and characters, and Keats for the actual writing, but the precise nature of the collaboration is not entirely clear. Brown describes the process of composition in his "Life" of Keats:

> At Shanklin [Keats] undertook a difficult task: I engaged to furnish him with the fable, characters, and dramatic conduct of a tragedy, and he was to embody it into poetry. The progress of this work was curious; for, while I sat opposite to him, he caught my description of each scene, entered into the characters to be brought forward, the events, and every thing connected with it. Thus he went on, scene after scene, never knowing nor inquiring into the scene which was to follow, until four acts were completed. It was then he required to know, at once, all the events which were to occupy the fifth act. I explained them to him; but, after a patient hearing, and some thought, he insisted on it that my incidents were too numerous, and, as he termed them, too melodramatic. He wrote the fifth act in accordance with his own view; and so enchanted was I with his poetry, that, at the time, and for a long time after, I thought he was in the right. (*KC*, II, 66)

Keats's letter to Taylor of 5 September, two weeks after completion of the play—"Brown likes the Tragedy very much: but he is not a fit judge, as I have only acted as Midwife to his plot, and of course he will be fond of his child" (*Letters*, II, 157)—confirms Brown's first sentence in the passage just quoted, but the subsequent details have to be modified somewhat, for Brown did not come to Shanklin until c. 22 July, by which time Keats presumably was well into or even finished with Act II. He would of course have been working with suggestions that Brown had given him before he left Hampstead toward the end of June, but the composition of "scene after scene" in the particular way that Brown pictures it must be taken to apply only to Acts III and IV. Brown perhaps gives himself more credit than he deserves for the "fable . . . and dramatic conduct"; on the other hand, he underplays his share in the actual writing, for he does not mention the many changes of wording that he initiated in the course of making a fair copy from Keats's draft, and he and Keats appear to have collaborated equally in the final revisions made in December and January.

The two authors wrote the play as "a joint money speculation" from which they hoped to make £200 each (*KC*, II, 105, and *Letters of Fanny Brawne to Fanny Keats*, ed. Fred Edgcumbe, New York, 1937, p. 34—Keats refers to his financial expectations in *Letters*, II, 143, 185–186, 210, 217), and their letters at the time convey an attitude of high spirits toward the work. Keats reported to Dilke on 31 July, "Brown and I are pretty well harnessed again to our dog-cart. I mean the Tragedy which goes on sinkingly—We are thinking of introducing an Elephant but have not historical referance within reach to determine us as to Otho's Menagerie. When Brown first mention'd this I took it for a Joke; however he brings such plausible reasons, and discourses so eloquently on the dramatic effect that I am giving it a serious consideration," and he told Fanny Brawne on 5 August, "I leave this minute a scene in our Tragedy and see you . . . through the mist of Plots speeches, counterplots and counter speeches—The Lover [Ludolph] is madder than I am" (*Letters*, II, 135, 137). Brown wrote to Dilke on 12 August,

> Keats is very industrious, but I swear . . . he is obstinately monstrous. What think you of Otho's threatening cold pig to the new-married couple? He says the Emperor must have a spice of drollery. His introduction of Grimm's adventure, lying three days on his back for love, though it spoils the unity of time, is not out of the way for the character of Ludolf, so I have consented to it; but I cannot endure his fancy of making the princess blow up her hair-dresser, for smearing her cheek with pomatum, and spoiling her rouge. It may be natural, as he observes, but so might many things. However, such as it is, it has advanced to nearly the end of the fourth act. (*The Letters of Charles Armitage Brown*, Cambridge, Mass., 1966, pp. 48–49)

For all this jocularity connected with the composition, however, Keats clearly took the work seriously. On 14 August, reporting the completion of Acts I–IV, he remarked to Bailey, "It was the opinion of most of my friends that I should never be able to [write] a [s]cene—I will endeavour to wipe awa[y the preju-dice]. . . . One of my Ambitions is to make as great a revolution in modern dramatic writing as Kean has done in acting" (*Letters*, II, 139), and indeed it was for Edmund Kean, the foremost tragic actor of the day, that he wrote the part of Ludolph: "he is the only actor that can do it—He will add to his own fame, and improve my fortune" (II, 217—see also II, 148, 149, 186, 237). He felt that successful production of the play would lift him "out of the mire . . . of a bad reputation which is continually rising against me. My name with the literary fashionables is vulgar. . . . a Tragedy would lift me out of this mess" (II, 186).

None of these hopes was realized. The play was offered to Drury Lane in October and after two months was accepted for the following or a later season, but the authors, impatient of delay, withdrew the MS and, after making further revisions, sent it in January to Covent Garden, whence, in Brown's words, "it was speedily returned with a note, in a boy's hand-writing, containing a negative. I have since had reason to believe [the MS] never was unrolled" (*KC*, II, 66–67—see also *Letters*, II, 229, 235, 237, 241). Brown apparently tried to get the play produced at a private theater in Rome in 1824, and Severn attempted the same in 1834, but without success (*Letters of Charles Armitage Brown*, pp. 331–332, 190 n.). It was first performed at St. Martin's Theatre, London, on 26 November 1950.

Otho (Otto I, called the Great, 912–973) became King of Germany in 936 and Holy Roman Emperor in 962. His son, Duke Ludolf of Swabia (d. 957), and his son-in-law, Conrad the Red of Lotharingia (d. 955), led a rebellion against him in 953–954, and the invading Hungarians (whom Ludolf and Conrad were accused of enlisting in their cause) were defeated in the battle of the Lechfeld, near Augsburg, on 10 August 955. These events form the background of the opening speeches of Act I, but the play does not attempt fidelity to dates or places, and most of the characters are nonhistorical.

I.i.83 ratio: Ration.   **II.i.133–134 Nimrod's . . . clouds:** A reference to the building of the Tower of Babel (Genesis 10:8–12, 11:1–9).   **III.i.16 Henry the Fowler:** Otho's father, Henry I.   **IV.ii.90 battailous:** Warlike, ready for battle.   **V.v.166 pight:** Settled, resolved (archaic past participle of "pitch").

Lamia

Written at Shanklin and Winchester in early July, late August, and perhaps also the first few days of September 1819, with further revisions in March 1820; first published in *1820*. There was a six-week interval between the completion of Part I and the commencement of Part II during which Keats composed, in order, Acts II–IV of *Otho,* part of *The Fall of Hyperion,* Act V of *Otho,* and part of the *King Stephen* fragment. As Gittings observes, *John Keats,* p. 336, "Technically, the process of completing *Lamia* was something he had never been able to do before; if he stopped in a poem, he habitually left it unfinished."

Like the immediately preceding work in this volume, *Lamia* was to an extent produced with an eye toward popularity and financial gain. Keats told Reynolds on 11 July that he had "great hopes of success, because I make use of my Judgment more deliberately than I yet have done" (*Letters*, II, 128). He wrote to his brother and sister-in-law on 18 September, "I am certain there is that sort of fire in [*Lamia*] which must take hold of people in some way—give them either pleasant or unpleasant sensation. What they want is a sensation of some sort" (II, 189). In a letter to Woodhouse, on 22 September, discussing *Isabella*'s "weak-sidedness" vis-à-vis "the Public," he commented, "There is no objection of this kind to Lamia" (II, 174). Woodhouse was pleased with the poem when Keats read it aloud to him on 12 September (see Woodhouse's plot summary for Taylor,

Letters, II, 164–165), but Taylor, when Keats sent him a 59-line extract from the draft of Part II in a letter of 5 September, reacted differently: "The Extract [Keats] gave me was from the Feast: I did not enter so well into it as to be qualified to criticise, but whether it be a want of Taste for such Subjects as Fairy Tales, or that I do not perceive true Poetry except it is in Conjunction with good Sentiment, I cannot tell, but it did not promise to please me" (*Letters,* II, 157–159, 183). Probably Taylor perceived the "true Poetry" when he read the whole poem, for he allowed it to appear as the opening piece in *1820.*

The story is from Burton's *Anatomy* (the passage appended to the last line of the poem in both *1820* and the present volume); the meter, as Woodhouse said, "is Drydenian heroic—with many triplets, & many alexandri[n]es. But this K. observed, & I agreed, was required, or rather quite in character with the lang[u]age & sentiment in those particular parts.—K. has a fine feeling when & where he may use poetical licences with effect" (*Letters,* II, 165). As to interpretation of the story, and Keats's intentions stylistically and otherwise, there is an extraordinarily wide range of opinions. We have another obvious use of dreaming as a metaphor for investment in a visionary ideal; a long introduction leading up to a statement about the reality of the dreams of gods and, by implication, the unreliability of the dreams of mortals (I.126–128, 145); an ironic apostrophe emphasizing the inseparability of pleasure and pain in human life (I.185–196); various indications to establish Lycius' character as a mortal acting under a magical spell (e.g., I.234–236, 241–242, 294–297, 347); and of course the unhappy awakening from illusion, too late, at the close. But there are complications at every turn. Along with enchantment from without, Lycius' own human vanity and perversity play a significant role in bringing about his undoing; the poem's attitudes are inconsistent (at times critical, at times highly sympathetic) toward both Lycius and Lamia; and by the end of the story all three principal characters are made to seem flawed: Lamia is again a snake-woman, Lycius is a hoodwinked dreamer, and Apollonius is the "cold" philosopher whose realistic perception has spoiled everything. The opening poem serves to introduce some basic Keatsian concerns in *1820* (dreaming, illusion, a mortal-nonmortal union, the separation of actual and ideal worlds, the impingement of reality), but appears to leave the conflicts unresolved.

Scholars are not comfortable with irresolution, and so there is an especially large body of critical writing on the poem. The most substantial discussions in books are those by Wasserman, *The Finer Tone,* pp. 158–174; Bernice Slote, *Keats and the Dramatic Principle* (Lincoln, Neb., 1958), pp. 138–163; David Perkins, *The Quest for Permanence* (Cambridge, Mass., 1959), pp. 263–276; Patterson, *The Daemonic in the Poetry of John Keats,* pp. 185–216 (with a useful summary of earlier work in the first four pages); and Sperry, *Keats the Poet,* pp. 292–309. Among the many articles see in particular Georgia S. Dunbar, *K-SJ,* 8 (1959), 17–26; Donald H. Reiman, *SEL,* 11 (1971), 659–669; Richard Benvenuto, *JEGP,* 71 (1972), 1–11; Warren Stevenson, *SIR,* 11 (1972), 241–252; William C. Stephenson, *Papers on Language and Literature,* 10 (1974), 35–50; Garrett Stewart, *SIR,* 15 (1976), 3–41; Gene M. Bernstein, *Papers on Language and Literature,* 15 (1979), 175–192; and Donald Pearce, *Yale Review,* 69 (1980), 212–233.

Part I.   58 Ariadne's tiar: Bacchus gave Ariadne a crown of seven stars that, after her death, was transformed into a constellation.   **78 Phœbean dart:** I.e., a ray of the sun.   **81 star of Lethe:** Hermes conducted the souls of the dead to Hades.   **114 psalterian:** Either like the sound of a psaltery (the stringed instrument) or in the style of the Psalter.   **155 volcanian:** Volcanic (here referring to the color of sulphur).   **174 Cenchreas:** The eastern harbor of Corinth, on the Saronic Gulf.   **176 Peræan:** Possibly not intended as a proper name. "Peraea" means literally "the country on the opposite side," and *Harper's Dictionary of Classical Literature and Antiquities* defines it as "a general name for any district belonging to or closely connected with a country, from the main part of which it was separated by a sea or river."   **179 Cleone:** A village on the road from Corinth to Argos.   **212 Mulciber:** Vulcan.   **288 complain:** Complaint.   **347 comprized:** Caught, wrapped up.   **396–397:** "Incredulous" can be read as modifying either "many a heart" or "busy world." The draft text ("'Twould humour many a heart, to close the door / Upon their happy days, incredulous of more") tends to connect it with the former.

    Part II.   81–83 She burnt . . . paramour: Keats told Woodhouse in September 1819, referring to this passage, "Women love to be forced to do a thing, by a fine fellow—*such as this* [Lycius] . . . *was*" (*Letters*, II, 164).   **160 daft:** Daunted, baffled.   **162 solve:** Dissolve.   **185 libbard:** Archaic spelling of "leopard."   **217 osier'd:** Twisted or woven like osiers.   **229–237 Do . . . rainbow:** Haydon records that at a dinner party on 28 December 1817 Lamb and Keats "agreed [Newton] had destroyed all the Poetry of the rainbow, by reducing it to a prism. . . . we drank 'Newton's health, and confusion to mathematics!'" (*The Diary of Benjamin Robert Haydon*, ed. W. B. Pope, Cambridge, Mass., 1960–1963, II, 173). In a lecture just sixteen days later, which Keats may have attended, Hazlitt said, "It cannot be concealed . . . that the progress of knowledge and refinement has a tendency to circumscribe the limits of the imagination, and to clip the wings of poetry. The province of the imagination is principally visionary, the unknown and undefined: the understanding restores things to their natural boundaries, and strips them of their fanciful pretensions. Hence the history of religious and poetical enthusiasm is much the same; and both have received a sensible shock from the progress of experimental philosophy" (*Complete Works of William Hazlitt*, ed. Howe, V, 9). As Sperry points out, *Keats the Poet*, p. 299 n., the theme is a common one in both Hazlitt's writings generally and the thought of the time.   **301 perceant:** Piercing.

Pensive they sit, and roll their languid eyes

Written at Winchester in a letter to George and Georgiana Keats on 17 September 1819; first published in the New York *World*, 25 June 1877. Describing his friend William Haslam's courtship of his future wife, Keats remarks,

> Nothing strikes me so forcibly with a sense of the rediculous as love—A Man in love . . . cuts the sorryest figure in the world—Even when I know a poor fool to be really in pain about it, I could burst out laughing in his face—His pathetic visage becomes irrisistable. Not that I take Haslam as a pattern for Lovers—he is a very worthy man and a good friend. His love is very amusing. Somewhere in the Spectator [No. 371, 6 May 1712] is related an account of a Man inviting a party of stutter-

[e]rs and squinters to his table. 't would please me more to scrape together a party of Lovers, not to dinner—no to tea. The[re] would be no
fighting as among Knights of old.

Keats then writes the present twenty-three lines of verse and adds, "You see I
cannot get on without writing as boys do at school a few nonsense verses—I begin
them and before I have written six the whim has pass'd—if there is any th[i]ng
deserving so respectable a name in them" (*Letters*, II, 187–188).

9 humane society: The Royal Humane Society (for the rescue of drowning
persons) was founded in 1774.   **10 Werter:** The name of Goethe's sentimental
hero in *Die Leiden des jungen Werthers* (1774), in English translations usually
spelled "Werter."   **16 winding-sheet:** A formation of tallow drippings down
the side of a candle "resembling a sheet folded in creases, and regarded in popular superstition as an omen of death or calamity" (*OED*). "Cauliflower" (15) probably refers to the shape of this formation at the top of the candle.   **17 Circus:**
Piccadilly Circus.   **23 Wapping:** In east London, near the docks.

To Autumn

Written at Winchester on 19 September 1819; first published in *1820*. Keats describes and dates the occasion in a letter to Reynolds on Tuesday the 21st: "How
beautiful the season is now—How fine the air. A temperate sharpness about it.
Really, without joking, chaste weather—Dian skies—I never lik'd stubble fields
so much as now—Aye better than the chilly green of the spring. Somehow a stubble plain looks warm—in the same way that some pictures look warm—this
struck me so much in my sunday's walk that I composed upon it" (*Letters*, II, 167).

This is almost certainly the latest of the great odes (see the note above to *Ode to
Psyche*), and it may be thought of, in a view of the odes as a group, as written out
of the experience of the earlier poems. From beginning to end it celebrates the
world of process—of "maturing," "ripeness," "budding"—not with innocent delight in the beauties of nature but rather with a philosophical understanding that
this is the only real world we have. A momentary yearning for the otherworlds of
the nightingale and the urn is expressed in the opening line of the third stanza,
but it is immediately countered by the line that follows ("Think not of them"),
and the remainder of the poem, even while hinting of death among the noises of
life, is for most readers unambiguously affirmative. See Arnold Davenport in
John Keats: A Reassessment, ed. Muir, pp. 95–101; B. C. Southam, *K-SJ*, 9 (1960),
91–98; James Lott, *SIR*, 9 (1970), 71–81; Geoffrey H. Hartman in *Literary Theory
and Structure: Essays in Honor of William K. Wimsatt*, ed. Frank Brady et al. (New
Haven, 1973), pp. 305–330 (the essay is reprinted in Hartman's *The Fate of Reading*, pp. 124–146, 324–327); and Virgil Nemoianu, *PMLA*, 93 (1978),
205–214.

The Fall of Hyperion

Begun as a revision of *Hyperion* probably at Shanklin toward the end of July 1819
and abandoned apparently for good by 21 September (but see the note below to
The Jealousies); first published in *Miscellanies of the Philobiblon Society*, 1857. Keats's

remarks to Reynolds on 21 September apply to both *Hyperion* and *The Fall* (they were of course considered a single project, the later version an attempt to redo the earlier):

> I have given up Hyperion—there were too many Miltonic inversions in it—Miltonic verse cannot be written but in an artful or rather artist's humour. I wish to give myself up to other sensations. English ought to be kept up. It may be interesting to you to pick out some lines from Hyperion and put a mark × to the false beauty proceeding from art, and one ‖ to the true voice of feeling. Upon my soul 'twas imagination I cannot make the distinction—Every now & then there is a Miltonic intonation—But I cannot make the division properly. (*Letters,* II, 167)

Almost certainly there were more reasons for abandoning the project than just the excess of Miltonic inversions (see the note above to *Hyperion*). In treatment of the original materials, the revision gets no further than *Hyperion* I.220.

The principal interest here is the personalized dream-vision introduction, entirely new in this revised version, in which Keats utters and dramatizes some serious thoughts about dreamers, visionaries, poetic creation, and the relation of poetry to humanitarian activity. Scholars have always had trouble sorting out the categories of poetic and nonpoetic types who are talked about in the dialogue between the poet and Moneta at I.136 ff. (and some textual complications at I.187–210 are a reminder that the work is unfinished all along, not just at the point of breaking off), but there is no mistaking the fervency of Keats's feelings about these matters. For a variety of useful explanations in specialized studies see Brian Wicker, *EC,* 7 (1957), 28–41; Stuart M. Sperry, *PMLA,* 77 (1962), 77–84 (the essay is reprinted in revised form in Sperry's *Keats the Poet,* pp. 310–335); Irene H. Chayes, *PQ,* 46 (1967), 499–515; Paul D. Sheats, *K-SJ,* 17 (1968), 75–88; Anne K. Mellor, *K-SJ,* 25 (1976), 65–80; K. K. Ruthven, *SIR,* 15 (1976), 445–459; and Warren U. Ober and W. K. Thomas, *K-SJ,* 29 (1980), 96–119.

Canto I.   1–11 Fanatics . . . enchantment: Keats quotes this passage in a letter to Woodhouse, 21 September 1819, as "a sort of induction" (*Letters,* II, 172). Critics usually take the "induction" to be either I.1–18 or I.1–293.   **48 caliphat:** Probably intended to mean one person (a caliph) rather than a collective group of rulers or their dominion (caliphate).   **70 faulture:** "Decayed remnants" (*OED,* citing this passage).   **75 in . . . corrupt:** In heaven (Matthew 6:19–20).   **96 One minist'ring:** The priestess Moneta, also (by mistake?) called Mnemosyne in I.331, II.50, but not the same as the character consistently named Mnemosyne in *Hyperion.*   **103 Maian:** Like that of May flowers (from Maia, the goddess whom Keats addresses in *Mother of Hermes*).   **135–136 As . . . heaven:** In Genesis 28:12.   **187–210:** As he noted on two transcripts, Woodhouse (probably because of the partial repetition of 187 and 194–198 in 211 and 216–220) thought that Keats "intended to erase" this passage.   **207–208 mock . . . verse:** Usually interpreted as a reference to Byron (cf. *Sleep and Poetry* 230–245).   **222 all spar'd:** All that is spared.   **246 electral:** Electric (electrically charged).   **294:** This is the first of 134 lines that Keats took over more or less verbatim from the then unpublished *Hyperion.* The present I.294–296 correspond to *Hyperion* I.1–3; I.310b–330 to I.7b–25; I.339–365 to I.37–63; I.367–383 to I.67–72, 74–82, 85–86; I.386–387 to I.87–88; I.400–403 to I.89–92; I.412b–417 to I.106b–108, 110–112; I.432b–438a to I.127b–133a; II.7–48 to I.158–173, 175–182a, 186–204; II.54–56 to I.218–220;II.58–61 to I.214–217.   **312 zoning:** Compass, duration.   **336 statuary:** Statuesqueness (with the modern implication of tallness of stature).   **425 Cybele:** Wife of Saturn and mother of the Olympian gods (the "babes" of 425 and the "imps" of 431).

Canto II.   6 legend-laden: In copying II.1–4, 6 for Woodhouse on 21 September 1819 Keats comments, "I will give you a few lines from Hyperion on account of a word in the last line of a fine sound." He then underscored "legend-laden" in the last of these lines (*Letters*, II, 171).   **20 even:** Evening.

The day is gone, and all its sweets are gone

Written in 1819, possibly toward the end of the year; first published in *PDWJ*, 4 October 1838. Probably this and the next two poems (and certainly the fourth, *To Fanny*) were addressed to Fanny Brawne.

I cry your mercy—pity—love!—aye, love

Written in 1819, perhaps toward the end of the year; first published in *1848*.

What can I do to drive away

Written probably in 1819; first published in *1848*. The poem is analyzed by Paul de Man in his introduction to the Signet Classic edition of Keats's *Selected Poetry* (New York, 1966), pp. xxvii–xxxiii, and by Ronald Primeau, *K-SJ*, 23 (1974), 106–118.
    17 throes: Is in throes, agonizes.

To Fanny

Written probably toward the end of 1819 or during the early months of 1820; first published in *1848*.
    40 blow-ball: "The globular seeding head of the dandelion and allied plants" (*OED*).

King Stephen

Begun at Winchester late in August 1819 and abandoned probably in November; first published in *1848*. In his "Life" of Keats Brown recalls that

> As soon as Keats had finished *Otho the great,* I pointed out to him a subject for an english historical tragedy in the reign of Stephen, beginning with his defeat by the Empress Maud, and ending with the death of his son Eustace, when Stephen yielded the succession to the crown to the

young Henry. He was struck with the variety of events and characters which must necessarily be introduced; and I offerred to give, as before [with *Otho*], their dramatic conduct. "The play must open", I began, "with the field of battle, when Stephen's forces are retreating—" "Stop!" he said, "stop! I have been already too long in leading-strings. I will do all this myself." He immediately set about it, and wrote two or three scenes, about 130 lines.

This second tragedy, never to be resumed, gave place to "Lamia", a poem which had been on hand for some months. (*KC*, II, 67)

Brown's account makes it clear that Keats began *King Stephen* in August, after the completion of *Otho* and before the writing of *Lamia* Part II, but does not square with the November dating in his partial transcript of *King Stephen;* nor does it square with the total of four scenes, amounting to 195 lines, in the work as we now have it. One must suppose that Keats did, contrary to Brown's recollection, take up the work again on a later occasion. The MS evidence indicates that the incomplete scene iii was written after the composition of scene iv (which is also obviously incomplete), and it seems most likely, if an August/November division is to be made among parts of the work, that Keats wrote i, ii, and what we have of iv (a total of 148 lines) in August and then resumed with the fresh attempt at scene iii in November. It was in this November (on the 17th) that he mentioned to Taylor "the writing of a few fine Plays—my greatest ambition—when I do feel ambitious. I am sorry to say that is very seldom" (*Letters*, II, 234).

The historical background of the fragment is the conflict between King Stephen (1097?–1154) and the Empress Matilda, or Maud (1102–1167), over the throne of England. The specific event is the decisive battle of 2 February 1141 in which forces led by Randulf, Earl of Chester (d. 1153), and his father-in-law, Robert, Earl of Gloucester (d. 1147), opposed Stephen at Lincoln Castle.

In the battle that ensued the bulk of Stephen's men "betrayed him and fled," and he was left with a mere handful of comrades in the midst of a host of enemies. The little band, all on foot, stood firm against charge after charge of the horsemen; and the life and soul of their resistance was the king himself, who "stood like a lion," cutting down every man who came within reach of his sword, or, when that was broken, of a battle-axe which a citizen of Lincoln gave him in its stead. When only four (or three) of his companions were left, he still fought on . . . till the axe too broke in his hands, probably from the force of a blow which had laid Randulf of Chester in the mire at his feet. . . . At last he fell, struck on the head by a stone; but even then he shook off a knight who sought to capture him, and would surrender to no one but Earl Robert. He was sent to Matilda at Gloucester, and thence to prison at Bristol. (*Dictionary of National Biography*, s.v. "Stephen")

In Henry of Huntingdon's description of the battle (one of the sources of the account just quoted) Stephen fights first with a battle-axe and then with a sword: "his heavy battle-axe gleamed like lightning, striking down some, bearing back others. At length it was shattered by repeated blows; then he drew his well-tried sword, with which he wrought wonders, until that, too, was broken" (*Chronicle,* trans. and ed. Thomas Forester, 1853, p. 279).   **I.i.6 plashy:** Marshy.   **I.i.13 flaunt:** Flaunted.   **I.i.19 De Redvers:** Historically Baldwin of Redvers (d. 1155) was an enemy of Stephen. Keats has mistakenly given his name to another Baldwin, of Clare (also called Baldwin Fitz-Gilbert), who fought valiantly on Stephen's side in this battle.   **I.ii.17 Duke of Bretagne:** Alan, Earl of Brittany, an ally of Stephen.   **I.ii.22 Like . . . Ilion:** In the *Iliad* (Chapman's translation) VII.17–18.   **I.ii.41 heft:** Variant spelling of "haft."   **I.ii.42 paunch'd:** Wounded in the paunch.   **I.iii.13 s.d. De Kaims:** Stephen's captor was William of Kahaines (also "de Cahaignes," "de Cahames," "de Kahains," "Dekains" in various sources).   **I.iv.1 Boulogne:** Stephen acquired this title when he married the daughter of Count Eustace of Boulogne.   **I.iv.17 brother:** Gloucester was her illegitimate half-brother. Their father (referred to in I.iv.40) was Henry I.   **I.iv.34 play . . . Darius:** Treat one's enemy magnanimously.

This living hand, now warm and capable

Written probably toward the end of 1819 (the lines appear on the sheet on which Keats later drafted stanzas 45–51 of *The Jealousies*); first published in Forman's one-volume edition of 1898.

The Jealousies

Written probably toward the end of 1819; first published (under the heading "The Cap and Bells; / Or, the Jealousies. / A Faëry Tale. Unfinished") in *1848* (lines 217–256 earlier in the *Indicator,* 23 August 1820). Brown says in his "Life" of Keats:

> By chance our conversation turned on the idea of a comic faery poem in the Spenser stanza, and I was glad to encourage it. He had not composed many stanzas before he proceeded in it with spirit. It was to be published under the feigned authorship of Lucy Vaughan Lloyd, and to bear the title of *The Cap and Bells,* or, which he preferred, *The Jealousies.* This occupied his mornings pleasantly. He wrote it with the greatest facility; in one instance I remember having copied (for I copied as he wrote) as many as twelve stanzas before dinner. In the evenings, at his own desire, he was alone in a separate sitting-room, deeply engaged in remodelling his poem of "Hyperion" into a "Vision." (*KC,* II, 71–72)

This account, circumstantial as it is, does not help much in dating. Brown places these events sometime after Keats returned to Hampstead from a short stay in lodgings by himself in Westminster in October 1819 and sometime before the severe hemorrhage of 3 February 1820 (*KC,* II, 71, 73–74). The reference to "remodelling" *Hyperion* is puzzling, since there is no confirming evidence that Keats worked on *The Fall* after abandoning it late in September 1819 (it is possible that he secluded himself "in a separate sitting-room" simply to get away from Brown's hearty chatter). Though he mentions intending to proceed with *The Jealousies* in letters of 28 February, 15 May, and c. 21 June 1820 (*Letters*, II, 268, 289–290, 299), it does not appear that he added anything after the initial period of composition described in Brown's account.

Keats's one remark of critical interest on the work occurs in a letter to Brown of August (?) 1820:

> The sale of my book [*1820*] is very slow, though it has been very highly rated. One of the causes, I understand from different quarters, of the unpopularity of this new book, and the others also, is the offence the ladies take at me. On thinking that matter over, I am certain that I have said nothing in a spirit to displease any woman I would care to please: but still there is a tendency to class women in my books with roses and sweetmeats,—they never see themselves dominant. If ever I come to publish "Lucy Vaughan Lloyd", there will be some delicate picking for squeamish stomachs.

Brown commented on this last sentence, "As for what he says respecting his poem by the supposed 'Lucy Vaughan Lloyd', there is nothing in the fragment he has left, nothing in the intended construction of the story, (for I knew all, and was to assist him in the machinery of one part,) but to the honour of women. Lord Byron, really popular among women, reduced them, to the offence of some men, to 'roses and sweetmeats'" (*Letters*, II, 327–328). In sending his transcript of the poem to Milnes on 29 March 1841 Brown explained that

> "Lucy Vaughan Lloyd" was written chiefly for amusement; it appeared to be a relaxation; and it was begun without framing laws in his mind for the supernatural. When I noticed certain startling contradictions, his answer used to be—"Never mind, Brown; all those matters will be properly harmonized, before we divide it into Cantoes." As failures in wit, I might point out such Stanzas as 16, 17, & 18; yet there is exquisite wit of a peculiar kind in other parts. And there are many enchanting poetical passages. Probably you will publish the fragment with omissions. What can be better than his description of a London hackney-coach [226–252]?—yet how much misplaced! (*KC*, II, 99)

Milnes published the work with the following note at the foot of the first page: "This Poem was written subject to future amendments and omissions: it was begun without a plan, and without any prescribed laws for the supernatural machinery.—CHARLES BROWN."

The most substantial interpretations (in terms of political, literary, and self-directed biographical satire) are those by Gittings, *The Mask of Keats*, pp. 115–143; Martin Halpern, *K-SJ*, 15 (1966), 69–86; and Howard O. Brogan, *Bulletin of the New York Public Library*, 77 (1974), 298–313.

1 Hydaspes: Ancient name for the Jhelum River (in Kashmir and Pakistan).   **4 Elfinan:** The name comes from *The Faerie Queene* II.x.72. His love interests here to an extent parallel those of the Prince Regent, who had married Princess Caroline of Brunswick in 1795 but soon separated from her to return to his mistress. The conflict between them was of course much in the news, as was that between Lord Byron and his wife, from whom he separated in 1816 (see 610–611).   **14 Zendervester:** Sacred scripture (from Zend-Avesta).   **29 Imaus:** "The name of a great mountain range of Asia; one of those terms which the ancient geographers appear to have used indefinitely for want of exact knowledge" (*Harper's Dictionary of Classical Literature and Antiquities*). The name occurs in *Paradise Lost* III.431, in a context that also includes "Hydaspes."   **31 Bellanaine:** Literally, "beautiful dwarf." Her journey to Panthea in 640 ff. parallels Princess Caroline's slow progress from Brunswick to England in December 1794–April 1795.   **38 sapphired:** Painted with sapphire blue.   **44 "promener à l'aile":** Literally, "take a walk on wings."   **90 Panthea:** The "faery city" of 3. Panthea is mentioned in *The Faerie Queene* II.x.73, six lines after the name "Elfinan" appears.   **90 Jubal's Head:** Jubal was "father of all such as handle the harp and organ" (Genesis 4:21).   **114 Angle-land:** England.   **157 cut-and-run:** Slang for getting away quickly.   **162 Biancopany:** Literally, "white bread," probably a reference to Samuel Whitbread (1758–1815), Princess Caroline's strongest supporter in the House of Commons.   **188 Hum:** Slang term for humbug, imposition, hoax (and also a name used by Shelley, Thomas Moore, and others for the Prince Regent).   **193 bowstrung:** Strangled (with a bowstring).   **196 neck'd:** Beheaded.   **215 scaith:** Variant spelling of "scathe."   **226 string:** Check-string, "a string by which the occupant of a carriage may signal to the driver to stop" (*OED*).   **227 jarvey:** A hackney coach and/or its driver.   **238 fiddle-faddle:** Being busy about petty trifles (i.e., wasting time).   **253 check:** Same as "string" in 226.   **283 Magazin des Modes:** Milliner's shop.   **288 cast . . . figure:** Calculate a horoscope.   **292 dentes sapientiae:** Wisdom teeth.   **295 grains of paradise:** "The capsules of *Amomum Meleguetta* of Western Africa . . . used as a spice and in medicine" (*OED*).   **297 douceur:** Gratuity, bribe.   **310 his . . . pair:** His room on the second floor.   **311 Salpietro:** Literally, "saltpeter" (here either an exclamation or the name of Hum's servant or dog).   **333 Man-Tiger-Organ:** "The famous mechanical tiger of Tipu Sultan tearing to pieces one of the East India Company's English officers. This . . . emits, together with the victim's movements, sounds in imitation of the cries of the man and growl of the tiger. It was found in the music room of the palace at Seringapatam and dispatched to England a few months after the fall of his fortress and the death of Tipu on 4 May 1799, and on 29 July 1808 received into the library at the East India House, Leadenhall Street, where it was kept in the public reading room" (Phyllis G. Mann, *K-SJ*, 6 [1957], 5, with black-and-white photograph facing opposite; for a two-page photo in color see *Horizon*, 3 [September 1960], 20–21).   **347 treen:** Archaic or dialectal plural of "tree."   **365 nantz:** A kind of brandy. The footnote to this line quotes from *Spectator* No. 317 (4 March 1712), which is Keats's source for the style of Crafticanto's diary in 642 ff.   **398 bam:** Slang for hoax or imposition.   **403 Cham:** The Biblical Shem. The footnote refers to the article on "Cham" in Pierre Bayle's *Dictionnaire historique et critique* (1697).   **416 Admiral De Witt:** Jan de Witt (1625–1672), grand pensionary of Holland, led the Dutch fleet against the English in the war of 1665–1667.   **429 Candy wine:** Wine from Crete (formerly "Candia," "Candy"), frequently mentioned in the works of Chapman, Jonson, Massinger, Beaumont and Fletcher, and other seventeenth-century dramatists.   **434 mago:** Magician.   **500** *Moore: Old Moore's Almanac,* the annual work started at the beginning of the eighteenth century by Francis Moore (1657–1715?).   **519 fainting fit:** Bertha in *The Eve of St. Mark* is similarly "Perplex'd," "dazed," "lost in dizzy maze"—in effect, driven to a fainting fit—by an old "volume, patch'd and torn" (*St. Mark* 25, 29, 56, and the canceled original text of 69–70). Critics note parallels between the decorations on the present Bertha's sampler in 447–450 and those on the earlier Bertha's screen in *St. Mark* 78–82, and the fact that both Berthas live in minster towns.   **539 cold pig:** "Give cold pig" means "to awaken by sluicing with cold water or by pulling off the bed-clothes" (Partridge, *A Dictionary of Slang and Unconventional English*). Here the "sluicing" element would be the oil of extreme unction.   **547 pigsney:** A term of endearment.   **554–560 Now . . . Now . . . now . . . nows:** Probably a private reference to Hunt's "A Now, Descriptive of a Hot Day" (*Indicator,* 28 June 1820, pp. 300–303), in which each sentence of the opening two paragraphs begins with "Now." Hunt said that this was "the paper . . . most liked by Keats. . . . He was with me while I was writing and reading it to him, and contributed one or two of the passages" (*Autobiography,* ed. J. E. Morpurgo, 1949, p. 281).   **567 mignionette:** Either a fragrant plant or, more probably, a piece of lace.   **602 invisible ring:** A ring that would make him invisible.   **610–611 Farewell . . . well:** Based on the opening lines of Byron's *Fare thee well,* written to his wife after their separation: "Fare thee well! and if for ever, / Still for ever, fare *thee well.*" The poem was privately printed for Byron in the first week of April 1816 and shortly afterward made public in several newspapers and magazines (beginning with the *Champion* on 14 April).   **620 scrutoire:** Escritoire.   **671 hoop:** Hoopskirt.   **679 Balk:** Balkh, in Afghanistan.   **690 Cinque-parted:** The term (literally "five-parted") may represent Keats's understanding or misunderstanding of "cinquepace," which is "a kind of lively dance much used for some time before and after 1500. From the name it is inferred that 'the steps were regulated by the number five'" (*OED*).   **694 kettle-drum:** The player of the kettledrum.   **770 ruffy-tuffy:** Disheveled.

In after time a sage of mickle lore

Written in 1820 (in a now lost copy of Spenser in a blank space at the end of *The Faerie Queene* V.ii); first published in *PDWJ,* 4 July 1839. In quoting the lines in a political article in *PDWJ,* Brown explains,

> Our modern poet Keats, under his death-stroke, to wile away the hours of sickness, was frequently reading his favourite Spenser. Upon one of these occasions, he wrote an extra-concluding stanza to the Canto [V.ii]. We give it not only on account of its intrinsic merit; but hitherto, it has

remained unpublished; and *it is the last stanza, of any kind, that he wrote before his lamented death.* Till then, he never wrote a line of a political tendency; yet it may be said, he died with his pen weilded in the cause of Reform. . . . If Typographus thought fit to disable the Justice and Law of the sixteenth century by blindness, he has certainly succeeded in opening the eyes of millions. Many thanks to Typographus!

The Contents of *1817* and *1820*

1817, printed by Charles Richards and published by Charles and James Ollier at the beginning of March 1817, consists of thirty-one items in four principal sections:

Dedication: To Leigh Hunt, Esq.

Poems: I stood tip-toe upon a little hill
               Specimen of an Induction to a Poem
               Calidore
               To Some Ladies
               On Receiving a Curious Shell, and a Copy of Verses, from the
                  Same Ladies
               Hadst thou liv'd in days of old
               To Hope
               Imitation of Spenser
               Woman! when I behold thee flippant, vain

Epistles: To George Felton Mathew
               To My Brother George
               To Charles Cowden Clarke

Sonnets: I. To My Brother George
              II. Had I a man's fair form, then might my sighs
           III. Written on the Day That Mr. Leigh Hunt Left Prison
           IV. How many bards gild the lapses of time
             V. To a Friend Who Sent Me Some Roses
            VI. To G. A. W.
           VII. O Solitude! if I must with thee dwell
          VIII. To My Brothers
            IX. Keen, fitful gusts are whisp'ring here and there
            X. To one who has been long in city pent
           XI. On First Looking into Chapman's Homer
          XII. On Leaving Some Friends at an Early Hour
        XIII. Addressed to Haydon
        XIV. Addressed to the Same
         XV. On the Grasshopper and Cricket
        XVI. To Kosciusko
       XVII. Happy is England! I could be content

Sleep and Poetry

The title page contains an epigraph from "*Fate of the Butterfly.*—Spenser" (*Muiopotmos* 209–210)—"What more felicity can fall to creature, / Than to enjoy delight with liberty"— and beneath this a vignette profile of the head and shoulder of an Elizabethan male crowned with laurel (usually identified as Spenser but instead probably intended to represent Shakespeare). A note in square brackets appears on the verso page opposite the beginning of *I stood tip-toe:* "The Short Pieces in the middle of the Book, as well as some of the Sonnets, were written at an earlier period than the rest of the Poems." The halftitle preceding the Epistles contains an epigraph from William Browne's *Britannia's Pastorals* II.iii.748–750:

> Among the rest a shepheard (though but young
> Yet hartned to his pipe) with all the skill
> His few yeeres could, began to fit his quill.

*   *   *

1820, printed by Thomas Davison and published by Taylor and Hessey in the last week of June 1820, consists of thirteen items in five principal sections:

          Lamia
          Isabella
          The Eve of St. Agnes
          Poems: Ode to a Nightingale
                    Ode on a Grecian Urn
                    Ode to Psyche
                    Fancy
                    Bards of passion and of mirth
                    Lines on the Mermaid Tavern
                    Robin Hood
                    To Autumn
                    Ode on Melancholy
          Hyperion

Keats is identified on the title page as "Author of Endymion." An Advertisement dated 26 June 1820 appears on the first recto page after the title: "If any apology be thought necessary for the appearance of the unfinished poem of HYPERION, the publishers beg to state that they alone are responsible, as it was printed at their particular request, and contrary to the wish of the author. The poem was intended to have been of equal length with ENDYMION, but the reception given to that work discouraged the author from proceeding" (for Woodhouse's draft of an earlier version see *KC*, I, 115–116). In the Harvard copy that he presented to Burridge Davenport, Keats crossed through the whole of this note, explaining that "This is none of my doing—I w[as] ill at the time," and he also separately commented on the last twelve words of the final sentence ("but . . . proceeding"): "This is a lie."

Index of Titles and First Lines

Page numbers in italics refer to the Commentary.